mental_floss *presents:*

Condensed Knowledge

mental_floss *presents:*

Condensed Knowledge

Edited by

Will Pearson, Mangesh Hattikudur, *and* **Elizabeth Hunt**

HarperResource
An Imprint of HarperCollinsPublishers

FIRST EDITION

Designed by Leah Carlson-Stanisic

Library of Congress Cataloging-in-Publication Data has been applied for.

ISBN 0-06-056806-2

05 06 07 08 WBC/RRD 10 9

To Jane Cee, Henley, Umesh-uncle and Chitra-auntie, and Barbara Roewe.

Acknowledgments

The editors would like to thank Abigail Myers, John Chernoff, Carol Hunt, Clif Hunt, Carla Kingery, Betsy Marsey, Patsy Jones, Terry Finley, Ellen Sullivan, Tom Gallagher, Jerry Footlick, Ceil Cleveland, and Jackie Leo.

Condensed_Knowledge

Try all 15 delicious varieties!

Introduction

mental_floss magazine was just one of a hundred semiamusing ideas that came out of our floor's late-night dorm room conversations at Duke University. There was, of course, the heated driveway company, that hoped to melt away morning frost and make snow shoveling a thing of the past. And the pet lobster farm, which not only intended to breed pedigree lobsters as domestic companions, but also carry fine lobster accessories . . . such as tiny leashes, sweaters, and mittens. And who could forget the Great American Pudding Truck? The idea was to get a cement mixing truck, fill it with pudding, and roam the country squirting gelatinous goodies into the pudgy hands of kids on every block. Brilliant, right? Well, if one thing was made abundantly clear to us in college, it was that there was a whole world of opportunities just waiting to be tapped by dreamers like ourselves. So, why then did we pursue *mental_floss*? Maybe because of all the ideas on the table, it's the one that made us grin the widest.

Statistically speaking, *mental_floss* never should have launched. Consider the facts: two 21-year-old kids with no industry experience, no journalism background, and no real money to throw around decide to start a national publication. Add to that the fact that the year we decided to launch was considered the worst economy for magazines since World War II. Ad money was down dramatically, and high profile publications like *Talk*, *George*, and *Mademoiselle* were all forced to close shop.

Not exactly the best timing. But when you're as quietly mischievous as we are, stats don't faze you. *mental_floss* was exactly the sort of magazine we wanted to find in our mailbox every month—something that was hip and quick and quirky and fun, but really left you feeling smarter. You know? A sort of bible for trivia addicts. A quick fix for knowledge junkies. Something that truly blurred the lines between education and entertainment. So we hunted for it. We scoured bookstores. We rummaged newsstands. And when we couldn't find the magazine we were looking for, we decided to go out and create it.

Fast forward a few years later, and *mental_*

floss still has us smiling. After all, we've managed to get away with a "Swimsuit" issue (featuring 15 geniuses, from Einstein to Eleanor Roosevelt stripped down to their skivvies), a "Saints and Sinners" issue (that had Mother Theresa, Gandhi, Nelson Mandela, and Madonna all fighting for cover space), and even a "Lies Your Mother Told You" issue featuring all the so-called facts people have been trying to slip past you for years. But now that we're growing older, wiser, maybe even a little more mature (emphasis on little), we're starting to branch out. *Condensed Knowledge* is *mental_floss's* first adventure in the book world, and well, we're pretty darn excited about it. We've gathered seventeen experts, thousands of facts, and slapped the work silly in typical *mental_floss* style. So go ahead: skim a few pages, ease into the paragraph of your choice. And if you're not hopelessly addicted in a matter of minutes, we'll do our best to understand. After all, we still have the pudding truck business to fall back on.

Happy flossing,
Will and Mangesh

A Feast for Hungry Minds

People love to feel smart, but would prefer not to have to work for the knowledge. There's a good reason we like the Dummies books, Cliff's Notes, and bulleted summaries; we're active people without a lot of time on our hands. It's the same reason fast food, insta-photos, and dry cleaning are so popular. We want it all, we want it quickly, and—if possible—we'd like it supersized (no mayo).

You think you have the time or energy to delve into ancient religious tomes to uncover

the basic tenets of Islam by yourself? We think not. Learning Arabic, even on tape, is a four-month process in and of itself. Besides, you've got better things to do.

Sadly, when it comes down to it, we're just not all that book-smart. We're fuzzy on the facts. We have trouble telling the Bill of Rights from a bill of lading, astronomy from astrology, or Madonna from, well, Madonna. Most people think Hercules is a pro wrestler, and Descartes a snail or dessert wine.

It's not our teachers' faults: our hormones were raging, we were bored out of our minds, hungry, afraid of the class bully, and looking to hitch a ride with the first trucker who'd take us far from our wretched neighborhood. And that was just elementary school.

We're not stupid, either; we used to know all kinds of stuff—we've just forgotten. Given our study habits, you can hardly blame us for our academic amnesia. Procrastination was the name of the scholastic game: we waited until ten minutes before class to attempt memorizing the names of every U.S. president, the 206 bones in the human body, that frickin' chemistry chart, or some Shakespearean sonnet—only to pass by the skin of our braced teeth. We crammed, we jammed, we purged.

The idea of *Condensed Knowledge* is for readers to stroll up to the buffet line of basics and take a heaping plateful of smart(aleck). And one helping surely won't be enough to fill that big noggin of yours, so like Pavlov's puppies, you'll ring the bell again and again. In this process, you will begin to make connections you never thought possible: like how the Industrial Revolution was critical to the invention of the snowboard, that without space travel there'd be no Twinkie, and that there are simple dance steps that can bring you closer to God.

Most of us are more interested in the big picture than in the microscopic minutiae of molecules, Sanskrit, or caloric intake; we leave that to folks like Einstein, Bill Gates, and Oprah. And now, thanks to the insanely bright crew of expert authors assembled here, critical events and ideas in fifteen fields of study have been distilled into easy Mc-Nugget-size chunks. Then it's up to you to connect the dots.

Confucius said, "To know that we know what we know, and that we do not know what we do not know, that is true knowledge." All we know is, that makes our heads hurt, and that Sir Francis Bacon (no relation to Kevin Bacon) said it better: "Knowledge is power."

You'll become top dog at the water cooler, a whiz at home Jeopardy!, an arbitrator of stupid bets your friends make. Kids will gather at your feet to hear your tales of wisdom, your lovers will finally be impressed, politicos will beg you to run for president. What you *do* with this newfound power is up to you. We hope you use it wisely.

Michael A. Stusser, a regular contributor, still remembers meeting the first issue of *mental_floss* magazine. The pair have worked happily ever after ever since, spending their waking hours making sweet, sweet, articles together.

mental_floss presents:

Condensed
Knowledge

by
Robert Cumming

Condensed ART HISTORY

Contains

5 Scandals That Rocked Art ✳ 7 Styles to Keep at Your Fingertips ✳ 6 Masters of the Modern ✳ 9 Champions of the Old School ✳ Wheeling and Dealing: 6 Dealers and Auctioneers the World Reveres ✳ 5 Greatest Sculptors of All Time ✳ 5 Bank-Breaking Works of Staggering Genius: The Priciest Artists in the World ✳ 4 Nudes You Ought to Know by Name (and Have as Fridge Magnets) ✳ 4 Artists (and 1 Exhibition) Bent On Shocking the Masses ✳ This Bold House: 5 Architects Who Defy Convention ✳

Scandals That Rocked Art

Forgeries, thefts, and outright vandalism? That's right. Art history's about to get a whole lot more interesting.

_01:: The Vermeer Forgeries

Every age sees art through its own eyes, and the cleverest forgers play up to this. One of the most notorious forgeries ever occurred in the 1930s. A Dutchman named Han van Meegeren (1889–1947) produced forgeries of early works by the Dutch 17th-century master Jan Vermeer. They were technically brilliant and faultless, using old canvas and the correct 17th-century pigments. Cunningly, van Meegeren chose religious imagery that some experts believed Vermeer had painted, but very few examples of which existed. Most (though not all) of the greatest experts were completely taken in, but when you see the paintings now, you'll wonder why. All the faces look like the great film stars of the 1930s, such as Marlene Dietrich and Douglas Fairbanks.

_02:: The *Mona Lisa* Theft

It's sometimes suggested that rich criminals arrange for famous works of art to be stolen so that they can have them exclusively to themselves in private. Such theories have never been proven, and the truth is usually just a bit simpler. One of the most bizarre thefts was of the *Mona Lisa* from the Louvre in 1911. An Italian workman, Vincenzo Perugia, walked into the gallery, took the painting off the wall, and carried it out. Security was nonexistent.

About two years later it was discovered in a trunk in his cheap lodging rooms in Florence. So, why did he take it? It was nothing to do with money. He said that as the painting was by an Italian, Leonardo da Vinci, it was part of Italy's national cultural heritage, and he was simply taking it back to where it belonged: Florence. (The painting was returned to the Louvre.)

_03:: The Auction Houses Scandal

The major commercial scandal of recent years has been the alleged collusion between the two big international auction houses Christie's and Sotheby's. As the supply of expensive masterpieces began to run out, competition between the two firms became increasingly fierce and each of them found it difficult to make a profit. They got together secretly to fix not the price of works of art themselves but the commission that they would each charge to sellers. In certain parts of the world, such an arrangement is quite legal but not in the United States. Eventually the practice came to light. The federal authorities imposed fines running into hundreds of millions of dollars, and prison sentences were also handed out.

_04:: The Portland Vase

Wanton acts of destruction in the art world are fortunately rare. One of the strangest occurred in 1845 in the British Museum, London, and is worthy of a Sherlock Holmes story. The Portland Vase, the most famous example of ancient Roman glass, decorated in dark-blue-and-white cameo technique, was brought from Italy in 1783 and purchased by the Duchess of Portland. A drunken young man entered the museum and without explanation smashed the vase and its glass display case. He was imprisoned for breaking the case but not the vase, as British law didn't impose penalties for destroying works of art of high value. The vase has since been repaired; however, you can still see the bruises.

_05:: Cellini's *Saltcellar*

A recent art world disaster/scandal occurred on May 13, 2003 (and it wasn't even a Friday!). Thieves climbed scaffolding and smashed windows to enter Vienna's Art History Museum and stole the *"Mona Lisa* of sculptures"—Cellini's *Saltcellar*. This intricate 16-centimeter-high sculpture was commissioned by François I, king of France, from Benvenuto Cellini (1500–1571), the Renaissance's most ingenious and gifted goldsmith. Crafted with amazingly rich detail and skill, its principal figures are a naked sea god and a woman who sit opposite each other, with legs entwined—a symbolic representation of the planet earth. The thieves set off the alarms,

---

What's the Difference?
FAKES VS. FORGERIES

While the two words are seemingly interchangeable, there's a real distinction here. A fake is a work of art that is deliberately made or altered so as to appear better, older, or other than what it is. When you go browsing round the stalls of the local flea markets and think you have found a bargain, be cautious because you may well be looking at a fake. A forgery, on the other hand, is something made in fraudulent imitation of another thing that already exists. Throughout history, people have come forward with what they claim are lost masterpieces by Leonardo or Vermeer, for example, which they themselves have created with great skill in their studios. Such works are not fakes but forgeries.

---

but these were ignored as false, and the theft remained undiscovered until 8:20 a.m. The reasons for the theft are as yet unknown. The fear is that these thieves will destroy the sculpture or melt it down, an act of vandalism that would be the equivalent of burning the *Mona Lisa*.

7 Styles to Keep at Your Fingertips

If you're looking to impress, you'll need to know more than just a handful of painters and their masterpieces—you're going to have to know some styles too. That's why we're giving you the lowdown—a revealing guide to the key movements and the reasons they matter.

_01:: Giving Birth to the Renaissance

Literally meaning "rebirth," the Renaissance ushered in the flowering of new ideas in Italian art between the 14th and 16th centuries, and the impact has been felt in the Western art world ever since. Like no style before it, the Renaissance brought three new ideas to the table and explored them with increasing sophistication. In this period you find art as a window on the world, with light and "real" space being continually explored; you find man as the measure of all things, from human scale and proportion to human emotions and ideals; and you find a strong reverence for Christianity, the Bible, and classical antiquity, with Christian messages from the Old and New Testaments along with the adaptation of classical Greek and Roman ideas incorporated into the style. If you want to see all of this together in one place and at its most magnificent, take a closer look at Michelangelo's ceiling in the Sistine Chapel, Rome.

_02:: Going for Baroque

The dominant style of the 17th century, the baroque period was filled with elaborate and ornate art, the theatrical world of illusion, endless drama, a love of rich color and materials, and, most important, heaviness, seriousness, and pomposity. The Catholic Church used the baroque style to illustrate Christian religious subjects and to proclaim the power of the established church as it fought back against austere Protestant ideals during the Reformation. Hence, the best examples of baroque style are found where the Catholic faith prevailed—Italy (especially Rome), Austria, southern Germany, central Europe, Spain, and France. Similarly, absolute monarchs used the baroque style for secular subjects to proclaim their worldly power, and to celebrate the richness of their possessions and lifestyles. Baroque's best work can be found in Bernini's churches and fountains in Rome and in the work of the Catholic monarchs' favorite artist, Rubens.

_03:: Cuckoo for Rococo

As the baroque began to fade, rococo art emerged as an 18th-century reaction to the heavy, ornate work that had characterized the previous century. Look for paintings, buildings, porcelains, sculpture, and furniture that are full of curves. You'll find an art style that is filled with pretty colors, playfulness, youthful exuberance, elegance, fine craftsmanship, extravagance, carefree attitudes, and references to real and fanciful nature (flowers, leaves, rocks, birds, monkeys, or dragons). Rococo reached its fullest expression in 18th-century France (it is the Louis XV style) and central Europe (Bohemia). In fact, it was Louis

XV's mistress, Madame de Pompadour, who encouraged the creation of rococo's most sumptuous and decorative masterpieces, such as the paintings of François Boucher and Sèvres porcelain.

_04:: Neoclassicism and Napoleon?

The fashionable art style from about 1770 to 1830, neoclassicism emphasized the spirit and appearance of classical Greece and Rome. While the style tends to be severe, authoritative, didactic, well made, and architectural (preferring straight lines), it originally trumpeted a more decorative and cerebral note. After the French Revolution and Napoleon, however, neoclassicism became heavy-handed, with an emphasis on magnificence and grandiosity. The style succeeds best in architecture, furniture, and sculpture, and can be seen at its finest in England (where it starts as the Adam style and ends up as Regency) and France (where it starts as the Louis XVI style and ends up as the Empire style). The key painter of the movement was Jacques-Louis David.

_05:: Isn't It Romantic?

The key movement in art, music, and literature in the late 18th and early 19th centuries, Romanticism produced some of the greatest and best-loved works of all time. The Romantics believed in new experiences, individuality, innovation, risk taking, heroism, freedom of imagination, love, and living life to the fullest. In painting and sculpture they introduced new and dramatic subjects, innovative styles and techniques, rich and vigorous colors and brushwork, and a tendency to see and experience everything as larger than life. Romanticism appealed particularly to the northern European temperament and flourished at its fullest in Germany, Britain, and France. Delacroix, one of the greatest painters of the Romantic movement, summed it all up in his well-known painting *Liberty Leading the People*, a key image celebrating the popular democratic uprising in Paris in 1830, whose spirit is celebrated in the hit musical *Les Misérables*.

_06:: Works That Leave an Impression

Impressionism was the famous progressive movement that started the dethronement of academic art and the traditions that had stemmed from the Renaissance. The impressionists ignored artistic "style" and went back to nature with the intention of painting only what the eye could see. They created small-scale works of contemporary scenes, notably landscapes, that were freely and directly painted *en plein air* ("out of doors"), portraits, and still lifes. The impressionists' trademark technique was short brush strokes and a rainbow palette. Talk about an explosive launch, though; the first impressionist exhibition took place in 1874 and featured the works of such heavyweights as Cézanne, Degas, Monet, Morisot, Pissarro, Renoir, and Sisley.

_07:: Modernism in a Modern Age

The great flowering of modern art occurred between 1880 and 1960, and it embraces all the avant-garde works produced at that time. Beginning with Manet and the impressionists, modernism continued on until Jackson Pollock and the New York school hit the scene. No doubt, modernism's greatest innovator and exponent was Picasso, whose style itself broached a variety of looks and feels. As modernism unfolded, three major characteristics

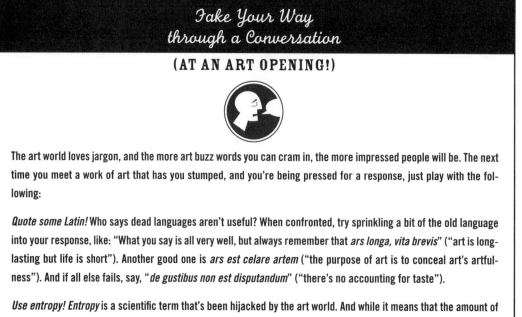

Fake Your Way through a Conversation
(AT AN ART OPENING!)

The art world loves jargon, and the more art buzz words you can cram in, the more impressed people will be. The next time you meet a work of art that has you stumped, and you're being pressed for a response, just play with the following:

Quote some Latin! Who says dead languages aren't useful? When confronted, try sprinkling a bit of the old language into your response, like: "What you say is all very well, but always remember that *ars longa, vita brevis*" ("art is long-lasting but life is short"). Another good one is *ars est celare artem* ("the purpose of art is to conceal art's artfulness"). And if all else fails, say, "*de gustibus non est disputandum*" ("there's no accounting for taste").

Use entropy! Entropy is a scientific term that's been hijacked by the art world. And while it means that the amount of disorder in the universe is bound to increase (this is the second law of thermodynamics: heat is disordered energy), it's pretty useful at openings. If the thing you're looking at appears to be irredeemably chaotic and incomprehensible, try saying, "The artist appears to be a supreme master of entropy." You will sound deeply knowledgeable while seeming to praise the work (when, in fact, you're cleverly condemning it!).

Isn't it ironic? Simply claim that "Fundamentally, this work is an extremely skillful use of irony." By definition, irony means to convey a meaning by expressing the opposite. If you have no idea what the artist is trying to say and suspect that the artist doesn't have an idea either, this is a crafty way of implying that you've penetrated to the heart of the work's nonexistent meaning. If you're asked what or where the irony is, look inscrutable, nod wisely, and walk away.

The final nod: If you find a work of art meaningless or someone's point of view incomprehensible, unacceptable, or futile, you can always shake your head and declare the whole issue to be "problematic." Just whatever you do, don't admit defeat or tell the truth.

---

emerged: (1) a strong desire to break with the past, unlike previous art movements that emphasized their inheritance from, or rejuvenation of, the art of the past; (2) a defiance of all art institutions and the creation of works of art that were intentionally "homeless," in the sense that they belonged in no official art institution; and (3) the incorporation of a plethora of styles and ideas. In essence, modern artists were at their most active in those places where freedom of speech and thought were newfound liberties, or in those places where those liberties were most actively fought for, such as late 19th- to early-20th-century France, post-Revolutionary Russia, interwar Germany, or post–World War II

United States. Modernism's two major homes, however, lay in France and the United States. Paris remained its center of gravity between 1880 and 1939, while New York was its home from 1945 to the 1960s.

6 Masters of the Modern

It's almost impossible to talk about modern art without tipping your hat to these greats. Here are the masters who gave birth to the modern.

_01:: Pablo Picasso (1881–1973)

Picasso is the undisputed master of the modern movement. You have to go back to Michelangelo to find anyone of equal genius or stature. Convivial and energetic, he had a voracious appetite for the female sex, although his relationships with women were not always happy. Creator of a vast output of work, he was equally inventive as a painter, sculptor, printmaker, ceramicist, and theater designer. His work displays a bewildering change of technical and stylistic originality with a wide-ranging Freudian response to the human condition, including many intimate references to sex and death, sometimes blissful, sometimes anguished. Always highly autobiographical, Picasso had the rare ability to turn self-comment into universal truths about mankind.

_02:: Henri Matisse (1869–1954)

Matisse was the king of color and celebrated the joy of living through the exploration of his palette. One of the founders of the modern movement, Matisse achieved a joyous combination of subject matter (notably the open window, the still life, and the female nude) and a glorious exploitation of color, and proclaimed a new freedom to do his own thing without necessarily imitating nature. Matisse explored color independently from subject matter and turned color into something you wanted to touch and feel. While he was at his best with paint and paper cutouts, he was also a brilliant and innovative printmaker and a gifted sculptor. As a personality, however, he was professorial, social, but a bit of a loner.

_03:: Wassily Kandinsky (1866–1944)

Kandinsky was one of the key pioneers of the modern movement and reputedly the creator of the first abstract picture. Russian born, he initially trained as a lawyer, which made him at ease with abstract modes of thought. Possessor of a complex, multifaceted personality, Kandinsky cultivated an intellectual rather than an instinctive approach to art, backed up by much theoretical writing. Starting as a figurative artist, he worked his way via freely painted abstracts to a complex geometrical form of abstraction. The common thread in all his work is color. He intellectualized his ideas and his art, but at the same time he had such a strong physical sensitivity to color that he could literally hear colors as well as see them (a phenomenon known as synesthesia; see page 289 in Psychology).

_04:: Piet Mondrian (1872–1944)

Mondrian was one of the pioneers of a pure abstract art. His most recognizable works have the simplest elements: black horizontal and vertical lines, a white background, and only the primary colors. His aim was to find and express a universal spiritual perfection, but his imagery had a profound influence on 20th-century commercial and architectural design and has been endlessly recycled with little or no understanding of its underlying purpose. As a personality he was austere and reclusive; he hated the green untidiness of nature but was addicted to jazz and dancing. Sadly, in his own lifetime he had no commercial success, but Mondrian was highly revered and tremendously influential on the movers and shakers of modern art and design.

_05:: Jackson Pollock (1912–1956)

"Jack the Dripper" was the leading artist of the pioneer New York school. He was a tortured, monosyllabic, alcohol-dependent soul, swinging between sensitivity and machismo, elation and despair. At his best he produced magnificent work that needs to be seen on a large scale to fully appreciate the passionate, heroic, and monumental nature of his achievement. When he rolled his canvases out on the floor and stood in the middle of them with a large can of house paint, he was literally and physically part of his work, thereby achieving an integration of the artist's personality and the activity of artistic creation that had never before been realized with such expressive freedom.

_06:: Andy Warhol (1928–1987)

Sure, Andy Warhol may have been a neurotic surrounded by drug addicts, but that doesn't mean he wasn't a key artistic figure. Warhol's work represents one of art's turning points because he changed the role model of the artist into one that all aspiring young contemporary artists now follow—no longer the solitary genius expressing intense and personal emotion (like Pollock) but the artist as businessman. He placed artists on a par with Hollywood film stars and Madison Avenue advertising executives. Understandably, he loved and exploited iconic images drawn from the world of glamour, mass media, and advertising, and you can still find his Campbell soup cans and Marilyn Monroe–themed prints everywhere. The son of Czech immigrants, Warhol acted out an oft-repeated American dream cycle—pursuing a driving need to be famous and rich (like his subjects) but destroying himself in the process.

Champions of the Old School

If you're waxing nostalgic for the good stuff, you can't go wrong with the classics. Here are some of the greatest men ever to wield a paintbrush, sorted by nationality.

_01:: Italy's Raphael (1483–1520)

So, why Raphael? Consider that Michelangelo was principally a sculptor, and Leonardo produced very few paintings. And while Giotto (ca. 1267–1337) first established a new level of realism in art, and Masaccio (1401–1428) pioneered deeply moving works with simple and profound human gestures and emotions, first place undoubtedly has to go to Raphael. A child prodigy, Raphael actually died young, but he had a complete mastery of all Renaissance techniques. In fact, he explored subjects and ideas and developed them with apparent ease, yet he managed to endow them with the deepest emotional and intellectual expression. Raphael projected an ideal at almost every level, which is why he was held up as the model for all ambitious artists to follow—until the overthrow of the Renaissance and academic traditions by the modern movement.

_02:: Spain's Diego Velásquez (1599–1660)

It's a close call between Velásquez and Goya, but we had to go with Velásquez, even though he wasn't prolific and his style changed considerably. Velásquez's early work is notable for its pinpoint-sharp realism, whereas his later works are loose and softly focused. By far, Velásquez's greatest achievements are his por-

traits, where he manages to balance grandeur, realism, and intimacy as no one has ever done before or since. And his sensitivity to light and sensational color harmonies were hugely influential on avant-garde painters (such as Manet) of the late 19th century. Goya (1746–1828), on the other hand, had a profound understanding of human character—youth and old age, hope and despair, sweet innocence and brutal savagery—yet he was never judgmental, simply showing human nature as it was (and still is). Nevertheless, the quality of Goya's work is variable, whereas Velásquez never seemed to put a foot wrong, which is why, by a hairbreadth, Velásquez takes the prize.

_03:: France's Nicolas Poussin (1594–1665)

Three names are in the frame here: Poussin, David, and Cézanne. Cézanne (1839–1906) is here because, although a solitary, pioneering, difficult workaholic who considered his life and work failures, he was nonetheless the mother and father of modern art. David (1748–1825) was the passionate, volatile founder of French neoclassical painting. Like his hero Napoleon, he was dictatorial, austere, and inflexible, and his art in the service of the state radiates a powerful ideological, political, and artistic commitment. Poussin was the founder of French classical painting, who lived and worked in Rome, creating complex allegorical subjects on moral themes that were severe, intense, highly intellectual, and composed with an underlying geometry of verticals, horizontals, and diagonals. So, why's he the greatest? For the simple reason that both Cézanne and David, both of whom knew what they were talking about, said he is.

The Low Countries'
_04:: Rubens (1577–1640) and
_05:: Rembrandt (1606–1669)

There needs to be a joint prize here because of national politics. In the 17th century the Low Countries split politically into the New Republic of Holland and Flanders (effectively modern Belgium). The greatest Flemish painter is Sir Peter Paul Rubens, the widely traveled man of many talents who was a painter, diplomat, businessman, and scholar. His studio had a huge output of large-scale altarpieces, ceiling decorations, and portraits, which were staunch favorites with the Catholic Church and monarchs wishing to proclaim the divine right of kings. The greatest Dutch master, on the other hand, is Rembrandt. His elusive work is completely different—out of the mainstream, gritty, and deeply personal. Fascinated by emotional crisis and moral dilemmas, Rembrandt's work makes you sense that he has genuinely experienced the intensity of the emotions he portrays.

_06:: Germany's Albrecht Dürer
(1471–1528)

The prize goes to Albrecht Dürer, the greatest Northern artist of the Renaissance (he was the same age as Michelangelo). Prolific, tenacious, and immensely ambitious, Dürer uniquely and subtly synthesized the old Northern medieval traditions and the new Italian humanist discoveries. His subjects include the New Testament, nudes, landscapes, and classical mythology, and he was equally fascinated by plants and animals. And though his oil paintings are skillful, they are clearly self-conscious. Dürer was more at ease with drawings and watercolors, and he excelled at printmaking, where his technical mastery of woodcut and engraving has never been equaled.

_07:: Britain's J. M. W. Turner (1775–1851)

There are only two contenders here: Turner and Constable (1776–1837). The British are probably more at ease with nature than they are with people, so not surprisingly they produced two of the world's pioneering landscape painters. Constable's peaceful, silvery green, dewy-fresh scenes of the English countryside were tremendously influential on the French, but he was a stay-at-home artist and didn't have the scope and originality of Turner in terms of subject matter and technique. Turner's travels took him all over Europe, where he saw the works of classical antiquity, and the Industrial Revolution fired his imagination. All of nature's moods and all her seasons are included in his work, and he was so innovative in his techniques with oils and watercolors that contemporary critics thought he must have gone mad.

_08:: U.S.A.'s Winslow Homer (1836–1910)

The two contenders for the American award are Winslow Homer and Thomas Eakins (1844–1916). Eakins was from Philadelphia and studied in Paris and Spain. Pragmatic but with an unyielding personality, he was little honored in his lifetime. He produced frank and candid portraits of matter-of-fact successful professionals (notably doctors and scientists). However, he lacks the masterly confidence of Winslow Homer who, although self-taught, produced satisfying, virile images that convincingly reflect the American pioneering spirit. Homer's work has a strong narrative content (he started as a magazine illustrator), and he's at his best with children and images of practical people coping with adversity. Homer lifted his art beyond the ordinary by infusing it with a sincerely felt underlying moral message.

_09:: Europe's Titian (ca. 1488–1576)

It may seem special pleading to classify Titian, who was Venetian born, as a European, but (with the exception of Raphael) he significantly influenced all the other artists selected here. Even in his own lifetime his influence and following were truly pan-European. He's also the only great master whose style and reputation over time have never been seriously questioned or suffered an eclipse. He is to painting what Shakespeare is to literature.

Alphabet Soup
(WITH ART-OFFICIAL FLAVORING!)

aesthete: [ES-theet] *n* Someone who claims to be particularly sensitive to beauty and who thinks as a result that he or she is superior to others (for example, Oscar Wilde).

vernissage: [ver-nih-SAZH] *n* French word for "varnishing," aka the day before an exhibition opened, when artists added the finishing touches to their work already hanging on the wall. Nowadays it's simply the chic word for a private viewing.

Both were masters of their craft, constantly innovative, producing thrilling new subjects or brilliant reinterpretations of classical themes, with a profoundly sympathetic response to the human condition.

Wheeling and Dealing:
Dealers and Auctioneers the World Reveres

6

What good's a great work of art if no one will buy the thing? Here are a few of history's slickest salesmen and their "off the wall" antics.

_01:: Jacopo Strada (1515–1588)

One of the cleverest and most successful dealers of the Renaissance, Jacopo dealt in statues, coins, drawings, and pictures. By luck or cleverness he had his portrait painted by Titian, the greatest master of portraiture, and so is remembered forever. Since Titian was brilliant at showing people's inner character, he shows Strada as a sly and cunning man with grasping hands. What's clear is that Titian did not like the guy, but he definitely needed his help to sell some pictures. The paintings in question had been done by studio assistants, but the crafty Titian wanted to pass them off as his own. Strada obliged, and Titian painted his portrait in return. Such deals have been done throughout the history of art, though usually not with such memorable artistic consequences.

_02:: James Christie (1730–1803)

Eighteenth-century London was thick with auctioneers, but James Christie soon established himself as the leading fine art auctioneer. In fact, he's the only one whose business has continued to the present day. (Sotheby's started as book auctioneers and did not deal in fine art until the 20th century.) Christie came from Ireland and had charming manners and a fluent tongue (he was known as the "specious orator"). A great favorite with the ladies, he would extemporize florid descriptions of the objects as he sold them from the auctioneer's box, literally talking the prices up as he took the bids. Such practices would now break every rule in the book. Since Christie's heyday, the art world has become more regulated and a little less colorful as a result.

_03:: Joseph Duveen (1869–1939)

Duveen was king of the commercial art world in the 1920s and 1930s, when dealers were the dominant force. He was the most successful art dealer ever and was the trusted agent of both the British aristocracy, who were forced sellers of their great treasures, and the new American industrial millionaires, who were enthusiastic buyers. One of Duveen's tricks was to refuse to sell to his American clients the thing they most wanted (e.g., a Rembrandt), telling them that they were not yet ready for such a fabulous masterpiece because they were not yet capable of appreciating it. He would then sell them lesser works, and when he finally announced that they were ready for the Rembrandt, they felt so honored by his judgment that they would pay almost any price for it.

_04:: Ambroise Vollard (1867–1939)

The best-known route to success as an art dealer is to think big, buy cheap, and sell expensive. The big money has always been in the big established names, but there are exceptions. Vollard supported the impressionists and the young modern avant-garde in their early penniless days, (e.g., Gauguin, Cézanne, Bonnard, Picasso). In retrospect, he was in the right place at the right time. He gave many of them their first shows when their work was basically impossible to sell, and he gave them contracts that paid them regular monthly allowances in anticipation of works to come. First and foremost Vollard believed in their art, and when his judgment was finally vindicated the financial rewards were considerable.

_05:: Peggy Guggenheim (1898–1979)

She was the grande dame of all 20th-century art dealers. Born into a wealthy dynasty with a famous name—Guggenheim's grandfather had made a fortune in mining, and her playboy father went down with the *Titanic*—Peggy opened her first gallery in London in 1938, but she made her reputation in New York with the Art of This Century Gallery, where she showed surrealist and abstract art. In fact, Jackson Pollock was one of her biggest discoveries. In 1947 she went to live permanently in Venice. And though her galleries thrived, Peggy's passions weren't restricted just to art. Once asked how many husbands she had had, Peggy replied, "Mine, or other people's?"

_06:: Peter Wilson (1913–1984)

Wilson was the suave aristocratic chairman of Sotheby's who, in the post–World War II era, turned fine art auctioneering into a multimillion-pound international phenomenon. Blessed with a true connoisseur's eye and a love of deals and risk taking, he was nevertheless better at recognizing a lost masterpiece than making money. His breakthrough came in 1958, when he held the first glamorous black-tie evening sale of just seven impressionist masterpieces from the Goldschmidt collection. Many of his partners were bitterly opposed to the project, fearing a disaster, but Wilson conducted a triumphantly successful sale, and the event launched a new and glamorous chapter in the history of auctioneering. He sold all the pictures in a mere 21 minutes.

5 Greatest Sculptors of All Time

Playing in two dimensions is easy enough, but what truly separates the men from the boys? Maybe it's when you give up your easel for a tool belt and get to work with a hammer and chisel. These amazing sculptors took their talents 3-D.

_01:: Donatello (1386?–1466)

Unquestionably the greatest sculptor of the early Renaissance, Donatello was born in Florence, though he traveled widely and was famous throughout Italy. Donatello had complete mastery of bronze, stone, wood, and terracotta, and nothing escaped his extraordinary capabilities: relief sculpture, nudes, equestrian statues, groups of figures, and single figures seated or standing. In fact, he reinvented the art of sculpture just as other contemporaries were reinventing the art of painting, and his innovations and discoveries were profoundly influential. Above all, Donatello seemed to be able to bring sculpture to life by his ability to tell a story, combine realism and powerful emotion, and create the impression that his figures were more than mere objects of beauty for passive contemplation, but creations filled with energy and thought, ready to spring into action.

_02:: Michelangelo (1475–1564)

Clearly an outstanding genius, Michelangelo's influence dominated European art until Picasso changed the rules. A sculptor first, painter and architect second, Michelangelo was a workaholic—a melancholic, temperamental, and lonely figure. He had a profound belief in the human form (especially the male nude) as the ultimate expression of human spirituality, sensibility, and beauty. In fact, Michelangelo's early work shows the human being as the measure of all things: idealized, muscular, confident, and quasi-divine. Gradually that image becomes more expressive, more human, less perfect, fallible, and flawed. He loved turning and twisting poses full of latent energy, and faces that expressed the full range of human emotion. Endlessly inventive, he never repeated a pose, although being a true Renaissance man, he was proud to borrow from Greek and Roman precedents.

_03:: Gian Lorenzo Bernini (1598–1680)

Bernini set sculpture free from its previous occupation with earthly gravity and intellectual emotion, allowing it to discover a new freedom that permitted it to move, soar, and have a visionary and theatrical quality. A child prodigy, Bernini had a sparkling personality and brilliant wit (he wrote comedies)—qualities that shine through his sculptures. He was also a true virtuoso technically, able to carve marble so as to make it seem to move or have the delicacy of the finest lace. At his best he blends sculpture, architecture, and painting into an extravagant theatrical ensemble, especially in his fountains, where the play of water and light over his larger-than-life human figures and animals creates a vision that is literally out of this world.

_04:: Auguste Rodin (1840–1917)

Rodin is the glorious, triumphant finale to the sculptural tradition that starts with Donatello. He is rightly spoken of in the same breath as Michelangelo, although they're very different: Michelangelo carved into marble whereas Rodin molded with clay. A shy workaholic, untidy, and physically enormous, Rodin emerged from impoverished beginnings. He became an international celebrity and was deeply attractive to smart women. Rodin was also well known for loving the fluidity of clay and plaster, and was able to retain this quality even when his work was cast in bronze, thereby magically releasing in his figures an extraordinary range of human feelings and a sense of the unknown forces of nature.

_05:: Constantin Brancusi (1876–1957)

Brancusi is one of the seminal figures of 20th-century art with a profound influence on sculpture and design. Born into a Romanian peasant family, he settled in Paris in 1904, becoming a student of Rodin. Amazingly, Brancusi remained indifferent to honor and fame. At the heart of his work is a tireless refinement and search for purity. Never abstract, his work always references something recognizable in nature. Brancusi believed in the maxim "Truth to materials," and he always brought out the inherent quality of each material that he used. The purity and simplicity of his

What's the Difference?

CONSERVATISM VS. RESTORATION

And you thought they were the same! As you well know, works of art are fragile and often made from organic materials, so even the most humble works need careful looking after. Conservation is the creation of the environment in which a work of art is properly looked after, without undue interference and without the need to restore and repair. A good example would be not hanging paintings on the wall above a radiator. Restoration, on the other hand, is the repairing of a work that has become damaged through accident, decay, or neglect. The science and technology of restoration are intricate, and the ethics are as complicated as medical ethics. How much transplanting, patching up, and cleaning can be done before the object dies aesthetically or becomes unrecognizable? The best motto is "If in doubt, leave well alone," because once a work is dead or ruined, there's nothing you can do. A terrifying number of paintings have been ruined by over-restoration in the last 50 years, and as yet no one has properly faced up to the fact. Case in point, *Mona Lisa* once had eyebrows—until an unwise restorer accidentally removed them.

forms touch something very basic in the human psyche, just as does, for example, the sound of the waves of the sea.

Bank-Breaking Works of Staggering Genius: The Priciest Artists in the World

If you take the 10 most expensive paintings ever sold at public auction, you'll find 5 names dominate the list.

_01:: Van Gogh

Van Gogh has three paintings on the list and holds the "honor" for the most expensive painting ever—the famous portrait of Doctor Gachet (1890). Van Gogh's doctor and an expert on melancholia, he asked Van Gogh to paint the picture, and it's one of the artist's last works (within eight weeks of completing it Van Gogh took his own life). In fact, he painted two versions, and the subsequent history of this one is extraordinary. Unsold at Van Gogh's death, it subsequently was owned by several different collectors, and in 1938 it belonged, astonishingly, to the Nazi supremo Hermann Göring. The Kramarsky family then acquired it, and they sold it at Christie's in 1990 for $82.5 million. The buyer was Japanese businessman Ryoei Saito, but he didn't get to enjoy his masterpiece for long. Shortly after his purchase the Japanese economy took a tumble, and Siato's businesses went down the plug, allowing the banks to take possession of his works of art. Van Gogh also pulls rank at number four with a self-portrait ($65 million) and at number eight with *Irises* ($49 million).

_02:: Renoir

Renoir weighs in at number two with *Au Moulin de la Galette*, selling for a cool $78.1 million. The piece is one of the most famous of all impressionist works, a busy open-air scene of an outdoor café, with Renoir's characteristic softly dappled sunlight. The café was an unpretentious meeting place with a happy holiday atmosphere attended by ordinary working-class people who liked to have a drink and a dance and eat the excellent little cake known as a galette. It was exactly the type of easy-on-the-eye picture that most appealed to speculative collectors at the height of the frenzied art market boom in the 1990s. The painting was sold by Sotheby's New York two days after Christie's sold Van Gogh's portrait of Doctor Gachet. Guess who the buyer was? None other than the same Mr. Ryoei Saito.

_03:: Rubens

The Flemish master Sir Peter Paul Rubens pulls in at number three with his *Massacre of the Innocents*. Painted between 1609 and 1611, the work is a huge and dynamic composition with plenty of naked flesh (a nudie pic!) illustrating the moment when Herod ordered the killing of innocent young babies because he'd been told that one of them would become king of the Jews. Part of the excitement was because the painting had sat unrecognized for over 100 years in the collection of a German family until a Sotheby's expert (in 2002) recognized it for what it was. The auction house predicted a price of $6–8 million and were as astonished as the owner when it eventually sold for a staggering $68.4 million.

_04:: Cézanne

Cézanne is at number four with a still life called *Curtain, Pitcher, and Bowl*. It's as different from the Rubens piece as can be imagined. A simple wooden table, a white tablecloth, an earthenware pitcher, a plate, a blue curtain in the background, and 20 or so apples and pears. But it came to the market at the right moment and was the star exhibit in a 1999 lot sale of 50 impressionist and modern art pieces in New York. The auction was held by the estate of a late New York socialite and philanthropist, Betsey Cushing Roosevelt Whitney, wife of the former American ambassador to London, John Hay Whitney. The sale was a huge success, and the painting fetched $55 million.

_05:: Picasso

Picasso can claim 4 out of the top 10. His most expensive is a Blue Period work (1905) called *The Marriage of Pierette*, painted when Picasso was living in poverty. The work was sold in Paris at the height of the 1989–1990 boom to, yes, another Japanese businessman, and the work is currently on the market waiting to be resold. The auctioneer who sold it for $51.72 million was a colorful character rumored to have owned the picture. In May 2000, however, he was arrested on charges of having forged auction sales documents in 1995. The other Picassos are a 1901–02 *Woman with Folded Arms* ($50 million in 2000), a 1938 portrait of his prewar mistress Dora Maar ($45 million in 1999), and an erotic 1932 portrait of his previous mistress, Marie-Thérèse Walter, asleep in a red armchair ($44 million in 1997).

Nudes You Ought to Know by Name (and Have as Fridge Magnets)

You've probably seen them out about town, and you've definitely witnessed them in all their glory. So, isn't it time you learned their names?

_01:: Michelangelo's *David*

This is the one you probably do have as a fridge magnet. In real life he's huge, 17 feet high, carved out of a single block of marble. Created by Michelangelo in 1501–1504, *David* stood outdoors in public view in the middle of Florence. The biblical hero is the little guy with a sling who killed the Philistine giant Goliath with a single shot. The Florentines revered him—he was the symbol of their small city-state, constantly under threat from bigger political powers. Artistically, however,

David is a mishmash, heroically ideal in the classical tradition, but in parts realistic (big veined hands, no fig leaf), imperfect (the head is too big), and also sexy (which is why your fridge magnet allows you to dress and undress him).

_02:: Venus de Milo

Once considered the perfect example of female beauty, Venus de Milo stands carved in white marble, naked from the waist up (her lower half is covered by a garment). She turns and seems to grow out of the cloth like an opening flower. Memorably, she has no arms because they were broken at some time, so you could have fun adding on your own to your fridge door. The statue is one of the most famous treasures in the Louvre, in Paris. Created during the Hellenistic period (fourth to first centuries BCE), the high point of ancient Greek art, she came to the Louvre in 1820, after she had been dug up on the island of Mílos by a Greek peasant.

_03:: Apollo Belvedere

Two hundred years ago the Apollo Belvedere was the most famous work of art in the world. Copies and replicas of the athletic young god were everywhere. Pulses raced at the sight of him stepping forward, left arm outstretched, with a cloak slung loosely over his shoulders and left arm. He wears a fig leaf, and both arms are broken, so a fridge magnet would give you scope to add and take away. Apollo, the son of Zeus and twin brother of Diana, was the god of prophecy and the ideal example of masculine beauty and rational civilized behavior. He is still one of the glories of the papal collections in the Vatican, but few visitors swoon before him now.

Strange but True

BRUSHES WITH CONTROVERSY

One of America's best-known artists, John James Audubon (1785–1851) (famous for his *Birds of America*, which illustrates in stunning detail and artistry 435 species), was the bastard son of a Haiti slave trader. To paint the birds, he first shot them and then wired their dead bodies into lifelike poses.

The painter and sculptor Daniele da Volterra (ca. 1509–1566) was nicknamed "braghettone" (i.e., "putter on of pants") because the Counter-Reformation pope Paul IV (1555–1559) employed him to cover up the most critical parts of the sacred nudes with decorous draperies, including Michelangelo's nudes on the Sistine Chapel ceiling.

The most faked and forged artist is probably Camille Corot (1796–1875). Over 10,000 fakes and forgeries have been recorded, and to complicate matters, Corot himself often added his signature to copies made by his pupils. When Corot died, the demand for his works was quite extraordinary, and there was a big market for unscrupulous dealers, who sold dozens of forgeries to foreign buyers, notably Americans.

The cherub-faced aristocrat and Italian artist Piero Manzoni (1933–1963), who died at the age of 29, created as a work of art a series of 30-gram tins containing "artist's shit." They were labeled with the same name and "naturally preserved," arranged in piles or randomly on a surface. Ninety versions were made, each designed to be sold for its weight in gold.

_04:: *Olympia*

Olympia became famous overnight in 1865. Exhibited at the Paris Salon, she was instantly condemned as indecent and disgusting. What was the problem? Pictures of naked women lying full length on a bed had been done by the greatest artists for centuries. Called Venus, goddess of love, they earned the highest praise. This picture was different, however. Although the subject was posed like a Venus, it was clear that this was no goddess.

With her fashionable shoe dangling on her foot, a come-hither look, a black ribbon round her neck, earrings, a black cat, and in a setting that is clearly a bedroom, Olympia is unmistakably a high-class prostitute. With one unforgettable picture, Manet destroyed all the old fictions and conventions, saying that art should show things (and people) to be as they are rather than dress them up to be what they are not. (Which is why you should have her on your fridge.)

Artists (and 1 Exhibition) Bent On Shocking the Masses

While refusing to decorate a saint's head with a halo or putting a toilet on display at a museum might seem tame by today's standards, these are the artists and events that pushed art forward. Take a closer look at the masters who sent the art world spinning.

_01:: Caravaggio (1571–1610) and Jesus

In spite of their reputations for unconventional behavior, most artists live peaceful and relatively uneventful lives. The only major artist with a serious criminal record is Caravaggio. He was regularly in trouble for hooliganism and was even charged with murder. Brilliantly talented as a painter, Caravaggio displayed a complete disregard for all the accepted proprieties and rules, and seems to have lived in a state of constant hyperexcitement. He loved sensational subjects, including severed heads, martyrdom, and corrupt-looking young men (although his tastes leaned to the heterosexual). He also caused deep offense by using peasant models for his images of Jesus Christ and the saints. This vexed plenty of people who thought that true art required idealization and that Christ and the saints needed to be depicted as superhuman angels instead of ordinary human beings.

_02:: Gustave Courbet (1819–1877) and the Working Masses

Courbet was a larger-than-life character, physically and mentally, who regularly shocked the bourgeoisie of the French Second Empire (1848–1870). Coming from a peasant background, Courbet established himself in Paris as a champion of realism. Courbet painted enormous pictures of working-class people doing humdrum, everyday things. To those who believed that art should be about pure beauty and that the working classes should be kept firmly in their place, this amounted to dangerous socialism and political revolution. In the end Courbet was put in jail for a brief period, but he won the argument for his art, and he became a model for the next generation of pioneers such as Degas, Toulouse-Lautrec, and Picasso.

_03:: Marcel Duchamp (1887–1968) and a Well-Lighted Urinal

Duchamp created very few works of art, and few of those are very interesting to look at. Today he's applauded as one of the great gurus and fathers of conceptual art. He was the first 20th-century artist to propose that the interest and stimulus of a work of art can lie solely in its intellectual content. The most famous example of this is his *Fountain Urinal* (1917). He took a used men's urinal, signed "R Mutt," and put it on display, saying, "Anything is a work of art if I, the artist, say it is." In 1917 this was a genuinely shocking idea, although now it's been repeated to the point of boredom.

_04:: America and the Scandalous Armory Show

The press loves scandal because it sells newspapers, and exhibition organizers enjoy it when it brings in the crowds. Both parties were satisfied at the famous Armory Show held in New York in 1913—so-called because it took place in the building of the 69th Regiment Armory, where half a million visitors turned up to gasp at and be shocked by the horrors of modern art. Cézanne, Picasso, Rodin, Brancusi, as well as the major impressionists were included in this show. It was, however, a turning point for art in America. The Metropolitan Museum bought its first Cézanne, and American artists realized that they had a long way to go to catch up with the latest developments in Europe. Half a century later, abstract expressionism and pop emerged, indicating that the Americans had not only caught up but actually overtaken the Europeans.

_05:: Picasso's *Guernica*

When Picasso painted *Guernica* he wanted to shock people—not to cause them offense but to wake them up to man's inhumanity. *Guernica* was first exhibited in the Spanish Pavilion at the International Exhibition in Paris in 1937. Its stark, terrifying, black-and-white imagery referred to the recent destruction of the Basque capital of Guernica in broad daylight in April 1937, when over 1,500 innocent civilians were killed. Nazi planes with German pilots under the command of General Franco carpet bombed the town so as to cause maximum death and devastation. Picasso kept the painting in his studio in Paris. In 1942 he was visited by some Nazi military officers who looked at the painting and asked Picasso, "Did you do this?" "No," replied Picasso, "you did it."

This Bold House:

Architects Who Defy Convention

If you're looking to renovate, forget the do-it-yourself approach. Instead, why not just contract out the job to one of the best? Here's a helpful guide for determining which architectural great deserves to design your dream home.

_01:: Frank Lloyd Wright (1867–1959)

A key figure in American architecture, Frank Lloyd Wright will build you a beautiful, harmonious house. It might have only a few rooms, but everything will be carefully integrated. The colors will be warm, and the materials natural and truthful. Daylight, of course, will be important, and it's a safe bet that the building will sit comfortably and easily in its natural setting. In fact, the house just might provoke gasps of admiration . . . but will you enjoy living in it? A stickler for his own views, Frank Lloyd Wright was obsessed with controlling everything, from the furniture to the ornaments to even the appliances—so much so that you may find you have a house in which Frank Lloyd Wright's personality is so dominant that you feel like a guest in your own home.

_02:: Andrea Palladio (1508–1580)

With Palladio, you've chosen not just the finest Renaissance domestic architect but one of the most skillful and intelligent architects of all time. The proportions will be so perfect and human that you will feel physically bigger and morally better the moment you step inside the front door. The classical details will be handled with the greatest understanding, but you will have a genuinely innovative house, not a pastiche of ancient architecture. Best of all, Palladio will have taken into account the full potential of your site, overcome any difficulties it presents, and created a design that fits your budget (well, he will be less tempted than most architects to spend your money as if it were in unlimited supply).

_03:: Le Corbusier (Charles-Edouard Jeanneret) (1887–1965)

Le Corbusier, one of the key pioneer architects of the modern movement, coined the phrase "a machine for living in," and that's exactly what his house will be. Simple in design, it will have minimal ornamentation, open plan spaces, white walls, and windows that run the full length of those walls like ribbons. But to appreciate your house to the fullest you'll need to have an understanding of his architectural and social theories, and be thrilled by the way they've been applied. You'll also need to dispense with clutter and have very few visible possessions; otherwise you'll be accused of desecrating the purity of his architectural principles.

_04:: Robert Adam (1728–1792)

Robert Adam was a canny Scotsman who became the architect of choice for the British nobility and gentry at the height of their powers. If your taste is for living in the grand manner with impressively proportioned rooms in the classical style (for receiving and impressing your guests, of course), then this guy's the architect for you. Especially good at converting existing houses, Adams pays breathtaking attention to detail and he would expect to design the furniture to go with your impressive rooms. He will also dictate the colors and the moldings, which are part of the overall scheme. Above all you'll require a taste for huge houses, an army of servants, deep pockets to keep the establishment going, and an overwhelming desire to entertain your guests in the style your house will lead them to expect.

_05:: Antonio Gaudí (1852–1926)

If your taste runs to the unusual and exotic, then Gaudí, the quirky Spanish interpreter of the art nouveau style, is probably the architect for you. You will see hardly a straight line on the outside, and your friends may think seeing too many old Disney movies has influenced your taste. Your house will look as though it's been molded rather than constructed, and don't be alarmed if you see the workers actually building it from rubble (one of Gaudí's favorite materials). The rubble will soon be covered in patterns made from brightly colored ceramic and glass. But be forewarned: you had better enjoy living on a building site, for it's highly probable that your house will never get finished.

by
Karen Bernd

Condensed
BIOLOGY

Contains

6 Critical Moments in the Fight against Diseases ✳ Slaphappy Science: 5 Great Reasons to Swat Mosquitoes ✳ 4 Ways Doctors Scope You Out ✳ Better Off Dead: 3 Parts of Your Body That Are Not Alive ✳ Biology That's Skin Deep: 3 Secrets to Unnatural Beauty ✳ 4 Things Your Boss Has in Common with Slime Mold ✳ Alien Invaders: 5 Guests That Overstayed Their Welcome ✳ 5 Extreme Mammals ✳ 7 Things Smarty-Plants Can Do ✳ 4 Excuses to Get a Prescription for Chocolate ✳ Behind the Equations: The Juicy Backstories on 5 Famous Biologists ✳

6 Critical Moments in the Fight against Diseases

In the Middle Ages a man considered himself lucky if he made it to the ripe old age of 35. Now, thanks to a few key health discoveries, the 30s are just a pit stop on the geriatric highway.

_01:: Bridging over Troubled Waters

The power of good plumbing is incredible. While good sanitation can't rid the world of all diseases, it has made a huge dent in epidemics caused by water-borne infectious diseases. Around 1700 BCE indoor plumbing came to royalty on the island of Crete. A millennium later Hippocrates (ca. 460–ca. 377 BCE) saw the importance of clean water and recommended that ancient Romans boil water to remove pollutants. The Romans hadn't a clue about bacteria and viruses, but we do. An easy way to pass bacterial diseases like cholera and intestinal infections is to come in contact with things that "pass through" people and animals. The moral: Don't wipe with the hand that feeds you.

_02:: Cider House Rules

Milk and cider are routinely pasteurized by a process developed by Louis Pasteur (1822–1895) in the 1860s. Sure, the name looks egomaniacal, but in fact, Pasteur's work deserves a namesake or two. Realizing that heat treatment of foods like milk could render "germs" harmless without altering the foods' taste was a big breakthrough. In addition to giving us fresh milk, Pasteur was the one who showed that spontaneous generation couldn't occur. Up until that point people believed that things appeared like magic—frogs in wet mud, maggots in meat. Showing that magic wasn't to blame, and that you could indeed keep maggots out of meat, was a major leap in preventing communicable diseases.

_03:: Pea-Brained Schemes

The saying that nothing in life is more important than good breeding holds true when it comes to diseases. Some diseases aren't caught; they're based on genes you got from your parents. Gregor Mendel (1822–1884) first noted the idea that living things had a genetic basis in 1865. At a time when people believed that babies grew from preformed beings, Mendel grew pea plants and studied the inheritance patterns of certain traits like height and seed shape. From simple, detailed observations he developed laws of inheritance showing a contribution from male and female plants. Knowing this made it possible to better understand appearance patterns for diseases like sickle cell disease, cancer, and Huntington's disease.

_04:: An Antibiotic Arsenal

Antibiotics kill bacteria. So, why can you ingest these things? Why don't they kill *you*? Many antibiotics are safe for humans because we aren't built like bacteria. Bacteria have cell walls protecting them from the environment (your gut). Antibiotics mess up cell wall synthesis or function. And while the drugs do little to our cells, they cause bacteria to lose their armor and die. And since bacteria are at the root of diseases ranging from colds to tetanus, syphilis, and leprosy, having the ability to zero in on their unique characteristics added a big gun to the antidisease arsenal. Note: antibiotics do not kill, maim, or even weaken viral infections, so don't bother asking for them if you've got the flu!

_05:: The Vaccination Emancipation

Prior to 1725 smallpox killed more than 100 million people. Today the virus lives only in laboratories. How did we get so lucky? It occurred to scientists to inject the virus that causes cowpox to fight smallpox. Makes a whole lot of sense, right? Turns out that the human immune system can remember being exposed to an invader and mount a better defense next time. Cowpox virus is very similar to smallpox virus, so a person who had a harmless case of cowpox would be immune to the much more harmful smallpox virus. Today vaccines are developed using mimic viruses (like cowpox for smallpox), heat-killed viruses, and even just bits of virus proteins. The vaccination causes your body to be ready so that the bad virus can't ambush it later in life.

_06:: DNA Cut-and-Paste

Mendel laid out the rules of genetic inheritance, and in 1952 Alfred Hershey and Martha Chase determined that you inherit DNA. James Watson and Francis Crick published the structure of DNA in 1953, and well, scientists have been studying it ever since. Recombinant DNA, however, is not the stuff of bad

sci-fi movies. It involves making new combinations of DNA in a test tube, much like using the cut-and-paste feature on your computer. So, why is this an advance in the fight against disease? Being able to manipulate virus genes has led to new vaccines that have no possibility of causing infections. Studying inherited diseases at the DNA level has led to better, more focused treatments and could possibly lead to cures.

Fake Your Way through a Conversation

(ABOUT GENES AND GENE EXPRESSION)

To use a construction analogy, genes are like blueprints for cellular parts. If you want to build a house (a protein) you go to an architect's office (the nucleus), which holds a collection of blueprints (the genome made of DNA). A copy of one blueprint is made (transcription of gene into mRNA, or messenger RNA) and given to a contractor (the ribosome). The contractor uses the paper plans to build your three-dimensional house out of brick (translation of mRNA into protein). The contractor may also make many other copies of that house (a subdivision) until the blueprint wears out. Every cell in your body contains the same genome, but not every cell has the same proteins. Just as branch offices of architectural firms can build subdivisions that look different, cells choose a subset of genes to express. The blueprints they pick determine what the cell contains and does.

Slaphappy Science:
Great Reasons to Swat Mosquitoes

Poor little mosquitoes. One minute they're just minding their own business, stopping to quench their thirst, and then whap! Suddenly their lives come to a screeching halt. Well, don't feel too sorry for the suckers. Here are five reasons to keep on swatting.

_01:: Malaria

Malaria occurs in more than 100 countries and territories and causes more than 1 million deaths each year. This disease comes from four species of *Plasmodium* parasites and is transmitted through, you guessed it, mosquito bites. In each case the mosquito picks up the invader when it bites an infected individual. The parasite then uses the mosquito as a reproduction center and food source (eww). After about a week, enough plasmodium to do some damage accumulates, and a little bit is passed along with the mosquito's saliva when it bites someone new. After multiplying in that person's liver, the parasite causes red blood cells to burst and releases toxins into the blood, making the person feel lousy. Hurray for citronella candles!

_02:: Dengue Fever and Dengue Hemorrhagic Fever

These sister diseases are caused by four related flaviviruses that use the *Aedes aegypti* mosquito as a flying hypodermic needle. Although the name *flavivirus* may sound yummy, a disease that causes you to hemorrhage probably isn't good dinner conversation. While infection sometimes results in only flulike symptoms, there are 50–100 million cases and more than 15,000 deaths from the diseases each year. The first reported epidemics occurred in Asia, Africa, and North America from 1779 to 1780; however, a current pandemic in Southeast Asia has brought the disease back to the forefront. The good news is that not all people hemorrhage and many immune systems can fight off the disease. The bad news is that the *aegypti* mosquito is currently in Texas and the southeastern United States, air travel makes disease movement easier, and there is no vaccine.

_03:: West Nile Virus

West Nile virus used to be found only in Africa, Eastern Europe, West Asia, and the Middle East. However, in 1999 cases were documented in the northeastern United States. That means that our generation is witnessing this disease's territory expand. Culex mosquitoes transmit the virus, and birds act as virus reservoirs, where the virus can multiply so more mosquitoes can pick it up. People are known as dead-end hosts because while we do get sick, we don't pass on the germs. Short-term symptoms of West Nile fever resemble the flu, and this form of the disease is more common because a healthy immune system can usually fight off the virus. And while West Nile encephalitis affects less than 1% of infected people, it is much more serious. In this form the membranes around the brain become inflamed, which can result in neurological damage or death.

_04:: St. Louis Encephalitis

If encephalitis is an inflammation of the brain, then St. Louis encephalitis refers to big-headed people from the Midwest, right? Actually, the disease is caused by another arbovirus—a virus transmitted by mosquitoes. The St. Louis part came, presumably, because of cases identified in that city. Symptoms range from fever and headaches to more severe infections resulting in stiffness, stupor, and spastic paralysis. There was a major epidemic of the disease during 1974–1977, but since then outbreaks have been sporadic and small. Like West Nile virus, the virus causing St. Louis encephalitis is a flavivirus passed through birds, which act as growth chambers, and transmitted by the *Culex* species of mosquitoes. Even though there are only about 128 cases per year, it still sounds like a good excuse for mosquito netting.

_05:: Yellow Fever

Yellow fever is perhaps the strongest advertisement for insect repellent—those infected can go from healthy to dead in three days. The symptoms include a progression from fever to extremity pain to "black vomit" (vomiting blood clots) to jaundice (making the skin yellow) to death. While not everyone dies, who wants to take the chance? Before we knew that only mosquitoes transmitted the virus (not human contact), yellow fever caused enforcement of strict quarantines. In 1793 yellow fever practically emptied Philadelphia. During the epidemic 5,000 Philadelphians died in three months, and many people—including notables like George Washington—fled the city in terror. The development of a vaccine against the disease has reduced the number of cases, but it still occurs widely in Africa and South America.

What's the Difference?
SEWAGE PLANTS VS. SEPTIC TANKS

While you probably don't want to be downwind of either a sewage treatment plant or a septic tank, you probably do want to know the difference. Though both have bacteria that eat waste, the two differ in the kinds of bacteria at work. Sewage treatment plants use large, open vats with moving multivalve spigots and rely on oxygen-loving (aerobic) bacteria. Constant stirring of the waste provides the aeration needed for aerobic bacteria to eat quickly and reduce the waste to filterable forms. Septic tanks, however, are built closed off and underground, an environment that spells death for aerobic bacteria. Septic tanks use oxygen-hating (anaerobic) bacteria, which are actually killed by oxygen. The anaerobic bacteria break down waste but are slower eaters than their aerobic cousins. Their slow-working nature and aversion to oxygen explain why septic tanks can fill up and why a hole in the tank can cause an awful stench. If the contents get out, the processing bacteria are killed and, well, yuck.

Ways Doctors Scope You Out

Doctor visits were always fun: paper gown with peek-a-boo flaps, cold stethoscopes up the back, annual weigh-ins. Just in case you're not feeling exposed enough, though, modern science has given us the scopes.

_01:: Endoscope: Glancing Where the Sun Don't Shine

Endoscopy refers to diagnostic devices that look into natural body orifices, like the ear, nose, and rectum, or cuts made by a surgeon's blade. The first designs, by Philip Bozini in 1805, consisted of a rigid shaft, a candle, and a concave mirror. Yoww! No flexibility and a lot of heat made insertion of this device unpleasurable, to say the least. Luckily, low light and poor visibility made it of minimal use to the physician, so the device fell out of favor. But not to worry. Two German physicians developed the semiflexible Wolf-Schindler gastroscope in 1933 and brought it to America. Modern forms use flexible shafts that contain video equipment within their mere 2.8-millimeter diameter—a big improvement for those on either end of the device.

_02:: Laparoscope: Tinier Scars in the OR

This device is the reason you can have your appendix removed without a scar above the bikini line. Laparoscopy is the younger cousin of endoscopy and refers to looking inside the abdomen. Although it was first performed in 1901, this procedure came into its own with the development of very small charge-coupled device (CCD) cameras and disposable laparoscopic instruments in the 1980s and 1990s. Currently, procedures ranging from gynecological to gall bladder surgeries can combine the visualization properties of endoscopy with high-tech laser surgery so that surgeons can remove a 6-inch-long organ through a 1-inch space.

_03:: Ophthalmoscope: For When the Eyes Have It

Looking into someone's pupils provides ways to monitor eye health. However, there is a basic problem—light enters and is reflected from the eye along the same path. If you want to look into someone's eye (at the retina), you have to put your eyes or a camera in front of the subject's. This gets complicated since the observer's head must necessarily block the light coming into the subject's eyes, leaving nothing to bounce back. Enter Hermann von Helmholtz. In 1851 Hermann developed an ophthalmoscope made of reflective plates and concave lenses, which provided indirect light while allowing a clear image of the retina. Besides exposing eye problems, the ophthalmoscope also helps in diagnosing a range of neurological, kidney, and heart disorders.

_04:: Microscope: For Looking Deep Within

To look beyond the organs and into the cells, a microscope is the way to go. Light microscopes in modern labs can make cells appear 1,000 times larger than they are. And though the microscope's inventor isn't known, its earliest descriptions date back to 1621. Original versions used a single glass lens and were plagued by problems with glass quality. How does the microscope work? The sample sits on a stage below a tube containing the lenses, and light shines up through the sample and into the tube to the user's eye. Modern light microscopes use glass of the highest specifications and exact curvatures. Compound microscopes can use up to three separate lenses and provide images with amazing details. Skin cells versus kidney cells, normal cells versus cancerous ones—a microscope can help you tell the difference.

Better Off Dead:
3 Parts of Your Body That Are Not Alive

If you think your hair is the only part of your body that isn't alive, maybe it's time you got a second opinion?

_01:: Cartilage

If you've had a nose job (don't worry, we won't tell), your plastic surgeon worked at least somewhat with a plasticlike tissue called cartilage. Chondrocyte cells make cartilage and then live in small pockets within the structure. The chondrocytes' secretions include a network of collagen and chondroitin sulfate that is strong enough to be the skeleton of humans during early development. Eventually, you develop a bone skeleton, but you still have cartilage in the flexible structures of the ear, nose, and windpipe.

_02:: Bone

The hard part of bone is a nonliving matrix of collagen and calcium phosphate. The catch is that the solid part of bones is nonliving, but it isn't unchanging. Just as you live in a house that you can renovate, osteoblasts and osteoclasts live in and remodel bone. When the diet is good and the bone is bearing weight, the osteoclasts are in charge of building, and new bone is laid down. It's why athletes have thicker bones than couch potatoes. On the other hand, cells use a lot of calcium and bones are the calcium store. If the body doesn't have enough dietary calcium or the bone is not bearing weight routinely, osteoclasts come in, tear down the matrix, and recycle the calcium to other parts of the body.

_03:: Tendons

Imagine a tow truck arrives to pull your car out of a ditch. If the driver uses a winch and a heavy rope, you'll be good to go. If he uses a

CLONING FROM THE COMFORT OF YOUR OWN HOME!

Public perception suggests that it's easy to clone animals and make perfect copies of the parent. But public perception is wrong. First, to create, say, a cow clone, you need two cells: the nucleus (containing the DNA) of a cell from cow 1 and an unfertilized egg from cow 2 that has had its own nucleus removed. The cow 1 nucleus is placed in the enucleated cow 2 egg and implanted into a third cow's uterus to develop—a highly inefficient process. Gathering eggs, removing nuclei, inserting "new" nuclei, and getting the egg to implant are each very difficult steps, and having them all work at the same time is rare. Then, even when the procedure works, the calf is not a truly complete genetic clone. While nuclei contain a majority of a cell's genetic material (DNA), mitochondria have small amounts. Because the cell contains many mitochondria, true genetic cloning requires that the nucleus and egg come from the same individual (which means the cloned animal can't be dead and can't be male—no egg).

winch and a rubber band, you're stuck. Tendons are the body's equivalent of that heavy rope. They connect muscles (the winch) to bones (your car) and are used to generate movement during muscle contractions. Each tendon is made of millions of tropocollagen strands, and each tropocollagen strand is made of collagen fibers. This is a different form of the same collagen used in collagen injections. Alone, each collagen molecule is short and somewhat weak. However, a collagen "rope" with a mere 1-millimeter diameter can support at least 10 kilograms (4.5 pounds) before breaking.

Biology That's Skin Deep:
Secrets to Unnatural Beauty

3

Helen of Troy may have awoken to her ship-launching beauty every day, but many of the rest of us turn to chemicals, rubs, and treatments for that "all-natural" look. Here's the dirt on why they work.

_01:: Exfoliants

Your skin has layers of dead cells making you look older (sorry), but exfoliants can come to the rescue. Exfoliants contain small abrasive particles, like bits of nutshells, rocks, or other exotic debris. When you rub the abrasives on the skin (in a circular motion, of course), they remove cells much the same way that sandpaper removes the top layer of a piece of wood. When used properly, the particles rub off only dead skin and result in the advertised healthy glow. Younger skin is revealed because skin cells are examples of epithelia—the same cells that line and cover every organ in your body and act as barriers and protectors. In every case the body knows that normal wear and tear damages this line of defense, and so new skin cells are always being made. The cells mature and end up on the surface when old cells on top of them die and fall off; it happens all the time. Rough exfoliation can cause their death, but correct use just speeds the cleanup process.

_02:: Perms

The grass is always greener on someone else's head. Those with curly hair spent hours smoothing it straight, while the straight-haired lot yearned wistfully for curls that wouldn't flop by happy hour. Then along came the invention of permanent waves and hair relaxers to address these serious issues. Both processes rely on the chemical structure of hair. Each hair is actually a bundle of proteins called keratins that are secreted from the hair follicle cell. The amount of bounce in your locks is a result of the pattern of cross-linking between keratins in a hair and protein components that contain sulfur. To make more lasting change in your hairdo, hairdressers use solutions that break the natural sulfide cross-links and reform them in a new way. When you get a whiff of the sulfur, you can be sure you're smelling biochemistry.

_03:: Botox Injections

Think of beauty and you probably don't conjure up images of food poisoning, but trends in cosmetics are sometimes unpredictable. Botox treatments are a case in point. Botox (botulinum toxin) is secreted by the *Clostridium botulinum* bacterium. If eaten, the bacterium lives in the gut, releases its toxin, and causes potentially fatal food poisoning. However, when injected (in small doses), it eliminates crow's-feet and worry lines. How? It causes paralysis. Botox inhibits neurons that normally tell muscles to relax. When the neurons can't signal, the muscle remains paralyzed in its contracted form. So it follows that injecting a small amount locally reduces wrinkles. However, injecting large amounts paralyzes vital organs and results in death—truly a case where dosage counts.

Things Your Boss Has in Common with Slime Mold

There have been times when you were sure your boss was a lower life form. Finally! Here's the biological proof you've always wanted.

_01:: They Both Respond to External Stimuli

Slime mold can, and does, move (a fact responsible for notorious B movie *The Blob*). The movement is known as chemotaxis because the slime mold senses a chemical (chemo) and moves (taxis). To understand the directional nature of the movement, think of freshly baked chocolate chip cookies and a skunk's smell. Anything the slime moves toward is a chemoattractant. If the mold moves away, the substance is a chemorepellant. Just as you follow the cookies' aroma to the kitchen or flee desperately from the skunk's spray, slime molds detect chemical gradients to determine the direction of their motion. Either the mold goes toward the higher concentration of an attractant chemical, or it slithers toward lower concentrations if the chemical is a repellant.

_02:: They're Both Eukaryotic

There are two basic cell types. Prokaryotic cells have an external membrane, and all their other parts float in the cytoplasm within it. Eukaryotic cells have an external membrane as well, but they also have smaller membrane sacks inside. The sacks are called organelles, and each kind of organelle is specialized for a different function. Slime mold (*Dictyostelium discoideum*) and your boss share this quality. Not only do they both have organelle-containing cells, but they also have the same kinds and similar numbers of each type of organelle.

_03:: They're Both Multicellular

Your boss started out as a single cell that divided to become the millions of different cells in the body. And while slime mold may look simple, it too has a multicellular stage in its life cycle. During times of plenty (food and moisture), each slime mold cell is an independent unit that lives as part of a swarm. However, when resources are scarce, these swarmer cells will clump and work together in a slug to produce reproductive structures called fruiting bodies. Just make sure to note two things: first, this slug is not the kind in your garden;

and second, unlike your boss, the slime mold "chooses" between single cell and multicellular existence, wherein all of the cells must work together for survival.

_04:: They Both Reproduce Sexually

This is true for humans certainly, since a sperm and egg must fuse to get things started. That fertilized egg, or zygote, will go on to divide thousands of times for the human body to develop. For humans, there's the hope of happily ever after, but not for slime molds. Once two swarmer slime mold cells fuse, the new cell goes on to divide two, and only two, times to produce four daughter cells. Each of these cells is a swarmer that can either remain solitary or clump with hundreds of others to form a slug. This mold can even do something your boss can't: it can reproduce asexually by having one swarmer cell divide in half to make two identical clones. Let's hope the boss never develops that ability!

Alien Invaders:
5 Guests That Overstayed Their Welcome

When these poor countries couldn't solve their own environmental dilemmas, they enlisted aid from overseas creatures. Here are a few foreign "friends" that didn't bother to help out, making the quick transition from guest to pest.

_01:: Cane Toads

Cane toads (*Bufo marinus*) aren't native to Australia, but they are becoming a large ecological problem there. The toads were introduced as a natural means of controlling the grayback beetle population that plagues the country's sugarcane fields. There are three slight problems. First, the toads reproduce very rapidly. Second, the cane toad has no natural predators to keep its population in check. And third, even though the toads have voracious appetites, they don't eat many of the beetles, because the grayback beetle lives inside the sugar cane and the toad can't get to it. Now instead of just an insect problem, Australia has beetles in the cane and toads underfoot.

_02:: European Starlings

Introducing a new animal to control an old pest seems to be a recurring theme. The European starling (*Sturnus vulgaris*) was brought to the United States as a means of controlling insects such as locusts. In 1890 a flock of 100 of the small black birds was released in New York City's Central Park. This small flock aggressively competed with native species for nesting cavities and food, and the birds are now found throughout the United States and Canada. This competition has resulted in declining numbers of native species, like the Eastern bluebird. As if that wasn't enough, starlings are responsible for damaging fruit crops as well. The upside is, at least they do eat locusts.

_03:: Zebra Mussels

Originally found in Europe, this freshwater mussel probably invaded the United States by stowing away in the ballast water of transatlantic ships. First seen in the Great Lakes, their range nearly doubled between 1986 and 1988. Since their larvae swim and the adults love boat hulls, they'll probably be found in more lakes soon. Zebra mussels are particularly unpopular with native clam lovers because the mussels compete with the clams for resources and space. Water intake structures don't fare well either: the cost of the damage from the adults' presence goes well into millions of dollars. On the other hand, the presence of millions of hungry filter feeders has led to a decrease in algae, allowing sunlight to penetrate into deeper water and helping some invertebrates and aquatic plants—a lot of power for a little mollusk.

_04:: House Sparrow

What is it about New Yorkers and birds? Like the European starling, the house sparrow (*Passer domesticus*) was released in New York City's Central Park in the 1800s. As settlers moved west across the United States, the house sparrows moved with them, and their range currently extends from sea to shining sea. This small brown, black, and white bird is a common sight at backyard birdfeeders since its diet consists of seeds. Its eating habits, however, have made it less than welcome on farms, where it can eat enough seed to reduce crop yields. Like many introduced species, house sparrows did muscle in on someone else's territory, so they too have been blamed for the population decline of some native bird species.

_05:: Kudzu

As interstate highways began crisscrossing the southern United States, a need developed for low-maintenance ways to control roadside erosion and beautify the landscape. Enter the kudzu (*Pueraria lobata*), a low-growing vine that requires basically no maintenance, can withstand hot southern summers, and has pretty green leaves and flowers in July. Problem is, kudzu is highly invasive and grows very quickly. A short visit to a southeastern state will introduce you to kudzu next to roads, in fields, and covering old barns. It may be picturesque and it does fight erosion, but it also outcompetes and kills all plant life in its path. There are even cases of livestock and pets wandering into kudzu fields, becoming entangled, and dying. On the other hand, kudzu is said to be quite tasty in salads.

5 Extreme Mammals

Mammals are warm-blooded, covered with hair, bear live young, and produce milk to feed them, and we like to think of ourselves as the best mammal around. However, in many categories other animals have us beat, paws down.

_01:: The Biggest

Some people argue that a vegetarian diet can't support a large life-form. They obviously haven't met the blue whale (*Balaenoptera musculus*), a massive creature that survives on plankton. Weighing in at 150 tons, the blue whale isn't only the largest mammal but, in fact, the largest animal known. Its ability to maintain life on such a grand scale is aided by its oceanic lifestyle. In comparison, the bull African elephant (*Loxodonta africana*) is the largest land animal, and it weighs a mere 12 tons.

_02:: The Smallest

The title "smallest mammal" is only slightly smaller than the animal it describes. A native of Thailand, measuring 1.14–1.3 inches and weighing 0.06–0.07 ounces, Kitti's hog-nosed bat (*Craseonycteris thonglongyai*), or bumble-bee bat, truly earns its title. The smallest land mammal, the pygmy shrew (*Suncus etruscus*), is only slightly larger, tilting the scales at a hefty 0.05–0.09 ounces. These pipsqueaks are so small that they're outweighed by two standard paper clips. Even though their diminutive stature places them eye to eye with many snails and insects, these two animals are true warm-blooded vertebrates: they are covered with hair, and their females produce milk—mammals to the core.

_03:: The Fastest

As might be expected, the winner in this category depends on the terrain. Mammals are found in the air, water, and land, and each domain requires different types of locomotion skills. The fastest air mammal is the big brown bat (*Eptesicus fuscus*), which can flap its way up to 15.5 miles per hour. The fastest water mammal reaches a significantly higher 34 miles per hour—and at this speed the killer whale (*Orcinus orca*) can definitely have its choice of the catch of the day. However, clocking in at 70 miles per hour, the overall fastest mammal is a land creature, the cheetah (*Acinonyx jubatus*). Due to the amazing amount of energy required, this cat can pour on the power only for short periods of time, but that's of little comfort to the gazelles it sets its sights on.

_04:: The Slowest

In a competition over slowness, three animals come to mind: the tortoise, the sloth, and the snail. Of these contestants the snail is definitely the winner hands down. The garden snail clocks in at a molasses-like 0.03 miles per hour. Moving at a steady pace, it would take the snail 12.5 hours to go around a standard city block. However, the category is the slowest mammal, and snails (and tortoises) aren't mammals. On that technicality the three-toed sloth (*Bradypus variegates*) pulls into the winner's circle. Three-toed sloths, believe it or not, have three toes and spend the vast majority of their lives in the rain forests of Central and South America. These speedsters register 0.15 miles per hour, making them 5 times faster than the garden snail but 467 times slower than the cheetah.

_05:: The Thickest

No, this award doesn't refer to mental capacity; that could be a much tougher call. The rhinoceros (*Diceros bicornis michgeli*) is the land mammal with the thickest skin. In fact, for its size, the rhino has the thickest skin of any animal. Rough boss, critical spouse—with 1-inch-thick skin, these tough guys can handle it all. Well, maybe not the boss.

Strange but True

X-TREME MATING

The male platypus is one of only two known venomous mammals. The venom, however, is delivered not by fangs but by retractable spurs on the male platypus's hind legs. Even more strange, these spurs aren't really used on predators and prey. Instead, platypus venom is reserved for battles with rival males during what must be an extreme mating season. In the very few documented cases where humans have been envenomed, the results were intense. The unfortunate victims reported tremendous pain that did not respond to morphine and lingered for months.

---

7 Things Smarty-Plants Can Do

Not to get you down, but plants can do everything you can do and then some.

_01:: Reproduce

Whoever argued that sex doesn't require a lot of brainpower was right. This applies not just for humans but for all plants as well—they reproduce without even having a brain. The way it works with plants is the same way it works with humans, with a few G-rated substitutions. The plant equivalent to sperm is pollen (think about that as you wash your car this spring), and the plant equivalent of an egg is an ovum. Pollination is the process of getting the pollen near the ovum. The pollen catches a ride on the wind or on a variety of insects like bees or moths. Once the pollen reaches its destination, it grows a tiny tube toward the ovum. When the tube penetrates the ovum, fertilization occurs, and a short time later the seeds are ready.

_02:: Reproduce All Alone

Most plants mate in pairs, but a few plants are monoecious (from the Greek "one house"), meaning that both sexes are present in the same plant. For example, one corn stalk can fertilize itself. This contrasts with the way animals and some plants, like oak trees, arrange things. Oak trees and people are dioecious (from the Greek "two houses"), meaning that different organisms produce the two types of sex cells. Being monoecious has some interesting consequences: it greatly promotes pollination by wind or even gravity, and it also favors inbreeding (believe it or not, intelligence is not a factor in that either).

_03:: Respond to Stress

What could a plant have to be stressed about? A lot. Once a seed begins to grow, the plant is quite literally rooted to the spot, unable to get up and move if the weather is lousy. Because of this, plants have developed ways of surviving abiotic stresses like drought, high salinity, heat, and chill. The defenses aren't always successful, though, and long-term stresses kill most plants. As an example, to combat drought, plants quite literally close up shop. Water pressure within plant cells provides much of their rigidity (called turgor), and without water the plant wilts. To combat wilting, cells harden their cell walls and leaves and shut their vent-like stomata to reduce water loss. Some plants have evolved amazing water conservation mechanisms, as errant houseplant owners know. However, most plants (both indoor and outdoor) will die during long droughts.

_04:: Produce Their Own Food

Forget TV dinners; plants know how to take in light and convert it to food. Translated into biology lingo, plants use photosynthesis to convert solar energy into usable chemical energy forms. Without thinking, the pigments in the chloroplasts of a leaf cell capture photons of light. The energy from those photons is passed through more than 10 protein complexes to produce glucose and other cellular building blocks. This process is a definite reason to go hug a tree. We humans need not only the end products but also what the plant considers waste—a gas called oxygen. Without plant life, we don't eat or breathe. Contrary to popular belief, without us they get along just fine (if not better).

_05:: Kill You

There's no reason to be paranoid. Plants aren't out to get you, personally, but many are killers. Some plant poisons are just plant waste products (think of the waste you produce). Others have developed because plants cannot run away from their predators. Toxins like ricin in castor beans or alkaloids from delphiniums make the animals that eat them sick or dead. Either way the animal is unlikely to eat leaves from that plant again. In a bizarre twist, humans are learning how to harness some of these poisons for medicinal purposes. Foxglove produces a toxic glycoside that in low doses is the heart medication digitalis. The power of opium poppies, a deadly alkaloid, has been used medicinally for centuries in the forms of morphine and codeine.

_06:: Coordinate Functions in an Organism More Than 100 Feet Tall

Sequoia trees tower overhead. Easily made up of many billions of cells, these giants, as well as all other plants, employ coordinated actions. Resources gathered through the roots or via photosynthetic leaves are shared throughout the plant. The organism bends toward the light and seems to know just when to do things like dropping leaves. And all this occurs without a brain, in part due to the plants' vascular system made of xylem and phloem. These tissues could be compared to the blood and lymph systems in the human body. Xylem is plant tissue that transports water and minerals up from the roots and provides support. Phloem moves the products of photosynthesis (food) from leaves to other sites for use or storage.

_07:: Fight Off Invaders

It may be surprising, but plants can actually detect invasion and mount counterattacks in a manner similar to humans' immune systems. When a fungus or bacteria attacks, the plant detects that something is amiss and does two things. First, cells around the infected cell die, forming a barrier that the original invader can't cross. Second, signals travel throughout the plant system warning other cells. The other cells change their content and functions so that they can resist invasion. The systemic nature of this signal is important because invaders usually don't come alone and plants can't run away. It is interesting to note that one of the chemicals in the resistance response is salicylic acid, the natural precursor of our painkiller aspirin.

What's the Difference?

MOLECULAR BIOLOGY VS. MICROBIOLOGY

There are enough subdisciplines in biology to choke the proverbial horse. Two of the most commonly confused are molecular biology and microbiology, and while both study cells, they maintain different approaches. Molecular biologists are like mechanics at a small-town garage—drive in any model of vehicle and they want to pop the hood to see what makes it run. Microbiologists are like dealership mechanics, working only on certain makes. Microbiologists specialize in microbes, microscopic organisms commonly called germs. They examine all aspects of single-celled organisms from beneficial and infectious bacteria to organisms like brewer's yeast. The type of vehicle (cell) determines their work. By contrast, molecular biologists are primarily interested in the cellular process, the cellular "engine," and may use any cell type. Because they study the way molecules interact (and all cells are made of molecules), plant, animal, and bacterial cells are fair game.

Excuses to Get a Prescription for Chocolate

It's true: chocolate is good for you, so why not stock up? (Unfortunately, there's nothing we can do about french fries.)

_01:: Love at First Chemical Reaction

Chocolate contains compounds like phenylethylamine (PEA), tryamine, and theobromine, all of which can make you feel swell. These compounds have mildly stimulatory and pleasure-causing effects because their shapes are similar to neurotransmitters, the brain chemicals that travel between nerve cells to help you interpret and react to your environment. Neurotransmitters like the catecholamines are responsible for feelings of well-being and contentment. Guess what? The chocolate compounds look a lot like these feel-good neurotransmitters. When PEA bumps into a nerve cell, a regular love-fest ensues, and all feels right with the world. Since the "love compounds" are present in only small amounts, you need to eat more, right?

_02:: Help Your Heart

A bar of dark chocolate contains 10 times as many phenols as an orange and 4 times as much as beets. Why calculate phenol content? Phenols have been shown to inhibit blood clots by thinning the blood. Thinner blood is easier for the heart to pump, and the decrease in clots means fewer heart attacks. And science is finally supporting what lovers have in-

---

Strange but True

EXERCISING'S "BURN" EXPOSED

While "Feel the burn" is the rallying cry of the exercise conscious, there are actually two burns. One signifies damage due to a muscle tear. The other indicates you're in oxygen debt and shouldn't overdo it. Muscles use oxygen as part of aerobic respiration, which consumes carbohydrates and produces cellular power. In times of exertion, even though your heart is pounding, power needs exceed the amount of oxygen your blood can deliver. When this happens, muscle cells use anaerobic respiration, an alternate power pathway that doesn't use oxygen but isn't as efficient. The burn then comes from the pathway's byproduct—lactic acid. Lactic acid is a weak acid, but it is an acid. If the blood doesn't remove enough and it accumulates in the muscle, it hurts. Too bad we don't use the anaerobic respiration pathway that yeast does—its byproduct isn't lactic acid but alcohol.

tuited for centuries—the gift of chocolate isn't only *from* the heart, it's also good *for* the heart. That being said, remember: moderation is the key. Some doctors now recommend a glass or two of red wine to add phenols to the diet, and eating only 1.5 ounces of dark chocolate will equal that phenol intake. Quadrupling that dosage is fun, but don't expect your doctor to recommend it.

_03:: Ward Off Magnesium Deficiency

Many of the enzymes (protein machines) in your cells require metals like magnesium to work. A magnesium deficiency can be a factor in anything from asthma to diabetes, migraines, stuttering, or even premenstrual syndrome. Food cravings can be the body's way of telling you about diet deficiencies, so to satisfy your craving, why not grab a chocolate bar and enjoy? It's a good source of magnesium. (For the record, so is broccoli, but broccoli cravings are less common for some reason.)

_04:: Put a Little Zip in Your Step

A "little" zip is the key part of this chocolate fact—chocolate contains caffeine. In a normal serving size of milk chocolate (about 6 ounces if you're feeling virtuous) there are 36 milligrams of the stimulant. You'd have to have almost three servings to compare with the jolt you'd get from a cup of coffee. Either way, candy bar or morning coffee, caffeine is the stimulant of choice, as it works to block the Off button for a stimulatory pathway found in all cells. When caffeine is around there's no signal to stop, so the pathway keeps on going and going and going—and so do you.

Behind the Equations: The Juicy Backstories on Famous Biologists

In most textbooks it seems like scientists just waltz into their labs, fiddle around for a bit, then wait for the Nobel Committee to call. Sadly, the road to discovery is rarely that simple, and speed bumps pop up constantly. Call it historical context or call it dirt; there's always more to the story.

_01:: Give Peas a Chance

Who would have guessed that Gregor Mendel (1822–1884), the "father of modern genetics," began his work in remedial training? In 1843 Mendel was an ordained priest attempting to get a job teaching natural science at a local school in Brno, Moravia. Problem was, he failed the teaching certificate exam. No social promotions allowed here; to fix him up, his abbot had Mendel attend the University of Vienna to study physical and biological sciences. Sticking with it seems to have worked.

At Vienna, Mendel began his legendary work with pea plants, which demonstrated that patterns of inheritance hold from peas to humans. Oh, and even though his work in genetics remained unrecognized by scientists until the 1900s, Mendel did achieve his goals. He finally received his teaching certificate, taught high school, and became the abbot of his monastery.

_02:: Naturally Selected

Charles Darwin (1809–1882), a young graduate from the University of Cambridge, almost didn't get to go on the 1831 voyage of the HMS *Beagle,* the five-year voyage that provided the basis for Darwin's historic *Origin of Species.* Initially, the ship's captain wanted to reject him based on the shape of his nose. It seems Captain Fitz-Roy judged a man's character by his profile, and Darwin's nose just didn't indicate "sufficient energy and determination." Also, Darwin's father thought the trip was a frivolous attempt to avoid getting a real job (like joining the clergy). What to do? A three-day test voyage with the captain and a well-worded letter from Darwin's uncle soon removed the barriers, and Darwin was on his way.

_03:: Rest in Peace Prize

Many people have heard about Watson and Crick, the dynamic duo of DNA. Fewer have heard of Rosalind Franklin, unless they've heard about the Nobel controversy. Franklin (1920–1958) took the X-ray photographs that are credited with making DNA structure clear to Watson and Crick and leading to the Nobel Prize the men shared with Maurice Wilkins. So, why didn't she just look at the picture and see it herself? Well, for one thing, an X-ray diffraction picture looks a lot like children's spin-art. Taking such pictures is difficult and interpreting them, an art. Also, many times breakthroughs require the perspectives of people from different areas. But was Rosalind Franklin denied a Nobel Prize due to sexism? Absolutely not. The proof: Watson, Crick, and Wilkins were awarded the Nobel Prize in 1962. Franklin died of ovarian cancer four years earlier, and Nobels are not awarded posthumously.

_04:: Albert in Wonderland

One safety rule for scientists is "Don't eat in lab." Albert Hofmann's (1908–) choice to ignore that rule took him not just down a different path but on a whole new kind of trip. In 1938, while trying to develop treatments for migraine headaches, Hofmann made a new chemical, but then had to leave work early due to feelings of "not unpleasant delirium." The next day he thought that there might be a connection between the chemical he inhaled accidentally and his altered mood, so he did the next logical (albeit crazy) thing. He ate some. The chemical was lysergic acid diethylamide, or LSD, and that day Hofmann became the first person ever to "drop acid." LSD has some therapeutic potential, but LSD abuse led Sandoz to stop producing it in 1966.

_05:: Cell Block

As a little guy, what do you do when your results fly in the face of current dogma? This was Leonard Hayflick's dilemma. In the 1960s scientists knew that if they put cells in a petri dish with the right nutrients and enough room, the cell culture would stay alive and keep dividing indefinitely. However, Leonard

Hayflick and Paul Moorhead had evidence that fibroblast cells in culture would divide only a certain number of times (about 50), and then they would die. To confirm their findings and convince skeptics, these young guns had colleagues working in leading labs, repeating their experiments. Good try, but it didn't work. Hayflick's first paper describing the work was rejected because it was contrary to the current line of thinking. Fortunately, the pair persevered and the paper was published in a different scientific journal. The evidence was so compelling that other researchers listened and the entire field of biogerontology, the study of how cells age, was born.

by
Joe Schwarcz

Condensed
CHEMISTRY

Contains

Elemental Floss: 4 Chemists Who Lived for the Lab ✳ 3 Sexy Insects ✳ Gills with Frills: 2 Fishy Health Benefits ✳ 3 Drugs That Save Lives ✳ 1 Backyard Narcotic ✳ 2 Religious Mysteries Solved by Chemistry ✳ 3 Fantastic Side Effects of Neutering ✳ Urine Trouble: 4 True Tales of Tee-Tee ✳ 3 Facts with Silver Linings ✳ 4 Metals That Meddle with Your Body ✳ Lady Killers: 3 Deadly Cosmetics ✳ 3 Tips for Brisk Business ✳ 4 Simple Cures Straight from Momma's Cupboard ✳ All Fired Up: 3 Smokey the Bear Nightmares ✳ Last Calls for Alcohol: 3 Tips for Imbibing ✳ 5 Facts in Poor Taste ✳

Elemental Floss:
Chemists Who Lived for the Lab

The life of a chemist isn't always easy . . . or safe for that matter. Hats off to these cats for braving the elements in the name of pushing science forward.

_01:: Antoine-Laurent Lavoisier
(1743–1794)

While Lavoisier was the father of modern chemistry, he certainly wasn't the father of *modest* chemistry. A brash Antoine once said, "I am young and avid for glory." He may have been somewhat full of himself, but he did deliver the goods. His contributions range from helping to light the streets of Paris to establishing the law of conservation of mass. And though he often took too much credit for the ideas of others, his own contributions have lasted as well. (He named oxygen and hydrogen—beat that!) Like all scientists, Lavoisier ran into some funding problems, so against the advice of his friends, he took a job as farmer-general (tax collector). That was his first mistake. His second was blackballing Jean-Paul Marat from the Academy of Science. During the French Revolution, the combination of Lavoisier's status as a tax collector for the government and Marat's influence landed Lavoisier at the guillotine. He supposedly begged for a few weeks to finish his experiments. Motion denied. Lavoisier was beheaded immediately. A fellow scientist who observed the tragic event commented that "it required only a moment to sever his head, and probably one hundred years will not suffice to produce another like it."

_02:: Henry Cavendish (1731–1810)

Cavendish was a notoriously shy, absent-minded English chemist and physicist with a pronounced fear of women (he had female servants but could communicate with them only through notes). Despite tons of experiments, he published only 20 articles, and many of his contributions weren't realized until they were rediscovered. Lavoisier (see above) repeated Cavendish's study of the collection of gases above water and renamed inflammable air—hydrogen. Similarly, James Maxwell repeated Cavendish's experiments on electricity, although he didn't go to quite the same lengths in the name of science. During his studies of capacitance (a measure of the ability to hold an electric charge), Cavendish shocked himself repeatedly and estimated the strength of a current by measuring the amount of pain he felt as it flowed through his body. Where would modern science be if a few crazy men hadn't been willing to shock themselves silly? The world may never know.

_03:: Marie Curie (1867–1934)

The Polish-born French chemist Marie Curie was the first person ever to win two Nobel Prizes: she shared the 1903 prize in physics with her husband, Pierre, and Henri Becquerel (for the discovery of radioactivity), and she later won the 1911 prize in chemistry (for the isolation of radium). But radiation turned out to be a poor friend to the Curies. In 1906 Pierre, sickened by his prolonged exposure to radiation, died when a horse-drawn wagon ran him over. Amid some controversy, Marie Curie accepted his physics chair at the Sorbonne and became the institute's first female professor. A classroom full of celebrities and politicians greeted her with a standing ovation, but of course, Marie skipped the niceties and began teaching her husband's lecture exactly where he left off. After a career of many more firsts, in 1934 Marie died of leukemia, likely brought on by exposure to high radiation levels during her research. The Radium Institute was renamed the Curie Institute in her honor.

_04:: Christian Friedrich Schönbein (1799–1868)

Note to spouses of chemists: hire your sweetie a babysitter. German chemist Christian Schönbein, who discovered ozone in 1840, didn't always listen to his wife's number-one rule: no experiments in the house. On an otherwise uneventful day in 1845, Schönbein accidentally spilled a mixture of nitric and sulfuric acids. He didn't want his wife to find out, so he quickly grabbed her apron to sop up the liquid. There was just enough time for the apron to dry out (over the stove) before his wife came home. All would have gone smoothly, except that the apron burst into flames and disappeared without producing any smoke. Fortunately, his wife wasn't wearing it at the time. On the bright side, Schönbein had discovered nitrocellulose (or guncotton), which effectively took the place of gunpowder on the battlefield.

3 Sexy Insects

If your cheesy pickup lines and B-grade courting tactics just aren't up to par, maybe it's time you took some tips from the Don Juans of the insect world.

_01:: Spanish Fly

Mention Spanish fly, and people's thoughts turn to carnal activities. Actually, Spanish fly isn't a fly at all, but a beetle that produces a compound called cantharidin, an irritant of the urogenital tract. While it isn't an aphrodisiac, Spanish fly can produce an erection. It can also pose a serious threat to human health. Luckily, it poses no threat to the male pyrochroid beetles, which rely on the stuff for mating purposes. During the mating ritual, the male secretes a gooey substance, which the female tastes. Only if she tastes cantharidin does mating become a possibility—a good example of chemical warfare and species survival. The female passes the cantharidin on to her eggs, which are then less appetizing to predators such as ladybugs.

_02:: Moths That Use Protection

Talk about clever dating tactics, the red male moth of the *Cosmosoma myrodora* species dines on the fluid from the leaves of the dog fennel plant and stores some of its chemical contents in a pair of pouches under his abdomen. Then, when the little guy goes a-courting, he discharges the pouch contents all over the female, sort of like nuptial confetti. The fluid contains a variety of alkaloids from the plant that repel predators, such as spiders. Indeed, virgin female moths coated with the stuff and placed into spiders' webs are quickly cut loose by the spider. This chemical protection seems vital since the moths spend up to nine hours copulating! The male wants to ensure that his mate doesn't become a meal while he attempts to impregnate her.

_03:: Meat and Greet

Plants use some fascinating techniques to spread their pollen. The voodoo lily, for example, depends on carrion beetles for pollination. Because these beetles normally feast on decaying flesh, the lily has evolved an ideal mechanism. Its fragrance is composed of two

Strange but True

OZONE AND CONDOMS

We think of ozone as a useful gas. And indeed it is, as long as it's up there in the stratosphere where it belongs. Ozone forms when oxygen is exposed to ultraviolet light, and it's a good thing because ozone's a great absorber of ultraviolet radiation, thus protecting us from skin cancer. At ground level, however, ozone is a pollutant, forming as a result of internal combustion in our car engines. It's also the characteristic smell you sniff around photocopiers or other electrical devices. While ozone irritates our lungs, it can also affect our sex lives. The most widely used condoms are made of natural rubber, a substance that degrades when exposed to ozone. In laymen's terms, this means that your protection needs protection if you're storing it around a photocopier.

delightful chemicals, putrescine and cadaverine, which smell just like rotten meat. And while they smell awful to humans, they're pretty appealing to carrion beetles. When the bugs come a-crawling in search of the odor, they are undoubtedly disappointed—no rotting meat in sight, only some weird flower. But as the beetles explore the plant they pick up pollen, which they then unwittingly spread around.

Gills with Frills:
Fishy Health Benefits

Stop heaping those ribs on your plate, put down that pork chop, and lay off the steak for just a sec! We've got the chemically justified reasons why you need to "go fish."

_01:: Fish for the Brain

Here's something to think about. Docosahexaenoic acid, or DHA for short, is a fatty acid. In fact, DHA is a major component of the brain, nerve, and eye tissue, and may just be the right substance for pregnant mothers to dose up on if they want brainy children. A British study showed that children born to mothers who ate oily fish such as sardines or mackerel at least once every two weeks showed superior brain development. In fact, the potential benefits of DHA are so great that there's talk of adding it to baby formula. Another encouraging finding is the reduction in the risk of dementia in people who eat fish at least once a week. It seems polyunsaturated fatty acids, such as DHA, reduce inflammation in the brain and aid in nerve cell regeneration. Holy mackerel!

_02:: And Fish for the Teeth?

Fish is so good for you that even its condiments have nutritional value. Along with your raw fish (sushi), try a little of the pungent, green horseradish known as wasabi. This spicy side might actually do more than just improve the taste: it could keep you smiling longer. Chemicals called isothiocyanates, found in a good dose in wasabi, have been shown effective at killing the bacteria that

cause tooth decay and likely fight other germs as well. Perhaps that's why wasabi evolved in the first place as a traditional accompaniment to raw fish! And if that wasn't enough, here's another sushi surprise: isothiocyanates also have anticancer properties, which should have you grinning even wider.

What's the Difference?
REAL OJ VS. FAKE OJ

The orange juice market is huge. Unfortunately, some processors try to cut corners by extending the juice with sugar, pulp wash, and water. But a true orange juice purist can detect the ruse with some clever science. Oxygen in nature occurs as two possible isotopes, O-16 and O-18, which differ slightly in mass. That's right: all water is not created equal. A juice diluted with water from nonbiological sources will have a different isotope distribution, and this can be detected by an instrument called a mass spectrometer. In fact, the authorities have already used this method to put the squeeze on some OJ fraud artists. They may fool the taste buds, but not the mass spectrometer.

Drugs That Save Lives

Sometimes the solutions to life's biggest problems (like tuberculosis) are found in the most unexpected places . . . like in the fungus at the back of a chicken's throat. Here's to unusual drugs from unusual sources that continue to save lives.

_01:: Aspirin and the Willow

It's a common belief that aspirin is found in the bark of willow trees. It's not! A related compound called salicin does indeed occur in willow bark, thereby explaining the traditional use of the bark as a medication. But salicin is irritating to the stomach, a problem that prompted the Bayer company to look for an alternative. When one of their chemists synthesized acetyl salicylic acid in 1898, he found it to be a great improvement over other salicylates—a triumph of chemistry over nature! Aspirin has since been found to do much more than alleviate pain. It's an excellent anti-inflammatory substance, as many arthritis patients will vouch. ASA, as it is commonly known, also has an anticoagulant, or blood-thinning, effect, which can reduce the risk of heart attacks. In fact, today more aspirin is consumed as a heart-attack preventer (generally in doses of about 80 mg a day) than as a painkiller!

_02:: Streptomycin and a Sick Chicken

In the 1930s Selman Waksman, working at Rutgers University, became interested in isolating antibiotics from fungi, hoping to find another penicillin. To aid his quest, he asked his colleagues to send him samples of any un-usual species they encountered. One day a farmer came to see a Rutgers veterinarian with a sick chicken in tow. All of his chickens, the farmer said, were suffering from the same kind of disease as the sample. The vet found that the bird had a fungal throat infection, but remembering Waksman's request, he sent him a throat swab. From a culture of this fungus, Waksman eventually isolated streptomycin, an antibiotic that revolutionized the treatment of infections, particularly tuberculosis.

_03:: Sister Morphine

When you're in pain, nothing else matters. Jobs, the vagaries of the stock market, and politics all take a backseat to dealing with the affliction. Unfortunately, about 10 million North Americans are permanently disabled by back pain, and nearly 75% of cancer patients experience severe pain. For these people, pain-killing medication can make life worth living. Oxycodone (OxyContin) is a semisynthetic analogue of morphine and is available in a time-release form for effective pain relief. But instructions must be carefully followed. Cutting a pill in half destroys the time-release effect, and all of the active ingredient is released at once, potentially causing a fatal overdose. Unfortunately, oxycodone has become a very popular drug for people who want to achieve a chemical high. They cut open tablets and chew, snort, or mainline the contents. Sadly, many have paid with their lives.

Backyard Narcotic

Not to get all Nancy Reagan on you, but it's probably best not to go around licking toads just to get a high. In fact, trial and error might not be the best policy when it comes to backyard narcotics. Here's a case that ended up in error.

_01:: Cane Toads Take a Licking

In the 1930s "sugarcane" toads were introduced into Australia from Hawaii with the idea that they would control the grayback beetle, a sugarcane pest (see Alien Invaders: 5 Guests That Overstayed Their Welcome, p. 33). Bizarrely enough, cane toads can secrete a toxic compound known as bufotenin from a couple of glands behind their eyes (when attacked by predators, of course). But the toxic goo is also a hallucinogen, albeit a dangerous one. In their endless quest to get high, Australian teenagers have taken to drinking the slime produced when toads are boiled. Clearly, emulating this behavior isn't the brightest idea, as two Canadian kids learned. They purchased a couple of toads from an exotic pet store and licked them, hoping for euphoria. They got hospital beds instead.

Religious Mysteries Solved by Chemistry

There are some mysteries that we just can't explain. Then again, there are plenty of others that make a lot more sense if you know a little chemistry.

_01:: Where the Hell Is It?

Does hell exist? The ancient Greeks thought so. They even knew where the entrance to the underworld could be found: right beside the temple of Apollo in Pamukkale, in what is now Turkey. The gateway looked like the entrance to a cavern, but this was no ordinary cavern. No animal or man who wandered into the misty cave ever returned. Today we have a good idea why—the area around the cave is permeated with subterranean hot streams. As the hot water flows over deposits of limestone, namely calcium carbonate, it liberates carbon dioxide into the water (sort of a natural carbonation process). Then as the carbonated water reaches the cave, the pressure is released and the gas escapes—kind of like opening a bottle of soda pop. Since carbon dioxide is heavier than air, it pushes the air out of the cave. So anyone entering is quickly overcome by a lack of oxygen . . . a hell of an explanation!

_02:: Popcorn's Devilish Origins

English colonists were introduced to popcorn at the first Thanksgiving in Plymouth by Quadequina, a Native American chief. They were told that popcorn pops because a demon living inside each kernel gets angry and has to escape when placed near heat. If you're looking for a better explanation, look to the steam. Each kernel of corn has a small amount of moisture inside that changes to steam when heated. Gases expand as the temperature increases so that pressure builds up inside the kernel until it can take it no more. Then there's a sudden explosion, and the kernel is

---

Alphabet Soup
FRESH OUT OF THE COVEN

belladonna: [bel-uh-DON-uh] *n* Derived from the Italian for "beautiful woman," belladonna was a favorite among witches, the forerunners of our modern chemists and physicians. In their attempts to make various poisons and potions, they discovered the physiological properties of many plants and herbs. An extract placed in the eye dilates the pupil and supposedly increases sex appeal. Similar compounds are used today by ophthalmologists when they examine the eyes. When belladonna is rubbed on the skin, its active ingredient, atropine, is absorbed and can give rise to hallucinations. That's why belladonna was incorporated into "witches' ointment," which was applied to the skin during coven meetings. Knowing that, it isn't hard to believe that witches really did fly (at least in a chemical fashion!).

---

literally blown inside out. If a small hole is bored into an unpopped kernel, it won't pop because the steam has a means of escaping.

Fantastic Side Effects of Neutering

There's always a silver lining, right?

_01:: Keep Your Hair

It may seem hard to believe, but as late as 1942 male patients in some mental hospitals were castrated to quiet them. And you thought what they did in *One Flew over the Cuckoo's Nest* was bad. As a result, Winfield State Hospital, a mental institution in Kansas, became an ideal place for Yale anatomist James Hamilton to conduct a study of castrated men. One day one of the patients who had been stripped of his manhood received a visitor, his identical twin. Dr. Hamilton was struck by the fact that the visitor was completely bald, while the inmate had a full head of hair. Could testosterone have something to do with baldness, the researcher wondered? To investigate this possibility, Hamilton got permission to inject the castrated man with testosterone. Within six months the mental patient became as bald as his brother, who had been progressively going bald over a 20-year period. The baldness was unfortunately irreversible, but Dr. Hamilton had demonstrated clearly that testosterone levels could be linked to hair growth.

_02:: Avoid Breast Cancer

The first scientific observation related to breast cancer was made in 1896, when it was noted that the disease sometimes regressed if the ovaries were removed. Eventually this con-nection was understood in terms of estrogen, the female hormone produced by the ovaries. Some types of breast cancer cells are stimulated to divide by estrogen, and so blocking this effect constitutes a form of treatment. In fact, many antiestrogen drugs have been tried

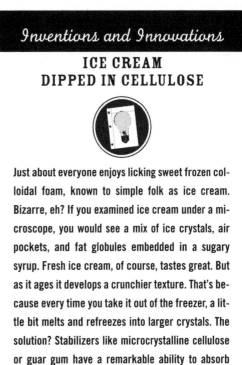

Inventions and Innovations

ICE CREAM DIPPED IN CELLULOSE

Just about everyone enjoys licking sweet frozen colloidal foam, known to simple folk as ice cream. Bizarre, eh? If you examined ice cream under a microscope, you would see a mix of ice crystals, air pockets, and fat globules embedded in a sugary syrup. Fresh ice cream, of course, tastes great. But as it ages it develops a crunchier texture. That's because every time you take it out of the freezer, a little bit melts and refreezes into larger crystals. The solution? Stabilizers like microcrystalline cellulose or guar gum have a remarkable ability to absorb moisture so that the water that forms as ice cream melts becomes unavailable for refreezing. The additives help you enjoy the product longer without worrying about the dreaded "heat shock."

with various degrees of effectiveness, and some plant products also contain compounds that can block the action of the body's estrogen. That's why soy beans and their derivatives, such as tofu, are being promoted as anticancer foods. Flaxseeds also contain antiestrogens, and a study at the University of Toronto showed that about 25 grams of flaxseed in a daily muffin improved the outcome for estrogen-sensitive breast cancers.

_03:: Prevent Prostate Cancer

We've known for a long time that eunuchs don't develop prostate cancer. Removing the testes lowers the level of male hormones in the blood—the same hormones that stimulate prostate cancer. Indeed, prostate cancer is sometimes treated by surgical removal of the testes, but it ain't the only way. Today there are also drugs, known as antiandrogens, that can block the action of male hormones. Of course diet can also play a role. Reducing the animal fat in your diet and increasing consumption of foods that contain the red pigment lycopene can offer protection against the disease. On that note, tomato products are the best source of lycopene, and the compound is made more available by cooking—a point well worth remembering for men who'd like to hang on to some important parts of their anatomy.

Urine Trouble:
4 True Tales of Tee-Tee

Who says there's no place in chemistry for bathroom humor? Here are four tales that should have you laughing all the way to the loo.

_01:: Peeing for Napoleon

When Napoleon ran short of gunpowder, he issued an ordinance for people to urinate on niter beds—or compost heaps, as we would now call them. Potassium nitrate, or saltpeter, is an essential component of gunpowder and forms as organic waste decomposes. The other main components of gunpowder, sulfur and charcoal, were abundantly available, so Napoleon had no worries there. Oddly enough, patriotic Frenchmen who increased their fluid intake to help the emperor's war effort may have reaped some unexpected benefits. A recent study has shown that men who pee more often have a reduced risk of bladder cancer. In fact, Israeli researchers have shown that rural men urinated more often and drank more fluids, while urban urine was more concentrated and stayed in the bladder longer, possibly promoting greater contact of carcinogens with the bladder.

_02:: Copper and Squatting Cowboys

A few cowboys were squatting around a campfire when one suddenly let out a painful yelp and grabbed his crotch. An excellent conductor of heat, the copper rivet in his jeans had apparently warmed up and burned the poor chap in a rather sensitive part of his anatomy. Levi Strauss, who had patented the riveted work pants made of denim in 1873, heard about the problem and issued an immediate order that copper rivets should be used only on pockets and not in the crotch. Thankfully, today's rivets are made of nickel coated with copper. The fact that copper is an excellent conductor of heat also explains why the most noted chefs use copper utensils. There are no hot spots on the bottoms of copper sauce pans, and the rate of heating the contents can be readily controlled.

_03:: Ben Franklin and Asparagus

Benjamin Franklin made many contributions to science, including bifocals, the Franklin stove, and lightning rods. But he was also the first to record that some people produced urine with a disagreeable odor after eating asparagus. You'll be grateful to know that the smell has now been identified and is due to sulfur-containing compounds produced when asparagus is metabolized. It seems, however, that not everyone can generate these compounds. A study examined the urine of 115 people who dined on the green vegetable, and only 46 produced the smell. Strangely, not everyone can smell it either.

_04:: Beets and Urine

You probably haven't given much thought to beets unless you've had an alarming bathroom experience after eating them. The naturally occurring pigment in beets, called betacyanin, is a deep red color, and it can give you quite a start if it shows up in your urine! Like asparagus, however, it doesn't affect everyone, only the folks who can't metabolize betacyanin. While this is a genetic trait, it has no health consequence other than to explain why some people will see red after eating beets and going to the restroom.

Facts with Silver Linings

We all know second place is the first loser. But if you're itching to justify all those second-place trophies on your shelf with stories of why silver's actually the best, look no further. Here are some reasons to get up with silver.

_01:: Scents and Sensibility

According to the legend, Sir Lancelot, who wooed Guinevere away from King Arthur, wore silver armor, while the king wore gold. Surely it was hot inside those suits, and conditions were conducive to bacterial growth. Amazingly, though, silver has an antibacterial effect, so Lancelot may not have smelled quite as ripe as Arthur. Today some water filters are impregnated with silver to kill bacteria. Silver-treated socks are also available for the control of foot odor, and experiments are even under way to determine if underarm aroma can be solved with a silver lining. In addition, some people claim that ingesting silver as a "colloidal" preparation destroys undesirable microbes in the body. While there's no scientific evidence that this is true, the practice may turn a person's skin color permanently gray.

_02:: Liquid Silver

The Romans named this element after Mercury, the messenger of the gods in mythology. Its symbol, Hg, is derived from the Latin *hydrargium*, meaning "liquid silver." Both of these refer to mercury's mobility, and indeed it's a mobile element in more ways than one. Liquid mercury scatters in an impressive way when hit, but mercury and mercury com-

pounds can also spread through the environment. Coal contains small amounts of mercury

Myths and Misconceptions

THE HUSBAND ALLERGY

Doctors used to laugh when ladies came in complaining that they must be allergic to their husbands, but now we know that you can develop an allergy to anything—including husbands! One lady became allergic to her hubby after 25 years of happy marriage. As soon as he came into the house she became uncomfortable with various aches and pains for which her physicians could find no solution. The couple was actually forced to live apart for months before the source of the problem was discovered: the husband was a dentist and had switched to a new type of anesthetic for his patients, and his unfortunate wife was reacting to the residues of these substances. So, how'd they solve their problems? Thorough washing by the dentist and a quick change of clothing before coming home restored their conjugal bliss.

compounds, which are released into the air when burned. They are then returned to lakes and oceans by rain, eventually concentrating in fish. Shark, swordfish, and mackerel can contain enough mercury to present a risk to pregnant women, nursing mothers, and young children. In fact, experts warn that even tuna shouldn't be eaten more than a couple of times a week, for fear of mercury's effect.

_03:: Hi Ho, Silver!

Everyone knows that the Lone Ranger fired silver bullets from his gun. Was this of any consequence? Maybe. If we compare a lead bullet and a silver bullet fired with the same amount of explosive charge, the silver bullet will get to its target faster. That's because silver is lighter than lead, so it's more readily accelerated by the exploding charge. While the silver bullet may get to its target a couple of milliseconds faster, it will likely do less damage than the softer lead, which spreads on impact. Since the Lone Ranger never actually shot anyone (and only knocked the gun out of the criminal's hand), the faster, harder, silver bullet was preferable.

4 Metals That Meddle with Your Body

Sure, they seem friendly enough when they're given cute Latin names and boxed neatly away on that periodic table you've got. But if you truly want to see these elements at their worst, here's a little metal floss to put things in perspective.

_01:: Putting the Mad in Mad Hatter

Danbury, Connecticut, used to be the center of the American hat industry. It was also known for the Danbury shakes, a condition that encompassed tremors, incoherent speech, difficulty in walking, and eventual feeble-mindedness. But why were the people of Danbury so prone to the disease? It seems the main victims of the shakes were hatters, or hat makers, who used mercury compounds in the processing of their felt. Oddly enough, this condition was also known in Europe, as evidenced by Lewis Carroll's Mad Hatter character in the famous *Alice in Wonderland* stories.

_02:: Mercury, Take II

The lighthouses along Canada's coasts are great tourist attractions. But some have recently been closed to the public because, of all things, mercury pollution. Virtually all lighthouses built in the 19th and early 20th centuries featured rotating lens assemblies that floated on a pool of mercury to reduce friction. At the time, the toxicity of mercury vapor wasn't recognized, and many a lighthouse keeper suffered ill effects such as tremors, delusions, and depression. In fact, the lighthouse on Rottnest Island in Australia is famous not only for being the first rotating beam lighthouse on that continent but also because its first three keepers all committed suicide! Today most exposure to mercury vapor comes from broken mercury thermometers.

_03:: Biting Humor

Anyone who's ever chomped on a piece of aluminum foil may have learned the hard way that dissimilar metals that come in contact can generate electric current. Since dental fillings contain metals, contact with aluminum can cause an intense jolt of pain. Imagine having such pain constantly! That's what happened to a lady who had a tooth filled next to a gold crown. Whenever she ate acidic foods, which provided the electrolyte needed to conduct current, she experienced intense facial pain, which at first was misdiagnosed as trigeminal neuralgia, a horrific neurological disease. When the filling was replaced with porcelain, the pain disappeared. This also provides a lesson for keeping cutlery made of dissimilar metals separate in the dishwasher. We're not worried about causing the cutlery pain, but the electric current will cause corrosion.

_04:: Around-the-Clock Dangers

In the 1920s the Radium Dial Company opened a new watch factory in the small town of Ottawa, Illinois. Many young women were hired to paint the numbers on the watch faces with glow-in-the-dark, radium-laced paint. They were told the paint was harmless even as they licked their paintbrushes into fine points. The paint *wasn't* harmless—radium is a radioactive element, which after prolonged exposure can accumulate in bones. It decays

---

Myths and Misconceptions
THE LEAD IN LEAD PENCILS

This may come as a shock to some people, but lead pencils do not, we repeat DO NOT, contain any lead. Never did. The so-called lead is actually a mixture of graphite and clay. The more graphite, the softer and darker the point. The mistake in terminology can be traced back to the ancient Romans, who actually used pieces of lead to draw lines on papyrus scrolls to guide them in writing with a tiny brush called a *pencillus*. Lead is a very soft metal and pieces readily rub off. The Romans never realized, however, that lead was potentially toxic. Of course, today we know that even tiny amounts ingested can result in poisoning. On the brighter side, though, it looks like you're not going to die of lead poisoning for chewing on your pencils way back in grade school.

---

by releasing alpha particles, which can destroy cells in the bone marrow, and it can often lead to bone cancer. Many factory workers developed health complications despite the team of doctors who routinely checked the women's radium levels. While few of the workers ever came forward with their complaints, the Radium Dial Company dealt with those that did—quickly and quietly. In a bizarre twist, as late as the 1940s radium was used by some physicians to treat arthritis. Not only was this treatment dangerous but it was also useless.

Lady Killers:
Deadly Cosmetics

Yeah, we all know beauty's in the eye of the beholder. And while a dab of makeup here and there generally helps the cause (Tammy Faye aside), the following are three cases where the price of beauty became excruciatingly high.

_01:: Dynamic Weight Loss

During World War I, French munitions workers manufacturing trinitrotoluene (TNT) commonly developed unusual sweating, fever, and weight loss. Apparently, inhaled TNT vapors increased their metabolic rate. And though TNT was too dangerous to use as a medication, in 1931 dinitrophenol, a chemical relative, was introduced in the United States to step up metabolic rate. It seemed so safe in small doses for weight loss that it was actually available without a prescription. But by 1935 toxic reactions involving the bone marrow and skin were noted, and eventually a few deaths were associated with the product. Dinitrophenol also caused cataracts, and about 100 users lost their sight. The drug is no longer legal in Canada or the United States but is still sometimes illegally obtained from Mexico.

_02:: Nail Files: Acetone vs. Acetonitrile

Acetone is the active ingredient in many nail polish removers, while acetonitrile is the active ingredient in the solution used to take off artificial nails. These two compounds are very different in their levels of toxicity. In an unfortunate case, a 16-month-old child ingested about 15–30 milliliters of the latter, and her panic-stricken mother immediately called a poison control center. The mother didn't transmit the information properly, and the doctor thought she was talking about nail polish remover. He informed her that there was no great risk. Had he realized that acetonitrile had been swallowed, he would have declared an emergency immediately because the compound releases cyanide once metabolized in the liver. Sadly, the child was found dead in the morning.

_03:: Perfume and Regurgitating Whales

Whales can finally relax! Today's chemists have learned how to mimic ambergris in the laboratory, causing high-pitched sighs of relief in oceans across the world. Ambergris, the waxy liquid coating the stomachs of sperm whales, protects them from the sharp bones of the cuttlefish they eat. When fresh, ambergris is soft and black and smells awful. When exposed to sun and water, it hardens, becomes lighter colored, and develops a pleasant smell. Bizarrely, ambergris is an excellent fixative that keeps perfume's scent from evaporating too quickly, and for this reason was once prize booty for whalers. A piece of ambergris weighing 922 pounds was once found floating in the ocean, making its discoverer instantly wealthy. But synthetic analogues have now eliminated the need to kill whales for perfume manufacturing. And ladies no longer have to cope with the notion of anointing themselves with whale regurgitation.

3 Tips for Brisk Business

While Kermit is no doubt right in singing that "it ain't easy being green," having green is another story. Here are a few tales of chemistry, business, and the pleasant effect they have when you mix 'em up just right.

_01:: The Brewing of Bluing

The real Mrs. Stewart did not want her face on the bottle of bluing. Too bad, because she missed out on immortality. Her husband, Al, a traveling salesman in the late 1800s, sold bottles of liquid bluing and thought that a kindly face on the label would increase sales. When his wife refused, he used a picture of his mother-in-law! As white fabrics age, they take on a yellow tinge. That's because they begin to absorb the blue wavelengths of light instead of reflecting them. The answer, as Mr. Stewart discovered, was to add a touch of ferric hexacyanoferrate, or Prussian blue, to the wash. Mrs. Stewart's bluing is still making clothes "whiter than white" today. And don't worry about the cyanide; it is tightly bound to iron and is harmless.

_02:: Tint of Brilliance

Proving that teachers really should watch what they say to impressionable youngsters, in 1856 an English schoolboy named William Henry Perkin (1838–1907) started experimenting in his home laboratory. His teacher had offhandedly remarked that a fortune could be made in synthetic quinine, so young Perkin went to work. Like most chemistry students, he ended up with little more than a failed experiment and a purple-tinted mess. Unlike most chemistry students, Perkin saw gold: he immediately left school and became a millionaire by opening a factory that produced the first synthetic dye.

_03:: About Face: Skin Peels and the Economy

Can the sales of trichloroacetic acid actually predict the state of the economy? Maybe. The chemical, used by dermatologists and plastic surgeons to carry out facial peels, is painted on to the skin. The skin immediately responds by trying to slough off the irritant. What results is a rapid turnover of cells whereby wrinkles are reduced, precancerous lesions are removed, and your skin is rejuvenated with a youthful glow. So what's this got to do with the economy? Skin peels aren't covered by medical insurance, and according to some doctors the number of patients desiring the procedure dropped dramatically before the recession in the early 1990s. So did the number of patients looking to have their breasts enlarged with implants. The same trend was repeated in the first couple of years of the 21st century.

Simple Cures Straight from Momma's Cupboard

No need to bother the doctor or visit the pharmacist; these are cures you'll find in the comfort of your own kitchen.

_01:: Dealing with Motion Sickness Gingerly

Motion sickness can be really unnerving. But would you believe that the solution might be as simple as ginger? A study at the University of Michigan Medical Center showed that subjects given about 1,000 mg of ground ginger fared much better than those on a placebo when placed on an amusement park–style ride famous for inducing motion sickness. And ginger may even help with the pain of arthritis. In India it's one of the most common remedies for the condition. How does it work? Ginger triggers the release of prostaglandins in the body, chemicals with anti-inflammatory properties. A word of caution though: People taking blood thinners have to be careful with ginger because it also has an anticoagulant (blood-thinning) effect. No need to worry about ginger ale, though, as there isn't much ginger in it.

_02:: Hyperventilation and the Paper Bag Trick

When we hyperventilate, we exhale abnormal amounts of carbon dioxide. And since carbon dioxide forms from carbonic acid in the blood, hyperventilation can affect our acid-base ratio and cause symptoms such as fainting. The ready remedy is to breathe into a bag so the exhaled carbon dioxide can be recycled. Of course, humans aren't the only ones left gasping for air—chickens can also hyperventilate, particularly in hot weather because they have no sweat glands. When they lose carbon dioxide, they start laying eggs with thinner shells. That's because eggshells are made of calcium carbonate. Less carbon dioxide in the blood means less carbonate available for eggs. The solution? Give the chickens carbonated water to drink. No need to pamper them with Perrier; cheap seltzer will do the trick.

_03:: Hate Hangovers? Drink Vodka!

Ever wonder what causes a hangover? It isn't the alcohol in the beverage—not the alcohol

What's the Difference?

ARTIFICIAL VS. NATURAL FLAVORING

Have you ever seen the phrase "natural flavor" under a list of ingredients on the side of a food or beverage? If you haven't, either you only shop organic or the term "natural" sounded so innocent you didn't pay attention. Go check your cupboard again—you might be surprised. As it turns out, there's nothing very natural about natural flavoring. In fact, it's pretty similar to artificial flavoring. Both are made by a flavorist, a scientist who blends chemical compounds to mimic perfectly a smell or taste found in nature. Natural flavors come from the chemical extracts of natural sources (plants, animals, oils, etc.), while artificial flavors come from synthetic sources. You're actually better off choosing artificial over natural, though, for two reasons. First, nature often sends us deadly poisons (there's a bit of cyanide in almonds, for instance), but the artificial version is calculated to be poison-free. Second, natural flavors cost more—sometimes it's expensive to find the right source, and consumers are willing to pay more just for the word *natural* on a product.

that most people think of, anyway. The alcohol that intoxicates is ethanol, but the stuff responsible for the hangover is a byproduct of fermentation known as methanol. Dark wines, cognac, fruit brandies, and whiskies contain the most methanol, while vodka has almost none. Enzymes in the body convert methanol to formaldehyde, which causes the symptoms. These enzymes actually prefer ethanol as their meal—hence the hair-of-the-dog treatment for hangovers. Taking another drink provides the enzymes with ethanol, and while they gorge on this, the methanol is excreted. In the doses found in beverages, methanol may be annoying but not dangerous. In high doses methanol can intoxicate and is sometimes passed off as regular alcohol by bootleggers, and in such amounts it can be lethal.

_04:: Cloves for the Breath

In the third century BCE officers of the court in China were required to carry cloves in their mouth when addressing the emperor. This was to prevent him from being exposed to bad breath. It was probably in this fashion that people discovered that cloves had local anesthetic properties. Eugenol, found in oil of cloves, is still used by dentists to anesthetize the gums before giving a needle, and in an emergency clove oil can be rubbed around an aching tooth for relief. Some interesting mythology surrounds cloves as well. Folklore suggests they have aphrodisiac properties because they resemble a certain part of the male anatomy. Not so. Cloves may improve your breath, but they won't leave you breathless.

All Fired Up:

Smokey the Bear Nightmares

Between the evolution of matches, mischievous children, and fiery fowl, there's plenty here to keep Smokey up all night.

_01:: The Stormy Petrel: A PETA Nightmare Too

The Shetland Islands are famous for sheep and wool. But did you know that they're also home to the stormy petrel? This unusual bird, so named because it was thought to appear before a storm, has a very high fat content. Fat, of course, is an excellent fuel and burns readily to produce carbon dioxide, water, heat, and light. Islanders used to catch the creatures, dry them, fix their feet in clay, and thread a wick through their beaks. Then they would light the wick and burn the dried bird for illumination. The Danes did the same with the great auk, a bird that has since become extinct. They inserted a wick into the dead bird's belly and burned it. The slightly less macabre were satisfied with burning whale oil.

_02:: Early Matches

We take many things in life for granted, like matches. Until the late 1700s if you wanted a flame, you had to be good with a flint and tinder. But then French chemist Claude Bertholet came along and discovered that a mixture of sugar and potassium chlorate could be ignited with a small drop of sulfuric acid. The first self-igniting matches had heads made of potassium chlorate, sugar, and gum, and were ignited by being dipped into a vial of sulfuric acid. The problem of carrying around open bottles of sulfuric acid was solved by sealing the acid in a glass tube that was wrapped in a paper saturated with the combustible chemicals. Small pliers were used to crush the tube and release the acid—which ignited the paper.

_03:: Mischievous Children and Methane

Children in Leeds, England, used to amuse themselves by throwing matches into the canal that was the receptacle for sewage output. However, the desired effect—a burst of flames—was seen only on very cold mornings. The decomposition of sewage due to the action of bacteria can generate lots of methane gas, and methane is highly flammable. While the spectacular display of flames angered bargemen on the canal and delighted wily children, it never lasted long. The gas is usually lighter than air, so it dissipates quickly. Only on very cold days did there seem to be enough lingering methane just above the surface of the water to cause the flaming effect.

Last Calls for Alcohol: Tips for Imbibing

Alcohol comes with enough of its own problems, so it seems unfair that people also have to worry about how they drink. Alas, here are some tips on getting tipsy.

_01:: Strong and Smooth with a Hint of Tungsten

There used to be a strange initiation rite for men drafted into an artillery regiment in France. Recruits had to drink a glass of white wine that had flowed through the barrel of a 155-millimeter gun after several shots had been fired. Then one day a 19-year-old soldier developed seizures and was taken to the hospital unconscious and unresponsive to stimuli. He had extremely high levels of tungsten in his blood, and doctors traced the source to the wine. It seems the composition of gun barrels had recently changed with the inclusion of tungsten for hardness, tungsten steel being especially hard. Other recruits were spared because they had vomited immediately after drinking the wine. Since then the French army has banned the hazing ritual.

_02:: Fill 'Er Up with Unleaded

An English couple moved to Spain and discovered the delights of sangria. To have some on hand all the time, they purchased a jug from a local potter that fit neatly into their fridge. Not a good move, as it turned out. Over a period of a few months the husband lost 25 kilograms (about 55 pounds) and began

---

Inventions and Innovations

SPRAY THAT UNFAITHFUL HUSBAND (S-CHECK)

For years people cheated on their spouses in the name of chemistry. Finally, chemistry is fighting back. Takeshi Makino, president of the Safety Detective Agency in Osaka, Japan, won the 1999 chemistry Ig Nobel Prize (for achievements that "cannot or should not be reproduced") for his unusual invention. His agency sells a pair of chemical sprays, called S-Check, that a wife can spray on her husband's underwear to see if he's been unfaithful. The sprays turn traces of semen bright green. And only showering will help. Unfortunately, the same company has also come up with a new idea for infidelity detection creams: the shower detector. Rub it into your mate's back, and a scab will form when he (or she) attempts to shower. Put it on socks or underwear, and they'll change color (from the change in temperature) if removed for longer than 15 minutes. When did cheating get so complicated?

to suffer from terrible abdominal cramps. Luckily, he called his brother, a British physician, who recognized the severity of the symptoms and urged him to get an immediate blood test. It showed toxic levels of lead! The jug had been improperly glazed, and the sangria leached lead from the decorative pigment. Immediate medical treatment to remove the lead from his system saved the man's life.

_03:: Meat, Fish, and the Color of Wine

Why does red wine go with meat and white with fish? The simplest explanation is that red wine has a more robust flavor and would overwhelm the delicate taste of fish. But if you're looking for more of a chemical explanation, here it is. Red grape skins contain plenty of tannic acid that ends up in the wine. Much of the flavor of red meat is due to compounds found in the fat, but unfortunately fat coats the taste buds so that subsequent bites don't taste as good as the first. This is where the tannic acid comes in. It has detergent properties, meaning that it can remove fat. So sipping red wine between bites cleans the palate. Fish has less fat, and tannic acid can also overpower the more subtle flavor. But contrary to what some may think, it isn't illegal to drink white wine with meat.

5 Facts in Poor Taste

Ever notice how some foods agree with you and some don't? Here are a few foods that aren't just out for an argument; they're looking to get the final word.

_01:: Bitter Cassava

Cassava roots have a bitter taste that prevents insects as well as hungry monkeys from eating them. This is great for African farmers, who grow a lot of cassava because it produces high yields in poor soil as well as in drought conditions. The bitter taste comes from a compound called linamarin, which the cassava root produces to protect itself from predators. How? By releasing cyanide of course! Amazingly, the cassava can cause human poisoning if the root is improperly prepared, so it has to be grated and soaked for days before being eaten. In fact, the resulting condition from eating raw cassava is known as konzo and is characterized by paralysis. Surprisingly, tapioca is actually made from cassava, but it contains no residual cyanide, so no need to worry about that pudding.

_02:: Bad Milk

One of the unfortunate victims of bad milk was Abraham Lincoln's mother, Nancy Hanks Lincoln, who died of milk sickness in 1818.

The sickness, which actually wiped out many pioneers, had nothing to do with bacteria and everything to do with a cow's diet. When the animals grazed on a plant called snakeroot, people who drank their milk got sick and often died. A naturally occurring substance in the milk called tremetone was converted by human body enzymes into a highly toxic substance. When chemists linked milk sickness to snakeroot early in the 20th century, farmers were counseled to rid their fields of the plant, and thus milk sickness was eliminated.

_03:: Hungry for Change

According to the *British Medical Journal*, coins are the most common items found after cremation of the human body. It seems some people ingest coins for good luck. Others think that they can correct dietary deficiencies in zinc or copper. Surgeons once removed $22.50 from a 31-year-old man who had been ingesting coins for 12 years and finally came down with zinc poisoning. Zinc reacts with hydrochloric acid in the stomach to form hydrogen gas and zinc chloride, which is very corrosive and can lead to ulcers. The world record for coin ingestion is 424, a feat outmatched only by the heartiest of piggy banks.

_04:: Beans, Beans, Good for the Heart . . .

Beans have been called the musical food because of their propensity to produce gas. That's because humans lack an enzyme needed to digest some of the carbohydrates in beans. Raffinose and stachyose are particularly problematic. Although we can't digest these compounds, microbes in our intestines can. Unfortunately, when the bugs eat the beans, they produce gas that eventually has to make a more or less dramatic exit. Now scientists have successfully isolated the required enzyme, alpha-galactosidase, which can be added to the first mouthful of beans (or broccoli or cabbage or stir-fry) to reduce the problem. And it's a good thing because beans are great. They're a wonderful source of fibers and also flavonoids, which can protect against cancer and heart disease.

_05:: A Mighty Wind

Restaurants often offer mints to their patrons after a meal. This is an old tradition because mint reduces the chance of untoward gaseous emissions (otherwise known as farting). You can get gas in your intestine in all sorts of ways. You can swallow air. Or carbon dioxide can be produced when the acid contents of your stomach mix with naturally occurring bicarbonate in the small bowel. However you get gas, the bottom line is the same: if there's a buildup of gas, it has to come out one way or another. And this is where mint works its charm. Peppermint contains natural oils that act as a carminative, meaning that they allow sphincter muscles to relax so that gases can be expelled steadily rather than in powerful explosive bursts. Long live the after-dinner mint!

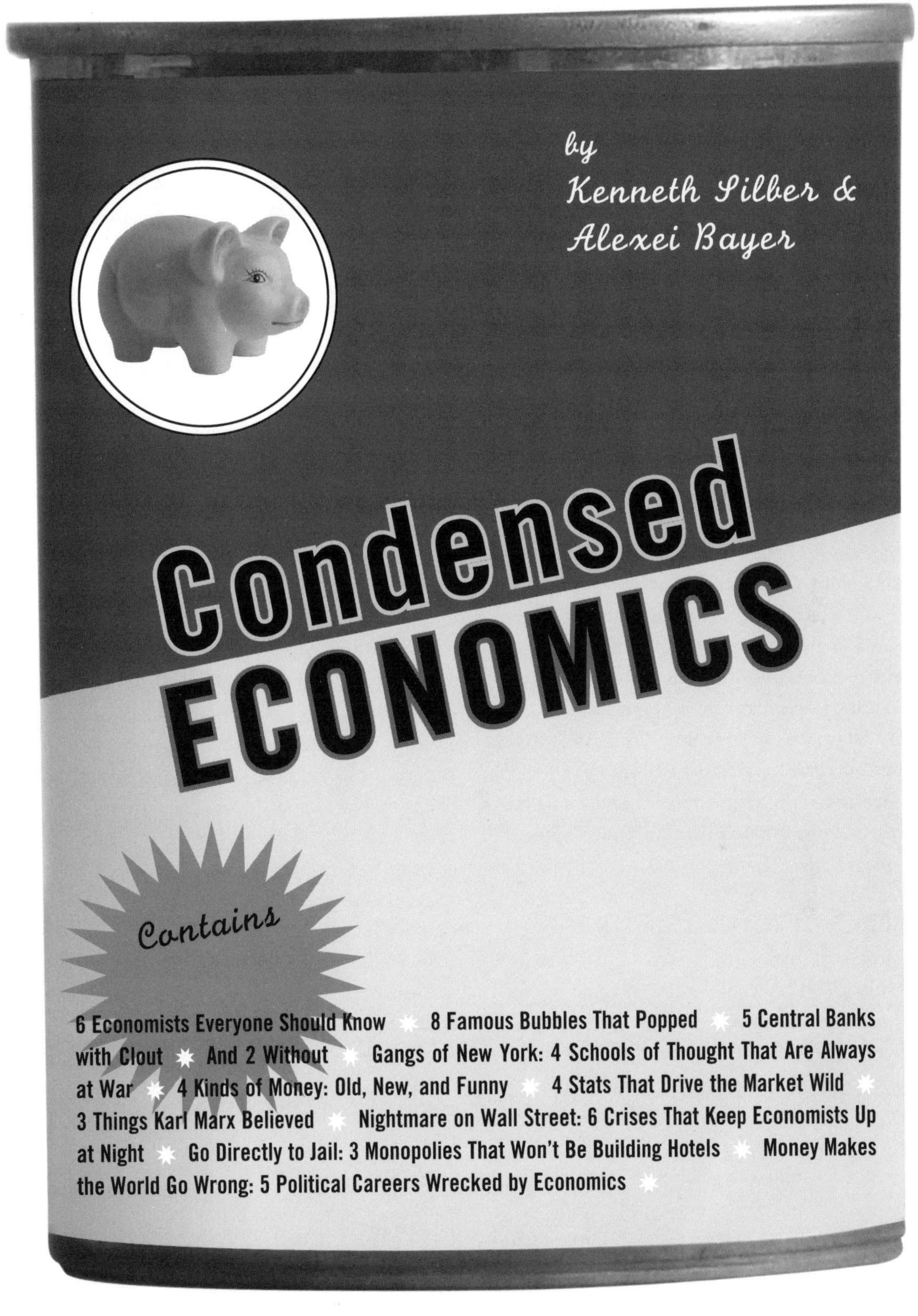

by
Kenneth Silber &
Alexei Bayer
Condensed
ECONOMICS
Contains
6 Economists Everyone Should Know * 8 Famous Bubbles That Popped * 5 Central Banks with Clout * And 2 Without * Gangs of New York: 4 Schools of Thought That Are Always at War * 4 Kinds of Money: Old, New, and Funny * 4 Stats That Drive the Market Wild * 3 Things Karl Marx Believed * Nightmare on Wall Street: 6 Crises That Keep Economists Up at Night * Go Directly to Jail: 3 Monopolies That Won't Be Building Hotels * Money Makes the World Go Wrong: 5 Political Careers Wrecked by Economics *

Economists Everyone Should Know

Sure, the next time you're laid off, salaried down, underbudgeted, or wearing hand-me-downs, you *could* blame the economy. But why pick on the economy when you can pick on the economist instead?

_01:: Adam Smith (1723–1790)

Ever felt a push from behind on your way to work, but when you turned around no one was there? It was probably Smith's "invisible hand," the force that leads individuals pursuing self-interest to provide useful goods and services for others. Champion of the free market, Smith pretty much founded economics as a systematic discipline, and his ideas echo through the profession to the present day. If you don't believe in economic forecasting, read Smith's masterwork, *The Wealth of Nations* (1776). Smith, a native Scot, argued that Great Britain couldn't afford to hold its rebellious American colonies—an impressive conjecture considering Britain's world domination at the time.

_02:: David Ricardo (1772–1823)

Ricardo became the poster boy for middle achievers everywhere when he came up with the idea of comparative advantage. He showed how free trade allows countries to specialize in what they do best—even if they're not very good at anything. The same principle explains why Michael Jordan doesn't fix roofs, even though he might be better at it than many roofers; it's more efficient for him to focus on basketball. Disinherited for marrying outside his family's Jewish faith, Ricardo was originally a successful banker in London, then a member of Parliament, before he became an economist. In his "Essay on the Influence of a Low Price of Corn on the Profits of Stock," Ricardo presented the law of diminishing returns, which explains how adding more labor and machinery to a piece of land (or other fixed asset) after a certain point is just unproductive.

_03:: John Maynard Keynes (1883–1946)

Before Keynes, economics was in its classical phase. After him, it was in its Keynesian phase (just as there was Newtonian physics before Albert Einstein came along). The Great Depression convinced Keynes that the government had to engage in deficit spending to combat unemployment, a major break from the economic thinking of the time. He first became well known after World War I when he quit his British Treasury job, complaining that the Treaty of Versailles would wreak economic havoc. (He was right.) He also helped set up the system of fixed exchange rates used for decades after World War II. Unlike the majority of economists, Keynes led the life of a celebrity: he married a Russian ballerina, drank Champagne with literary figures, and made a fortune in the stock market. Keynes once said, "I would rather be vaguely right than precisely wrong," which may account for continued arguments between "new Keynesian" and "new classical" economists.

_04:: Joseph Schumpeter (1883–1950)

Schumpeter, born in Austria, reportedly vowed to become the best economist, horseman, and lover in Vienna—and later regretted not meeting the horseman goal. He argued that economists' traditional idea of competition (similar companies competing on price) was much less important than "creative destruction," whereby entrepreneurs create new products and industries. He predicted that capitalism would be undermined by its own success. But unlike Karl Marx, Schumpeter didn't look forward to the system's demise. He wrote, "If a doctor predicts that his patient will die presently, this does not mean that he desires it."

_05:: John Kenneth Galbraith (1908–)

Galbraith once said, "The only function of economic forecasting is to make astrology look respectable." A prolific author and adept debater, Galbraith stands among the economists best known outside the economics profession. The Canadian-born Galbraith moved to the United States in the 1930s and worked as a price controller in World War II, a Harvard professor, an advisor to President John F. Kennedy, and eventually a U.S. ambassador to India. A persistent concern of his long career has been with corporate power. In such books as *The Affluent Society* (1958) and *The New Industrial State* (1967), he argued that big companies have little to fear from competitors and exercise lots of influence over consumers. Not everyone likes the thesis, of course; critics have pointed out that big companies sometimes lose market share and go out of business.

_06:: Milton Friedman (1912–)

Friedman advocated free-floating exchange rates, school vouchers, the shift from the draft to a volunteer military, and for doctors to be allowed to practice medicine without a license. A proponent of free markets and limited government, Friedman challenged the Keynesian ideas that dominated economics in the decades after World War II and instead supported monetarism, an emphasis on the

---

Strange but True

THE STONE MONEY OF YAP

If you're frustrated by the market and you're looking for a currency that can stand the test of time, look no further. In the Caroline Islands in the South Pacific, there's an island named Yap (or Uap). In 1903 an American anthropologist named Henry Furness III visited the islanders and found they had an unusual system of currency. It consisted of carved stone wheels called *fei*, ranging in diameter from a foot to 12 feet. Because the stones were heavy, the islanders didn't normally carry their money around with them. After a transaction the *fei* might remain on a previous owner's premises, but it was understood who owned what. One family's *fei*, Furness was told, had been lost at sea many years earlier while being transported from a nearby island during a storm. But that stone was still used as currency, even though it was unseen and irretrievable beneath hundreds of feet of water.

role of money in the economy. Born to immigrants in New York City, Friedman spent much of his career at the University of Chicago. In 1976 he won the Nobel Prize for economics for, among other things, "his demonstration of the complexity of stabilization policy"—meaning, why government has

so much trouble keeping the economy on an even keel. His fame, however, only grew. In 1979 Friedman's book *Free to Choose* (coauthored by his wife and accompanied by a public-television series) reached a worldwide audience.

Famous Bubbles That Popped

Everyone loves bubbles, right? Bubble gum, bubble tea, bubble baths. Fun, fun, fun! That is, until your lousy stockbroker calls up from Boca Raton to tell you that the surefire stock tip he gave you just bottomed out, and now he's going back to school to pursue his law degree. That's when bubbles are less fun—when they're of the economic nature and leave you cursing in the poorhouse. Here's a tribute to eight of the worst bubbles ever to pop.

_01:: The Ponzi Scheme

Being a scam artist is bad enough; having a type of scam named after you is a perverse sort of immortality. Consider the case of Charles Ponzi, who showed great chutzpah even by 1920s standards. Promising investors a return rate of 100% in just 90 days, Ponzi lured trusting thousands into his Security and Exchange Company (no relation to the Securities and Exchange Commission, which regulates U.S. financial markets). But the supposed whiz kid merely used the new funds to pay off existing investors, a practice now known as a Ponzi scheme. The arrangement collapsed when the authorities began investigating, and after doing a stint in the slammer, "the Ponz" finally got a real job—working for Alitalia, the Italian national airline.

_02:: The South Sea and
_03:: Mississippi Bubble

Don't you just love globalization? In the early 18th century this double bubble grew on both sides of the English Channel at the same time, probably the first example of globalization in financial markets. In England, investors snatched up shares of the South Sea Company, a firm that was supposed to monopolize trade with the Americas, while in France money flowed into a company set up by Englishman John Law to operate in the Mississippi Valley and other French colonial areas. Share prices of the companies rose so much that it became necessary to invent a new word for those who grew rich in the bubble: millionaires. Somehow the South Sea Company never made a profit; claims that Louisiana had mountains of gold turned out to be a little less than accurate. After share prices collapsed in 1720, France had a government crisis, and England passed the Bubble Law, forbidding companies to issue stock.

_04:: Florida's Real Estate Boom

President Andrew Jackson—whose face graces the $20 bill—won Florida for the United States in 1821, but for 100 years Americans couldn't quite figure out what to do with it (aside from removing the Native American population). But in the early 1920s developers descended en masse on the Sunshine State, realizing its potential as a giant vacationland for winter-weary northerners. A huge boom ensued, with prices rocketing to $1,000 per acre, a hefty sum of money in those days. At one point, an amazing one-third of Miami's population had become real estate agents. Right idea but bad timing—Florida weather helped burst the bubble with severe hurricanes in 1926 and 1928.

_05:: The Roaring '20s Stock Market

In the 1920s stocks could be purchased like real estate, by putting 10% down and taking out a 90% loan from the broker, secured by the value of the shares. This huge margin provided fantastic leverage—when stocks appreciated. And appreciate they did. The Dow Jones industrial average rocketed 344% between 1923 and 1929, and more and more Americans got caught up in the stock market frenzy. It was not all speculation or a pyramid scheme: there were legitimate reasons for investors to be optimistic. The '20s were a period of rapid economic growth and development of new technologies: radio, electricity, automobiles, and airplanes. Nevertheless, the bubble

burst in October 1929, and the Dow lost nearly 25% in just two days. The crash was promptly followed by the Great Depression, and the market bottomed a few years later, at just 11% of its 1929 peak.

_06:: Japan's Stock Bubble

In the 1980s Japanese companies could do no wrong, as far as investors were concerned. The Nikkei 225 index of the Tokyo stock market rose dramatically throughout the decade—dipping briefly only during the 1987 Black Monday crash—to hit almost 40,000 in 1989. Its market capitalization peaked at 611 trillion yen—larger than the New York Stock Exchange's. So convinced was everybody that stock prices had nowhere to go but up, Japanese stockbrokers offered their big clients guaranteed returns on their stock portfolios. It all came to an end when growth in Japanese exports failed to keep pace with investors' expectations, and for over 10 years the Nikkei slumped—ultimately giving up all the gains of the late 1980s and returning to the pre-bubble level of around 7,800 in early 2003.

_07:: Russia's Notorious MMM

When the Soviet Union collapsed in 1991, Russians were naive about financial markets. So, when in 1994 an obscure company called MMM (not to be confused with the 3M Company, the American blue chip) opened offices in Moscow and other Russian cities and began offering fantastic returns on its shares, Russians pulled their hard-earned rubles out of their mattresses. They didn't ask how MMM was going to earn such returns; after years of Communist propaganda, they had an unshakable faith in the capitalist system. Sergey

Mavrodi, MMM's founder, even got elected to the Russian parliament. The damage from the pyramid was relatively small; when the scheme collapsed in 1995, MMM had stolen an estimated $100 million, a mere pittance by the standards of Enron. But the number of Russians taken in was enormous; since record keeping was spotty, estimates ran as high as 50 million—which would make it the largest fraud of its kind in history.

_08:: The Internet Bubble

American investors have none of the excuses the Russian investors had. They're supposed to be the hard-nosed capitalists and the most sophisticated investors in the world. But in the second half of the 1990s they got caught in the Internet bubble on NASDAQ. This wasn't all that different from a pyramid scheme, even though it was touted by hotshot analysts working for the world's most re-spected investment banks. Internet companies that never made a profit were valued by the market at hundreds of times their annual rev-enues. The NASDAQ composite index, which traded at 1,500 in 1998, rocketed to over 5,000

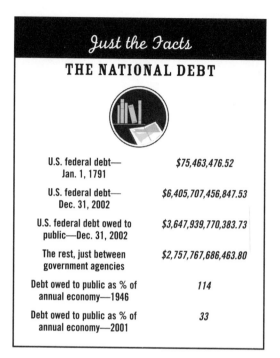

Just the Facts
THE NATIONAL DEBT

U.S. federal debt— Jan. 1, 1791	$75,463,476.52
U.S. federal debt— Dec. 31, 2002	$6,405,707,456,847.53
U.S. federal debt owed to public—Dec. 31, 2002	$3,647,939,770,383.73
The rest, just between government agencies	$2,757,767,686,463.80
Debt owed to public as % of annual economy—1946	114
Debt owed to public as % of annual economy—2001	33

by March 2000, and serious analysts began measuring the number of mouse clicks visi-tors made at different Web sites. As in other bubbles, though, the fall was precipitous, and the shares of those few Internet start-ups that survived fell to a tiny fraction of their peak values.

Central Banks with Clout

William McChesney Martin, former chairman of the U.S. Federal Reserve, once claimed that central banks are like bad party hosts: they "take away the punch bowl just when the party gets going." The following are five of the worst party hosts around.

_01:: The Fed (the Leader)

U.S. dollars make up about 70% of central bank reserves around the world so, big surprise, the U.S. Federal Reserve holds the rank of world's leading central bank. The Fed sets American interest rates, controls the U.S. money supply, and regulates the country's commercial banks. If a commercial bank can't get money anywhere else, the Fed serves as the lender of last resort. Working for the Fed may not seem like the most glamorous job, but Fed chairman Alan Greenspan has certainly gotten his share of the limelight since taking office in 1987 (he's lasted through four presidents). Although Greenspan gets just one vote on the 12-member Federal Open Market Committee, the chairman's views usually carry a lot of weight, as was true of those of Greenspan's cigar-chomping predecessor, Paul Volcker.

_02:: The European Central Bank (the New Kid)

Don't discount the European Central Bank (ECB) just because it's the new kid on the chopping block. Since it was founded in 1998, the ECB has conducted monetary policy for the 12 countries that have adopted the euro, the single European currency. The ECB sets interest rates for the entire euro zone, but—wouldn't you know it—in highly bureaucra-

tized Europe, all countries still have their own national central banks. All of them, plus the ECB, are part of another organization called the European System of Central Banks. Setting a single interest rate for an entire continent is a pretty thankless task since not all countries are likely to be satisfied, so the ECB gets pulled different ways by political pressures. Even the location of ECB headquarters—Frankfurt, Germany's financial center, rather than Paris—was a matter of political horse trading.

_03:: The Bank of England (the Old Guard)

Nicknamed the Old Lady of Threadneedle Street, after its headquarters in London's financial district, the Bank of England stands as one of the world's oldest central banks—only the Swedish central bank is older. Founded way back in 1694 and nationalized in 1946, the Bank of England gained its operational independence only in 1997. In an ironic twist, it was the Labor government—the putative socialists—that finally decided not to meddle in the interest-rate-setting process. Although the pound is no longer the currency of an empire over which the sun never sets, London still acts as Europe's largest financial hub. As a member of the European Union, Britain is eligible to join the euro zone but has so far followed the conservative path of holding on to the pound—thus the Bank of England remains a force to be reckoned with.

_04:: The Swiss National Bank (the Safety Zone)

You know you're watching a good movie when the crook/tyrant/heiress utters the phrase "numbered Swiss bank account." The Swiss franc acts as the quintessential safe-haven currency—a reassuringly stable thing to invest in during times of crisis and turmoil. The Swiss National Bank maintains that sense of security, and the franc's safe-haven role has acquired even greater appeal for many investors since September 11, 2001. However, before hiding your money and heading for the border, you should know that Swiss bank secrecy laws have weakened in recent years.

_05:: The Bank for International Settlements (the Go-Between)

Sometimes you just need a go-between, and that's where the BIS comes in. A central bankers' bank, the BIS serves as a counterparty, or trading partner, for financial transactions between banks. The ultimate purpose of the BIS is to foster cooperation among central banks to ensure stability in the world's financial and banking systems. Located in Basel, Switzerland, the BIS was originally formed in 1930 to deal with the issue of German reparations after World War I, and it's been a fixture of global finance ever since. In contrast to the World Bank and the International Monetary Fund, however, you rarely hear about the BIS being targeted by antiglobalization protesters. Sometimes keeping a low profile keeps you out of trouble.

And **Without**

_01:: The Bank of Japan (the Has-Been)

For a while in the 1980s, the Japanese central bank trampled close on the heels of the U.S. Fed. The Japanese economy, the world's second largest, gained on its rival, and the yen won acceptance as a reserve currency, especially in Southeast Asia. But it all came a-cropper in the 1990s, when the speculative bubble in Japanese stocks and real estate burst. The Japanese economy entered a long period of stagnation, and Japanese banks, once the world's largest, became a weak link in the world financial system. The Bank of Japan has been powerless in reviving the economy—even though it has pushed interest rates down to zero.

_02:: The People's Bank of China (the Lame Duck)

The People's Bank of China is China's central bank (whereas the Central Bank of China is the central bank of Taiwan). Whether or not the institution really belongs to the people, the People's Bank has responsibility for the financial system of a nation with more than 1.2 billion people. The Chinese economy grows by 7–8% each year and will probably become the world's biggest sometime in the 21st century. But unlike other major central banks, the People's Bank doesn't really make key decisions about monetary policy. Interest rates in increasingly capitalist China are still set by bureaucrats in the Communist Party.

Gangs of New York:
4 Schools of Thought That Are Always at War

Winston Churchill once said, "If you put two economists in a room, you get two opinions, unless one of them is Lord Keynes, in which case you get three." Clearly, the legacy of Keynes lives on.

_01:: Keynesianism

In the world of economics, you're cool only as long as you're right. Based on the ideas of British economist John Maynard Keynes, Keynesianism dominated economics for several decades after his death in 1946. Keynesians focus on aggregate demand, or total spending in the economy by consumers, industry, and government. When there's a recession, in their view, consumers and industry aren't spending enough, so government should spend more to take up the slack. By the 1960s Keynesians had grown confident that government could fine-tune the economy, nicely smoothing out the business cycle. But 1970s stagflation (economic stagnation combined with high inflation) was a major blow to this confidence. You still see Keynesian prescriptions at work, though, whenever governments ramp up public-works projects to push the economy out of recession.

_02:: Monetarism (or How to Stand Up to Keynes 101)

If your date tells you that "money matters," simply tell her you don't associate with monetarists. It might sound like a dirty word, but in fact monetarists just believe that economies are profoundly affected by how much cur-

rency is in circulation. Led by economist Milton Friedman, the monetarists shredded Keynesian theory and argued that the Keynesian tolerance of inflation as a way of keeping unemployment low would result in escalating inflation—and lousy unemployment figures too. The experience of the 1970s gave monetarists considerable intellectual cachet, and in the early 1980s economic policy in the United States and Britain had a strong monetarist tinge. But monetarism ran into some trouble when it became clear just how hard it is to measure the money supply. (Do you count just cash? Also checking accounts? What about other financial instruments?) Moreover, central bankers were never entirely enthused about the idea of limiting their own decision-making power by adopting clear, stable rules for managing the money supply.

_03:: Supply-Side Economics (If You Trust the Man with the Napkin)

Nothing's better for a new school of economic thought than a bad economy. Similar to the monetarists, the supply-siders spent the late 1970s arguing that the Keynesians had made a mess of the economy. Of course, they thought that monetarist ideas were at best a partial solution. The supply-siders put their emphasis on tax cuts, and especially on reducing marginal tax rates (the high rates at which income above a certain level is taxed). Using a curve initially drawn on a napkin by economist Arthur Laffer (yes, the Laffer curve), the supply-siders argued that tax revenues could increase if rates were reduced, since people would work and invest more. The supply-siders hit a peak of influence in the 1980s, inspiring tax cuts in the United States and other countries. The results were controversial, with the supply-siders claiming to have boosted economic growth, while critics complained they had boosted government budget deficits.

_04:: Post-Keynesianism (When in Doubt, Recycle)

Garnish your Keynes with a hint of Marx, and you'll find you get a post-Keynesian. The post-Keynesians emphasize the uncertainty, instability, and problems of capitalist economies, drawing on Karl Marx's ideas about class struggle. They think that Keynes was on to something in seeing how markets can fail, but that regular Keynesianism doesn't sufficiently explore those insights. And although they may all look alike, post-Keynesians are a pretty diverse group. They're generally on the political left, but they don't rally around a specific set of policy proposals. Nor are there well-defined theoretical tenets that they all share. They don't even really agree on where they stand in relation to Keynes. Some post-Keynesians see themselves as building on the man's work.

Pure Genius

FRIEDRICH HAYEK

Friedrich August Hayek (1899–1992) knew a lot. He was a Nobel Prize–winning economist who also contributed to political science and psychology. But a key part of his work was pointing out that no one knows all that much because knowledge and data are scattered among numerous individuals and institutions. That, Hayek explained, is why socialist central planners can't run a halfway decent economy—they don't have the info. During the Great Depression, Hayek argued with British economist John Maynard Keynes about what makes economies go boom and bust. Many economists agreed with Keynes, but decades later Hayek's insights got new respect. By the 1940s Hayek was deep in the debate over socialism. In his book *The Road to Serfdom*, he argued that government control of the economy erodes political liberties. And although he was a hero to many conservatives, one of his most famous writings is an essay entitled "Why I Am Not a Conservative."

Spending over a decade at the University of Chicago, then later moving to Germany and finally back to Austria, Hayek shared the 1974 Nobel Prize and was still publishing at age 89.

Others think of themselves as truly *post-Keynesian*, moving beyond Keynes's ideas.

Kinds of Money: Old, New, and Funny

Sure, we believe all people are created equal. It's just that some of their currencies are created more equal than others.

_01:: Ecuador's Vanished Sucre

Nations like having their own currencies. First of all, they can print the portraits of great political leaders, or at least honor their famous writers and painters—or sexpots, if they're living in France. If they can't pay their bills, governments can also run the printing press and produce as much money as they need. But Ecuador is an exception to this rule. Until 2000 it had its own currency, the sucre, which existed for 116 years. But runaway inflation, the flight of capital, and entrenched economic crisis convinced the government that it would do better to adopt the U.S. dollar as its national currency. Inflation promptly fell and the economy began to grow. Panama is the only other sovereign state that uses the greenback in its domestic economy—although it never bothered to remove the balboa, its own currency, from circulation.

_02:: The Euro

After nearly a decade of preparation, the euro began circulating January 1, 2002. The euro replaced the national currencies of 12 nations of the European Union. Such venerable currencies as the German mark, the French franc, and the Greek drachma are gone. But three nations eligible to join the euro zone—Britain, Sweden, and Denmark—have so far opted not to do so. While euro banknotes are identical across euro-land, every nation mints its own coins, with its own national symbols on the

What's the Difference?
DISINFLATION VS. DEFLATION

Disinflation means the rate of inflation is going down. In other words, when there's disinflation, prices continue to rise but at a slowing pace. The United States has seen a good deal of disinflation since the late 1970s, which is usually regarded as a good thing.

Deflation, on the other hand, means that prices are going down. It's not just lower inflation but actually negative inflation. Deflation isn't considered a good thing at all. Like inflation, it creates uncertainty, distorts decision making, and transfers wealth in arbitrary ways. Deflation erodes the value of collateral, while the real value of loans goes up—which gives borrowers a good reason not to pay the money back. Take for example Japan, which has experienced deflation in recent years, exacerbating the country's economic woes. Not surprisingly, Japanese banks have ended up with a lot of dud loans on their hands.

flip side. There's even a Vatican euro, with a depiction of Pope John Paul II. Currency unions are nothing new in Europe, but the current European Monetary Union is the first attempt to introduce a single currency for some 300 million people at once.

_03:: Brazilian Money

In the 1970s and 1980s Latin America went through a nasty bout of hyperinflation. With prices rocketing by up to 3,000% per year in Brazil, its currency, the cruzeiro, disintegrated. In 1986 the government came up with the cruzado, which fared little better. In 1989 this had to be replaced with the new cruzado, then back to the cruzeiro, and then to the cruzeiro real. Since 1994 Brazilians have had yet another currency—the real—which so far

has been a bit more real. Because of inflation, the real, when it was introduced, was worth 2.75 billion 1986 cruzados. By the way, *real* is pronounced "ray-owl" by people who want to sound Brazilian, though true Brazilians call it something closer to "he-ow."

_04:: The Turkish Lira

The Turkish lira has the unfortunate distinction of having the highest exchange rate per dollar. The greenback was worth about 1,400,000 liras in 2003. Since Turkey's per capita gross domestic product is approximately $2,800, it means that each and every Turk—man, woman, and child—is on average a lira billionaire. It wasn't always that way. In 1980 the lira exchange rate was a modest 70 liras per dollar.

4 Stats That Drive the Market Wild

British prime minister Benjamin Disraeli once claimed, "There are three kinds of lies: lies, damned lies, and statistics." And, well, statistically speaking, economic data is rarely perfect. Here are just a few of the figures that make the markets move.

_01:: The Unemployment Rate

Here's how to tell if you're part of the unemployment rate: if you're out of work and looking, the U.S. Department of Labor counts you as unemployed; if you're out of work but just sitting around on the couch all day, it does not. (No one keeps statistics on laziness as of yet.) Every month the U.S. Department of Labor uses surveys and statistical methods to measure how many civilians are out of work, and

that percentage is known as the unemployment rate. When the unemployment rate goes up, investors tend to get nervous. It doesn't help that the rate is considered a "lagging indicator," meaning that it can stay high (bad) even after the economy starts to get better.

_02:: Gross Domestic Product

Financial traders across the world dash for their desks at 8:30 a.m. eastern time the last day of each quarter. No, no one's passing out discount stock coupons. Rather, it's the time of year when the U.S. Department of Labor releases the GDP figures. The GDP is the total output of goods and services within the United States, which includes spending by consumers, companies, and government, plus the trade balance (exports minus imports). So it's a big-picture look at how the economy is doing. The figure includes all goods and services produced inside the borders of the United States, regardless of the nationality of the producer. And while economists used to focus on Gross *National* Product, or GNP, which includes products made by U.S. companies abroad (and excludes stuff made by foreign-owned producers in the United States), in these days of globalization, the GDP is seen as the more meaningful figure.

_03:: Housing Starts

If you want to know which sectors of the economy are likely to thrive, check out the housing starts figures. Compiled by the U.S. Census Bureau, these figures show the number of residential units that start construction each month. When homes are built, it means work for construction workers, demand for lumber, and even potential refrigerator purchases. During troubled economic times in the first few years of the 21st century, the relatively strong housing sector helped keep the economy from sinking into a deeper downturn.

_04:: Consumer Confidence

Consumer confidence can be a tricky thing to measure; just ask the Conference Board, an organization that puts out a monthly index of consumer attitudes based on surveys of 5,000 households. The numbers reflect how consumers feel about their present economic situation, as well as their expectations for the next six months. Consumer spending accounts for two-thirds of the economy, so high consumer confidence is an indication that corporate profits and stock prices are likely to be healthy. Then again, bond traders sometimes start selling if it looks as if consumer confidence is getting too high—because that could mean that inflation will soon show up and erode the value of fixed-income bonds.

Stump the Expert

HOW HIGH IS NAIRU?

Economists believe in something called the NAIRU, or Non-Accelerating Inflation Rate of Unemployment. It's a level of unemployment at which inflation is stable. That means if the unemployment rate falls below the NAIRU, inflation will increase (the economy is booming, so companies hike prices and workers demand raises).

It would be nice to have an exact number for NAIRU, since this would allow for better economic forecasting and help policy makers steer the economy. But economists can only make estimates based on actual unemployment and inflation. Also, NAIRU changes over time, due to shifts in demography, productivity, and other factors. Some economists think the current U.S. NAIRU is around 5 percent, but no one knows for sure. And though the NAIRU has also been called the natural rate of unemployment, economists now tend to avoid implying that unemployment is a natural, or good, thing.

Things Karl Marx Believed

If you're sick and tired of free markets and Adam Smith's invisible hand waving at you with one finger, maybe you should consider joining the throngs of Marxists who think capitalism's beat. Here are three theories that should have you seeing red in no time.

_01:: A Working Theory

Karl Marx (1818–1883) wasn't all that radical for his day; earlier 19th-century economists, notably David Ricardo, held similar views on some subjects, but Marx took the ideas one step further. According to his labor theory of value, the value of a commodity is determined by how many hours of labor went into producing it. So, if it takes twice as long to make a combat boot as a stiletto-heeled shoe, then the boots will cost twice as much as the shoes, at least in the long run. Marx argued that la-

Fake Your Way through a Conversation
(ON RATIONAL EXPECTATIONS)

Mentioning "rational expectations" is an excellent way to demonstrate that you have some familiarity with economic theory. The idea of rational expectations, put forward by some economists, is that people are pretty smart when it comes to predicting economic phenomena (such as inflation or stock prices or their own incomes). That doesn't mean the predictions will be accurate, but it means they won't be off target in any regular or predictable way.

If your conversation partner asks, "So what?" point out that the rational-expectations theory sets limits on what government is able to do. For instance, in a recession, the government might cut taxes to get people to spend more. But if taxpayers have rational expectations, they'll realize the tax cut is temporary, and they'll keep their spending low in anticipation of the budget deficits and higher taxes coming next year.

At this point your conversation partner may express skepticism, questioning whether people in a shopping mall are really performing complex calculations about government policy. Don't worry, we've got an effective counter! Just note that some economists share these doubts, and then mention the alternative view of adaptive expectations, which says people form expectations based on the past. So, if inflation was high last year, shoppers will expect it to be high next year, even if the Fed is now gung-ho about stopping inflation.

bor, too, is a commodity, its value determined by how many labor hours society puts into getting a worker ready for work. This raises a question: how do capitalists make profits? Marx's answer: they do it by exploiting workers, squeezing "surplus value" out of them. His political ideas took a big hit when the Soviet Union collapsed in 1991, causing economists to reject his economic critique of capitalist society; however, he remains influential in sociology and political science and among lefty intellectuals everywhere.

_02:: A Falling Rate of Profit

As capitalists exploit their workers and compete against one another, profits generally tend to decline, according to Marx. This idea follows logically once you've accepted everything in Marx's labor theory of value. The capitalists take the surplus value they get from the workers and reinvest it in factories and machinery. But this means that exploiting the workers gets them less value than it used

to, in comparison to the overall size of their operations. So what do you do if you're a capitalist? Exploit the workers even harder, of course!

_03:: A Concentration of Wealth

Try as they might, many capitalists can't prop up that falling rate of profit for very long. Instead, they are beaten by their competitors and end up falling into the working class. The capitalists who remain on top, however, are increasingly wealthy. They form monopolies that dominate their markets. The trouble is, there are fewer and fewer successful capitalists, while the numbers of workers are growing—as is their misery. Therefore, Marx thought, history was moving inevitably toward revolution. Workers would rise up and displace the capitalist class, creating socialist societies instead. But he expected this to happen first in the most advanced economies, such as his native Germany, not in relatively backward places like Russia.

Nightmare on Wall Street:
6 Crises That Keep Economists Up at Night

Thomas Carlyle once called economics "a dismal science." Indeed, economists tend to be cautious and pedestrian, but can you blame them? After all, who could sleep easy after hearing these scary stories?

_01:: The Irish Potato Famine

When you think of economics, think of food. Until the late 1800s economic crisis usually meant agricultural crisis, with famine a not-

so-infrequent consequence. Before the advent of industrial agricultural methods, weather conditions and infestations of various kinds had the power to hold the economy hostage.

In 1845 a new fungus, *Phytophthora infestans*, struck the potato—the mainstay of Ireland's food supply. Although the blight lasted only a few years, its effects were far reaching. As many as 1.5 million died as a direct result of the famine, and many more emigrated in the second half of the 19th century. Even today, only half as many people live in Ireland as did before the famine.

_02:: German Hyperinflation

By November 1923 in Germany, $1 in the United States equaled 4.2 billion German marks, and even daily staples had to be purchased with wheelbarrows of cash. How did this happen? In 1918 Germany lost World War I, suffered a revolution, and became a republic when Emperor Wilhelm II was forced to abdicate. The Treaty of Versailles, signed a year later, saddled Germany with 6.6 billion British pounds' worth of reparations. With the German treasury empty, the government could pay—and conduct its ongoing business—only by printing lots of money: the quickest recipe for inflation. At the height of inflation in 1923, prices rose 40% *per day*. People rushed to the stores as soon as they were paid, before their money became worthless. The frightful experience of the early 1920s scarred the German national psyche and undermined faith in the Weimar Republic, which helped pave the way for Adolf Hitler and the Nazi Party. In fact, Hitler's early grab for power—the Beer Hall Putsch in Munich—came on November 8, 1923.

_03:: The Great Depression

During the Roaring '20s in the United States, the wealthy spent a lot of money they had, and the not-so-wealthy spent a lot of money they didn't have. The Great Depression began soon after the stock market crashed in October 1929, but economists still argue whether the bursting of the 1920s financial bubble caused the Depression or merely foretold the coming economic slump. Either way, by 1932 the economy contracted by 31%, and some 13 million were left jobless—a quarter of the workforce. When President Franklin Delano Roosevelt took office in 1932, he started the New Deal, a set of policies to boost federal spending and create government-financed jobs. Although the economy began growing again in the mid-1930s, the effects of the Depression lingered on until Pearl Harbor. The number of unemployed fell to 7.6 million in 1936 but rose again to 10 million in 1938—the same number of men drafted into the armed forces during World War II.

_04:: The '70s Oil Crisis

The price of oil tends to be slippery—something the economists forgot in the early 1970s when they confidently predicted that crude prices could fall as low as the cost of pumping oil out of the Saudi desert (estimated at less than $1 per barrel). Instead, following the Yom Kippur War between Israel and its Arab neighbors in October 1973, Arab oil producers declared an embargo. Oil prices tripled to more than $10 per barrel, and gasoline shortages ensued. By December President Nixon had to announce that because of the energy crisis, the White House Christmas tree would not be lighted. The 1979 Iranian revolution brought a second oil shock, and oil prices eventually peaked at around $35 per barrel. The oil crisis helped bring on a period of stagflation—meaning that even though the U.S. economy barely dragged along, inflation continued to rise.

_05:: The Asian Flu

The domino-like collapse of several Asian economies in the late 1990s seemed to come out of nowhere. The "tiger" economies of Southeast Asia had been booming for years, and the region widely expected to stay an economic powerhouse straight into the upcoming millennium. Yet in July 1997 things went spectacularly wrong. Thailand became the catalyst for the crisis, when severe pressure from speculators brought down its currency, the baht. The Philippine peso and the Malaysian ringgit fell next. Then the Indonesian rupiah was devalued in August, ushering in political and social turmoil. Finally, even South Korea, one of the strongest economies in east Asia, nearly went bankrupt and had to be bailed out. Economists were at a loss to fully explain the crisis. But as country after country succumbed to the financial bug, one lesson seemed clear: an interconnected global economy can transmit panic just as well as it can goods and services.

_06:: Argentina's Peso Crisis

During the 1990s Argentina was the star pupil of the International Monetary Fund. After two decades of runaway inflation and collapsing currencies, the Argentine government finally turned over a new economic leaf in 1992. Economy minister Domingo Cavallo helped set up a new currency, the peso, and firmly linked it to the U.S. dollar. The government decreed that one peso could always be exchanged for one dollar and that it would print only as many pesos as were backed by dollar reserves. The system functioned extremely well for a few years, but by late 1997 the overvalued peso and restrictive monetary policies helped bring on a prolonged recession, accompanied by turmoil in financial markets. Successive economy ministers and presidents could find no solution. In December 2001 the Argentine peso was devalued, and the government defaulted on some $140 billion in debt, the biggest default on record.

Go Directly to Jail:
Monopolies That Won't Be Building Hotels

We all played the board game. But real-life monopoly is a serious matter, at least as far as the government is concerned. Here are three giants that got some unwanted face time with Uncle Sam.

_01:: Standard Oil

Around the turn of the 20th century, Standard Oil was practically synonymous with ruthless corporate power. John D. Rockefeller's company cut secret deals with railroads, undermined its competitors, and gained control of some 90% of U.S. oil-refining capacity. In 1906 the federal government filed a lawsuit against Standard Oil under the Sherman Antitrust Act—a law designed to combat monopoly power and unfair business practices. The Supreme Court ruled in the government's favor in 1911, ordering the giant company to be broken up into relatively minuscule pieces such as Esso (later known as Exxon) and Socal (later known as Chevron). Oddly, though, the company's assets turned out to be worth more after the dissolution, so Rockefeller became even richer than before.

_02:: AT&T

Remember the days when there were no long-distance telephone commercials? For decades, if you wanted to make a phone call, you had little choice but to go to American Telephone & Telegraph, which handled the overwhelming majority of long-distance and local calls and also built most of the phones and telecom equipment. The Justice Department wrestled with Ma Bell in court in the early 1950s but achieved only minor limits on the company's monopolistic practices. The feds filed suit again in 1974, and eight years later AT&T was ordered to divest itself of its local phone operations; the reorganization took effect in 1984, and the regional "Baby Bells" were born.

_03:: Microsoft

For a while, it looked as though the software company founded by Bill Gates might be broken into "Baby Bills," but this never happened. An antitrust case filed by the Justice Department and state governments in 1998 accused Microsoft of abusing its dominance of operating systems (software that lets computers operate) so as to stifle competitors and take advantage of consumers. In November 2000 Judge Thomas Penfield Jackson ruled against

---

Timeline

FOLLOW THE BOUNCING INCOME TAX RATE

1913 The federal income tax begins. It's progressive, meaning that income at higher levels is taxed at higher rates. The top marginal rate (or highest tax bracket) is set at 7%.

1918 The United States needs money to fight World War I. Top rate jumps to 77%.

1929 Tax rates lowered throughout the Roaring '20s. Top rate bottoms out at 24%.

1933 Great Depression. Top rate goes to 63%, but you're lucky if you have any income.

1944 World War II is going on. Highest U.S. top rate ever: 94%.

1963 The war is long over. Why is the top rate 91%?

1965 Tax cuts initiated by President John F. Kennedy take effect. Top rate: 70%.

1982 "Reaganomics" means tax cuts. Top rate: 50%.

1986 Tax reform. Close the loopholes and lower the rates. Top rate drops to 28%.

1991 President George H. W. Bush breaks his "no new taxes" pledge. Top rate: 31%.

1993 "Clintonomics" means tax hikes. Top rate: 39.6%.

2003 President George W. Bush's tax plan would cut top rate to 35%.

Microsoft, but his decision was overturned on appeal. A settlement reached in November 2001 and modified the following year set some restrictions on Microsoft's practices but left the company fully intact. It's no surprise then that a number of state governments, not to mention Microsoft's corporate rivals, complained that the software goliath had gotten off with a slap on the wrist.

Money Makes the World Go Wrong: Political Careers Wrecked by Economics

It's often said that people vote with their pocketbooks. Well, it's no doubt that thinning wallets and receding purse lines definitely played a big role in shoving these cats out of office.

_01:: Herbert Hoover

Considered a wonder boy of American politics, Hoover (1874–1964) organized relief efforts that fed millions around the world after World War I. In fact, he was a well-regarded secretary of commerce in the 1920s and was elected president in 1928 with a mandate to manage the nicely humming American economy. The next year, however, saw the stock market crash and the start of Great Depression. And Hoover's policies—such as keeping the budget in balance and imposing high tariffs on imported goods—seemed only to deepen the crisis. It didn't help that he had a gloomy demeanor, which led one historian to call him the Great Depressive. Hoover was trounced in the 1932 election by the upbeat Franklin D. Roosevelt, who adopted the more activist policies of the New Deal. And while Hoover got the Hoover Dam named after him, as well as the Hoover Institution, the famous vacuum cleaner brand bears no relation.

_02:: Jimmy Carter

In the years after the Watergate scandal, Americans were pretty sour about their political leaders. That's why former Georgia governor (and nuclear engineer turned peanut farmer) Jimmy Carter's reputation for honesty swept him into the White House in 1976. "I'll never lie to you," he told the public—and apparently he never did. When the economy tanked during his presidency, Carter was up-front about it, saying the country was in crisis in what came to be known as "the malaise speech." (Actually, Carter never used that word, but it was in a memo he'd gotten from a political consultant.) But things kept getting worse, and Carter didn't seem to have an answer. Inflation rose each year of his presidency, hitting 13.5% in 1980. And the "misery index" (which you get by adding inflation and unemployment) went to 20%. Carter lost the 1980 presidential race but won the 2002 Nobel Peace Prize for his international good works.

_03:: George H. W. Bush

The 41st U.S. president learned the hard way that success overseas isn't enough to get you reelected when the economy goes south. After a victory in the first Persian Gulf War in early 1991, Mr. Bush's approval ratings soared as high as 91%. Only 1 American in 10 didn't love him, and leading Democrats chose to sit out the 1992 presidential election for fear of being mauled by a popular incumbent. But the economy perversely went into recession— in part because of high oil prices before the war. Unemployment, which stood at 5.3% in 1989, rocketed to 7.5% by 1992. The president compounded his problems by appearing insensitive—fielding questions about the economy at the golf course. Defeated 18 months later by a cheeky unknown named Bill Clinton, Bush changed from the glorious war victor into another one-term wonder.

_04:: John Major

Becoming British prime minister in November 1990, after 11 years of often controversial rule by iron lady Margaret Thatcher, Major promised conservatism with a human face. His youthful enthusiasm appealed to British voters, and he led the Conservative Party (also known as the Tories) to an unprecedented third straight election victory in 1992. But then, in September of that year, selling of the pound by financial speculators forced the gov-ernment to ignominiously devalue the currency and abandon its link to continental European currencies. Inflation soared and unemployment peaked at 10.5% two months later. Major endured as a lame duck for another four and a half years—simply because the British parliamentary system didn't require him to hold elections. When the voters finally got a chance to vent their anger at the Tories, Major was defeated in a landslide by the bright new light of the Labor Party, Tony Blair.

_05:: Marie Antoinette

By the time Marie Antoinette became queen of France in 1774, at the ripe age of 19, she had already been married for five years. She was never popular because of her Austrian origins, but her extravagant ways and lavish lifestyle earned her the nickname Madam Deficit from her subjects. In fact, she was squarely blamed for the country's financial crisis, though the true cause was heavy debt from the Seven Years War (1756–1763) and French support for the American Revolution. More than half of the government budget went to service that debt, and inflation was massive. By the time the French Revolution broke out in 1789, over 80% of the average peasant's income was spent on bread. When told that her subjects had no bread to eat, Marie Antoinette reportedly replied, "Let them eat cake." (Historians doubt she ever said this, but the point is the peasants thought she had.) The monarchy was abolished in 1792, and in January 1793 King Louis XVI was guillotined. Madam Deficit followed her husband to the scaffold in October of that year.

by
Curry Guinn

Condensed
GENERAL SCIENCE

Contains

The Naked Truth: 4 Bizarre Revelations about Sex ✳ Fun for the Feeble-Minded: 6 Useless Studies ✳ 4 Mind-Boggling Facts You'd Never Have Guessed ✳ 6 Little-Known Scientists (Who've Contributed as Much as Einstein) ✳ Accidents Waiting to Happen: 5 Mistakes That Became Medical Miracles ✳ And 6 That Became Marketable Merchandise ✳ 7 Technologies That Will Change the World (as Soon as We Invent Them) ✳ They Blinded Me with Science: 10 Frauds and Hoaxes That Duped the Masses ✳

The Naked Truth:
Bizarre Revelations about Sex

Don't look so smug, Casanova. Just when you thought you had the birds and the bees all figured out, it turns out Ma and Pa shorted you on the details. Here are four little-known sex facts every cad needs to add to his or her repertoire.

_01:: Even Cockroaches Have Standards

British scientists at the University of Manchester have determined that female cockroaches will lower their standards for a mate as their biological breeding clock begins to tick. By looking at the amount of cockroach wooing required by a male (similar to what's observed on college campuses worldwide), the researchers documented that females became less selective as their reproductive potential decreased. Males, however, seemed to show no difference in mating practices regardless of the female cockroach's age.

_02:: Are You My Lover? (Confused Birds without Bees)

Charles Paxton of St. Andrews University gave this sage advice: "You would not want to go into a pen with an amorous ostrich." And right he is! When Paxton set out to determine why ostriches on British farms weren't laying eggs despite their obvious mating displays, he quickly realized that the poor birds were "sexually confused." It turns out the species-curious ostriches were pointing their "affections" in the wrong direction, mistakenly directing their courtship behaviors toward the human farmers. In perhaps a sign of truly unconditional love, the ostriches seemed to be able to work up their mojo irrespective of the farmer's sex.

_03:: 7 Degrees of Separation

Forget Kevin Bacon; using DNA analysis, Professor Bryan Sykes of Oxford University has traced 95% of the people living in Europe back to one of seven women who lived approximately 11,000 to 45,000 years ago. Amazingly, he's bringing people one giant

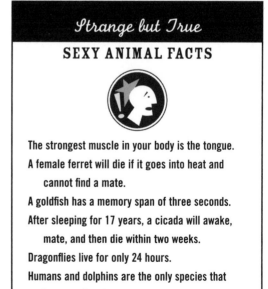

Strange but True

SEXY ANIMAL FACTS

The strongest muscle in your body is the tongue.

A female ferret will die if it goes into heat and cannot find a mate.

A goldfish has a memory span of three seconds.

After sleeping for 17 years, a cicada will awake, mate, and then die within two weeks.

Dragonflies live for only 24 hours.

Humans and dolphins are the only species that have sex for pleasure.

step closer to answering that eternal question, "Where do we come from?" By examining mitochondrial DNA—a genetic material that is passed on only by mothers—Sykes has been able to establish direct maternal links back to these "seven daughters of Eve." Though his research has focused on Europe and these seven clans in particular, Sykes estimates that there are 36 different clans around the world.

_04:: You Know What They Say . . .

It's time to squash those rumors! Despite what you may have heard, two Canadian scientists, Jerald Bain and Kerry Siminoski, studied the relationship between height, foot size, and pe-

nile length and found no significant correlation, seemingly disproving the myth. In addition, Chris McManus of University College London set out to determine once and for all the question of testicle asymmetry in reality versus ancient art. His "nutcase" study was based on the observation of 107 ancient nude statues. Despite previous research claiming that male testicles tend to be symmetrical, McManus observed that on real men, the right side of the scrotal sac is higher, but not lighter (as it is incorrectly portrayed in ancient Greek statues). Both studies won the Ig Nobel Prize (1 of 10 annual awards for research "that cannot, or should not, be repeated").

6 Fun for the Feeble-Minded: Useless Studies

Do you ever get mad when you hear stories of scientists who were paid thousands of dollars to research, say, how many people can walk and chew gum at the same time? Well, we do! After all, we had to sit through 12 years of Career Days, and no one ever said science was this easy.

_01:: Sudden-Death Can Lead to Sudden Death

Scientists at Utrecht University in the Netherlands analyzed the incidence of death on the five days prior to, the day of, and the five days after the 1996 semifinals between the Netherlands and France in soccer. The game was particularly exciting, going to overtime before being decided by penalty kicks. (France ultimately won.) The average number of male deaths in the Netherlands by heart attack or

stroke on the days surrounding the match: 150; on the day of the match: 173. It isn't known what the French death rate was during and after the match. Guess that means they'll have to do more research.

_02:: The Wave Factor

Did you know that the stadium wave, where eager fans jump out of their seats, throw their arms in the air, and then quickly sit back down, travels on average 40 feet per second?

Or that the average width of a stadium wave is 15 seats? Or how about that on average it takes roughly 30 fans to set a wave in motion? Well, thanks to Hungarian scientist Tamas Vicsek and his team of researchers, these numbers are now quantifiable science. In a study done in 2002, Vicsek and his team watched videotape of Mexican soccer matches (sounds exhausting) to create a mathematical model. Just useless science? Not according to Vicsek. The research might actually be used to help predict how and when soccer fans will riot.

_03:: The Trouble with Stubble

Are you (or if you are female, your husband) having trouble relating to your cat? Perhaps you should think about shaving. A study led by Fairfield University indicates that cats re-

---

Alphabet Soup
(WITH JUST A PINCH OF TECHNOLOGY)

ambimousterous [AM-bee-MOUS-ter-ihs]: *adj* Proficient using a mouse with both the left and right hand.

Aunt Tillie [ANT TIL-lee]: *n* The quintessential naive user that must be taken into account when designing software. To pass the Aunt Tillie test means the software is idiotproof.

Batman factor [BAT-man FAK-tur]: *n* A measure of electronic geekness that looks at the size and number of items attached to one's belt. For instance, having a Palm Pilot, a cell phone, and a walkie-talkie would grant you a very high Batman factor.

bogosity [bo-GOS-ih-tee]: *n* The degree to which something is bogus.

chickenboner [CHIK-en BO-nur]: *n* A spammer generally thought to be a redneck in a darkened trailer with a litter of KFC chicken bones surrounding the workstation.

dancing frog [DAN-sing FROG]: *n* A computer bug that will not manifest itself when someone else is watching over your shoulder. (Remember the Warner Brothers frog that sang and danced for only one person?)

geekasm [GEE-KAS-em]: *n* Best understood by reading this quote by MIT professor Alex Slocum: "When they build a machine, if they do the calculations right, the machine works and you get this intense . . . uhh . . . just like a geekasm, from knowing that what you created in your mind and on the computer is actually doing what you told it to do."

kilogoogle [KIH-lo-GOO-gul]: *n* Unit of measurement to indicate the number of hits made on a term by a Google search. "mental floss" has 7.5 kilogoogles.

teledildonics [TEL-uh-dil-DON-iks]: *n* Virtual-reality sex.

zipperhead [ZIP-ur-HED]: *n* Someone with a closed mind.

act negatively to men with long, dark beards. They seem rather indifferent to short beards or unshaven men. In another study, Robert Bork's distinctive partial beard caused disorientation and paralysis in some cats. Of course, now all we need is a study to figure out *why* cats don't like facial hair. It will probably require a hefty chunk of grant money, but we're sure it would be worth it.

_04:: That Whole Shakespeare-Monkey Thing

If a million monkeys typed on a million typewriters for a million years, would they produce a work of Shakespeare by chance? This notion has been used to indicate how, over the vastness of time, complex creations could arise from chance. Well, researchers at Plymouth University in England have carried out a small-scale experiment by placing a computer in an enclosure with six macaques (short-tailed monkeys). After pounding on it with a rock, defecating on it, and urinating on it, some of the monkeys did hit a few keystrokes, producing mostly a lot of *S*s. Theoretically, the hypothesis defies statistics. The odds of striking the correct sequence is so small that you'd have to have a million monkeys typing at a rate of 31,000,000 strokes a year (one per second) each for a million years, and then multiply that amount by itself almost 200 times.

_05:: Toast Really Does Fall Butter-Side Down

Led by physicist Robert Matthews of Aston University, British schoolchildren dropped thousands of buttered and unbuttered pieces of toast from their tables. The results are in: the butter side will hit the ground first more often. In fact, the side of the toast facing up on the plate would hit the floor first more often than not, even if it has no butter. Simply put, when the bread falls, it begins to flip. It generally only has time to flip over before it hits the floor, given average kitchen table height. In a related experiment, when the toast is dropped from a significantly higher height, the unbuttered side would, on average, hit first.

_06:: Navel Academy

A study by Karl Kruszelnicki of the University of Sydney seems to raise more questions than it answers. In a survey of 4,799 people, Kruszelnicki determined that two-thirds of those surveyed detected the presence of belly button lint (BBL). A much higher percentage of men (72%) reported BBL as opposed to women (27%). But curiously, the color of the belly button lint didn't always seem to correspond to the clothes that people wore. The main question this study raises is, why?

Mind-Boggling Facts You'd Never Have Guessed

Some things are just too strange to be coincidence. Maybe the universe is more interconnected than we think?

_01:: There Are as Many Chess Games as Particles in the Universe

Want to know why the best human chess players can still beat the best computers? The secret, brought to you in math-speak, is that the primary game-tree search algorithm in chess faces a massive combinatorial problem. More simply, on average there are 40 moves for each chess turn. And chess games can last up to 70 turns (although most good players will resign well before if they see their position is lost). So the resulting tree describing all chess games is 10^{73}. Estimates for the number of particles in the universe range from 10^{70} to 10^{80}, which means the two are actually pretty close!

_02:: Happy as a Clam

Believe it or not, Gettysburg College researcher Peter Fong decided to dope up his subjects, fingernail clams, by putting them on antidepressants. And while the phrase "happy as a clam" didn't exactly originate with Fong's research, his unique Prozac prescription has kick-started their social lives. Prozac decreases the uptake of serotonin, making more of the neurosecretion available to the nervous system. In the bivalves' case, this led to an overwhelming urge for synchronous spawning, a boon both for clam farmers and gawky teenage clams alike.

_03:: You're Bananas!

If you took bio in high school, you learned that humans are primates. Fine. We accept that we have things in common with other animals—but not the produce aisle! DNA, the building block of life, is a common strand in all living organisms on earth. If the DNA in your body were stretched out it would be 500 million miles long, its average thickness 10 atoms. Here's the strange part, though: humans and bananas share approximately 60% of the same DNA structure. Of course, there are closer comparisons. Humans and mice share about 97% of the same structure, while humans and chimps, perhaps our closest relatives, share about 98%.

_04:: Spooky Particles

Albert Einstein called it "spooky action at a distance." The quantum process known as entanglement (also known as the Einstein/Podolsky/Rosen [EPR] effect, though it should be the ESP effect) allows one particle to "know" the change of state of another particle instantaneously. What's that mean? When paired quantum particles are sent off in different directions, and then one of the particles changes its spin, its pair immediately senses the change and alters its own spin. Eerily enough, experiments have confirmed that this "communication" across distance occurs faster than the speed of light.

6 Little-Known Scientists (Who've Contributed as Much as Einstein)

Sure, Albert Einstein and Marie Curie might have hogged the limelight back in the classroom (showoffs!), but they certainly weren't the only scientists on the scene. Here are six geniuses who deserve equal attention.

_01:: The Guy Who First Realized We've Been Drifting Apart

In geology, Alfred Wegener (1880–1930) is recognized as the father of continental drift. His theory, introduced in 1915, then ridiculed for years, was a paradigm-shifting idea that led to all of modern-day geology. In fact, you've probably seen simulations of what the world looked like back when all of the continents were joined together. Wegener's understanding of continental drift and plate tectonics has helped to explain phenomena such as earthquakes, volcanoes, and other action within the earth's crust. Further, his ideas have shed considerable light on how plants and animals have evolved and spread across the globe.

_02:: The Guy You Should Thank for Must-See TV

Philo T. Farnsworth (1906–1971) single-handedly dreamed up the cathode ray tube, which led to the invention of the television. By scanning and transmitting images in horizontal lines, the young eccentric pioneered an entirely new medium. Sadly, his claim to fame was quietly usurped. At just 21, Farnsworth presented his research to RCA executive David Sarnoff and Russian scientist Vladimir Zworykin. Zworykin and Sarnoff then replicated the technology and revised it. Using their resources at RCA, the two then began to dominate the marketing of this new technology. Farnsworth sued and seemingly won in court, but the power of the corporation proved mightier, and Farnsworth was never able to profit from the industry he helped launch.

_03:: The Guy Responsible for Your Speedy PC

William Shockley (1910–1989) and other scientists at Bell Labs were the first to use semiconductors to replace vacuum tubes in 1951. In fact, the use of transistors completely revolutionized modern computers. Shockley's use of the technology both as a transmitter of information, converting sound waves to electronic information, and as a resistor, to control the electronic current (spelling it out— TRANSmit + resISTOR), was unique. Transistors could perform the same function as vacuum tubes at one-millionth the energy required. The technology quickly became ubiquitous in electronic equipment, leading to revolutions in size, speed, and capabilities. Sadly, however, the genius tarnished his reputation in later years by espousing some shockingly racist theories.

_04:: The Guy You Should Thank for the World Wide Web (and We're Not Talking Al Gore!)

Tim Berners-Lee (1955–   ) helped launch an information revolution that has forever altered society. While the Internet is the product of many people's creative genius, the World Wide Web (WWW) itself has a unique parent. In 1980 Berners-Lee struck on the idea of having hyperlinked text available to him on his computer so he could easily follow his thoughts while working. But he didn't want to access data and information on just his own computer; he wanted information available from other computers on the network. And ultimately, that means the entire network of computers out there. Berners-Lee created the first language for Web pages, HTML, which is still the primary language of the WWW. In 1991 the WWW was introduced, and the whole world's gone dot-mad every since.

_05:: Just One Word—Plastic

Is there any substance that is more ubiquitous and more representative of the past 40 years than plastic? It's inexpensive, moldable, and incredibly functional, and we've got a genius named Leo Baekeland (1863–1944) to thank for it. In fact, Leo saw the immense potential for the fully synthetic material when he first invented it, way back in 1907. Dubbing his creation Bakelite, the inventor spent his life dominating the world of synthetic plastics, even subduing rival Thomas Edison. Bakelite itself became a predecessor to more advanced and malleable plastics (you can still find Bakelite products and collectors on eBay!), and his legacy clearly lives on: during this year alone, over 50 million tons of plastics will be produced.

_06:: The Guy Who Chose to Breed Flies instead of Swatting Them

Theodosius Dobzhansky (1900–1975) isn't a name that rolls off the tongue (or that immediately springs to mind when we think of the world's greatest scientists), but his contribution to the field of genetics is immense. Dobzhansky took Darwinian concepts of evolution and began studying them in terms of genes and gene pools. His research focused on the humble fruit fly, but his results weren't humble at all. He's credited with having first demonstrated evolution in action by showing how the genetic makeup of fruit flies changed to adapt to different environments. For the first time evolutionary theorists could point to the hard science of genetics to bolster their claims. No small feat, Dobzhansky laid the groundwork for all future science in evolution and genetics.

Strange but True

EINSTEIN'S PICKLED BRAIN

While Albert Einstein's cranium is now safely stored at Princeton Hospital, the genius's cranium was actually kept in a mason jar in a Wichita, Kansas, laboratory for many years. The brain, which has been subject to plenty of postmortem study, measures surprisingly smaller than average brains. It is, however, markedly denser in some of the regions associated with mathematical ability, and neuroscientists disagree over whether these differences are significant.

Accidents Waiting to Happen:
Mistakes That Became Medical Miracles

Mama always said you should learn from your mistakes. But did she really mean that you should take your daily gaffes and turn them into groundbreaking, earthshaking revelations in science? Here are a couple of cats who did just that.

_01:: That Stuff in the Back of Your Fridge

In 1928 Alexander Fleming famously left a culture of *Staphylococcus aureus* bacteria out under a microscope for too long. By chance, some mold spores landed on the culture and began to grow. Preparing to throw the culture out, Fleming noted something truly peculiar: the bizarre mold had killed all of the bacteria. Fleming capitalized on his mistake when he realized that the mold was nontoxic to animals, going on to develop the first truly effective antibiotic. The medicine, which you now know as penicillin, has saved millions of lives over the years.

_02:: The Original X-Man

Wilhelm Roentgen was setting up a primitive cathode ray generator projected through a glass vacuum tube when he noticed a faint green light on the wall across the room. The light was shining directly on a barium-platinocyanide-coated screen (isn't that always the case?). What was more astonishing, the light from the cathode ray generator seemed to travel through a variety of materials such as wood and paper. As Roentgen began putting various objects in front of the generator, he noticed the outline of the bones of his hand on the wall. For the next few weeks, Roentgen stayed in seclusion studying his accidental phenomenon, which he later dubbed X (for unknown)-rays.

_03:: The Reason You Don't Have a Larger Family

In 1951 Carl Djerassi was attempting to synthesize estradiol, a steroid primarily used to treat inflammatory disease. In the process, however, he accidentally produced a chemical that was similar to progesterone, only more active. Playing with his new product, Djerassi modified the chemical so that it could be taken orally. What resulted wasn't just any ordinary pill; it was the Pill. Still in wide use across the globe, the birth control drug Djerassi created had one of the most sweeping social impacts on the world in the 20th century. Djerassi went on to become a crusader for birth control, publishing and lecturing widely on the subject.

_04:: A Poodle's Piddle

Who could have known that a puddle of dog urine would spur a cure for diabetes? That's right! In studying the function of the pancreas (which wasn't well understood in 1889), two professors from the University of Strasbourg decided to remove the pancreas from a living dog. Later, flies were seen swarming around the canine's urine. Curious as to the cause, the professors analyzed the sample and found that it contained a higher than normal amount of sugar. The doggone discovery led the scientists to determine a relationship between the pancreas and its control of insulin. In turn, this led to the first effective treatment of diabetes through insulin injections.

_05:: Something to Stop the Burning!

German scientist Paul Ehrlich was looking for a treatment for sleeping sickness, an infection that can eventually lead to coma. Looking for an arsenic compound that would kill the disease without harming the patient, Ehrlich stumbled across a compound known as 606. The drug did little for sleeping sickness, but it did work wonders on syphilis. At the time (1999), syphilis was a hugely disabling and extraordinarily prevalent—though little talked about—disease. Ehrlich and his colleagues tested 606 on syphilitic mice, guinea pigs, and rabbits. Surprisingly, within just

Just the Facts

BODY-BASED STATISTICS

Amount of time it takes blood to make a complete circuit through your body: 60 seconds

Amount of saliva produced per day: 2 quarts

Length human hair grows on top of head in a month: 1 inch

Average number of blinks per minute: 25

Average number of blinks per year: 13,140,000

Number of bones a human is born with: 300

Number of bones an adult human has: 206

Increase in life expectancy if cardiovascular disease were eliminated: 9.78 years

three weeks, the animals emerged cured. The resulting drug, Salvarsan (606), sold brilliantly across the globe and put Germany at the top of chemical and drug production.

And

6 That Became Marketable Merchandise

Forget the hard work and hours of research. If you want to make a lot of money as a scientist, maybe your best bet is a lucky lab find.

_01:: This Is What Happens When You Don't Wash Your Dishes!

In an act repeated thousands of times in thousands of science labs across the world, in 1903 Edouard Benedictus knocked a flask off a shelf and onto the floor. The glass shattered, but oddly, the container retained its shape. Upon questioning his lab assistant, Fast Eddy learned that the flask had contained cellulose nitrate. And while it had appeared empty (his assistant had done a shoddy cleanup job), the residue from this liquid plastic clung to the inside of the vial. Quick on the uptake, Benedictus realized that he could insert a layer of the celluloid between two sheets of glass, such that the composite would fracture yet retain its shape. The discovery led to safety glass being used in car windshields as well as thousands of other applications.

_02:: Bring the Heat

Corning scientist Dr. Eugene Stookey was experimenting with photosensitive glass. Unbeknownst to him, though, the oven he was working with malfunctioned and heated the glass to a much higher temperature than intended. Instead of finding a puddle of melted glass, though, Stookey opened the oven door to a hard milky white substance. As he pulled the overheated glass out, he accidentally dropped the material—but it didn't break! So, what's become of his discovery? Stookey and company used the process to create a little line of plates and pans you probably know as Corning Ware.

_03:: Is That a Candy Bar in Your Pocket or . . . ?

Radar and microwave technologies developed during World War II were credited with helping to turn the tide in the battle in Europe. But after the war, scientists like Percy Spencer stumbled across all sorts of new applications for the technologies. Percy, who was working for Raytheon at the time, happened to be in the path of powerful radiation emitted from a magnetron (ouch) when he noticed that the candy bar in his pocket had melted. He then, believe it or not, put popcorn kernels in front of the device and watched in fascination as the popcorn popped. He also demonstrated cooking an egg from inside out. (Don't do this at home, they tend to explode!) Of course, using low-density microwave energy to cook is now commonplace, and Spencer's use of popcorn as an early experimental substance was prescient—today the United States produces 500,000 tons of popcorn, most of which is cooked in microwave ovens.

_04:: A Weak Solution

Spencer Silver of 3M was experimenting with superstrong adhesives in 1970. One combination disappointingly led to something only mildly adhesive. In fact, the adhesive was so weak that it couldn't even be used to hold two pieces of paper firmly together! Finding no good use for it, Silver tossed the pitiful glue aside and continued to work. A few years later another 3M employee, Arthur Fry, was frus-

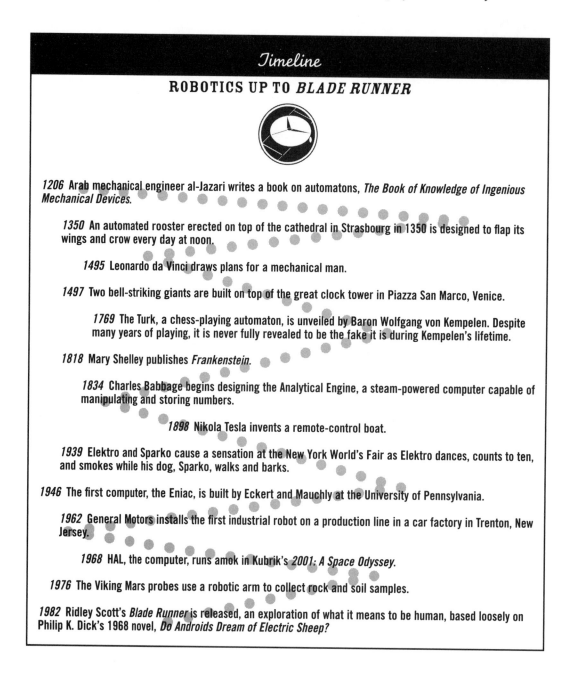

Timeline

ROBOTICS UP TO *BLADE RUNNER*

1206 Arab mechanical engineer al-Jazari writes a book on automatons, *The Book of Knowledge of Ingenious Mechanical Devices.*

1350 An automated rooster erected on top of the cathedral in Strasbourg in 1350 is designed to flap its wings and crow every day at noon.

1495 Leonardo da Vinci draws plans for a mechanical man.

1497 Two bell-striking giants are built on top of the great clock tower in Piazza San Marco, Venice.

1769 The Turk, a chess-playing automaton, is unveiled by Baron Wolfgang von Kempelen. Despite many years of playing, it is never fully revealed to be the fake it is during Kempelen's lifetime.

1818 Mary Shelley publishes *Frankenstein.*

1834 Charles Babbage begins designing the Analytical Engine, a steam-powered computer capable of manipulating and storing numbers.

1898 Nikola Tesla invents a remote-control boat.

1939 Elektro and Sparko cause a sensation at the New York World's Fair as Elektro dances, counts to ten, and smokes while his dog, Sparko, walks and barks.

1946 The first computer, the Eniac, is built by Eckert and Mauchly at the University of Pennsylvania.

1962 General Motors installs the first industrial robot on a production line in a car factory in Trenton, New Jersey.

1968 HAL, the computer, runs amok in Kubrik's *2001: A Space Odyssey.*

1976 The Viking Mars probes use a robotic arm to collect rock and soil samples.

1982 Ridley Scott's *Blade Runner* is released, an exploration of what it means to be human, based loosely on Philip K. Dick's 1968 novel, *Do Androids Dream of Electric Sheep?*

trated that his little paper markers wouldn't stay in place in his choir hymnal. Borrowing some of Silver's adhesive, Fry found that his markers would stay in place, and he could lift them off without damaging his book at all. Post-it notes were first marketed in 1980, spurring a whole revolution for office organizers and to-do list makers the world over.

_05:: Fishing for Answers

Roy Plunkett discovered Teflon (tetrafluoroethylene) in a Du Pont lab in 1938 during the search for a new refrigerating coolant. However, much like Spencer Silver's 3M solution (see above), it was tossed aside for lack of application. In fact, it wasn't even considered for commercial production until a Frenchman named Marc Gregoire went fishing. Gregoire found that the substance worked great on his tackle to reduce tangling. Of course, now Teflon is used in everything from car brakes to space suits to replacement arteries for the human heart. It's also used on microchips and

rockets, and surprisingly, it's even rubbed liberally on the Statue of Liberty's arthritic joints (Teflon apparently slows down the aging process in statues).

_06:: Delicious and Refreshing (Not to Mention Good for Your Teeth?)

Did you know that Coca-Cola started out as a medicinal syrup? It's absolutely true. In the late 1800s pharmacists frequently mixed up and sold cure-all potions. One such pharmacist, a guy named John Pemberton, stirred up a batch of what he thought was an excellent tonic for tiredness, nervousness, and sore teeth. He and his assistant then mixed the solution with ice water, tried it, and decided they wanted more than just a spoonful. In their next batch, though, Pemberton's assistant accidentally used carbonated water, and wow, a soft-drink giant was born! So, just how popular is Coke? According to the Coca-Cola company, the only word more commonly used than *Coca-Cola* in the *world* is *OK*.

7 Technologies That Will Change the World (as Soon as We Invent Them)

We know Louis Armstrong likes to sing about "What a Wonderful World" we've got, but seriously! Just think of how much better things will be when we finally get these objectives crossed off our list.

_01:: No More Flu!

Penicillin changed the state of health care for the entire world by helping to control bacterial infections. Viral infections, on the other hand, are still mostly untreatable. There's a

good deal of evidence to suggest that this will change in this century, though. Today's scientists have had some success in controlling viral fusion by inserting genetic material into healthy host cells in a class of envelope viruses (a class that includes HIV, influenza, rhinoviruses, and Ebola). The research definitely looks promising. And given these advances, it's not hard to see a future where many of the most common viral ailments are as treatable as common infections.

_02:: No More Fat!

While genetic engineering is becoming commonplace in agriculture (producing things like tear-free onions and nutritionally enhanced rice), this technology is only just starting in the treatment of humans. The real revolution in genetic engineering will occur when genes are routinely manipulated to eliminate the onset of heart disease, obesity, and cancer. Scientists have identified approximately 2,000 single-gene diseases that will one day be stopped through gene therapy. So, why isn't the technology commonplace yet? The problem is that often the manipulated gene fails to show up when inserted in the host. As we better understand the human genome sequence, though, it will become far easier to insert as well as delete genes without endangering the function of other chromosomes.

_03:: No More Memory Loss!

Think Keanu Reeves in *The Matrix* or *Johnny Mnemonic*. In both films he had a socket in the back of his head where information could be downloaded or uploaded. Believe it or not, this sort of technology will no longer be science fiction in the 21st century. Currently about 6,000 people have cochlear implants, electrodes that stimulate the auditory fibers in the brain. Amazingly, this technology gives the profoundly deaf the ability to actually

hear sounds. But that's just the start. At Emory University patients with an implanted computer chip connected to the cortical node can use the chip to move an object on a computer screen. Of course, this technology brings up huge debates about the line between man and machine, but the sheer scope of its application is staggering.

_04:: No More Automobile Accidents!

With trains in Japan and Europe routinely having no human operators, it seems only a matter of time before our highway systems will no longer be under the control of the 100 million drivers who take to the road every day. And considering the statistics, it seems like a logical step forward. Every year 50,000 road deaths occur, but does that mean people will be ready to turn the wheel over to their PC? If computer drivers had the same fatality rate as humans, would you get in the automated car? Probably not. How about if automated cars had a fatality rate of 20,000 lives? What about 10,000 lives? Or even 300 lives? Most people's gut reaction is that the fatality rate must be very, very low to give up that control. Of course, we're willing to take far greater risks and are far more accepting when it comes to human gaffes than when technology's to blame.

_05:: No More Blackouts!

Promises of pollution-free, unlimited power have been looming for a while. The idea is that we should be able to obtain energy by extracting hydrogen from water. And it sounds ideal. The reality is that if fusion can be harnessed in a safe way, our dependence on fossil fuels will be a thing of the past. Unfortunately, the power it takes to create nuclear fusion (1) either is higher than the power it creates or (2) necessitates a fission nuclear reaction. Plasma technologies, magnetic confinement, and laser-induced fusion are the most likely candidates for efficiently producing a fusion reaction that can be converted to useful power. But don't rule out hope, yet! The next leap forward will come soon, as the European Union continues the development of the Tokamak fusion reactor, which will create a self-sustaining fusion reaction.

_06:: No More Age Spots!

In the 21st century the ability to replace worn-out organs will become commonplace by cloning new organs and cells from the host body. But more than just performing transplants, scientists will also be able to slow or halt the aging process in many cells. Current theories on aging indicate that the interaction of free radicals (reactive oxygen species) causes cells to degenerate over time. By neutralizing these free radicals, significant delays can occur in the aging of cells. So, what's that mean exactly? The natural lifespan might be increased to well over 100 years, and those later years might still be as productive (perhaps even reproductive) as earlier years. Such a change would revolutionize the way we structure society.

_07:: No More (Exorbitant) Power Bills!

Superconductors allow the transmission of electricity without any loss of energy, so scientists continue to strive toward making room temperature semiconductors. And why are room temperature semiconductors important to your well being? The end result of such

Fake Your Way Through a Conversation

NANOTECHNOLOGY'S GONNA CHANGE EVERYTHING!

It's confirmed—nanotechnology is one of the hottest buzzwords since ... well, the buzzword *buzzword*. And the good part is that faking your way through a discussion of it is easy once you understand only a few things. First off, nanotechnology implies building things with atoms and molecules. The scale is obviously very, very small, a nanometer being a billionth of a meter. By comparison, a human hair is about 50,000 nanometers wide. But what exactly's the payoff? If you're arguing for the technology, just keep these things in mind: by applying it to medicine, nanomachines will actually be able to enter the body to destroy viruses, remove arterial plaque, and excise cancer cells. Even more amazingly, nanomachines will have the ability to build other nanomachines in a completely pollution-free production process, and the potential for these tiny machines is enormous. Of course, if you're lobbying against the technology, the potential for overreplication is a real threat. So, if you want to kill the conversation ASAP, just bring up the Terminator scenario: nanotech weapons have the potential to self-replicate as targeted killing machines to kill any sort of host system available (from computers to crops to livestock to humans). It should help you switch topics quickly.

technology will be an enormous increase in our ability to miniaturize devices. Computers, power transmission, and communication technology would become smaller and, as a result, faster. Further, billions of dollars will be saved as energy is conserved rather than lost in heat.

(See 4 Reasons to Have Your Physics Super-Sized on page 240 for more on superconductors.)

They Blinded Me with Science:
10 Frauds and Hoaxes That Duped the Masses

Sometimes scientists are brazen, sometimes they're power hungry, and sometimes they're just plain wrong. Hey, if you can't believe a scientist, who can you trust?

_01:: The Cold Fusion Incident

Fusion power has been heralded as the solution to our future power needs. After all, it promises to provide a nearly limitless supply of energy with minimal environmental impact. The current problem, though, is that it takes a tremendous amount of energy to fuse together nuclei. So, when Stanley Pons and Martin Fleischmann announced to a hungry scientific world that they'd discovered cold fusion in 1989 (a process that supposedly used much less energy), the duo were welcomed with splashy headlines. Other scientists were dubious, and when Pons and Fleischmann withdrew their paper from *Nature* magazine and refused to answer questions, charges of fraud were made. Pons and Fleischmann never gave enough details of the experiment to allow others to replicate it, and more than 10 years later no one has been able to replicate their results. There are still scientists who believe Pons and Fleischmann were on to something, but the premature claims of cold fusion

cast such doubt on these two researchers that they were doomed to ignominy.

_02:: Scientist in on God's Prank

In the early 18th century Dr. Johann Beringer of the University of Würzburg devoted his research to the discovery of fossils that seemed to indicate prehistoric life. Beringer, however, believed that these fossils were "capricious fabrications of God," used to test man's faith. His beliefs seemed confirmed when at one site he discovered fossils of birds, beetles, moons, and stars. Little did he know that two mean-spirited colleagues had planted the fake fossils. Perhaps trying to get caught, they even planted tablets inscribed with the Hebrew and Arabic words for God. Beringer published a book, *Lithographia Wirceburgensis*, in 1726 describing his findings and his theory. But then he made another discovery: a similar buried tablet inscribed with his own name. He immediately began trying to buy back all the available copies of his book, but it was too late. Because of the hoax, his book became a bestseller.

_03:: George and the Cardiff Giant

George Hull had no patience with fools, but he exhibited great patience for making a fool of others. After arguing with a clergyman who claimed that giants had walked the earth because the Bible said so, Hull proceeded to carve a 10-foot gypsum statue of a man. He then buried his creation on a neighboring New York farm. In 1869, a full year later, Hull hired some well diggers, who discovered his stone man on the job. Of course people gathered to see this oddity, and rumors began to spread that it was a fossilized human of gigantic proportions. Many saw it for the hoax it was, but when two Yale professors declared it genuine, the proof of giants on earth became set in stone. Eventually Hull had to admit it was a fake after he sued P. T. Barnum for exhibiting a copy of it. Barnum claimed his statue was just a hoax of a hoax and was found not guilty.

_04:: The Most Unnatural of Selections

In the mid-1800s pollution from factories in Britain was darkening trees by killing the lichen, and scientists also noted a decline in the ratio between lighter-colored peppered moths and darker varieties. It was hypothesized that the lighter moths were easier to spot and thus were eaten more by birds. Here was evolution in action. Bernard Kettlewell sat in the woods and watched to see whether birds preferred the lighter version to darker, and he reported that indeed they were twice as likely to eat the lighter moths. Three problems, though: (1) Kettlewell was responsible

for nailing dead moths to the trees for the birds to feed on, (2) peppered moths rarely alight on tree trunks, and (3) birds don't normally feed on moths that are on the side of trees. Even after scientists were informed of these inconsistencies, many still clung to the validity of the experiment, perhaps because they wanted to believe it as the canonical example of observed natural selection.

_05:: Sex and the Seedy

Alfred Kinsey's landmark studies of the 1950s, known as the Kinsey Reports, were the major emphasis on late-20th-century views of human sexuality. The incidence of homosexuality, bisexuality, adultery, and childhood sexual behavior were higher than previously thought, which helped lead to different views of adult and childhood sexual behavior. According to Judith Reisman, however, Kinsey's research was fraught with very bad scientific method and possibly fraud. He obtained much of his data by interviewing prisoners, his interviewing technique was biased, and he used reports from pedophiles to hypothesize about childhood sexual behavior. Kinsey's estimates on the extent of homosexual behavior (38.7% in males ages 36–40) have not been validated in subsequent studies. In contrast, a Batelle report found that 2.3% of men reported having sex with another man. Nonetheless, Kinsey's landmark study still remains one of the primary sources for current sexuality discussions.

_06:: Anything for Albert

Arthur Eddington was so convinced of the theory of general relativity that he altered his data to support it. Eddington set out to put

Einstein to the test by carefully measuring how light was bent during a solar eclipse. But apparently the examiner went soft. When the results were in, Eddington threw out 16 photographic plates that didn't support Einstein's theory. Even worse, he then published his research without those 16 plates and showed how Einstein's theory accurately predicted the resulting data. It was this experiment that helped launch the public acceptability of relativity. Strangely enough, the hoax still has legs. You can still find the experiment listed in current textbooks as "proof" of Einstein's theory.

_07:: Errors of a Graphic Nature

A more recent incident of fraudulent science concerns Jan Hendrik Schön, a physicist at Bell Laboratories. Considered brilliant, Schön was on the fast track in the field of nanoelectronics. His name was even mentioned for a possible Nobel Prize. But his rate of publication (40 a year) and his amazing results began to make some colleagues curious. Eventually Schön was caught falsifying data when he presented identical graphs in two different papers—and the graphs were supposed to be on different topics. Bell Labs themselves initiated an investigation and were rightfully horrified to find gross misconduct.

_08:: The Great Tasaday Hoax

One of the most startling anthropological discoveries of the 20th century was the discovery of a primitive, cave-dwelling society in the Philippines in 1971. The Tasadays, as they were called, were a find of enormous proportions because they lived a life undisturbed by hundreds of years of society. And to many an academic's delight, anthropologists could now directly observe how people lived in such societies. The Tasadays even used stone tools. If you're thinking it's impossible that such an isolated group could exist in the Philippines as late at the 1970s, you're right. It turns out that their "discoverer," PANAMIN (Private Association National Minorities) secretary Manuel Elizalde Jr., paid local farmers to live in the caves, take off their clothes, and appear Stone Age. In return he gave them money and security from counterinsurgency and tribal fighting. The fact that the Tasadays were a hoax was not confirmed until the fall of Marcos in 1983, invalidating, no doubt, many PhD dissertations that had been written in the interim.

_09:: Don't Worry about the EMF, but Please Don't Talk and Drive

Concerns about the dangers of living close to high-tension wires or of frequent use of cell phones have been hot topics for the past decade. Unfortunately, one of the studies that warned about the dangers of electromagnetic field (EMF) damage was a case of fraudulent science. Robert P. Liburdy, a cell biologist at the Lawrence Berkeley National Laboratory, was a leading researcher looking into the dangers of EMF. No study up to that point had shown any increase in risk due to electromagnetic fields. Liburdy set out to change that, however, as his papers claimed that the fields could cause a disruption in calcium, which is important to cell function. According to external reviewers, however, Liburdy left out, manipulated, and otherwise misrepresented the data to support the conclusions he was looking for. While the intense debate about the possible dangers of EMF will continue, it will do so without Liburdy's findings.

_10:: Further Proof That Scientific Education Is Essential

The Quadro Corporation of Harleyville, South Carolina, had an impressive client list: public schools, police agencies, the U.S. Customs office, and Inspector General's offices to name a few. The product they sold, the top of the line Quadro QRS 250G (also known as the Quadro Tracker, available for $1,000), boasted the ability to find drugs, weapons, or virtually anything worth looking for. The small plastic box supposedly contained frequency chips of an advanced sort not known to regular science. Driven by static electricity, the Quadro would resonate at exactly the same frequency as the searched-for item. When the FBI opened the box, however, they found nothing inside. Quadro threatened to sue Sandia Laboratories when Sandia suggested that the device was fraudulent, but eventually Quadro became the bigger company, and just closed shop.

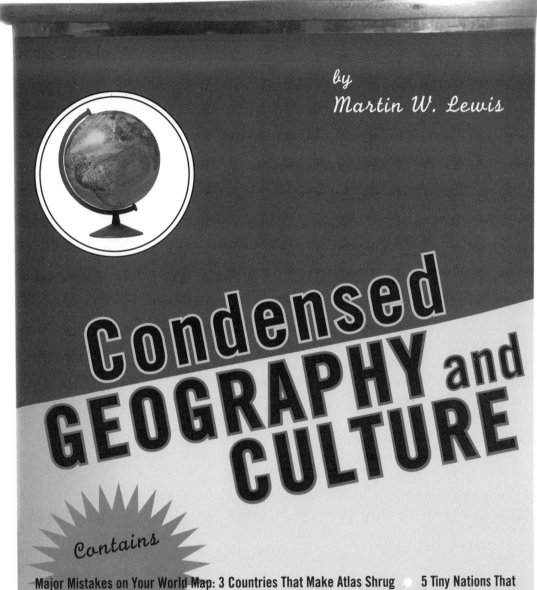

by
Martin W. Lewis

Condensed GEOGRAPHY and CULTURE

Contains

Major Mistakes on Your World Map: 3 Countries That Make Atlas Shrug ✳ 5 Tiny Nations That Get No Respect ✳ Home Alone: 4 Places That'll Make Any Misanthrope Smile ✳ 3 Swarming Megacities Where People Just Won't Leave! ✳ 3 Countries That Don't Take American Express (Don't Even Get Them Started on Travelers Cheques) ✳ 4 Places That Will Never See a Club Med ✳ Dysfunction Junction: 5 Crime and Kidnapping Capitals ✳ Sex and the Cities: 3 International Hubs of Prostitution ✳ English as a 102nd Language: 4 Places Where Subtitles Would Definitely Help ✳ 6 Lands Where Gods Collide ✳ 5 Assumptions That'll Help You Lose Friends ✳ 6 Places to Meet New People and Chew Their Saliva ✳

Major Mistakes on Your World Map:
Countries That Make Atlas Shrug

3

Forget about trying to find Waldo; what about Somalia? That's right! While your world map no doubt looks authoritative—with all those fancy colors and heavy lines—there seems to be a real problem locating some of these so-called countries on the ground.

_01:: Somalia

Somalia isn't really a country, but you can still find it on most world political maps. You can read all about in the reference books too: they'll tell you that almost all of the people of Somalia share the same ethnicity, speak Somali, and follow the Sunni Islam religion. Of course, the books usually forget to mention that Somalia hasn't been a unified state for years. After bouncing around as a pawn in Cold War geopolitics (first as a Soviet ally and then an American one), Somalia collapsed catastrophically in 1991. Now its "central government" doesn't even control all of its capital city, Mogadishu. As for the rest of Somalia, it's basically divided into squabbling clan territories.

_02:: Republic of Somaliland

The new, stronger government in northern Somalia transcends the squabbling clans to rule the Republic of Somaliland. So, what's the catch? The Republic of Somaliland is a phantom country—it hasn't received any international recognition, so it's almost impossible to locate in the reference works. Oddly enough, you can find Somaliland on the world map if you have a map made during the first half of the 20th century. At that time, northern Somalia was a British colony—called British Somaliland—and Italy ruled the rest of Somalia. It's surprising that arbitrary European-imposed boundaries have shown such staying power.

_03:: Democratic Republic of the Congo

The Democratic Republic of the Congo is another challenge to the geographically literate because (1) it's not democratic; (2) it's not a functioning republic; (3) it's not the same place as its neighbor, Congo; and (4) it goes through lots of name changes (Belgian Congo, Congo Leopoldville, Congo Kinshasa, Zaire). So, good luck with the atlas. Unfortunately, by the time we figure it all out, the Democratic Republic might not exist anymore. Its economy and infrastructure have been decaying for decades, and the government just doesn't control much of the territory. During the Cold War, Belgium, France, and the United States propped up the brutal and corrupt regime of Mobutu Sese-Seko, but subsequent coups and foreign invasions have turned the country into an empty shell.

Tiny Nations That Get No Respect

Every sovereign state deserves its own seat in the community of nations, right? But what happens when you make size a factor? These countries help put an end to the debate over whether size really does matter.

_01:: Luxembourg

With 448,000 people inhabiting 2,500 square kilometers, Luxembourg is a small place indeed. Luxembourg could easily fit into Russia 6,600 times, and the population of Luxembourg would have to be multiplied by more than 2,000 to equal China's. But Luxembourg counts as a significant member of the European Union and other international organizations—and it ranks as the world's richest country on a per capita basis (at US$43,000). Luxembourg also stands as something of a giant when contrasted with the world's true microstates. These are the internationally recognized sovereign entities that you might not find on a world map for the simple reason that they're too small (for example, the feudal remnants of Europe and a few of the islands of the Caribbean and Pacific).

_02:: Principality of Monaco

Everyone knows that American movie star Grace Kelly became Princess of Monaco, but what exactly is Monaco? The quintessential European microstate, Monaco could fit into tiny Luxembourg about 1,400 times. Covering less than two square kilometers, Monaco boasts a total population of 32,000 (fewer people than you could find at a large U.S. university). Of that small number, only 16% are actually classified as Monegasque; the rest are mostly French and Italian. So, what's so special about Monaco? For one thing, it has Monte Carlo, a well-known gambling haven for Europe's dissolute elite.

_03:: Nauru

Composed of 10,000 people on an island less than one-eighth the size of the District of Columbia, the nation of Nauru is both interesting and sad. In the 1970s Nauru was one of the most prosperous countries in the world, and the large profits from its phosphate industry were spread widely among its small number of citizens. The problem? The phosphate deposits are mostly gone, and with them went most of the country. What remains is largely a desolate, stripped-out wasteland. The people of Nauru now face an uncertain future, surviving on mismanaged trusts left over from the days of the phosphate boom. The government of Nauru, however, hopes to reinvent the island as an off-shore banking center.

_04:: Pacific Atoll Countries

Although the islands of Tuvalu and Kiribati are tiny specks, both states control vast expanses of the Pacific Ocean, with substantial fisheries and potentially significant mineral resources. Kiribati is only about four times the size of the District of Columbia, but it extends across more than 3,000 miles of sea space—a substantial "territory" for its 78,600 inhabitants. Patrolling this expanse, however, is a rather large challenge. And looming over Kiribati and Tuvalu—as well as the Marshall Islands and the Maldives—is the threat of global warming. If sea levels rise as some models predict, the low coralline atolls of these countries will simply vanish beneath the waves.

_05:: Vatican City: The Holy See

Even such minuscule countries as Nauru and Monaco are substantial when contrasted with the world's smallest sovereign state: Vatican City. The Vatican (or the Holy See, as it is more properly called) is little more than a cluster of buildings in Rome, covering less than half a square kilometer. This speck of land, roughly three quarters the size of Washington's Mall, is all that remains of the Roman Catholic Church's once substantial territorial holdings. Here one can find a true, if tiny, theocracy: the pope enjoys full executive, judicial, and legislative powers, and the legal system is based on canon law. But despite its limited size, the Holy See is a highly international place, receiving pilgrims and financial contributions from Catholic churches all over the world.

Home Alone:

Places That'll Make Any Misanthrope Smile

The most remote destination on earth is undoubtedly the center of Antarctica. Guarded by thousands of miles of rugged glacial terrain, not to mention the roughest seas on the planet, you're pretty likely to find all the alone time you need there. But if you're simply looking for a hiding spot, here are a couple other places no one will think to seek.

_01:: Tristan de Cunha

If you'd like to see another person or two, your best bet is probably Tristan de Cunha, in the south Atlantic. Tristan de Cunha, population 300 or so, is a rugged volcanic island largely ringed by sea cliffs up to 600 meters high. The best way to get to the island is by taking a fishing boat out of Cape Town, South Africa. Tristan is a dependency of the almost equally isolated St. Helena (population 7,300), famous as Napoleon's final place of exile. But St. Helena, itself one of Britain's last remaining colonies, lies over 1,500 miles away. The people of Tristan make a decent living by fishing and growing a few crops (mostly potatoes); the island's main exports are saltwater crayfish and postage stamps.

_02:: Pitcairn

The Pacific also contains a number of remote islands. One of the most famous is Pitcairn, another British territory. As oceanic islands go, Pitcairn is not that isolated, being only a few hundred miles from the Isles Gambier in French Polynesia, but it is rugged and lacks an anchorage site. In fact, it was selected as a refuge by Fletcher Christian and the other mutineers from the *Bounty*—along with their Polynesian wives—precisely for this reason. The subsequent history of Pitcairn was grim and bloody, resulting in a highly limited gene pool. Its population, moreover, is in serious decline; from a height of 233 in 1937, it now stands at only 47. Pitcairn's main export is (again!) postage stamps, and it's probably the only place in the world where everyone is a Seventh-Day Adventist.

_03:: Kyrgyzstan

Outside of the polar reaches, the world's most remote lands lie in Central Asia. Here one can find a number of landlocked countries far removed from the cosmopolitan cities and sealanes of global commerce. One could do little better that Kyrgyzstan, a former Soviet republic dominated by rugged mountains and deep canyons. It also boasts one of the most scenic lakes in the world, the 115-mile-long Issyk Kul. Kyrgyzstan joins four other landlocked states (Kazakhstan, Turkmenistan, Tajikistan, and Afghanistan) in surrounding Uzbekistan, making it the world's only double-landlocked country. Surprisingly, traveling to Kyrgyzstan is remarkably easy. The government is now encouraging tourism, and one can fly to Kyrgyzstan's capital, Bishkek, from a number of major airports. Flights on British Airways leave London several times a week, but if you're feeling more adventurous, try Kyrgyzstan Airlines flying out of Stuttgart, Germany.

_04:: Tuva

Even more isolated than Kyrgyzstan, however, is Tuva, an internal Russian republic nestled behind mountain barriers along the Mongolian border. Lying at the very heart of the Eurasian continent, Tuva is an odd geographical and cultural mélange. The Tuvinians speak a language related to Turkish, practice Tibetan Buddhism, and are famous (to ethnomusicologists, at least) for their throat singing. But access to Tuva is tough. Be prepared to pay top dollar if you want to book a flight to their capital, Kyzyl. (No shortage of the letters *k*, *y*, and *z* in Central Asia!)

3 Swarming Megacities Where People Just Won't Leave!

Some people seek solace in the world's empty lands, but making yourself another face in the crowd can be just as effective. Take your pick from hiding spots among urban populations exploding across most of the Third World.

_01:: São Paulo, Brazil

Most reference works inform us that greater Tokyo, with some 26 million inhabitants, is the largest urban cluster on the planet. Such a figure is somewhat misleading, however, because it fails to capture the greater density of settlement and rates of growth typically found in Third World megacities. Latin America already has some of the world's largest urban clusters, with both greater Mexico City and São Paulo containing roughly 18 million residents. São Paulo, the commercial, financial, and industrial center of Brazil, has seen particularly explosive growth. From a "mere" 8 million inhabitants in 1970, São Paulo is predicted to soon surpass 25 million. Its industrial suburbs were widely reputed to be the most polluted places in the world in the 1980s, but recent measures have resulted in some improvement.

_02:: Lagos, Nigeria

Megacities in other parts of the Third World are catching up with those of Latin America. Lagos, Nigeria, for example, was a small and manageable city of roughly 1 million inhabitants in 1960, but it had reached 12 million by 2000 and is predicted to top 23 million by 2015. As early as the 1970s, however, the city was becoming unmanageable, and at present conditions are often nightmarish: commute times of three to four hours are common, crime is surging, and the basic infrastructure isn't even close to keeping pace with the burgeoning population. Owing partly to the chaos of Lagos, the Nigerian government decided in 1976 to build a new capital at Abuja, in the center of the country. Although it has done little to halt the expansion of Lagos, Abuja's growth has also been impressive, if not frightening. From some 400,000 in 1991, when it officially became Nigeria's capital, Abuja had reached a population of nearly 4 million by 2003.

_03:: Calcutta

Third World urbanism in its starkest form—with the largest and most impoverished crowds—can be found in Calcutta (Kalikata). Greater Calcutta's 15 million inhabitants squeeze into a relatively small area, giving an average population density of 85,000 people per square mile. Millions live in crude plywood and plastic shacks—luxury homes compared to such housing units as small stretches of concrete piping or simply the sidewalks. Most of the city has a strong stench, and after the monsoon rains hit, much of the city floods, compounding the sanitation problem. But the common image of Calcutta—Mother Teresa caring for a leprous child—conveys only a half-truth. Despite its squalor and misery, Calcutta is culturally sophisticated. Not all of its people are impoverished, and even quite a few of its poor are well educated. Some reports claim that Calcutta has the highest level of cultural output—measured by such features as the amount of poetry published annually—in the world.

Countries That Don't Take American Express (Don't Even Get Them Started on Travelers Cheques)

If you're sick of traveling halfway around the globe just to see a McDonald's, a Starbucks, and an ad for American Express, here are a couple of spots to add to your itinerary. But be wary: leaving globalization behind may cost you.

_01:: Burma (Myanmar)

If you're looking for an entire country that until quite recently opted out of the global economic system, try Burma. But remember that opposition to globalization also means skepticism about international tourism, so don't expect an easy time. And don't necessarily expect a nice place; isolation is maintained in countries such as Burma (which now calls itself Myanmar) and North Korea by stringent repression. Up until the 1980s the Burmese government strictly limited tourism, but it's now encouraging it. Expect friendly people; a leisurely pace of life; a relatively unsullied natural environment; some of the world's most impressive temples, monuments, and ruins—and a nasty police state that still wants to limit your contact with its citizens.

_02:: Bhutan

A more enticing option is Bhutan. Nestled along the southern slopes of the Himalayas adjacent to northeastern India, Bhutan is a lightly populated, environmentally pristine country noted for its stupendous mountains, Buddhist temples and monasteries, and determination to keep the modern world at bay. The Bhutanese government, however, recognizes that some forms of development are desirable, and it now looks to tourists as a potential source of revenue. But it has no desire to see mass tourism, which it views as culturally destabilizing, much less to welcome the throngs of hippie backpackers that once swarmed through nearby Nepal. Bhutan, therefore, invites well-heeled and short-term guests. Tourists in groups of three or more are required to spend at least $165 a day, and single tourists are levied an additional fee of $40 a day.

_03:: North Korea

If you really want to escape globalization, you might try sneaking into North Korea. Of course, you'll probably be arrested and executed, and you may even be captured and eaten by villagers. (Between one and three million North Koreans have starved to death over the past decade, and reports of cannibalism are growing.) But if you do survive the ordeal, you can bear witness to the most extravagant personality cult in history, one that makes the efforts of Hitler, Stalin, and Saddam Hussein look rather modest in comparison. Kim-Il Sung, the country's founding dictator, is still its official president—even though he died in 1994. (Why be president for life when you can have the position for all eternity?) His son, Kim Jong-Ill, now the country's "dear leader," is evidently doing his best to follow in his father's footsteps.

Places That Will Never See a Club Med

What exactly is the worst climate in the world? Whether a given climate is good or bad is subjective; to a native of northern Alaska, for instance, 75°F can seem miserably hot. But, in general, what makes for the worst climate depends on what you dread the most: fire or ice.

_01:: Jacobabad, Pakistan

Those averse to fire should avoid spending a summer in Death Valley, California, where the average July temperature is 101°F, or Marble Bar, Australia, which once recorded 161 days in a row when the mercury topped 100°F. Even hotter—or at least more sticky—times can be had in Jacobabad, Pakistan. Here the average June high temperature is 114°F, with relative humidity averaging nearly 60% in the morning hours. Dust storms are also frequent at this time of the year. Add to that the prevalence of Islamic extremism and clan feuds in the area, and Jacobabad might not be the ideal place for resort development.

_02:: Djibouti, Africa

At least Jacobabad, like Death Valley and Marble Bar, has relatively pleasant winters. For year-round heat and general unpleasantness, the best selection is probably Djibouti, in northeastern Africa, where it's always hot, always humid, and hardly ever rains. Djibouti's winters are marginally bearable, with average high temperatures in the mid-80s Fahrenheit and relative humidity at midday hovering at 70%, but the rest of the year is something else. By July expect a temperature range from 87°F at night to 106°F in the afternoon, with early morning relative humidity around 60%. The people of

---

Inventions and Innovation

THE CHRONOMETER

Early mapmakers and navigators had no problem determining latitude, which is fairly easily calculated on the basis of the height of the midday sun. Longitude, however, was mostly a matter of guesswork, resulting in distorted maps and innumerable shipwrecks. Geographers had long realized that the problem could be solved by a highly accurate clock; if it were noon onboard ship (determined by simple observation) and midnight at Greenwich, England (as revealed by the chronometer), then you had to be halfway around the world from Britain's Royal Observatory. But no one could build a clock that would remain accurate enough through rolling waves and temperature and humidity extremes, despite the lure of a £20,000 award promised by the British government. No one, that is, until the task was taken up by an ill-educated British craftsman named John Harrison (1693–1776). In 1773 Harrison was belatedly awarded the full prize much to the chagrin of a few gentleman scientists who continued to look down on Harrison with pure class contempt.

Djibouti are especially inclined to seek shelter during the summer months when the khamsin wind blows in from the desert, compounding the heat with ample quantities of dust and grit.

_03:: Sakha, Siberia

Ice haters should avoid the polar areas, but that's easy enough, since no humans live there. Roughly 1 million people, on the other hand, live in Sakha (or Yakutia) in east-central Siberia. In its capital city of Yakutsk, the average January temperature is −45.4°F. Further north, Verkhoyansk enjoys an average January high temperature of −54°F. Cultural practices exacerbate the nastiness: in the winter, the local people traditionally live with their horses and cattle, subsisting on milk tar—an intriguing blend of fish, berries, bones, and the inner bark of pine trees conveniently dissolved in sour milk. Not surprisingly, Russia's Czarist and Communist authorities used to enjoy exiling troublesome intellectuals to this region. But partially as a result, the people of

Sakha are now noted for their intellectual and political sophistication.

_04:: Kerguelen

Despite its winter frigidity, Sakha's brief summers are sweet. For incessant unpleasantness, look to maritime locations between 50° and 60° latitude, where raw temperatures; brisk winds; and rain, sleet, and snow predominate year-round. Alaska's Aleutian Islands certainly fit the bill, but the best example is probably Kerguelen, a sizable French-owned archipelago in the southern Indian Ocean. Kerguelen experiences precipitation on more than 300 days a year, and its average temperatures range from 35.6°F in July to 45.5°F in January. Kerguelen has no flying insects—not too surprising considering its average wind speed of 35 kph, which would quickly send the hapless butterfly far out to sea. Thus even the ubiquitous Kerguelen cabbage, a former godsend for scurvy-racked whalers, has adapted to being pollinated by wind rather than insects.

Dysfunction Junction:
5 Crime and Kidnapping Capitals

If pickpockets, purse snatchers, and petty thieves just don't get your heart racing the way they used to, maybe you should take a trip to these five exciting locales. Of course, there's no guarantee that you'll ever return.

_01:: Yemen

In Yemen, kidnapping is culturally institutionalized. Yemen's tribal groups, which tend to be militantly independent, have long used

hostages as a tool for negotiating with the central government. Outsiders are simply grabbed and held until the authorities make promises or deliver the goods. Traditionally, the victims are treated with courtesy, and a few have reported that they rather enjoyed the ordeal. But don't expect such treatment anymore, especially if you hold a U.S. passport. Yemen is the ancestral home of Osama bin Laden, and sympathy for Al Qaeda runs rather high throughout the country.

_02:: Colombia

Although kidnapping in Colombia doesn't have such deep cultural roots, it's widely prevalent and extremely dangerous. Ransom figures are often exorbitant, and murder is a relatively common outcome. Beset with several competing leftist revolutionary and rightist paramilitary organizations—all of which now seem more interested in the narcotics trade than in political action—Colombia has a well-deserved reputation for being the most violent, crime-ridden country in the world. But while the drug trade has greatly exacerbated the problem, violence, especially political violence, is nothing new. The period between 1948 and 1962, when some 200,000 Colombians perished, is commonly referred to in history texts simply as *la violencia*.

_03:: Sierra Leone

Maybe it's unfair to highlight Colombia's crime rate, as a number of places are actually far more dangerous. Colombia does have, after all, a competent government, police force, and judicial system—which is more than a lot of countries. In contrast, the western African states of Liberia and Sierra Leone have been torn apart by brutal rebel armies over the past decade. Rival warlords have sought control of lucrative diamond fields, and they've been joined in the gem and arms businesses by several questionable international organizations—

including Al Qaeda. Visitors to Sierra Leone will likely see many handless people, as hand-chopping has been a favorite technique of rebel leaders for instilling fear in, and ensuring cooperation from, wary villagers.

_04:: Liberia

In neighboring Liberia, on the other hand, the violence continues. Charles Taylor, a one-time guerrilla leader who was "elected" president in 1997, terrorized his own people while supporting brutal rebel movements in neighboring countries. Taylor, in turn, was challenged by the delightfully named LURD: Liberians United for Reconciliation and Democracy. Some observers believe that LURD is serious about democracy and reconciliation; others are skeptical, leery of a militia in which commanders sport such names as Dragon Master and Nasty Duke and favor American "gangster chic."

_05:: Ituri, Democratic Republic of the Congo

The Democratic Republic of the Congo, as noted on p. 108, is a textbook case of a failed state. It's important to note, however, that parts of this country have failed rather more spectacularly than others. In fact, nowhere is the violence and general mayhem more extreme than in the northeastern province of Ituri. After Uganda withdrew its pillaging troops in early 2003, the region's two main ethnic groups, the Hemas and the Lendus, set upon each other with ferocity. Numerous reports of cannibalism, conducted more for reasons of magic than of hunger, soon reached the global media. (When corpses are missing their hearts, livers, and brains, you can assume that *something* fishy is going on.) According to some reports, many Pygmies—innocent bystanders to the region's ethnic carnage—had been hunted down and partially eaten. Colombia and Yemen are looking better all the time, no?

Sex and the Cities:
International Hubs of Prostitution

Like it or not, the world's oldest profession shows no sign of slowing down. And while your Lonely Planet guide probably won't clue you in to just how lonely some of this planet gets, the truth is sexual tourism remains a booming global business.

_01:: Bangkok, Thailand

Thailand supposedly has the largest number of prostitutes per capita in the world. While most Thai prostitutes cater to a domestic clientele, many in Bangkok are oriented to the international sex tourists coming from such countries as Germany, Japan, and the United States. Technically speaking, prostitution is illegal in Thailand—but that just makes it a highly lucrative source of income for corrupt policemen and army officers. This situation is nothing new, though. The Thai government evidently began to draw significant funding from prostitution in the 1680s after the king awarded a monopoly in the field to a state official, who in turn employed over 600 enslaved women for the purpose.

_02:: Angeles City, Philippines

While Manila has its share of prostitution, far more insidious is Angeles City, former site of a major U.S. Air Force base. After the United States pulled out and volcanic Mt. Pinatubo catastrophically exploded, many experts predicted disaster for Angeles City. But instead of withering away, the city turned to one of the special "industries" that had arisen to serve the "needs" of American military personnel. Web sites advertise ever more lavish clubs, indicating that Angeles City may be seeking to emulate Las Vegas as an international adult playground, albeit one focusing on sex rather than gambling.

_03:: Havana, Cuba

In the 1950s the world's premier sin city, offering both gambling and sex, was probably Havana. When Castro came to power, however, all such aspects of "bourgeois decadence" were supposedly swept away, and Cuba was soon pronounced free of prostitution. But after the Soviet Union collapsed, bringing down the Cuban economy with it, the old ways returned with alacrity. As the government turned to foreign tourism as an income source, it soon became clear that the

Just the Facts

WHERE'S THE BEST PLACE TO BE A WOMAN?

Most female populations (# men per 100 women)*: Latvia, 83; Ukraine, 87; Russia, 88

Highest female life expectancy at birth:** Japan, 84.4; France, 82.4; Sweden, 82.2

Largest gender discrepancies in longevity (number of years women outlive men):** Russia, 13; Belarus, 12; Ukraine, 11

Female unemployment rate as % of male unemployment rate*:** South Korea, 71; UK, 79; Sweden, 87

Female professional and technical workers as % of total*:** Lithuania, 70; Latvia, 67; Estonia, 67; Moldova, 67

Ratio of estimated female to male earned income*:** Latvia, 0.72; Denmark, 0.70; Finland, 0.70

Women in Parliament, % of Total*:** Sweden, 42.7; Denmark, 38; Finland, 36.5

Women in government at ministerial level, % of total*:** Sweden, 55; Colombia, 47; Denmark, 45

Female students as % of male students in secondary education*:** Lesotho, 194; Namibia, 148; Uruguay, 136

Composite gender empowerment index (women in important decision-making capacity), top three countries*:** Norway, Iceland, Sweden

(Sources: *The Economist*, Pocket World in Figures, 2001; **L. Rowntree et al., *Diversity Amid Globalization*, Prentice Hall, 2003; ***UN Human Development Reports: http://hdr.undp.org/reports/global/2002/en/indicator/indicator.cfm?File=index_indicators.html)

one commodity that would bring in substantial sums of hard currency was sex. *Jinateras*, as Cuban streetwalkers are commonly called, soon became a ubiquitous sight. Subsequently, the embarrassed Cuban regime began to crack down, but the underlying dynamics remain. Once again prostitution is shoring up the Cuban state.

English as a 102nd Language:
Places Where Subtitles Would Definitely Help

4

Sure, languages of business, like English, Spanish, and Chinese, are taking the world by storm. But don't throw out your pocket translators just yet! Since 3,000–4,000 distinct languages are still in existence, you might want to get, say, 30 or 40 more languages under your belt before you visit these places.

_01:: Papua New Guinea

No country has more linguistic diversity than Papua New Guinea (PNG). Over 800 languages are currently spoken in the country, and no one linguistic group contains more than a small percentage of the population. Many languages of the interior are poorly known, although missionary linguists are working hard to record them in preparation for bible translation. How does Papua New Guinea function as a country, considering this welter of tongues? Some form of common speech is necessary, and PNG has one in English. Well, not exactly English as we know it, but Melanesian Pidgin English, based on a simplified vocabulary and local grammatical and sound structures. Thus a foreign tourist would generally be labeled a *man bilong longwe ples* (or "man belong long-way place").

_02:: Caucasus Mountains

Even greater linguistic complexity is found in the Caucasus Mountains, stretching between the Black and Caspian seas. Some of its languages belong to large, widespread families that extend far beyond the area, such as Armenian and Ossetian (which belong, like English, to the Indo-European family). Most, however, fit into three totally distinct linguistic families that exist nowhere else in the world. A few Caucasian languages are nationally significant. Georgian, for example, is the official language of an independent country. Spoken by some 5 million people, it has an ancient and rich literary tradition. Most others, however, are never written, and many are limited to a single isolated valley. Complexity reaches its apogee in the small Russian internal republic of Dagestan in the northeast, where more than 50 distinct languages are still spoken.

_03:: Yunnan, China

Another linguistically intriguing area is the province of Yunnan in south-central China. Here the fertile valleys and plateaus are populated by people speaking Mandarin Chinese, but on the steep slopes and rugged hills one can find more than 20 separate languages belonging to three linguistic families. A similar situation exists across the border to the south, where the lowlanders speak the national languages of Vietnam, Burma, Laos, and Thailand but the hill tribes retain their own tongues. Laos alone has some 82 distinct languages. Such patterns are linked to a centuries-old process of Chinese expansion. Peoples who did not wish to be overwhelmed by the Chinese fled to the rugged slopes or moved southward along the ridgelines into Southeast Asia. Today this area—known as the Golden Triangle—is notoriously difficult to control, owing both to its rugged topography and to its ethnic complexity. Not surprisingly, it remains one of the world's main opium-growing zones.

_04:: Salt Lake City, Utah

Although the United States is one of the most monolingual parts of the world, certain parts of it—those attracting large numbers of immigrants—are truly polyglot: try standing on a corner in New York and counting the languages heard on the street. One of the most unexpectedly multilingual parts of the U.S., however, is Salt Lake City, which as a result now boasts a number of translation services. Linguistic diversity here derives not from ethnic complexity or from immigration, but rather from missionary activity. As the center of the globally expanding religion of Mormonism, Salt Lake City is home to tens of thousands of returned Mormon missionaries. And Mormon missionaries are famous not merely for walking around obscure Third World cities in their starched white shirts but also for assiduously learning the languages of their host societies. Since most young Mormon men go on missions, the resulting linguistic resources of Salt Lake City are impressive indeed.

6 Lands Where Gods Collide

Most world atlases divide the planet into large blocks of faith, showing a Muslim Middle East, a Hindu India, a Christian Europe, and so on. These maps are useful at the global scale, but they often prove misleading when you're looking at the smaller picture.

_01:: Kerala

In India's southwestern state of Kerala, roughly half the people follow Hinduism, and the rest are evenly divided between Islam and Christianity. Although Kerala is one of the few parts of India that was never under sustained Muslim rule, trade connections across the Arabian Sea brought Islam to the state centuries ago. Christianity came as early as the third century CE, and in the 1500s the Portuguese made another round of converts. The two Christian groups remained separate, however, and the older Syrian Christian community is still considered to have a much higher caste ranking than the Roman Catholics. (So much for caste being exclusive to Hinduism!) Kerala once had a thriving Jewish community as well, but all but a handful of its Jews have long since decamped for Israel. To make matters even more complicated, Kerala also has a substantial antireligious (or is it quasi-religious?) movement: that of Marxian communism. Hammer and sickle emblems are just as common as temples, mosques, and churches across the lush and densely populated landscapes of "Red Kerala."

_02:: Brazil

South America has surprising religious diversity. Even though Roman Catholicism still reigns in most areas, evangelical Protestantism has been spreading rapidly in recent years. Many Brazilians practice a variety of syncretic (or mixed) faiths that are more deeply rooted in traditional West African religious practices than in Christianity. The most widespread African faith in Brazil is probably Candomblé, which can be directly traced back to the Yoruba country of southwestern Nigeria. Candomblé, like other mixed faiths with African roots, involves the use of a wide variety of ritual plants, some of which are apparently intoxicating.

_03:: Suriname

South American religious diversity reaches its extreme in Suriname, a former Dutch colony north of Brazil. Both Roman Catholic and Protestant Christianity are well represented (at roughly 23% and 25% of the populace, respectively), but so are Islam and Hinduism (20% and 27%). (Under colonialism, many workers were imported from Indonesia and India to cut sugarcane, hence the Muslim and Hindu elements). In the interior, a sizable number of indigenous people practice traditional animism, worshiping nature spirits and their ancestors. The so-called bush blacks—people whose enslaved ancestors escaped to the interior rain forests—generally follow an African syncretic faith. To round things out, Suriname's small but commercially important

Chinese community tends, not surprisingly, toward Buddhism, Taoism, and Confucianism.

_04:: Lebanon

The Middle East is widely noted for its religious conflicts rather than its religious diversity. Lebanon, however, is fairly evenly divided between Sunni Muslims, Shiite Muslims, and Christians—and its Christians belong to roughly a dozen distinct sects. Throughout much of the Middle East, Christianity is both widespread and diverse; the re-

---

Myths and Misconceptions
EUROPE AS A CONTINENT

Textbook definitions tell us that Europe is a continent, bounded on the east by the unimpressive Ural Mountains and Ural River, which means that not only Russia and Turkey but also Kazakhstan lie partly in Europe but mostly in Asia. But reference works also tell us that continents are supposed to be mostly separated from each other by seas and oceans, disqualifying Europe from the category. Europe is thus perhaps best defined as a region, but regions are by their very nature slippery categories. Is Russia part of Europe? If so, Europe borders North Korea; if not, shouldn't Ukraine have to be excluded as well? (You can make such an argument, but it wouldn't make you very popular in Kiev.) Alternatively, one can redefine Europe as the collection of countries belonging to, or seeking to belong to, the European Union. No problem—provided that you are willing to exclude Switzerland and Norway.

ligion originated here, and certain forms survived that were stamped out as heretical in the West.

_05:: Turkey and Syria

Islam also exhibits marked diversity, especially in the region extending from southeastern Turkey through the mountains of coastal Syria and Lebanon. The Alevi of Turkey and the Alawites of Syria—who number in the millions—view the pillars of their faith metaphorically, and hence have no problem with such un-Islamic practices as drinking alcohol. The Druze take Islamic heterodoxy to an extreme, but it is hard to say what they really believe, since they purposely dissemble to outsiders while limiting knowledge of their innermost doctrine to a select few.

_06:: Iraq

Iraq is a religiously diverse country, with many Christians (an estimated 4% of the total population) as well as both Shiite and Sunni Muslims. More significantly, in northern Iraq and adjacent lands one can find some 150,000 Kurdish-speaking Yezidis, members of a profoundly antidualist faith who revere Satan, God's chief angel, in the form of a peacock. (The Yezidis cannot be considered Satanists, however, because in their version the rebellious devil later repented and was brought back into the fold by the benevolent deity.) Although the Yezidis have suffered periodic persecution, they have generally been allowed to worship in peace. Just imagine what their fate would have been had they lived in Europe during the Middle Ages or Renaissance!

Assumptions That'll Help You Lose Friends

Stereotyping is an indispensable part of geographical analysis, but it sure won't make you popular. The following misconceptions are five easy ways to lose footing on new grounds.

_01:: All Nicaraguans Speak Spanish

Surely Nicaragua is a typical Spanish-speaking, Latin American country, no? Visit the Caribbean shore of Nicaragua—the idyllically named Mosquito Coast—however, and you will find that English, Caribbean-style, is the dominant tongue, a legacy of the days of British imperialism. (Even Colombia has an English-speaking zone in the nearby islands of San Andrés and Providencia.) In the 1980s Nicaragua's leftist

Sandinista rulers discovered to their chagrin just how deeply entrenched their country's cultural divide was. When they tried to root out English as the language of imperialism, the Caribbean coast quickly rose up in rebellion.

_02:: All Europeans Are Traditionally Christian

Latin America isn't the only part of the world with zones of unexpected cultural juxtaposition. We do not tend to think of Tibetan Buddhism as a European religion, for example, but Europe includes within its supposed continental boundaries a community of some 150,000 Mongolian-speaking Tibetan Buddhists, the Kalmyks. The Kalmyks, whose internal Russian republic of Kalmykia lies to the northwest of the Caspian Sea, have formed a well-established European community for

several hundred years. Today the republic is noted for its charismatic, and perhaps criminal, leader, Kirsan Ilyumzhinov. A former chief of the World Chess Federation, Ilyumzhinov has engaged in such stunts as locking up drunks in iron cages along the streets of the capital for public humiliation.

_03:: There Aren't Any Jews in Ethiopia

Other such cultural oddities are much larger and much older. Most of the people of the central highlands of Ethiopia, numbering more than 25 million, speak Semitic languages that are more closely related to Hebrew than they are to the other languages of sub-Saharan (south of the Sahara) Africa. The central Ethiopians, moreover, began practicing Christianity roughly 1700 years ago, much earlier than did the people of northern Europe. Until recently Ethiopia also had a thriving Jewish community, that of the Falashas. The Falashas had long been isolated from other Jewish groups, and as a result they held only a small portion of the Jewish Holy Scriptures. A debate ensued over whether they should therefore be considered true Jews. Once the issue was decided in the affirmative, virtually the entire community migrated to Israel.

_04:: . . . Or in Zimbabwe for That Matter!

Jewish connections to sub-Saharan Africa do not end with the Falashas. More intriguing is the case of the Lemba, a tribal group from Zimbabwe. The Lemba have long been noted for a number of seemingly Jewish cultural practices, particularly those associated with diet and animal slaughter. Their own oral legends, moreover, point to a Middle Eastern origin. Recent analysis of genetic markers on the

---

Myths and Misconceptions

THE FLAT EARTH OF MEDIEVAL EUROPE

We all know that medieval Europeans believed the earth to be flat, a misconception conveniently put to rest by Christopher Columbus. Wrong! Not only did ancient Greek geographers know that the world was (roughly) spherical, but one of them (Eratosthenes) even worked out a fairly close approximation of its size. As heirs to the Greek intellectual tradition, medieval European scholars had good access to such information, and most fully accepted it. There were actually only a few eccentric thinkers who denied sphericity, most prominent among them being Cosmas Idicopleustes, author of *Christian Topography*. Columbus's major geographical departure was to argue for a small world, allowing easy access to Asia by sailing to the west. Here, of course, he was completely wrong. So why do most of us think that flat-earthers once prevailed? Simply put, during the battle over evolution in the late 1800s a few of Darwin's supporters got a bit carried away in denouncing the intellectual obstinacy of the Christian tradition.

Y chromosome indicates that many Lemba, particularly those of one clan, can indeed trace part of their ancestry back to ancient Jewish peoples. How they ended up in southern Africa, however, remains quite a mystery.

_05:: Islands That Were Never Colonized Follow Native Religions

The kingdom of Tonga was the only major archipelago in the South Pacific that was never colonized by a western power (although it was a British protectorate for many years), and it is still considered to be one of the most traditional parts of Polynesia. But don't expect such tradition goes particularly deep when it comes to religion. Tonga is now one of the most devoutly Christian places in the world, resulting in a virtual shutdown of the country every Sunday. Four separate Methodist churches account for a majority of church attendance, but Mormonism is growing fast. By some accounts, up to one-third of Tongans are now Latter-Day Saints, making Tonga the most Mormon place—outside of Utah—in the world. Not surprisingly, Salt Lake City now has its own thriving Tongan community.

6

Places to Meet New People and Chew Their Saliva

If you're a firm believer in the "when in Rome, do as the Romans do" travel philosophy, be prepared to ingest some highly unusual substances when traveling to these places.

_01:: The South Pacific Saliva High

In much of the Pacific, kava is the traditional drug of choice. Kava supposedly reduces inhibitions and enhances conviviality, much like alcohol. However, it isn't the drug itself, so much as the traditional mode of preparation that often dismays outsiders. The active substance in kava is apparently released in interaction with chemicals contained in human saliva. Kava roots are thus thoroughly chewed, the masticated mass is wrung out in a twisted cloth, and the resulting liquid is then ready for drinking. Even though young people with good teeth and fresh breath are usually the designated chewers, kava drinking is still likely to put off the fastidious traveler.

_02:: Meet the Betels: A Southeast Asian Alternative

Kava drinking is, however, declining in parts of the western Pacific, where it is being gradually supplanted by betel chewing. Betel nut, actually the seed of a certain palm, chewed in combination with the leaf of a certain vine, is by some reports the third most popular recreational drug in the world (after alcohol and tobacco). From India through Southeast Asia and well into the Pacific, this mild intoxicant is often the drug of choice. Chewing it makes the saliva flow freely while coloring it deeply; if you see gloppy masses of red spittle all over the sidewalks, you know that you are in betel country. In many tribal societies of Southeast Asia, betel is a cornerstone of sociability; sharing one's stash is how friendships are cemented and courtships initiated. Whether it's good for the teeth, however, is a matter of some debate.

_03:: West African Cola

In much of West Africa, another area of habitual chewing, the drug of choice is cola. A mild stimulant, the main active ingredient of which is caffeine, cola has given its name—but not much more—to the common carbonated beverage of world renown. (Minute quantities of cola are, however, used in some colas.) Extremely bitter, cola itself has never found much favor outside of its place of origin. But West African history cannot be understood without reference to the nut. In earlier days, major caravans were organized to carry cola quickly from areas of production to areas of consumption, and major political struggles over the cola plantations were not unknown.

_04:: Leaves from the Andes

Coca-Cola itself derives its name, obviously, from coca as well as cola. Coca is the source of cocaine, but while the original recipe did indeed employ the real thing, the modern beverage uses only drug-free traces of coca extract. In the Andes Mountains, on the other hand, coca leaves are habitually chewed precisely for their stimulating effect. But a lot of patient chewing is required for even a fairly mild buzz, which prevents coca from causing

the kinds of psychological and social problems associated with cocaine. As a result, coca is fully legal in much of the Andes and is widely consumed. Intriguingly, in the days of the Incas coca chewing was tightly restricted, but when the Spanish came in its use was encouraged: the more the Indians chewed, the more silver they could mine.

Fake Your Way through a Conversation

THE ARMCHAIR GEOGRAPHER AS WORLD TRAVELER

There are few better ways to fake your way through cocktail party conversations than by learning geography. As people talk about their vacations to distant and exciting places, simply ask a few informed questions—and drop a few obscure place names—and they will tend to assume that you have been there yourself. If you really want to impress, you might focus on amusing place-names, especially if the conversation is focused on the British Isles. "When you visited Ireland," one might venture, "did you climb Macgillicuddy's Reeks or fish in the River Suck? It is especially noted for its pike, you know." "The Isle of Man is no doubt delightful, but the Calf of Man is really quite special." "My favorite Scottish islands are the threesome of Rhum, Eigg, and Muck, right off the Sound of Sleat." Or one can also compare Scotland's various firths, the best-named undoubtedly being the Firth of Forth. My own personal choice, however, has got to be the northernmost point of the Outer Hebrides: the Butt of Lewis.

_05:: Yemen's National Pastime

A somewhat similar drug of the Middle East is qat, the national obsession of Yemen. Every afternoon, much of Yemen simply shuts down as men gather together to chew great wads of qat and convivially discuss events. A few writers have gone so far as to blame Yemen's persistent poverty on the drug, largely because chewing it simply eats up so much time. A more reasonable concern is that qat cultivation is undermining Yemen's agriculture, as other crops are being abandoned in favor of the much more profitable drug. Yemen was once the world's major supplier of coffee, but those days are long gone. The Yemenis evidently think that they have found a better stimulant, even if most of the rest of the world begs to differ.

_06:: Siberian Mushrooms and More!

Qat, kava, cola, coca, and betel are all rather mild drugs that do little to truly alter one's consciousness. More powerful drugs, however, are central to a number of tribal societies across much of the world. The greatest diversity of psychoactive substances is found in the Amazonian rain forest, but the weirdest drug cult is probably that of fly agaric, a beautiful red-and-white mushroom. In Siberia and Lappland, shamans have traditionally used fly agaric to obtain sacred knowledge. In some Siberian societies, it is also popular with laypeople, but the mushrooms are rare and difficult to obtain. The poor thus sometimes take advantage of the fact that the active ingredient passes with almost full potency through the urinary tract (use your imagination!). The suggestion has even been made that the fly agaric cult infuses American popular culture in the person of a Lapp shaman nicely repackaged as Santa Claus. That would explain, after all, the flying reindeer.

by
Peter Haugen

Condensed
HISTORY

Contains

4 Civilizations Nobody Remembers ✳ 4 Regular Words with Epic Roots ✳ 3 Great Explorers You've Never Heard Of ✳ Bad Credit: 4 Bumbling Explorers History Still Adores ✳ A Row Is a Row Is a Row: 6 Misnamed Wars ✳ 4 Historical Commodities Brought to You by the Letter *S* ✳ 5 Women Who Proved to Be the Right Man for the Job ✳ 5 Women with Chops on the Battlefield ✳ You Say You Want a Revolutionary: 4 Reluctant Leaders ✳ 3 African Rulers Who Built Formidable (If Now Forgotten) Nations ✳ Rotten to the Corps: 8 Tyrants with Horrific Rap Sheets ✳ 7 World Leaders You Don't Know by Name ✳

Civilizations Nobody Remembers

Sure, you've got your Mesopotamians, your Egyptians, your classical Greeks, but the checklist of early civilizations—from military and trade powers to technological innovators—stretches quite a bit further. Here are four ancient cultures that rarely get their names dropped.

_01:: The Minoan Civilization

Around 3000 BCE a rich and resilient civilization arose on the Mediterranean island of Crete. The Minoans thrived there and on nearby isles for many centuries. While invaders, possibly sailing from Mycenae (an early Greek city-state) did prey on them, this civilization's death blow actually came from a massive volcanic explosion around 1500 BCE. It triggered tidal waves and released sky-choking clouds of ash. Some say the legend of Atlantis is based on this sea-swamped culture. Its ruins lay forgotten until 1900 CE, when British archaeologist Arthur Evans dug up Crete's fabulous palace of Knossos. Evans followed in the footsteps of Heinrich Schliemann, an inspired amateur who had earlier unearthed Troy, showing that the legendary city wasn't mere legend and that there really were lost civilizations.

_02:: The Hittites

By 1700 BCE these people, originally migrants from beyond the Black Sea, were thriving in Asia Minor (today's Turkey), where they built an empire that at its peak stretched east into Iraq and south to Syria. In the 1300s BCE Hittite power and wealth rivaled that of Egypt, the Hittites' sometime enemy. About 100 years later, the Hittite civilization suffered a sudden, steep decline as Sea Peoples, who were raiding sailors, migrated into Hittite territories. Hittites kept historical records, but they stopped abruptly, so nobody today knows the details of their downfall. A few linguists even think that the Hittite language (they call it Indo-Hittite) was the root of all later Indo-European languages such as the various Germanic and Celtic tongues.

_03:: Sea Peoples

These marine raiders were like the Vikings, except much, much earlier (1200s and 1100s BCE instead of the 700s through 900s CE) and based in the Mediterranean. Sea Peoples terrorized far-flung ports for fun and profit and even waged wars against foes as formidable as Egypt. No one knows exactly who they were or why they were so aggressive, but these sailors most likely included Greeks and Sardinians—people from places with limited fertile land. This probably encouraged them to look elsewhere for economic advantage. In fact, one reason Hittites are little known is that invading Sea Peoples appear to have wiped out their empire.

_04:: The Nazca

From a plane flying over the Palpa Valley of southern Peru, you can make out figures of animals and geometric shapes made from massive lines etched in the earth atop surrounding mesas. A people called the Nazca dug them. Contemporary with the technologically advanced Moche people to their north (South American civilizations didn't begin with the Inca), the Nazca also made beautiful ceramics, paintings, and sophisticated fabrics woven of alpaca wool and cotton from about 1 to 900 CE. Their giant dirt sculptures, which can be recognized only from the air, have been cited as evidence of long-ago visits from other planets. More likely, they were laid out in accordance with astronomical observations and were meant to be viewed by sky gods.

4 Regular Words with Epic Roots

If you want to see your old professor swell with pride, try garnishing your sentences with some of this historically laced vocab.

_01:: Draconian

In the late 600s BCE the Greek city-state of Athens got a new set of laws, drawn up by an official called Draco. These weren't the first Athenian laws, or even the first to be written down, but they were systematic and codified as never before. They were also cruel. Even minor offenses were punishable by death. Draco himself died after guests at a reception in his honor showered him with their cloaks—a gesture of respect. He suffocated. Not long after, another lawgiver, Solon, struck down Draco's code in favor of a more compassionate system. Draco's laws may have been short-lived, but his name lives on as the adjective *draconian*, meaning unusually harsh. Solon's name is an English synonym for legislator.

_02:: Justice

Flavius Petrus Sabbatius (483–565 CE) was just a poor boy from Illyria (today's Albania) who became Byzantine emperor. Adopted by his uncle, the emperor Justin, young Flavius added *Justinianus* to his name and succeeded to the throne as Justinian I. Considered a great ruler, Justinian fought barbarians in Italy and corruption in Constantinople, but he is best remembered for collecting and organizing the best Roman statutes in the *Codex constitutionum* in 529 CE. (The Byzantine Empire was a latter-day, eastern extension of the Roman Empire.) Known as Justinian's Code, this system underlies many laws still used today. It's also a source of our modern concept of impartial judgment and fair punishment. Justinian's name, by way of Latin and French, became a word for that concept.

_03:: Guy

Guy Fawkes (1570–1606) almost succeeded in blowing up James I and the king's entire government in 1605. Although he was born in Yorkshire, Fawkes's pro-Catholic sentiments led him to a career in the Spanish army. When Catholic activists in England grew desperate over government persecution, they sent for Fawkes to attempt their assassination plan, the Gunpowder Plot. Caught in a Parliament cellar full of explosives, Fawkes was arrested, tortured, and executed. The English commemorate his arrest every November 5, Guy Fawkes Day, by burning him in effigy. Over the centuries, the word *guy* meant one of these effigies, then it evolved to mean any stuffed dummy, then a dull man, then a regular bloke. Now just about everybody is a guy.

_04:: Sandwich

Before it was food, Sandwich was a town in England. When Edward Montagu, an English admiral, was made an earl in 1660, he took the place name as part of his title. A century later his descendant John Montagu, fourth Earl of Sandwich (1718–1792), sat down to a game of cards and didn't leave the table for the next 24 hours. For this dedicated gambler, sleep was as nothing. Food, however, was another matter. To keep up his strength, he called for chunks of meat between two slices of bread. Voilà, a cuisine was born.

What's the Difference?
SPOTTING BC FROM BCE

On the one hand you've got the BC and AD camp, and on the other you've got BCE and CE supporters. So, what's the difference? As a young John Lennon once said about his flowing hair, "It's just fashion." If you grew up with BC and AD and now find yourself dealing with BCE and CE, remember that academic styles change. Late in the 20th century, some historians decided that BC and AD wouldn't do anymore. Those initials go back to Dionysius Exiguus (Denny the Little), who invented the modern calendar in 525 (AD or CE). As a Christian abbot, he keyed everything to Jesus's birth. AD, for *anno Domini* (year of Our Lord), counted forward from that date. BC, or Before Christ, counted backward. Recent scholars, however, felt the system was too centered on just one religion, so they changed AD to CE, for Common Era, and BC to BCE, for Before the Common Era. And wisely, they left the year numbers alone. So, doesn't that mean that the years still count from when Jesus was born? It would, except that Denny miscalculated. Most scholars now think that Jesus was born between 4 and 6 BCE.

3 Great Explorers You've Never Heard Of

Some guys have all the luck: Columbus got his own day, Lewis and Clark got their own university, and Marco Polo got his own water game. Sure, the following explorers were a little press-shy, but that doesn't mean you shouldn't know them.

_01:: Pytheas (ca. 300 BCE)

In the period just after Alexander the Great, a Greek sailor ventured through the Strait of Gibraltar, into the Atlantic, and up the coast of Europe. The Greeks were masterful navigators, who had planted their colonies all around the Mediterranean, but Pytheas (he lived in Marseilles) went far beyond their world. He reached Cornwall, explored the British Isles, and continued on, probably to the Baltic Sea and Norway, which he called Ultima Thule. Some historians think Pytheas might have landed on Iceland. Pytheas chronicled his travels in his book *On the Ocean*. While it hasn't survived, the historian Polybius wrote about Pytheas in the 100s BCE. That's how we know about his observations, including his accurate distance measurements, astronomical readings, and reports on fair-haired northern folk.

_02:: Abdullah Muhammad ibn Battuta (1304–1368 or 1369)

In 1325 this well-born young man left his native Tangier, in North Africa, for a pilgrimage to Mecca. Going by way of Egypt, where he studied to be an Islamic judge, Ibn Battuta was bitten by wanderlust. Over succeeding decades he logged an estimated 75,000 miles—more than any other traveler before the steam age—visiting every part of the Muslim world and beyond, ranging as far as Sumatra and China to the east, Georgia to the north, Granada in Spain, and across the Sahara Desert to Sudan. Back home in 1353, Ibn Battuta hired a Moroccan poet to help him write his richly detailed travelogue, *Rihlih*. It vividly describes 60 rulers he met, including the treacherous sultan of Mogul India, Muhammad ibn Tughluq.

_03:: Cheng Ho (ca. 1371–ca. 1473)

In 1381 the Ming dynasty conquered the last Mongol stronghold in China. Ming soldiers captured Mongol boys, castrated them, and placed them in the emperor's service. Apparently holding no grudge, one of those boys grew up to command the emperor's great naval expeditions in the early 1400s—sailing to India, the Persian Gulf, and Africa. Cheng Ho (sometimes spelled Zheng He) made seven voyages, visiting capitals in Arabia, Egypt, and even Mozambique. Some modern theorists, notably British author Gavin Menzies and the Zheng He Association in London, argue that certain shipwrecks in the Caribbean, stone inscriptions in the Americas, and even a 1424 navigational chart prove that the Chinese traveled much farther, circumnavigating the earth a century before Magellan did.

Bad Credit:
Bumbling Explorers History Still Adores

So much for honesty being the best policy. These cats fell woefully short of their destinations but still nabbed the credit.

_01:: Christopher Columbus (1451–1506)

Columbus insisted throughout his life that he had found some fringe of Asia. He had no interest in discovering new continents in 1492. He wanted storied lands of old. China, India, and Indonesia were the prize destinations sought by European explorers of the late 1400s, not wild new places. Columbus took some comfort and derived a bit of wealth from the gold he found in the Caribbean, but through the troubled rest of his life, including two more voyages to the New World, he never gave up on the idea that Haiti must be Japan, Cuba was China itself, and South America could be a biblical earthly paradise. Imagining India nearby, he kept seeking a passage to it.

_02:: Ferdinand Magellan (ca. 1480–1521)

Everybody learns in school that Ferdinand Magellan was the first sailor to go around the world, proving that the world is, indeed, round. Few remember that he conceived the voyage and commanded the mission but never completed it. Magellan died in May 1521 when he unwisely got involved in a fight between two tribes of natives in the Philippines. Late the next year only one of his five ships, captained by Juan Sebastián de Elcano and manned by a tattered, starving skeleton crew, arrived back in Spain. Still, it had been Magellan's determination that got them through the treacherous strait (named for him) at the southern end of

---

Fake Your Way through a Conversation

WHY WE'LL TAKE VASCO DA GAMA OVER COLUMBUS ANY DAY

Love him for "discovering" America or hate him for despoiling it, Christopher Columbus today ranks as main man among explorers of the late 1400s, while Vasco da Gama of Portugal gets honorable mention. Yet in their time it was Gama, not Columbus, who grabbed more glory. How? It's simple. Both Columbus in 1492 and Gama in 1497 went looking for a sea route from Europe to the rich trading ports of Asia. Columbus, sailing west, ran into a strange part of the globe that nobody cared about—not yet, anyway. Gama, on the other hand, hit pay dirt. Heading south around Africa and then north and east, he landed in Calicut, on the west coast of India. In other words, he accomplished what he set out to do. By that standard, Columbus failed miserably.

South America and across the Pacific, which he named, mistakenly, for its "calm" waters.

_03:: Juan Ponce de León (1460–1521)

After joining Columbus on his second voyage to the Americas in 1493, Ponce de León became Spanish governor of both Hispaniola (the island that today includes the Dominican Republic and Haiti) and then Puerto Rico. Puerto Rican natives told him a legend of a spring on the island of Bimini in the Bahamas that would make anyone who drank its water young again. Trying to find this island and its miraculous fountain of youth, Ponce de León landed instead on the east coast of Florida. Not knowing he had found the North American continent, he named the new "island" for the time of year and for its lush plant life (*Pascua Florida* is Spanish for "flowers Easter"). On his next visit to Florida, Ponce's quest for the fountain of youth was tragically cut short when he was hit by a Seminole arrow.

_04:: Sir John Franklin (1786–1847)

Franklin, late in his career as a British navy officer and explorer, set off in 1845 to find the Northwest Passage, a northern water route from the Atlantic to the Pacific. He died lost midway between the oceans. By 1850 every member of his expedition was starving or frozen. After ice trapped their two ships, sinking one, crew members set off on foot. Remains of a few were found years later near a waterway that connected with the Pacific. Franklin failed, but the many expeditions sent to find his missing party learned a great deal more about the geography of the far north. So, indirectly, his voyage proved the Northwest Passage really existed. Roald Amundsen of Norway finally sailed it successfully in 1905.

Timeline

COME AND KNOCK ON MY DOOR (WHEN ADVENTUROUS OUTSIDERS FIRST GOT THERE)

326 BCE Alexander the Great leads his army east across the Indus River and invades India.

300 BCE Greek navigator Pytheas sails west from Massalia, Gaul (Marseilles, France), past Gibraltar, heads north, and ends up in Norway.

55 BCE Julius Caesar invades Britain.

1000 CE Norse sailors from Greenland, led by Leif Eriksson, land in North America.

1265 Venetian brothers Niccolò and Maffeo Polo visit Mongol emperor Kublai Khan in Shangdu, Inner Mongolia. (Niccolò's son, Marco, will accompany the merchants on their next trek east.)

1413 Admiral Cheng Ho of China, having already visited Arabia and Egypt, sails to Malindi (in what is now Kenya).

1492 Columbus lands on his first New World island, probably San Salvador in the Bahamas.

1498 Vasco da Gama sails into the port of Calicut, in southwestern India.

1616 Dirk Hartog of Holland, a sea captain on his way to Indonesia, sets foot on the west coast of Australia. Seeing nothing of interest, he sails away.

1642 Dutch navigator Abel Janszoon Tasman lands on New Zealand. Islanders attack his landing party and kill several crewmen.

1980 Hollywood actor Harrison Ford moves to Jackson Hole, Wyoming.

6 A Row Is a Row Is a Row: Misnamed Wars

Sometimes not everybody agrees on what to call a war. Sometimes the name choices seem deliberately calculated to confuse you on a history test. The following wars came out with mixed-up monikers.

_01:: The Hundred Years War

Depending how you do the math, the war took more or less than a century. From 1337 to 1453, the English kept attacking France. But the foes didn't fight the whole time. The war started as a quarrel over English-held lands on the European continent. Also, England's Edward III thought he should rule France. Naturally, French king Philip VI disagreed. Phil tried to snatch Aquitaine, a French region ruled by Ed. This led to generations' worth of battles, but there were truces—some quite long. Peace broke out in 1360, for example, and lasted nine years. In 1396 England's Richard II married the daughter of France's Charles VI. That truce lasted 28 years. It finally took an internal conflict called the Wars of the Roses (see below) for England to give up the cause.

_02:: The Wars of the Roses

A battle over bouquets? Nope. The Wars (or War) of the Roses consisted of a fight between Yorks and Lancasters—two English families descended from Edward III (see above). They battled from 1455 to 1487. After Henry VI, a Lancaster, had a mental breakdown, his cousin Richard, Duke of York, took over as Protector of the Crown. Henry recovered. Richard, cit-

ing his own hereditary claim to the throne, refused to hand back the reins. Richard's son became Edward IV, whose rule was interrupted when Henry briefly regained power. So it went for decades, getting even more sordid in 1483. That's when Richard III (a York) came to power, but only after he had his little nephew Edward V (another York) declared illegitimate and then allegedly murdered the boy. Finally, Henry Tudor, a Lancaster on his mother's side, defeated Richard III in battle and became Henry VII. So, how did Hank restore the peace? He married a York. Oh, and those roses? They were family symbols—red for Lancaster, white for York.

_03:: The War of Jenkins's Ear

By some accounts, he was a slave trader, smuggler, and pub brawler. Others paint Robert Jenkins as a respectable English sea captain. As Jenkins told it, Spanish coast guards in 1731—trying to keep the British from trading in Spain's Caribbean colonies—boarded his ship, *Rebecca*; seized the captain; and cut off one of his ears. Doubters charged that he had lost the appendage in a drunken melee. Either way, Jenkins saved his ear in a jar of alcohol. The memento came in handy in 1738 when London politicians, arguing in favor of war with Spain, displayed both Jenkins and the severed ear before the House of Commons. It worked. Britain declared war. Fought in the West Indies from 1739 to 1741, this naval conflict blended into the more wide-ranging King George's War (see below).

_04:: French and Indian/Seven Years' War

Colonists in America named the 1754–1763 fight after the enemy (French troops and their Native American allies), but math-impaired Londoners named it for its duration. Actually, the F&I War was the final episode of a four-part struggle between France and England for control of North America. Marked by shifts in alliances and fought in Europe and Asia as well as in the New World, these wars would be confusing even if every one *didn't* have a different name on either side of the Atlantic. They also included:

> 1689–1697 King William's War (America)/ the War of the Grand Alliance (Europe)
> 1701–1713 Queen Anne's War (America)/ the War of the Spanish Succession (Europe)
> 1744–1748 King George's War (America)/ the War of the Austrian Succession (Europe)

In the end, the British emerged victorious, gaining French Canada and other territories.

_05:: The Civil War/War Between the States/The War for Southern Independence

The brutal 1861–1865 conflict, in which the U.S. government fought to reign in a breakaway region, is best known as the Civil War. But many southerners prefer War between the States or, among the real Dixie diehards, the War for southern independence. If you're an American using the term *Civil War*, remember that other countries, England and Spain among them, have suffered their own internal uprisings. It could be a good idea to specify which civil war you mean.

_06:: World War I/The Great War

It wasn't called World War I until World War II came along. In the intervening decades this massive, Europe-centered fight was generally referred to as the Great War (*great* in the sense of *big*, not *extra good*). Lasting from 1914 to 1918, this war—fought largely from hand-dug defensive trenches—pitted the Central powers (Germany, Austro-Hungary, and the Ottoman Empire) against the Allied powers (Britain, France, Russia, Italy, and the United States, which finally waded into the brawl in 1917). Some old-timers continued to call the hostilities "the big one," even during and after the second big one. Another popular phrase, coined by U.S. President Woodrow Wilson, was "a war to end all wars." Obviously, that didn't work out.

4 Historical Commodities Brought to You by the Letter *S*

Just as the petroleum oil trade plays a major part in coloring today's international politics, it's tough to understand history without considering the crucial role these four *S*-words have played.

_01:: Silk

By 2500 BCE China already had a silk industry. By about 1000 BCE they were exporting silk to India, Turkistan, and Persia. More than any other commodity, silk was the basis of early trade along a 4,000-mile caravan track from China to the Mediterranean still known as the Silk Route (or Silk Road). Silk's value was such that you could buy livestock or pay taxes with it. The ability to make silk became such an economic advantage that in the 500s CE Byzantine emperor Justinian I sent two Persian monks on an undercover mission to smuggle silkworms out of China. During the Song dynasty (960–1279 CE), Chinese emperors doled out more than 500,000 bales of silk annually to bordering rulers, buying their goodwill.

_02:: Spices

Along with silk, spices such as cinnamon and ginger traveled overland from the Far East to the Middle East from early times. But even in the Renaissance, spices were rare and expensive farther west. Merchants of Venice, which ruled a small empire in the eastern Mediterranean, got very rich bringing spices to western Europe in the 1300s and 1400s. That's why Spain and Portugal wanted sea routes to India

and why Columbus tried to sail to China. Magellan's round-the-world quest was such a success because the one ship that made it home in 1522 (out of five that set out in 1519) carried a fortune in cloves. Sailors on pepper ships later had their pockets sewn shut so they wouldn't steal the pricey cargo.

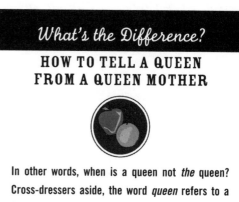

What's the Difference?
HOW TO TELL A QUEEN FROM A QUEEN MOTHER

In other words, when is a queen not *the* queen? Cross-dressers aside, the word *queen* refers to a female ruler, such as England's Queen Elizabeth I of the 1500s. The current Elizabeth's late mother was also considered a queen, but not *the* queen. As George VI's wife, she was queen consort, or spouse. When George died, his daughter Elizabeth succeeded him, so her mom (also named Elizabeth) then changed from queen consort to queen mother. While there's no such thing as a king consort, Elizabeth has given her husband, Philip, the title "prince of the United Kingdom."

_03:: Salt

An essential part of the human and animal diet and a crucial tool in preserving meat, fish, and dairy products, salt has been a lynchpin economic and strategic commodity throughout history. Soldiers of the Roman Empire even received an allowance of salt (the origin of the English word *salary*). In various eras people in Ethiopia and other parts of Africa have used cakes of salt to pay their debts. "Without salt they cannot make bacon and salt beef," said Union general William Tecumseh Sherman about his enemy in the U.S. Civil War. "Salt is eminently contraband, because [of] its use in curing meats, without which armies cannot be subsisted." In fact, Sherman even charged one of his captains with aiding the enemy for letting the rebels acquire the seasoning.

_04:: Slaves

What's most distressing about slavery is how widespread and common it was. Egyptians kept and dealt in slaves. So did classical Greeks, Romans, Arabs, and Vikings. Although rooted in warfare (prisoners of war were among the first slaves), economic advantage sustained slaving. In the 1500s and 1600s, colonists in the Americas looked to Africa for a forced labor base. Portuguese ships (followed by Spanish, English, and Dutch) obliged. A triangular trade developed in which molasses, rum, and tobacco went to Europe (or New England), where profits bought manufactured goods that were traded in West Africa for slaves to be shipped back to the Americas. It was usually more complicated than that (isn't it always), but to the traders, human beings were just another commodity.

Women Who Proved to Be the Right Man for the Job

Turns out, there isn't a correlation between testosterone and brain power after all. Who knew?

_01:: Elizabeth I of England (1533–1603)

Her daddy, Henry VIII, wanted a boy to succeed him (his life, not to mention England's history, was notoriously complicated by this desire), and young Bess didn't seem destined to rule. She was the third of Henry's children to wear the crown. Yet she proved the only one with a talent for government. Unlike her sickly half-brother, Edward, and unlike their spendthrift half-sister, Mary, known as Bloody Mary for her persecution of the Protestants, Bess knew how to manage people. Over a long reign, from 1558 to 1603, the Virgin Queen used sharp political instincts to solidify her power at home and internationally. Her firm rule gave foundation to a golden age, as English sea power, world exploration, trade, and arts (including the playwright Shakespeare) ascended.

_02:: Jinga Mbandi of Ndongo
(ca. 1580–1663)

She preferred the title "king," and she kept a harem of young men, whom she dressed in women's clothes. This monarch of west central Africa made her mark first in nervy negotiations with the encroaching Portuguese, but she was just as adept at the use of force. Over the course of a long, eventful reign, she personally led forces into battle both against neighboring tribes and against encroaching Europeans. Jinga came to power only after her brother, who preceded her as ruler, met a mysterious death. Legend says she killed both him and his young son to secure the throne. Far from delicate in her sensibilities, she reportedly devoured the slain prince's heart and drank human blood.

_03:: Nellie Bly (1867–1922)

Elizabeth Cochrane was a poor Pennsylvania teenager in 1885 when she wrote an angry letter to the *Pittsburgh Dispatch*, responding to an article saying women were meant for housework and child rearing. The *Dispatch* editor hired her and even sent her to Mexico to write about poverty. Soon, her byline—taken from a Stephen Foster song—caught the eye of Joseph Pulitzer. He hired "Nellie Bly" for his sensationalist *New York World*. Pulitzer made his star reporter the best-known American woman of a century ago. Most celebrated for a Pulitzer stunt—a 73-day trip around the world, beating author Jules Verne's fictional 80-day trip—Bly also wrote exposés of incompetence and corruption in mental asylums, jails, and sweatshops, and her stories prompted reform.

_04:: Golda Meir (1898–1978)

A wife and mother of two, Goldie Mabovitch Myerson dedicated her public life to the dream of a strong, independent Israel. Born in Russia, she grew up in Wisconsin, and after a stint as a Milwaukee schoolteacher, she moved with her husband to a kibbutz, or communal farm, in what was then British Palestine. She began rising through decades of labor union, political, and government positions—including legislator, envoy, and foreign minister. Golda Meir (as she renamed herself) became Israeli prime minister in 1968. Renowned for tough-mindedness, she nevertheless took the blame after a concerted attack by Arab nations caught Israel unprepared in the Yom Kippur War of 1973. At great cost, Israel won the war. Meir's party won that year's elections, but she soon resigned.

_05:: Indira Gandhi (1917–1984)

The daughter of independent India's first prime minister, Jawaharlal Nehru, Indira Gandhi served as his official state hostess. After the death of her politician husband, she won election to India's Parliament in 1964 and two years later became prime minister. She quickly won great popularity—especially after India defeated Pakistan in a 1971 border war. But she also made enemies and mistakes. Convicted of illegal campaigning, she defied a 1975 court order to resign. Instead she suspended civil rights, censored the media, and persecuted critics. Although voted out of office in 1977, she won the prime minister's post again three years later. Fighting a separatist movement, she ordered a military attack on a Sikh shrine in 1984. Two of her bodyguards, militant Sikhs, took revenge, assassinating her.

5 Women with Chops on the Battlefield

A few women leaders have taken a distinctly hands-on—not to mention violent—approach to conflict. Here's the dirt on women who were much happier playing the field than cheering from the sidelines.

_01:: Trung Trac and her sister,
_02:: Trung Nhi (birth dates unknown, died 43 CE)

In 39 CE two noblewomen led Vietnamese aristocrats in an armed march against their Chinese rulers. Trung Trac took up the cause after a Chinese officer killed her husband, a local lord, for plotting against China's Han dynasty. First, Trac and Nhi drove out the Chinese general in charge of Lien Lau. Within a year they conquered 65 other Chinese strongholds. They ruled as queens until 43 CE, when China attacked. With neither a professional army nor peasant support, Vietnam's nobles could not withstand the assault. The Trungs fought the invasion near present-day Hanoi, then retreated and regrouped for one last battle. Defeated, the sisters refused to surrender. Instead, they held hands, jumped into a river together, and drowned.

_03:: Boudicca (died 60 CE)

Romans in 60 CE Britain didn't know whom they were messing with. When tribal king Prasutagus (in what is now Norfolk) died leaving no male heir, the Romans grabbed his kingdom. They persecuted his family and the chiefs that had been under Prasutagus's protection. The king's angry widow, Boudicca, responded by rallying locals and charging through East Anglia, slaughtering thousands of Romans (and Britons who supported them) and burning towns from Camulodunum (Colchester) to the Roman outpost of Londinium (London). Boudicca's rebels sliced to pieces the Roman Ninth Legion. Finally the Roman governor, Suetonius Paulinus, who had been out of the country, came back with troops enough to beat her, although it was a tough fight. Boudicca died soon after, most probably after drinking poison.

_04:: Joan of Arc (ca. 1412–1431)

France's national heroine was an earnest teenager who heard saints telling her to fight for Charles, heir to the French throne. Pious and persistent at only 16, she convinced Charles (later Charles VII) to let her lead troops in the Hundred Years War. In 1429 she shrewdly took advantage of a military diversion to enter the besieged city of Orléans with much-needed supplies. Then she led successful attacks on surrounding English forts. This swung the war's momentum in Charles's favor. Later captured, Joan endured a torturous trial by French church officials aligned with the English. They convicted her of crimes that included heresy and wearing men's clothes. Burned as a heretic, she became a martyr. The Vatican later rescinded the heresy verdict and finally, almost five centuries after she died, consecrated her as a saint.

_05:: Lakshmi Bai (died 1858)

When the maharaja of Jhansi, a principality in northern India, died in 1853, the British governor general announced that since the ruler had left no heir, Britain would annex Jhansi. If the governor had studied his own country's history (see Boudicca, above) he might have seen what would happen next. The maharaja's widow (her title was maharani or rani for short) tried reason, pointing out that she and her late husband had an infant son. The governor said the boy didn't count because he was adopted. Angered, Rani Lakshmi Bai assembled an army to defend Jhansi. They fought valiantly but eventually fell to the overwhelming British onslaught. Instead of surrendering, the maharani slipped away on horseback and led a wide-scale Indian rebellion. She died in battle.

You Say You Want a Revolutionary: Reluctant Leaders

4

Some men are born revolutionaries, some men achieve revolutions, and some men have revolutions thrust upon them. The following can be lumped with the last.

_01:: Martin Luther (1483–1586)

A Catholic priest and university professor, Luther nailed his 95 Theses (arguments against the sale of indulgences, a Church method of raising money) on a church door in Wittenberg in 1517 as a call for debate. Instead, he triggered the Protestant Reformation, an upheaval not just of religious practice but also of Europe's entire power structure. At first Luther was appalled at the popular revolt, but when Holy Roman Emperor Charles V asked him to recant, Luther refused with a line that became famous: "Here I stand. I can do no other. God help me. Amen." He meant "nope." Expecting to be arrested and killed, Luther instead found himself kidnapped— not by the emperor, but by the sympathetic prince Frederick the Wise of Saxony. Fred snatched Luther for his own protection and kept him safely locked away in a cozy castle, where Luther wrote more arguments against Church excesses.

_02:: Benjamin Franklin (1706–1790)

For most of his prolific career as a printer, publisher, author, scientist, and inventor, Franklin remained a devoted British subject. He lived in London briefly as a young man and again for 17 years (1757–1775) just before the American Revolution. Although proud of his colonial origin, he referred to himself as "an Old England man" and artfully negotiated the post of British royal governor of New Jersey for his son, making Will Franklin the first American-born appointee to such an office. Ben Franklin tried to avert the split with Britain, but he was alarmed when some colonists tried to blame him for the hated British tax law called the Stamp Act. When Ben saw the inevitable, he sided with his fellow Americans.

_03:: Simón Bolívar (1783–1830)

Inspired by some of the same ideas that fired the American and French revolutions, Bolívar led South Americans in Venezuela, Ecuador, Colombia, Bolivia, and Peru as they threw off Spanish rule in the early 1800s. Yet "the Liberator" (as he was known) never quite embraced democracy. A wealthy aristocrat by birth and upbringing, Bolívar envisioned Hispanic-American republics in which hereditary power—as in the British House of Lords—restrained the popular will. And he argued that the office of president should be held for life. As president himself (in both Gran Colombia—later split into Venezuela, Ecuador, and Colombia—and Peru), he was more dictator than public servant. When he drafted a constitution for Bolivia (named for him), Bolívar restricted the right to vote to an elite class.

_04:: Robert E. Lee (1807–1870)

The Confederacy's greatest general started out as an opponent of Southern secession. As a U.S. Army officer and the son of a Revolutionary War hero ("Light-Horse Harry" Lee),

Strange but True

BEN FRANKLIN LIKED TO WORK IN THE BUFF!

It's true! Benjamin Franklin sat around naked, usually with the window open for the breeze. In a 1768 letter to a friend, Jacques Barbeu-Dubourg, Franklin described his "air bath" ritual in detail: "I rise early almost every morning, and sit in my chamber, without any clothes whatever, half an hour or an hour, according to the season, either reading or writing. This practice is not in the least painful, but on the contrary, agreeable; and if I return to bed afterwards, before I dress myself, as sometimes happens, I make a supplement to my night's rest, of one or two hours of the most pleasing sleep that can be imagined. I find no ill consequences whatever resulting from it."

Robert E. Lee felt strong allegiance to the United States. Yet he also felt that the nation should *not* go to war against its breakaway states. In 1861 Lee was offered command of a U.S. force being assembled to attack the Southern rebels. He turned it down. Later that year, after his beloved home state, Virginia, joined the Confederacy, Lee regretfully resigned his U.S. Army commission after 36 years of service and offered his allegiance to the South.

African Rulers Who Built Formidable (If Now Forgotten) Nations

In the 1800s the African map became a colonial patchwork of European flags, obscuring the memory of what had come before. But whites didn't just march in and take over; they had to deal with accomplished home-grown leaders.

_01:: Usman dan Fodio (1754–1817)

In the early 1800s Usman, an Islamic teacher and philosopher descended from the nomadic Fulani people, accused the king of Gobir (in what is now northern Nigeria) of failing to rule by Muslim law. Winning widespread support, Usman led a revolt that brought down the king and allied rulers of the region. He became caliph of a theocratic Fulani empire encompassing much of Nigeria and parts of Mali, Niger, Cameroon, and Chad. More interested in religious practice than administration, the pious Usman put his brother and son in charge of running the empire's emirates while he continued to teach. Decades of British pressure eventually wore away Fulani rule. The emirate of Sokoto, last bastion of Fulani power, finally fell to Britain in 1903.

_02:: Shaka (ca. 1787–1828)

Shaka's parents were of different tribes but the same clan, which broke a taboo in what is now South Africa. During his late-1700s boyhood, members of his mother's Langeni tribe persecuted Shaka for her sin, instilling in him a deep rage. In 1816 Shaka succeeded his father as chief of the small Zulu tribe. He quickly reorganized its army into a ruthless

---

Strange but True

ALEXANDER THE GREAT'S SWEETER SIDE

It can't be proved, but tradition says that after he died, Alexander the Great's body was preserved in honey. Why? As the most famous, most powerful person in the world, an elaborate funeral carriage was commissioned to escort his body from Babylon, where he died, to his birthplace in Macedon. This ornate hearse took two years to build—24 months in a hot climate, 24 centuries before refrigeration. And that's where the honey probably came in. The thick, sweet substance works as a natural preservative, admitting no oxygen, so the young conqueror's body maintained that dewy-fresh look (as opposed to mummification, which involves drying). As it turned out, though, the corpse never got home. Ptolemy Sotor, Alexander's appointed governor in Egypt, hijacked the funeral caravan to Memphis (not the one in Tennessee) and put his body on display before entombing it.

force that wiped out rivals and absorbed survivors of other tribes, including the Langeni. More bold and arrogant than shrewd, Shaka allowed Europeans to come ashore at Durban because he considered his own culture so far superior that the strangers presented no threat. Becoming murderously insane after his mother's 1827 death, Shaka angered his top officers, including his two half-brothers. They assassinated him. The Zulus finally fell to the British in 1879.

_03:: Samory Touré (ca. 1830–1900)

A West African reformer, religious leader, and military commander, Touré, a Muslim from a Mande village in what is today Guinea, proclaimed himself a chief in 1868 and by the 1880s had put together a big, rich, well-run kingdom. Trading gold and ivory for guns, he attacked and defeated neighboring chiefs, and also fought the French, whose growing African empire was threatening to nibble away at his borders. After his forces failed to turn back a French attack in 1883, he accepted French dominance, but only temporarily. He turned on the Europeans again in 1891. Eventually they pushed Touré out of his territory and then, when he tried to set up a new coastal kingdom, captured him in 1898. Exiled to Gabon, he died two years later.

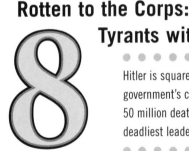

Rotten to the Corps:
Tyrants with Horrific Rap Sheets

Hitler is squarely to blame for the six million Jews shot, gassed, or worked to death in his government's concentration camps, but should he also be charged with *all* the estimated 50 million deaths in World War II, a conflict he started? It's impossible to rank the world's deadliest leaders, but all these guys would make the list.

_01:: Adolf Hitler (1889–1945)

He wasn't crazy but calculatingly brutal. No surviving document shows that Hitler personally ordered the deaths of millions of Jews, Romany (Gypsies), homosexuals, the disabled, and other "defectives" in the Nazi camps, but it's clear that he did it. Hitler revealed his ambition for a Germany purged of Jews in many speeches and conversations, later collected in book form and in other writings, including his autobiography, *Mein Kampf*. In a way, he actually did create the New Germany he dreamed about. The Jewish population of Europe was drastically reduced, not only through mass murder but through emigration—before, during, and after the war. When Jewish survivors were finally liberated from the death camps, many had nobody left and nowhere to return. Their families were dead, their houses confiscated or destroyed.

The Nazis had wiped out entire villages. Of course, Hitler did not limit himself to picking on the powerless. He also took on rivals such as Ernst Röhm, commander of the Nazi storm troopers. In 1934, after they had helped bring him to power, Hitler ordered the murders of Röhm and dozens of other *Sturmtruppen* leaders.

_02:: Joseph Stalin (1879–1953)

As secretary-general of the Communist Party of the Soviet Union (1922–1953) and Soviet premier (1941–1953), "Uncle Joe" ruthlessly asserted his will. When his program to turn Russia's farms into collectives met resistance, he sent soldiers to shoot uncooperative peasants, killing perhaps 100,000 of them. When he sought to consolidate his power, he arranged for the murder of Sergei Kirov, his chief rival. Then, on the pretext of rooting out the assassins, he had his former party comrades sent to death camps, along with millions of other Russians perceived as threats to his absolute authority. The Soviet Union lost not just party bosses and farmers but military leaders, government officials, industry managers, diplomats, artists, and more. Nobody knows exactly how many Stalin killed. Estimates range from ten million to three times that.

_03:: Mao Ze-dong (1893–1976)

Unlike Stalin, he never ordered assassinations; unlike Hitler, he did not attempt genocide. The peasant-born Mao became a revolutionary as a young man, took over leadership of the Chinese Communist Party in 1931, served as chairman (head of state) of the newly declared People's Republic of China from 1949 to 1959, and remained party chair until his death. By pushing endless class warfare and ordering violent political and social reforms, Chairman Mao brought about horrible famines in which some starving peasant families resorted to cannibalism. He inspired repression, torture, and widespread humiliation that led to mass suicides. Victims of his Great Leap Forward—a failed attempt to build a rural industrial base in the 1950s—and his Cultural Revolution—a mass attack on intellectuals and the privileged in the 1960s and 1970s—probably number in the tens of millions.

_04:: Ismail Enver Pasa (1881–1922), _05:: Mehmed Talat Pasa (1871–1921), and _06:: Ahmed Cemal Pasa (1872–1922)

The Young Turk revolution of 1908 brought this triumvirate to power in the Ottoman Empire (Turkey) before World War I. ("Pasa" or "pasha" is a Turkish title of high rank and respect.) In 1915 and 1916 perhaps 600,000 (some estimates range as high as 2 million) members of the country's Armenian population died during a forced relocation. Armenian activists and the Turkish government still disagree over what caused the deaths—a deliberate genocidal drive carried out against a minority group or an unfortunate side effect of harsh wartime necessity. Some historians blame Talat; as minister of the interior, he directed the forced relocation. But there's plenty of responsibility to go around. All three fled Turkey in 1918, and all three were assassinated. Talat's killer was an Armenian seeking revenge.

_07:: Pol Pot (1925 or 1928–1998)

As prime minister of Cambodia's Khmer Rouge government between 1975 and 1979, Pol Pot enacted radical reforms that forced city dwellers into the countryside to work as farm slaves of the state. A million people died of starvation and disease. Pol Pot's government thugs tortured and executed many more, starting with anybody who resisted or dissented. After Vietnam invaded Cambodia in 1979, forcing him into hiding in the mountains, Pol Pot directed Khmer Rouge guerrillas against the new Hanoi-supported government. Although he officially lost his job as Khmer Rouge top boss in 1985, he continued to play a leadership role in a disintegrating Khmer Rouge until 1997, when his former comrades placed him under house arrest. He died without having been called to account for the people he killed.

_08:: Idi Amin (1924 or 1925–2003)

The head of Uganda's armed forces seized control of the country in 1971. At first Amin's strong leadership was welcomed by Ugandans, as well as by observing nations such as Britain, which had feared his predecessor Milton Obote's flirtation with socialism. But Amin's idea of statesmanship was to slaughter anyone who opposed him. Dependent on the support of his own Kakwa ethnic group, he ordered the persecution of other tribes. Amin's Uganda was notorious for torture chambers, cruel prisons, and executions numbering in the hundreds of thousands. He won popularity by deporting thousands of Asian Ugandans. But the Asians had run much of the economy, which then collapsed. After his 1978 invasion of Tanzania backfired (thousands of Ugandan exiles helped the Tanzanians), Amin fled to Libya and then to exile in Saudi Arabia.

World Leaders You Don't Know by Name

Be it an identity crisis, canny marketing, or simply a way to fool the authorities, many powerful people have gone by names their parents didn't give them. Here are seven leaders you know by their aliases.

_01:: Akhenaton aka Amenhotep IV (died 1336 BCE)

In the 1300s BCE a new king shook up Egypt by abandoning the centuries-old state religion. Forsaking other gods, he fixed on one only—the formerly obscure god of the sun disk, Aton. Polytheistic priests held enormous power in ancient Egypt, and Amenhotep may have been trying to slip their influence. He moved his capital from Thebes to a new site, far to the north, which he called Akhetaton, or "place of Aton's power," and renamed himself Akhenaton, or "useful to Aton." His radical changes ultimately failed as the military faltered and the empire withered. When son-in-law Tutankhaton became king, he changed his name to Tutankhamen (dropping the reference to Aton) and moved the capital back to Thebes. Tutankhamen died young but left a great-looking mummy.

_02:: Augustus Caesar aka Gaius Octavian (63 BCE–14 CE)

Only 18 when his great-uncle Julius Caesar was stabbed to death in 44 BCE, the boy learned that he was the Roman dictator's designated heir. Although Caesar's aide Mark Antony also wanted the job and had more experience and clout, the kid went for it. As Uncle Julius's adoptive son, Octavian changed his name to Gaius Julius Caesar Octavianus. After more than a decade of turbulent fighting among co-rulers and rivals, he emerged as unchallenged boss of the Roman Empire. His new government paid homage to old Roman republican institutions, but it rested entirely in Octavian's hands as emperor. In 27 BCE the Roman Senate, which he controlled, renamed him Augustus, connoting superhuman or even godlike stature.

_03:: James I of England aka James VI of Scotland (1566–1625)

When Elizabeth I of England died in 1603, she left no heir. The best claim came from James VI of Scotland. That's because James's great-grandmother was the sister of Elizabeth's father, Henry VIII. James also remained ruler of Scotland, but the scholarly king (he actually wrote a book) is better known as James I, England's first Stuart king. When he moved south he was not quite 37 but already long-accustomed to rule. He put on his own country's crown (figuratively, anyway) when he was a baby. That was after his mom, Mary Queen of Scots, had to skip the country. (The nobles didn't like it that she had married for a third time to a man suspected of killing her second husband, baby James's dad.) James the boy king began making state decisions as a teen. Once he got to England he called himself King of Great Britain (although legally, there wasn't any such nation yet), and he tended to argue with Parliament, who found him high-handed. Whatever the number after his name, James firmly believed in his own absolute power.

_04:: Vladimir Lenin aka Vladimir Ilich Ulyanov (1870–1924)

Raised in middle-class comfort, young Ulyanov and his four siblings all joined the revolutionary movement in Russia in the late 1800s. When Vladimir was only 17, his older brother, Aleksandr, a college student, was accused of conspiring to assassinate the czar and was hanged. Vladimir became a lawyer, but in 1895 he was arrested for trying to publish a revolutionary newspaper. After questioning him for more than a year, the government sent him into exile in Siberia. He kept up the radical journalism, however, publishing the book *The Development of Capitalism in Russia* in 1899 and founding the leftist newspaper *Iskra*. In 1901 be began writing under the by-line Lenin. At first the pen name was meant to cloak his identity, but the name stuck so well that the Soviet Union's founding leader will always be remembered by it.

_05:: Ho Chi Minh aka Nguyen Sinh Cung (1890–1969)

The Vietnamese leader used many aliases. Signing on as Ba, the former schoolmaster, also known as Nguyen That Thanh, he took a berth as cook on a French steamer in 1911 and sailed around the world. Settling in France in 1917 and becoming a socialist organizer, he went by the name Nguyen Ai Quoc, or "Nguyen the patriot." Around 1940 he called

himself Ho Chi Minh ("he who enlightens"). As Ho, he declared Vietnam independent of France in 1945. He fought the French, who withdrew in 1954, leaving a partitioned Vietnam with pro-French nationals headquartered in the south. With U.S. support, South Vietnamese leaders scuttled a scheduled 1956 election that would have reunited Vietnam under the popular Ho. During the civil war that followed, the north sent weapons to its southern guerrilla allies, the Viet Cong, by way of a jungle path, the Ho Chi Minh Trail. After the north won the Vietnam War in 1975

Myths and Misconceptions

A LOPPING MISTAKE

Dr. Joseph-Ignace Guillotin (1738–1814) did *not* invent the guillotine, a French execution machine named for him. The doctor's name was Guillotin, with no final *e*, and he was deputy to the French Estates General in 1789. A supporter of capital punishment, he thought it should be done uniformly, with merciful efficiency, and proposed a head-chopping device. Of course, such machines had been around for centuries. After the Estates General became the revolutionary General Assembly, French Procureur General Pierre-Louis Roederer turned not to Guillotin but to another doctor, Antoine Louis, for a design. And in fact it was a German engineer who built the first working model. While it's not clear how the machine came to be named for Guillotin, we do know why it's spelled that way. The final *e* was added to make it easier to rhyme within revolutionary ballads.

(more than five years after Ho's death), the former southern capital, Saigon, became Ho Chi Minh City.

_06:: Marshal Tito aka Josip Broz
(1892–1980)

In 1928 Yugoslav police found bombs in Broz's apartment in Zagreb, Croatia. They accused the sometime mechanic of working for a Soviet-sponsored revolutionary group. (Broz had embraced Marxism while in a Russian prisoner-of-war camp during World War I.) Convicted of conspiracy against the Yugoslav monarchy, he served five years in jail. When he got out, he used aliases to avoid another arrest. Under one of those names, Tito, he was brought into the politburo, or controlling committee, of the Communist Party of Yugoslavia (CPY). When Germany and Italy occupied Yugoslavia in World War II, the royal government fled, leaving the CPY, now led by Tito, as the only effective Yugoslav resistance. This drove the exiled royals into an alliance with the Axis powers. When the Allies won the war, the CPY and Tito took control, creating the Federal People's Republic of Yugoslavia. As leader until his death, he held offices including party chair and president, but was best known by his preferred title, Marshal Tito.

_07:: Gerald Ford aka Leslie Lynch King
Jr. (1913–)

Born in Omaha, he was named for his dad, Les King. But when Leslie Jr. was very young, his parents divorced. Mom moved to Grand Rapids, Michigan, and married Gerald Rudolph Ford, who adopted the baby. They decided to rename the little guy Jerry Jr. Jerry won a seat in the House of Representatives in 1948, became House minority leader in 1965, and in 1973, President Richard Nixon appointed him vice president, replacing the disgraced Spiro T. Agnew. The next year Nixon himself, also disgraced, resigned from office, and Ford stepped up. That's how a Ford, not a King, came to occupy the White House from 1974 to 1977. Ford is the only U.S. chief executive never elected either president or vice president. Ex-pres Bill Clinton, born William Jefferson Blythe, also uses a stepfather's surname.

by
John Timpane

Condensed
LITERATURE

Contains

7 Literary Works That Changed Everything ✳ What a Famous Thing to Say: 6 Quotable Lines and How to Use 'Em ✳ Girls Just Want to Have Fame: 5 Female Authors You Need to Know ✳ High Art: 5 Classics Written under the influence ✳ 6 Writers Who Didn't Need No Degree ✳ Arrest That Writer!: 6 Authors Too Dangerous to Let Loose ✳ 15 for All Time: The Ultimate Desert Island Reading List ✳

7 Literary Works That Changed Everything

If you're looking for a cheat sheet of lit's movers and shakers, you've come to the right paragraph. Here are seven figures that shifted paradigms on the strength of their pens.

_01:: *Sonnets to Laura* by Francesco Petrarch (1304–1374)

A poet becomes obsessed with a young woman and makes her his ideal, his way to God through love. In many ways this tale is still the paradigm for the love story. Now, did Petrarch *invent* the love poem? A good question, and one that people still fight over. Some feel that the Roman poet Catullus was the first to write poems we would call love poems. Others say that love (and love poetry) as we know it arose among the troubadour poets of 11th- and 12th-century France. And some cast their vote solidly with Petrarch. In any case, he certainly did show centuries of poets how to write about very personal emotions, and his influence can be seen in almost every love song written ever since.

_02:: *The Canterbury Tales* by Geoffrey Chaucer (1343–1400)

We think he spells his first name the cool way too. It's no mean trick to write a long series of narrative poems that stay fresh and funny and full of life for 600 years. And, at first glance, you wouldn't think a pilgrimage to a saint's shrine would make such great reading. But the *Tales* did do something that was new and different: they portrayed people as people often are. Some call it realism; some simply call

it honesty. Chaucer had an eye for human foibles, and he presents them in comic detail, with an attitude that's both honest and sympathetic. As his characters pose, steal, lie, fornicate, and mess up, he looks on them all with a forgiving, amused detachment. The *Tales* aren't modern, but they sometimes feel like it. They really began the history of the English language (Chaucer wrote in what we now call Middle English) as a powerful literary device.

_03:: *Les Fleurs du Mal* ("Flowers of Evil") by Charles Baudelaire (1821–1867)

Baudelaire's book is important because it showed that a poet can create his own intense, suggestive world by weaving symbols into a new emotional language. This became a poetic movement called Symbolism, and it's still going strong. (This is different from the small-*s* symbolism—that's just the use of symbols. We all do that. Large-*S* Symbolism, which only poets and other writers do, is a whole way of creating a language and a landscape out of symbolic language. Sometimes the symbols will really refer to things, as most symbols do, and sometimes no one, not even the poet, will know the precise meaning of the symbols that emerge from the unconscious.) He fearlessly explored the underside of life, the perversities, the sensual overloads, the almost painful longings. Baudelaire is everywhere.

_04:: *Ulysses* by James Joyce
(1882–1941)

Joyce did not (we repeat, DID NOT!) invent the stream of consciousness technique. That honor goes to the novelist Dorothy Richardson, whom you should read. And in fact, other writers, such as Virginia Woolf and William Faulkner, may have done it better. (Your pick.) But Joyce certainly helped perfect it. We watch the world slide in front of the brain of Leopold and Molly Bloom and Stephen Dedalus. All the time, they're thinking to themselves of this and that. Outer and inner worlds intersect and combine. One of the beautiful things in this novel is how the forces of time and history make their appearance in the supposedly private thoughts of individuals. Also, getting behind people's eyes turns out to be a great way to see them at their frankest. Although difficult for the untrained reader, this book is a taste of life itself, a comic masterpiece if ever there was one.

_05:: Short Stories by Ernest Hemingway
(1899–1961)

If Hemingway didn't invent it, he certainly perfected a new way to tell tales, showing us action but refraining from interpreting it, letting us figure out the significance of things for ourselves—as we have to do much of the time in the nonliterary life. In his story "Hills Like White Elephants," a man and a woman have a conversation. But we're not told the topic. We figure it out by *listening*. Little by little, the painful ironies we're observing draw us in, involve us as if we were seeing this angry chat going on in front of us. Hemingway's stories walk a tense tightrope strung between hopelessness and the ecstatic celebration of strength and courage. The standoff between the sexes has never been presented so uncompromisingly. And has there ever been a better appreciator of nature? Probably not. Ever since Ernest took hold of his number two pencil, fiction just hasn't been the same.

_06:: *Howl* by Allen Ginsberg
(1926–1997)

The madness of postwar America; sex and drugs; beatific, crazy exaltation. Ginsberg's poem was the opening of the Beat era, and also its high point. His poetry, his embrace of the forbidden, and his nutty, beatific energy have had a great deal of influence on music and the arts. In fact, many people cite *Howl* as the beginning of the counterculture years: the years of free thinking; sex, drugs, and rock and roll; and social ferment. Years when the civil rights movement swelled, antiwar protests built, and the general standoff between an older generation with their hands on the reins of power and a younger generation looking for a newer, wider world came to a head. Now, one poem can't be responsible for all that. But it *did* free many writers to think more expansively, with less fear, with more possibilities. And it still retains its haunting, mad power.

_07:: *One Hundred Years of Solitude*, by Gabriel García Márquez
(1928–)

In the 20th century the world of literature stopped being almost exclusively the province

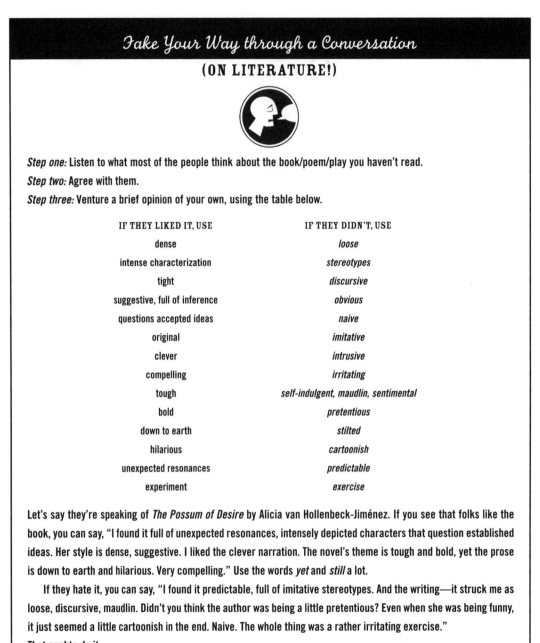

Fake Your Way through a Conversation

(ON LITERATURE!)

Step one: Listen to what most of the people think about the book/poem/play you haven't read.

Step two: Agree with them.

Step three: Venture a brief opinion of your own, using the table below.

IF THEY LIKED IT, USE	IF THEY DIDN'T, USE
dense	*loose*
intense characterization	*stereotypes*
tight	*discursive*
suggestive, full of inference	*obvious*
questions accepted ideas	*naive*
original	*imitative*
clever	*intrusive*
compelling	*irritating*
tough	*self-indulgent, maudlin, sentimental*
bold	*pretentious*
down to earth	*stilted*
hilarious	*cartoonish*
unexpected resonances	*predictable*
experiment	*exercise*

Let's say they're speaking of *The Possum of Desire* by Alicia van Hollenbeck-Jiménez. If you see that folks like the book, you can say, "I found it full of unexpected resonances, intensely depicted characters that question established ideas. Her style is dense, suggestive. I liked the clever narration. The novel's theme is tough and bold, yet the prose is down to earth and hilarious. Very compelling." Use the words *yet* and *still* a lot.

If they hate it, you can say, "I found it predictable, full of imitative stereotypes. And the writing—it struck me as loose, discursive, maudlin. Didn't you think the author was being a little pretentious? Even when she was being funny, it just seemed a little cartoonish in the end. Naive. The whole thing was a rather irritating exercise."

That oughta do it.

of Europe and the United States, as new lit from across the globe elbowed its way to the table. *One Hundred Years of Solitude* by Colombian author Márquez was a worldwide smash, and its success helped bring the Central and South American voice into the world theater. What's different about that voice? Well, it's exotic: its view of history (and its environment—the steamy, mysterious, mythical rain forests and jungles of Central America) is wholly different from that of Europe. Of course, Europe's in there, but you also have the indigenous imagination, the postcolonial present, the beliefs of the past, and the disbe-lief of the present. Márquez's mind seems to be a fountain of stories. For many readers, his novel introduced magic realism, a world in which reality and our sense of the magical find new ways to interact.

What a Famous Thing to Say:
Quotable Lines and How to Use 'Em

6

The great thing is, when you drop these lines at your next cocktail party and people ask, "Where's that from?" you're actually going to know!

_01:: "Rule a large country as you'd cook a small fish."—Lao-tzu, *The Way of the Tao*

Very little is known about Lao-tzu. The very name actually means "old master," so it may simply be a name—like Homer, or the Preacher in the book of Ecclesiastes—as-cribed to someone supposed to have written an ancient, famous work. There's even some doubt as to whether Lao-tzu, or any one per-son, wrote *The Way of the Tao*. Still, this work founded a religion/way of life followed by 20 million people today. The famous line, with its piquant terseness, even a trace of humor, ap-pears to counsel political moderation and wisdom. The wise governor governs least, in-terferes least. Use this line whenever folks are discussing taxation, welfare, or other social programs. Heck, use it whenever an extremely big thing must be done with extreme care.

_02:: "Abandon all hope, you who enter here!"—Dante, *The Inferno*

This is the slogan written over the main en-trance into Inferno. The message is clear. Hell is pretty definitively The End. If this is where you end up, ain't no bus out. You know how most of the time, if stuff gets you down, your friends will say, "Hey, come on, cheer up. It'll get better. Just you wait"? Well, not here. This is the ultimate Line to Use When Things Are Irretrievably Bad. Use it whenever you or your friends are about to go into some doubt-ful place, such as an Internal Revenue Service office, a bar, a dentist's office, or a draft office in wartime. And remember, it also comes in handy just before entering the dwellings of parents-in-law, loan officers, or difficult lovers.

_03:: "Now is the winter of our discontent."—William Shakespeare, first line of *Richard III*

Most people don't realize that Richard III, the guy who speaks this line, is a *villain*. The next line—"Made glorious summer by this sun of York"—is totally sarcastic, directed at the present resident of the throne, which Richard really really really wants. Richard III is a scheming, morally challenged evildoer who compounds outrage upon outrage in his quest for power. He seduces a woman by the casket of her husband (one that Richie killed), drowns his brother in a cask of wine, and performs other charming stunts along the way. So this line is the all-time expression of virulent impatience. Use it whenever you or someone you know has entered a stretch of misfortune, bad luck, or frustration. Makes a nice statement of empathy. Suppose your pal says, "Man, I haven't had a date in 20 years." Nod your head sympathetically and say, "Now is the winter of our discontent!"

_04:: "It was the best of times, it was the worst of times." —Charles Dickens, *A Tale of Two Cities*

This line hits maximum potential when you use it to describe your childhood, a party, your family, a class reunion, or any other event about which you are completely ambivalent. "How was the boss's Christmas party last night?" "Oh, it was the best of times, it was the worst of times." "Daddy, what was it like growing up in 1974?" "Oh, Junior, it was the best of times, it was the worst of times." So many memories and gatherings inspire ambivalence that folks will probably never stop using this line. (Note: *A Tale of Two Cities* also has a pretty great ending, which contains the line "It is a far, far better thing I do, than I have ever done." You can say this aloud when you want to be praised for some selfless deed you're about to perform.)

_05:: "Things fall apart; the center cannot hold."—William Butler Yeats, "The Second Coming"

Throughout recorded history, human beings have looked around at the world and exclaimed, "Everything is falling apart!" And

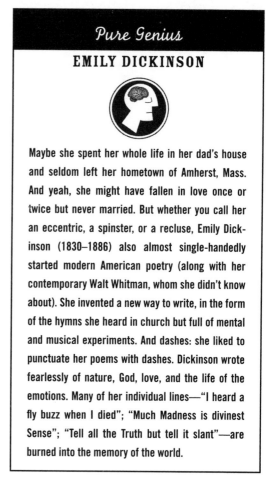

Pure Genius
EMILY DICKINSON

Maybe she spent her whole life in her dad's house and seldom left her hometown of Amherst, Mass. And yeah, she might have fallen in love once or twice but never married. But whether you call her an eccentric, a spinster, or a recluse, Emily Dickinson (1830–1886) also almost single-handedly started modern American poetry (along with her contemporary Walt Whitman, whom she didn't know about). She invented a new way to write, in the form of the hymns she heard in church but full of mental and musical experiments. And dashes: she liked to punctuate her poems with dashes. Dickinson wrote fearlessly of nature, God, love, and the life of the emotions. Many of her individual lines—"I heard a fly buzz when I died"; "Much Madness is divinest Sense"; "Tell all the Truth but tell it slant"—are burned into the memory of the world.

they have always been wrong. The sun rose in the morning, and there was a world. Maybe not the greatest world, but *a* world. Still, that nagging human sense remains: things are getting bad, and they can only get worse. The 20th century was like that, personally and internationally. That may be why Yeats's line is possibly the most-quoted line of modern poetry. Use it vigorously whenever everything is just crumbling around you. (Boss: "We lost our biggest account!" You: "Things fall apart; the center cannot hold.") Also good when a very embarrassing situation happens, such as, for example, when someone's brassiere falls open, someone's pants fall down, or a plant comes crashing down from a mantelpiece.

_06:: "Never laugh at live dragons." —J. R. R. Tolkien, *The Hobbit*

This line is a version of Shakespeare's famous "Discretion is the better part of valor." It's not a good idea to dare forces that are stronger than you are—especially if those forces don't have anything holding them back. In other words, don't play chicken with a universe that doesn't have your best interests at heart. Don't dance in front of the onrushing train; you might get caught on the tracks. Use this wise and hilarious line when it's better to be quiet than confrontational. "Let's go tell the boss she's a pain in the butt." "Ah, never laugh at live dragons." "Let's go to the police station and tell them we aren't paying that drunk-driving ticket." "Ah, never laugh at live dragons."

Girls Just Want to Have Fame:
5 Female Authors You Need to Know

Sure, you might have overheard their names in classrooms or at cocktail parties, but isn't it time you were formally introduced? Don't be shy—these are ladies everyone needs to know.

_01:: Enheduanna: Hymns for Nanna

"Who?" you might ask. Well, we're both shocked *and* disappointed. Enheduanna was only the earliest poet ever recorded. The daughter of Sargon, a great ruler of Mesopotamia (2350–2330 BCE) and the guy who founded the kingdom of Akkad (as in the Akkadians), this princess spent her days penning dreamy poems. And while we don't know her given name, we do have her official name: pronounced En-head-WAN-na, which means "high priestess of Nanna." And basically, that was her job: to preside over ceremonies and write official hymns to Nanna, the moon goddess. Amazingly enough, several of these hymns have made their way down to us, and they're among the oldest poems known. The hymns show a powerful incantatory quality, possibly with a call-and-response thing going on.

_02:: Sappho: The Barry White of Her Day

If you're hunting for the roots of the poetry of love, look no further. One of the earliest Greek lyric poets, Sappho lived on the island of Lesbos around 600 BCE. And evidently she had quite a nice business running a school for women and writing wedding songs. Today most of her poetry survives in fragments; in one, the speaker undergoes the mania of love and describes herself as "paler than grass." In another, the speaker longs for her loved one and watches the Pleiades crawl across the sky. Because her love poems are directed to both men and women, she's become an eminent symbol of same-sex love, but really it's best to understand her as one of the first great love poets of all time, of all love.

_03:: Jane Austen's Powers (1775–1817)

After reading a Jane Austen novel, you realize two things: (1) It would have been humbling to know this woman, because she was sharp—she noticed *every* nuance about people. And (2) hers is about as female an art as you could wish for. Some people think her world is too restricted: middle-class women in the early 1800s trying to find themselves and find mates. Within that world, however, Austen unlocks our interior universes: what we pretend to be vs. what we really are. Prejudice is one of her great themes; in her three major novels (*Pride and Prejudice*, *Emma*, and *Persuasion*), a person has to unlearn those prejudices somehow. Oh, and did we mention that her stories make great movies?

_04:: Colette, the Original Vagabond (1873–1954)

Colette's life is almost as famous as her writings. But we shouldn't let the former overshadow the latter. Colette is the great chronicler of women in the world of love. Her worlds are full of humor and disappointment, revelation and bitterness. The Chéri novels portray the attempts of an older woman to hold on to a younger man, even after his marriage. *The Vagabond* may be Colette's best, as it follows a lonely single woman through the bruising turns of her theatrical career; it's pretty close to an autobiography. The Claudine novels, originally written as a kind of penny-porn under the brutal regime of her first husband, the infamous Willi, amount to an epic about a woman's sexual coming of age. Here we first see a theme running throughout Colette's work: loving men is so painful that it's no wonder women turn to other women. Melodramatic at times, perverse at others, Colette definitely created a world worth entering.

_05:: Virginia Woolf: Be Afraid! (1882–1941)

Her quiet, insistent, original voice has a way of staying on your mind. She is, let's face it, a modernist, meaning that for many readers her writing takes some getting used to. It seems difficult until you get the hang of it: that it's really being told from within people's minds, and that we're hearing the flow of their interior thoughts. We also encounter fascinating characters, such as the Ramsay family and Lily Briscoe of *To the Lighthouse*. If anyone wants a short segment that shows what great writing can do, how it can embrace time and passion and give us a new vision of our lives, you can't do better than the "Time Passes" passage of this novel. *Mrs. Dalloway* is just about as good. The high point of her technique and vision is *The Waves*, a series of internal monologues by a group of friends as they pass through time. And Woolf's last novel, *Between the Acts*, is her funniest and most frightening, a stroke of genius to end a singular career.

High Art:

5

Classics Written under the Influence

Many writers seek extreme experiences, including getting drunk/high/ecstatic/wasted/buzzed. And while we're not exactly advocating altered states here, it did seem to take the edge off their writer's block.

_01:: Collected Poetry, Li Po (701–762)

One of the best of the T'ang dynasty poets in seventh-century China, Li Po wrote many poems about drinking. In his poems and in many poems of the classic era of Chinese poetry, alcohol has two functions. First of all, it brings friends together to sing, to reminisce, to have great little parties at which everybody gets tight and starts having poetry contests. Well, great! Second, it acts as a muse, a way to relax and release the poet into fantasies and mediations that are good for the creation of poetry. See? Nothing new. Artists have been saying for centuries that if you take drugs, you make better art. They've often felt that the perceptual expansion offered by drugs lets them have better, more surprising insights. Or at least *think* they do! Li Po and his pals obviously felt that wine helped you be a better poet. Of course, being continuously sozzled comes with its own problems. Legend has it that Li died when, in a drunken state, he tried to embrace the reflection of the moon in a lake and fell in.

_02:: "Kubla Khan," Samuel Taylor Coleridge (1772–1834)

After smoking opium, Coleridge fell asleep, and when he awoke he was on fire with images. He set to writing at a white-hot pace—until he was interrupted. When he returned to the poem an hour later, the vision was gone. He'd lost the moment. The result is one of the wildest, most puzzling poems of all time. A lot of people like the fact that it was written under the influence: it had a period of great popularity in the 1960s. And back when it was published (1816), people took it as *the* quintessential Romantic poem: passionate, spontaneous, beyond conscious control. They also liked how "he had it all there—and then lost it," which is a nice little fable about how fleeting inspiration is.

_03:: *The Sun Also Rises*, Ernest Hemingway (1899–1961)

Like many famous writers, Hemingway battled alcoholism all his life. In *The Sun Also Rises*, one of his best novels, almost every character drinks continually. They're trying to ignore the realities of life after World War I, trying to ignore their hangovers, and, often, just having a great party. War has torn apart the old ways, and the new ways—ways of nation building, ways of writing, ways of love, ways of being men and women—are full of pain and uncertainty. And these people, though they're adults, in many ways are incomplete, crippled. Jake Barnes, the protagonist, has suffered a war wound greatly compromising his sexual function (how's that for a delicate way to put it?), and the wound becomes a metaphor for the incompleteness that everyone's drinking to forget.

_04:: *Being and Nothingness*, Jean-Paul Sartre (1905–1980)

Sartre apparently was a big ingester of mescaline to get him, er, up to speed. He also took downers to let him sleep. These facts create a big question for the history of philosophy, don't they? Now, many readers have felt that despite his fame as the inventor of existentialism and despite his importance in many fields of literature, thought, and politics, he's completely unreadable. *Being and Nothingness* is supposed to be Sartre's great investigation of the experience of the absurdity and lack of intrinsic meaning in existence. When you discover nothingness, it's like a huge turning point, and there's no turning back. Sure wish the *book* was better. This thing is a twisty-turny, pompous, sloppy, contradictory mess, written in a celebratedly bad prose, whether

---

Strange but True

WRITERS IS THE CRAZIEST PEOPLE

While living in a hotel room in Brussels, Belgium, French poet Charles Baudelaire (1821–1867) captured a bat in a nearby graveyard, brought it back to his room, and kept it as a pet, feeding it bread and milk.

Russian playwright and fiction writer Anton Chekhov (1860–1904) didn't have long to live. His doctor bought a bottle of Champagne and poured Chekhov a glass. He drank it down with great appreciation and remarked: "It has been so long since I've had Champagne." Then he rolled over, and Chekhov checked out.

One of the strangest novels ever written may be *Gates of Paradise* by Polish writer Jerzy Andrzejewski (1909–1983). It is one-sentence long, unpunctuated, 40,000 words.

Speaking of strange, how about *Pugna Porcorum* ("Battle of the Pigs"), published by the Dominican monk Léon Plaisant (Placentius) in 1530? The poem extends to more than 250 verses, and *every word begins with the letter* P! Talk about pig Latin. Playful priest produces porky poetry!

French poet Gérard de Nerval (1808–1855) had a pet lobster that he took for walks, guiding it through the park of the Palais Royal on a pale blue ribbon.

Irish novelist James Joyce (1882–1941) wore five wristwatches on his arm, each set to a different time.

French or English. It may be a brilliant book, but it's not a good one. Maybe, applying the Li Po principle above, Sartre should have taken *more* drugs.

_05:: *Naked Lunch*, William Burroughs
(1914–1997)

Burroughs was a Beat writer and a heroin addict. His surrealistic novel influenced poets, musicians, and other addicts for the rest of the 20th century. This may be the ultimate in underground cult novels. You'll find its influence in everything from the art of Keith Haring to the poetry of Jack Kerouac to the lyrics of Steely Dan. One thing that's very impressive (besides the amount of drugs Burroughs reputedly took while compiling *Naked Lunch*) is how Burroughs uses addiction as a key metaphor for human existence. Everyone is a junkie for something—and everyone is also a narc, an agent of judgment and punishment. It's a brilliant insight, and it emerges from the jumble of this novel like a flash of drug-induced wisdom. Now, how many films have you seen that explore this theme? *Naked Lunch* is often called a novel, but it's really a collection of scenes and characters held together by the aforesaid metaphor. In fact, it doesn't hold together. Its existence is more important than its actual worth as literature. But its impact, which continues today in artists, writers, and filmmakers all over the world, is, well, psychedelic.

Writers Who Didn't Need No Degree

"Never let your schooling interfere with your education." And while Mark Twain might have said it, these cats definitely lived it. Here are six writers who skipped the degree and still did pretty OK for themselves.

_01:: Homer (ca. ninth century BCE)

"Well, OK," you say. "There were no colleges then, and Homer is just a name, not a person." True on the former; on the latter, scholars disagree. Many readers believe that the *Iliad* and the *Odyssey* are compilations of stories well-known around the Mediterranean world. The notion is that itinerant businessmen spread these stories around, along with the Greek language, and that after a while someone wrote them all down. But there's another idea: the name *Homer* may derive from an ancient word meaning "black," which leads some scholars to believe that Homer may have been a real person—an African businessman who spoke Greek, had a wide-open mind and a sharp ear, and wrote down tales that travelers around the Mediterranean told to while away those long nights between business deals. Who needs college when you have a road trip for a life?

_02:: William Shakespeare (1564–1616)

There's no evidence that this guy went to *any* school. Makes you sick, doesn't it? We don't know much about his youth in the provincial town of Stratford-upon-Avon, but one interesting guess is that he left town with a traveling acting troupe. With the troupe, Shakespeare may have worked his way to London and caught on with a band of actors there. Of course, living in London in the explosive last 20 years of the 16th century was bound to educate anyone. It was a world capital of trade, power—and theater. When Shakespeare became a playwright, he also became a literary bandit, cribbing tales and characters from wherever he could find them, from ancient Greek and Latin authors to contemporary (for him) tales from Italy, Spain, and France. Not a single book he owned has come down to us—so he must have been quite a borrower.

_03:: Leo Tolstoy (1828–1910)

Tolstoy has a reputation as an encyclopedic writer—a writer likely to allude to philosophy, history, industrial methods, military lore, social and educational theory, almost anything that's relevant to his story, and some that, well . . . isn't. So, how did he get such an encyclopedic mind? Not in college. He got a pretty good private education but dropped out of university. He hung out in Moscow and St. Petersburg, had a wild time, and developed venereal disease and a gambling habit. Then he joined the army, where among other things he commanded an artillery unit and witnessed the siege of Sebastopol. He traveled to Europe, started a school for kids, went back to Europe to learn about education, and read his head off. (He also married a woman who bore him 13 chil-

Alphabet Soup
WITH MULTISYLLABLE WORDS

Literary studies have some of the most jawbreaking technical language you can find. What's funny is how these hard words (*anacephalaeosis*) sometimes have simple meanings ("recap").

hendiadys: [hen-DIE-uh-diss] *n* You know how you say *good and mad* when you mean *very mad*, or *nice and soft* when you mean, er, *nicely soft*? You've expressed an idea in two words connected by *and* when you could've used just two words (a word and its modifier) to do it. So, what's a really crazed Greek word we could use for that? Oh, we know: hendiadys.

homoioteleuton: [ho-mee-oh-te-LOOT-on] *n* Again, a big, hard word for a pretty simple thing. This refers to the trick of using several adjacent words with the same ending: "He sneezed mightily, showered cheerfully, ate hungrily, dressed carelessly, and drove crazily."

Now for the one that everyone learns, the word that makes you *know* you've really learned something about literature:

onomatopoeia: [oh-no-mah-to-po-EE-ah] *n* The naming of something by imitating a sound associated with that thing, such as when we write *hiss* when we want to name a, er, a hiss. Or a sonic *boom*. People get apoplectic over another use, which many swear isn't really onomatopoeia, but who cares? That's the use of words that sound like the thing they stand for, such as *moan*, *dribble*, *bounce*, and so forth.

dren and was his secretary.) In the process, Tolstoy kept a huge personal diary and mined it for his earliest fiction. His experience in the army furnished some of the foundations for his masterwork, *War and Peace*, and a spiritual turning point later in life led to his later mystical writings. So, once again one of literature's most educated writers got that education almost anywhere but in school.

_04:: W. B. Yeats (1865–1939)

OK, he went to art school, but does that *really* count? Like many of the people on our list, Yeats was largely privately and self-taught. His interest in mythology and spiritualism led to intense reading in those directions and informed his poetry throughout his life. His interest in theater and politics helped lead to the founding of the Irish National Theatre, and he wrote most of his best-known plays (most of them based on Irish mythology) for performance there. His self-taughtness also led to a rejuvenation of his poetry in the early decades of the 20th century, when he found a new, harder, modern voice, partly through meeting Ezra Pound and other modern poets. Another engine for his muse was Ireland's struggle for independence. Writing powerful poetry of the highest order well into his seventies, Yeats was brilliant at continually reinventing his style and work.

_05:: Robert Frost (1874–1963)

This guy came pretty close to being a total failure. He dropped out of Dartmouth, taught school, was a newspaper man, worked in a factory, dropped out of Harvard, bought and ran a number of farms. Of course, none of these pursuits made him rich or famous. He published a poem here and there, but in one of the riskier life decisions you'll find in any poet's biography, Frost up and packed his family off to England. That's where he got his first two books of poetry published. And he was in his forties—so he was no spring chicken. England's where Frost met Ezra Pound and many other fine contemporary poets. They spread the word: this guy was the real thing. Upon returning to the United States, Frost became famous and then became a college professor (though not a college graduate).

_06:: Maya Angelou (1928–)

To continue our theme, who needs college when you have life? Angelou has been an actress, a nightclub singer, a civil rights activist, a screenwriter, a producer and director, a playwright and . . . a lot of other things. She's lived in Egypt, Ghana, Arkansas, and California. And the time she didn't have for college she's more than lavished on her writing, her poetry, and her memoirs. And that's a good thing. She was one of the first black cable car conductors in San Francisco; joined in the civil rights movement in the United States (she had already been involved in African civil rights) as a regional coordinator for the Southern Christian Leadership Conference; was associate editor of a newspaper in Cairo; and became an eminent poet, teacher, and writer. Once again, an incredible life. The gal ended up teaching college rather than attending it!

Arrest That Writer!:
6 Authors Too Dangerous to Let Loose

Writers agree that pens are mightier than swords. And apparently, tyrants and despots agree that jails are mightier than pens. The following are a few of the writers, poets, and playwrights who ended up behind bars just when their writing started to get interesting.

_01:: Ovid

In 8 BCE the Roman poet Publius Ovidius Naso, better known to us as Ovid, was banished from Rome by the emperor Augustus. Why? Tradition says the cause was the immorality of his verses. That might be, since Ovid was a very accomplished erotic poet—although his erotic poems are seldom if ever pornographic. But Augustus was a bit of a prude, and (alas for Ovid) the most powerful person in the world. He also had been a friend and supporter of Ovid's, in the days when Ovid was writing the *Metamorphoses* and other works based on myth and more "moral" stuff. So, this is the story not just of a political punishment but also of the breakdown of a friendship. In fact, we're not even sure why he was banished, but banished Ovid was—to the town of Tomi on the Black Sea. Ovid desperately tried to change his ways, tried to produce poetry that was less, er, racy, but in fact, he never saw Rome again.

_02:: John Milton (1608–1674)

It's hard to imagine that the author of *Paradise Lost* was ever anything but saintly and studious. But in fact, he had a tumultuous life. Milton was a convinced, aggressive Puritan.

And the Puritans weren't exactly fond of the Church of England or the king. With Milton as one of their main firebrands in print, they fomented a revolution that led to the beheading of Charles I in 1649. When the Puritans took power, Milton was appointed Latin secretary to the ruling Council of State. But the rule of the Puritans lasted a scant decade. When their government collapsed in 1659, so did Milton's fortunes. He was imprisoned between October and December 1660, and his works burned in public bonfires. After his release, he lived under modified house arrest for the rest of his life. What to do? He kept himself occupied by penning *Paradise Lost* (1667), *Paradise Regained* (1671), and *Samson Agonistes* (1671).

_03:: The Marquis de Sade (1740–1814)

How great would it be to have sadism named after you? Of course, you'd have to go to certain lengths, as this fellow did. His family married him off to a woman for the money, and he immediately began to busy himself (quite publicly) with prostitutes and with a sister-in-law. His mother-in-law didn't like that, and she had him imprisoned. So he spent 14 years in jail, including being condemned to death in the town of Aix for his sexual practices. Yet somehow he got out of that one. Then he was again imprisoned in 1777, and again for six years at the Bastille in Paris in 1784. Imprisonment gave him lots of time to keep churning out the vigorous pornography that made him famous. In fact, the marquis spent his last 12 years in the insane asylum at Charenton, where he wrote and directed plays starring the staff and inmates.

_04:: Václav Havel (1936–)

This brave poet and playwright was jailed repeatedly in the 1970s for works critical of the communist government in then-Czechoslovakia. With civil unrest rising, he was jailed in February 1989 but kept turning out influential plays, poems, and essays, and even winning literary awards. Set free in May, he helped stoke a peaceful resistance movement known as the Velvet Revolution. Havel became the focal point of a largely peaceful revolution, where large crowds of nonviolent demonstrators showed their disapproval of the ruling communists. Havel addressed crowds that sometimes numbered almost a million. By the end of the year, the communist government was out and Havel had been elected president. He served as president of Czechoslovakia—and later, when the country split in two, of the Czech Republic—for 13 years, retiring in 2003. The tally? Poetry 1, communism 0!

_05:: Salman Rushdie (1947–)

A lot of people think literature is just, well, a particularly brainy sort of fun, not dangerous at all. But woe to those who step out of line. In 1989 Indian novelist Salman Rushdie published a novel titled *The Satanic Verses*. On

Inventions and Innovations

KEEPING LIT LIT

It's about recording and reproduction, baby. The root word of *literature* means "letter." That figures: if you can't write a piece of literature down, it stays *talk*—which is fine if people have great memories, but less fine for stretches of longer than, say, 30 minutes. So all the inventions that have helped people set words down in locatable form—papyrus, the Gutenberg press, the Internet—they keep lit lit. And like any human endeavor, literature has been full of inventions. How about the novel? That's a good one. Scholars disagree about what and when the first novel was (Was it *The Golden Ass* by Lucius Apuleius, of around 150 CE? Was it *The Tale of Genji* by Murasaki Shikibu, of around 1000? Was it *Don Quixote* by Miguel de Cervantes, of around 1605?), but the progression is pretty clear. As of 1400 you really didn't have that many; as of 2003 you see tens of thousands of new ones every year. At one time poetry reigned supreme; now prose is king.

October 14, 1989, Ayatollah Khomeini, theocratic ruler of Iran, published a *hukm* against Rushdie for his novel because some parts were considered blasphemous against certain tenets of Islam. The text of the *hukm* was pretty serious: "I call on all zealous Muslims to execute [Rushdie and all those involved in publishing the book] quickly, wherever they may be found, so that no one else will dare to insult the Muslim sanctities." Rushdie was forced to go into hiding for several years, but he continued to publish. The bounty on his head was raised to more than $5 million. With the death of Khomeini and comparative relaxation of Iranian politics, however, Rushdie's begun to make public appearances again.

_06:: María Elena Cruz Varela (1953–)

A Cuban poet, Varela was self-taught, a true flower of the countryside. She won Cuba's National Award for Poetry in 1989. In May 1991, however, she and nine other writers wrote a letter to Fidel Castro, calling for greater openness in Cuba, direct elections, and the release of political prisoners. State-run newspapers attacked these writers as agents of the CIA. Then a state security brigade broke into her apartment, where she lived with her husband, daughter, and son. She was dragged by her hair into the street and made to eat some of her published work. Then she was thrown into jail, beaten, and starved. She was released in 1994 and went into exile in Puerto Rico.

15

for All Time: The Ultimate Desert Island Reading List

A miniature history of world literature fits into a good-sized trunk. Here are fifteen titles to keep you occupied while Skipper and the Professor try to fix the hole in that boat.

_01:: *The Iliad* and *The Odyssey* by Homer

These got Western Civ started; might as well keep it going! The two epics are very different. The *Iliad* portrays the nine-year battle of Troy as a series of individual battles. The sorrow and pity of war has never been as well portrayed. It's told in the most elevated of all voices—and yet, its concerns always stay close to the human heart. If ever there was a cast of characters that were epic, this one has it: Paris, Priam, Hektor, Odysseus, Menelaos, Agamemnon, Akhilles, Patroklos, Ajax, and old whatsername, Helen of Troy. The *Odyssey* follows Odysseus on a trip around the world, encountering (and surviving his encounters with) a range of gods and monsters. Meanwhile, his patient wife, Penelope, waits for him and fends off suitors who want her hand and her land. Both books are worth reading if only for the moment Odysseus's dog, Argos, recognizes his master when he finally returns, and then the faithful pet dies.

_02:: *The Tale of Genji* by Lady Murasaki Shikibu

A panoramic, passionate story of Japanese courtly life, *The Tale of Genji* is thought of by many as the first novel. Its central character is a man known as Genji. He is never the emperor, but he is the most admired, most desired, most accomplished man in the court. Yet he isn't exactly the most self-aware person in the world; he doesn't always know why he does things. Which may be why he makes love to so many different women and thus causes confusion and heartache of all sorts. One of this book's many delights is the delicate, reserved tone of the narrator. Another is the way lovers exchange tanka (short poems) to allude to their feelings; this practice makes *Genji* an anthology of poetry as well as a novel. Like many great works, this ancient book often strikes us as fresh and aware in a contemporary way.

_03:: *The Divine Comedy* by Dante Alighieri (1265–1321)

Hell, purgatory, and paradise—who could ask for anything more? Dante grew up in the city-state of Florence, and he strove to reach the top of the society that bore him. But in the political battles that tore Florence apart in the late 13th century, Dante was expelled from his home (1302) and forced to be a gypsy-exile-scholar for the rest of his life, during which he tried to make sense of this cataclysm. In the poems that came to be known as *The Divine Comedy*, Dante goes on a guided tour (his guide is the great Roman poet Virgil) of, well, those three places. The *Inferno* is best known: that's because, as the cliché goes, it's easier to imagine hell than heaven. Dante makes the poem sort of an autobiography, putting many of his enemies and rivals in the heated place and elevating Beatrice, the love of his life, to the apex of divine realization in the *Paradiso*. The story remains one of the most sustained examples of the sublime in any language.

_04:: *Don Quixote* by Miguel de Cervantes (1547–1616)

Self-delusion is one of the greatest themes a writer can wade into. It's at once what is very funny about people and very tragic about them. The good don, also known as the Knight of the Doleful Countenance, believes that the era of knights and damsels and dragons and such still exists, and that he can win glory and fame by defending the weak and attacking the evil. His sidekick, Sancho Panza, tries to talk him out of his deluded ways, but a combination of nearsightedness and a simple refusal to believe all available evidence makes Quixote impregnable to good sense. It's a huge collection of stories, many of them taken from Cervantes' own painful, eventful life, but it feels like a novel because it has a great, arching coherence to it. It gives us a great hero, a great sadness, and much laughter in the bargain.

_05:: Shakespeare's Collected Works

Without them, you might as well not have anything else. If you take this with you to your desert island, you will have the company of hundreds of characters trooping across the stage of life, matching wits, swords, passions, and words. You'll see Hamlet in the graveyard, Othello in the bedroom, Julius Caesar on the ground, Sir John Falstaff on the battlefield (hiding), Juliet up there and Romeo down there. You'll encounter hundreds of lines and phrases you didn't know you knew ("Oh, *that's* where that's from?"). And in the sonnets you will meet one of the most compelling and perplexing triangles ever created: the speaker, the beloved gentleman, and the Dark Lady. And running through it all like a rainbow river, the unconscious, superlative music of Shakespeare's poetry. We're not saying it's any good. But it may help you while away the time before getting rescued.

_06:: The King James Version of the Bible

Even the least religious reader can savor the words and tales; you know many of them already, as well as the great phrases reverberating throughout the English language. It is famously divided into the Old Testament, a collection of sacred scriptures of the Jewish people, dating from between about 1000 BCE and 200 BCE; and the New Testament, a collection of writings about the life of Jesus Christ and the works of his followers. So why not treat the Bible as it is: the greatest anthology of prose and poetry ever? Read the book of Job tonight, then 2 Corinthians tomorrow night. Read the book of Psalms for a couple of weeks, savoring it psalm by psalm; then read the book of Matthew. Go from the lovely, erotic Song of Songs to the book of John. From Ruth to Paul, from Isaiah to Luke, from Genesis to the book of Revelations. It'd be worth rowing to an island just to have the privilege.

_07:: *Tom Jones* by Henry Fielding (1707–1754)

What is life without laughter, and plenty of it? Several of our desert-island books have yuks in them, but none of them have more than *Tom Jones*. There's a wide-open good nature to the humor, an energetic affection for the characters, that comes through on every page. We meet Tom, an orphan who has a lot of life in him, meaning he gets into a lot of

beds, a lot of trouble, and a lot of hearts. Mr. Allworthy is his kind benefactor. Tom is in love with the virtuous Sophie Western, but because of the sneaky Blifil, Tom is expelled from Mr. Allworthy's affections and hits the road. (See *The Odyssey*.) It's really a story about sin and forgiveness: Tom sins a whole lot, but deep down inside, he's a good person, as we (and Sophie) can see. Many people have said that the plot of this wonderful, racy book is one of the best ever concocted. The film *Tom Jones* is also a good intro to the book (if your island is somehow equipped with DVD), but it's certainly no replacement for it.

_08:: *Eugene Onegin* by Aleksandr Pushkin (1799–1837)

It's sometimes said that Russian literature begins and ends with Pushkin, especially with this exquisite novel in verse. As with Shakespeare in English and Ghalib in Urdu, lines and phrases of Pushkin's are on Russian lips every moment. Eugene Onegin is a young man with all the advantages. He's in the midst of society, the midst of luxury. And then it hits him—he loses his taste for life. Everything suddenly bores him. He can find no savor in existence. Natalya is a young girl who falls passionately, romantically in love with Eugene, and even though he is drawn to her, he is unable to come out of his boredom to respond to her. It's one of the most poignantly frustrating frustrated loves in all of literature. Considering the fate of their relationship, the fate of Eugene's friendship with the proud poet Lensky, and the fate of life itself—there's a profound perfection to this tale that has seldom been equaled.

Myths and Misconceptions

ANOTHER MAN BY SHAKESPEARE'S NAME?

At the turn of the 20th century, certain folks started whipping themselves into a lather over the notion that Shakespeare had not written his plays. They started reading between the lines, smelling a rat. The favorite theory was and is that a nobleman wrote the plays—the Earl of Oxford, maybe, or Francis Bacon—and didn't want people to know he'd indulged in this disgraceful pursuit. So he tapped Shakespeare as the front man. Some pretty famous people got into the act, including that all-time sleuther-behind-the-scenes, Sigmund Freud.

Here are a few of the reasons people think Shakespeare didn't write his plays:

1. There's no record that he ever went to any school.
2. Many of his plays were published without his name on them.
3. The plays are too smart to have been written by a middle-class guy with no university education.
4. There are clues in the plays that other people wrote them.
5. If Shakespeare wrote all this great stuff, why don't we know more about him?

Maybe they're right. Maybe we should tell the old joke: "Shakespeare didn't write his plays—it was another man by the same name." But there are pretty good replies to these notions:

1. Records were pretty bad back then, so that might be why there's no record of him in school.
2. True. So what? Later they were. And it's possible he didn't want them published (come pay to see *Hamlet*; don't buy the book), didn't care, or didn't want his name on them. And we have a fair number of contemporaries who say he did write many of these plays.
3. There really isn't much in the plays that a voracious reader couldn't have learned. We know a lot of the books and stories the "author of Shakespeare's plays" ransacked for plots and ideas. You didn't need to be an upper-class university student to read them.
4. Most of these "clues" are clues only if you want to see them that way.
5. Shakespeare isn't that mysterious a figure. We actually know a lot about the guy for a nonroyal person of 400-plus years ago.

_09:: *Little Dorrit* by Charles Dickens
(1812–1870)

Dickens wrote so many wonderful novels that this one might come as a surprise choice. And, hey, if you'd rather take *Oliver Twist, David Copperfield, The Pickwick Papers, Bleak House, A Tale of Two Cities,* or *Great Expectations,* well, fine. But to Dickens fans this choice will be no surprise. The novel has all the Dickens hallmarks: the sweeping sense of teeming human life in the midst of history; biting satire on unfeeling government institutions in the Circumlocution Office; stories of class snobbery and true love; wacky humor; a mystery to be solved; and a (fairly) happy ending tempered by the wisdom that life, even at its best, is pretty hard. *Little Dorrit*, like many Dickens novels, invites us not only to read it but also to live it.

_10:: *The Brothers Karamazov* by Fyodor Dostoevsky (1821–1881)

There are a few novels—and this is certainly one—that are so huge you can't pin a meaning on them. You can find lots and lots of meanings, but not a single strand. *The Brothers K* is the best of one of the very best writers ever. As many of the greatest literary works do, this book concerns the cataclysmic forces within a family: father Fyodor Karamazov and his sons Dmitri, Ivan, and Alyosha. This huge novel has that obsessive (and obsessing), dry-mouthed, feverish intensity for which Dostoevsky is famous. Again and again, we keep colliding with the profoundest themes in life: What are good and evil? Can human sin be redeemed? Is love possible? Where, if anywhere, is God? (In this regard, the high point of the novel is the segment titled *The Grand Inquisitor*, an interrogation of Christ come back to earth.) Reading this book feels like living an intense, maddening, poetic life.

_11:: *The Adventures of Huckleberry Finn* by Mark Twain (1835–1910)

This is one of the funniest books you'll read while on the island, yet it's no less profound for all that. It's got the Mississippi River—the ultimate symbol of freedom—life on the road, the American dream. It's got the tension between young and old, slave and free, black and white. It has perhaps the most likable cast of characters to be encountered in any novel, including Huck, Tom Sawyer, the slave Jim, and the whole rogues' gallery of swindlers, killers, would-be's, has-been's, and never-will-be's all along the river. During the novel Huck realizes that living his kind of life is a way to hell in some people's eyes. All right, then, he says, I'll go to hell. It's an act of courage, and a shocking one at the time. But it's also the ultimate moral act, as this surprisingly subtle novel shows us. Warning: This novel is much different and much more perplexing than advertised. All aboard.

_12:: *Light in August* by William Faulkner (1897–1962)

Faulkner created dozens of novels and stories we could have recommended, most of them set in the mythical southern county of Yoknapatawpha. The central figure of *Light in August* is a fugitive named Joe Christmas. Uh-oh! Red lights, sirens, SWAT teams of the mind: Christ figure Christ figure Christ figure. Well, all right, but in Faulkner's hands, even this most overdone of symbols assumes new meanings in the early-20th-century South. Joe is an orphan and doesn't really know where he's from, but he believes he's part black. That means he never fits in anywhere and is doomed. We also meet the similarly symbolic and out-of-place Joanna Burden. Everyone has his or her own special burden in this novel: the burden of memory, identity, history, and race. Out of the wreckage emerges the human will to endure. Not a bad message for an island castaway.

_13:: *The Plague* by Albert Camus
(1913–1960)

OK, the existentialists were good at thinking, or at least in talking in cafés, but were they good writers? Answer: not always! Jean-Paul Sartre, for example, is wholly overrated. But one born writer who would have been a genius whether he'd been an existentialist or not is Albert Camus. *The Plague* is one of his widest-ranging myths. Bubonic plague grips a small Algerian town, and Dr. Rieux battles the disease even though he can't really stop it and can't really help people once they're infected. So, why carry on? There's an answer: We try to help one another bear the burden of a universe without answers. We battle against evil in protest against evil, in solidarity with one another. It's sad, it's grueling, but it's ultimately a beautiful exploration of how friendship can redeem the worst of experience.

_14:: *Catch-22* by Joseph Heller
(1923–1999)

This book is still hanging around. Why? For one thing, it is funny. Brilliantly funny. And it does gets serious about three-quarters of the way through, but then thinks better of it and ends on a genius high note. *Catch-22* is a war novel, and much of the humor is black humor. The main character is a guy by the name of Yossarian who is afraid to die and is trying to get out of flying dangerous bombing missions. But the true central character is the Catch-22 itself: that the only way you can't go on the bombing run is if you're crazy, and if you're crazy, you are normal, so off you go. Some catch. Along the way we get great satire: of the American Organization Man, of the McCarthy hearings, of organized and disorganized religion, and, above all, of the army.

_15:: *The Color Purple* by Alice Walker
(1944–)

Alice Walker's novel operates on many levels at once. It's a story about how whites oppress blacks and how men oppress women. It's also a story about how a woman who does not value herself learns to love herself. And it's also a story about what's valuable and singular about being an American of African descent, about the birthright of pain and joy waiting for the black person willing to acknowledge it. And on top, in between, and underneath all that, this is an intensely religious novel, at least in the sense of discovering what God is: the principle of beauty waiting for us to pay attention to it. God is, in a lot of ways, the color purple. But there's no seeing that until we've seen our way through history, self, family, sex, and culture. Enough joy here to make the whole island happy.

by
Bill Hauser &
Scott Speck

Condensed
MUSIC

Contains

6 Classical Scandals Straight from the Tabloids* ✳ My 4 Dads: Men Who Sired Rock and Roll ✳ 3 Country Outlaws Who Became Folk Heroes ✳ 9 Composers Who Pull Our Strings* ✳ 3 Bandleaders Who Made Swing the Thing ✳ 5 Classical Tunes You Know from the Movies* ✳ 3 Rock Gods Who Died at 27 ✳ Miles Ahead: 4 Candidates for the Miles Davis Cosmic Jazz Combo ✳ 2 Reasons Why Motown Saved America ✳ The Great Divides: 4 Breaks in Classical Music* ✳ 3 Skirts Who Shook the Music World ✳ 6 Political Moments in Rock and Roll ✳

*Written by Scott Speck

Classical Scandals Straight from the Tabloids

Every generation thinks it invented sex and scandal, but that just isn't true. Musicians, even the classical ones, have always walked on the wilder side.

_01:: First Conductor Dies from Conducting!

Jean-Baptiste Lully (1632–1687) was the first documented conductor. Before him, most musical groups followed their first violinist or their keyboard player. Lully was the first musician ever to use a baton. However, his "baton" was a heavy staff six feet long, which he pounded on the ground in time to the music. Unfortunately, this staff proved to be his undoing. One day, while merrily beating time (in a concert to celebrate the king's return to health), he stuck the staff into his foot by mistake. He developed gangrene and died. Not a good role model for conductors worldwide.

_02:: Haydn Nearly Castrated!

Franz Joseph Haydn (1732–1809) was the father of the symphony as we know it. During more than 30 years of experimentation, he came up with the form that has influenced composers to this day. But as a little boy, Haydn was known for something else—his beautiful voice. He was the star soprano in his church choir. As he got older and his voice was about to change, his choirmaster came to him with a little proposition. If he would consent to a small operation, he could keep his beautiful soprano voice forever. Haydn read-

ily agreed and was just about to undergo the surgery when his father found out and put a stop to the whole thing.

_03:: Paganini Allegedly Sells Soul to Devil! (Fetches Good Price)

The Italian violinist and composer Niccolò Paganini (1782–1840) was one of the most astounding virtuosos of all time. He had amazing technique and enormous passion. He also promoted himself shamelessly, doing tricks to astonish his audience. Often before a concert he would saw partway through three of the four strings on his violin. In performance, those three strings broke, forcing him to play an entire piece on one string. Rumors flew that Paganini had sold his soul to the devil in order to play so well. Sometimes Paganini would order the lights dimmed while he played particularly spooky music. Everybody fainted—when the candles were lit again, the room appeared to be full of dead bodies, sprawled everywhere. (It didn't take much to make an audience faint in those days.)

_04:: Cross-Dressing Berlioz Nearly Snuffs Out Rival!

The renowned French composer Hector Berlioz (1803–1869) was, among other things, wacky. While away in Rome studying on a scholarship, he heard that his beloved girl-friend, Camille, back in Paris, had started seeing another guy. Furious, he resolved to kill his rival. But he needed to disguise himself. So he bought a gun, put on a dress, and boarded a train for Paris. Halfway home, however, Berlioz chickened out and threw himself into the Mediterranean. Luckily for us, and for music, he was fished out (minus the gun).

_05:: Liszt's Lucky Fans Receive Canine Surprise!

There's a reason musicians give out only autographs these days. The Hungarian Franz Liszt (1811–1886), a virtuoso in the tradition of Paganini, played the piano and created a sensation all throughout Europe. Everywhere he played, women swooned—and he sometimes swooned himself. Liszt was one of the first rock stars, and the word *Lisztomania* was coined during his lifetime. He received so many requests for a lock of his hair that he finally bought a dog, snipping off patches of fur to send to his admirers—an unexpected use for your best friend.

_06:: Peter Tchaikovsky Nearly Loses Head!

The magnificent Russian composer Peter Tchaikovsky (1840–1893) was yet another in the line of geniuses who sometimes came unhinged. Tchaikovsky loved to compose, but he hated to conduct. Unfortunately, conducting opportunities came up way too often for him—including the gala opening concert of Carnegie Hall in 1891. Neurotic to the core, Tchaikovsky conducted with one hand firmly on top of his head, in the desperate belief that otherwise his head would fall off.

My 4 Dads: Men Who Sired Rock and Roll

When rhythm and blues went on the sly, it gave birth to rock and roll. In the paternity suit that followed, a few too many men claimed to be the father.

_01:: Chuck Berry

Roll over, Beethoven; Chuck Berry (1926–) straddled the racial chasm in music, blending blues, country, and teenage pop music, and tailoring performances to black or white crowds. Berry's witty lyrics, entertaining stage presence, and signature "duck walk" made him one of the most sought-after early rock performers of the 1950s. Berry didn't even have a demo tape when Muddy Waters sent him to meet Leonard Chess, co-owner of Chess Records, in 1955. But within a week he'd written four songs, including "Maybellene," his first Top 10 hit. Unfortunately, his celebrity made him a target, and after a racially charged trial in 1959 Berry spent two years in prison for "transporting a minor across state lines for immoral purposes." He went right back to recording afterward, though, and over the past 50 years Berry's songs have influenced countless rock musicians, from the Beatles to the Stones.

_02:: Little Richard

At a time of political and social conservatism, Little Richard's frantic piano pounding, falsetto singing, and no-holds-barred stage presence were enough to drive teenagers into a frenzy, and their parents into cardiac arrest. His appearance—mascara-coated eyelashes and pompadour hairdo—was, well, different and personified the sexuality and rebelliousness of the new music called rock and roll. During the 1950s he recorded classics like "Tutti-Frutti," "Lucille," and "Good Golly, Miss Molly." However, the performances, lyrics, and even his race helped to fire the 1950s backlash against rock and roll. The music didn't go away, but in 1957, at the height of his success, Little Richard did: he had a premonition of his own damnation and quit rock and roll to become a minister. Luckily for rock fans, he returned in 1964.

_03:: Bill Haley

Originally the lead country singer of the Saddlemen, Bill Haley tossed his cowboy hat in 1952 and renamed the group Bill Haley and His Comets. A year later Haley's "Crazy Man Crazy" became the first rock and roll record to make the *Billboard* pop chart. However, his

"Rock around the Clock" had only moderate sales until it was rereleased in 1955 as part of the soundtrack for *Blackboard Jungle* (a movie about juvenile delinquents). Rock and roll and the movies have been inseparable ever since. With hits like "Shake, Rattle, and Roll" and "See You Later Alligator," Haley was considered the most popular rock performer in the world in the mid-1950s. By the early

---

Inventions and Innovations
WHY LES PAUL IS GOD

Where would rock and roll be without the electric guitar? Blame it on Lester Polfus. Lester, better known as Les Paul, created the solid-body electric guitar and is the innovator of many of the recording techniques used today. In the early 1930s Les was already working on a rudimentary guitar pickup using pieces from his ham radio set. By 1941 he had built a solid-body electric guitar that consisted of a four-foot wooden board, strings, plug, and pickup. In 1945 he created the recording process of multitracking in a recording studio he built in his garage. Later, as part of a very successful duet with his wife, Mary Ford, he perfected the technique of multitracking Ford's voice responding to his guitar. But Paul's technological genius didn't end there. In the 1950s Paul built the first 8-track recorder and invented the process of overdubbing. Inducted into the Rock and Roll Hall of Fame in 1988, Les Paul continues to take the recording industry higher and higher.

1960s Haley's star had sunk in the United States, but it grew even stronger in England, where he was viewed as a young rebel. By that time Haley was middle-aged and nearly bald.

_04:: Ike Turner

Despite notoriety as the ex-spouse of Anna Mae Bullock (Tina Turner), Ike Turner should be remembered for his early contributions to rock and roll. Considered one of the best session guitarists, talent scouts, and producers of the 1950s, Turner landed gigs on many early R&B and rock and roll recordings but often got stiffed on the credits. He recorded a song in 1951 called "Rocket 88" at Sam Phillips's Sun Records studio in Memphis, Tennessee, with saxophonist Jackie Brenston of the Delta Cats performing the lead vocals. The Delta Cats, not Turner, got the label credit, and "Rocket 88" became a number one R&B hit—considered by many the first rock and roll recording.

Country Outlaws Who Became Folk Heroes

"There's always that other 20% who just don't fit in. That's what happened to me, and it happened to Johnny Cash, and it happened to Willie Nelson. We just couldn't do it the way it was set up."—Waylon Jennings on the Nashville scene.

_01:: Johnny Cash

Think Ozzy Osbourne's "bad"? You must not have met the "Man in Black." When Johnny Cash first sang, "I shot a man in Reno/Just to watch him die," he wasn't serenading radio listeners; he was playing to a roaring crowd at Folsom State Prison. True to the outlaw mantra, Cash crooned on both sides of the bars: in 1965 he was nabbed at the Mexican border for trying to smuggle drugs into the States in his guitar case. Despite doing some time (or maybe because of it), Cash still had enough mainstream clout in 1969 to host his own prime-time variety show, showcasing the talents of artists like Bob Dylan. By the fall of '69 Cash's *Folsom Prison* and *San Quentin* albums had outsold even the Beatles.

_02:: Waylon Jennings

Waylon Jennings barely escaped "the day the music died"—February 3, 1959—by giving up his plane seat to the Big Bopper. The flight crashed, killing the Big Bopper, Buddy Holly, and Richie Valens, but Jennings survived to found the "outlaw" country music movement. In the 1970s he twisted out of Nashville's grasp and started singing a more rebellious style that mixed country, rock, and rockabilly. His recording of "The Eagle" in 1991 became the anthem for troops in Operation Desert

Storm, solidifying his hero status. But by 1988 hard living caught up with Jennings, and he had to undergo triple bypass surgery (partner in crime Johnny Cash had heart surgery across the hall at the same time). Jennings recuperated to perform nearly 100 shows a year.

_03:: Willie Nelson

The man in braids, Willie Nelson, grew up working the cotton fields of Texas and selling Bibles door to door. As an adult, he often played honky-tonk bars Saturday nights and taught Sunday school the next morning. But when told to choose between the two, Nelson couldn't resist the honky-tonks. He moved from Texas to Nashville, where his songwriting skills created hits for Patsy Cline, Faron Young, and Roy Orbison. By the 1970s Nelson's own singing career skyrocketed with a string of solo hits, duets with Waylon Jennings, and collaborations with the Highwaymen, all blending redneck country with rock. True to the outlaw spirit, Willie didn't get along with "the man," and in 1991 the IRS presented him with a past-due tax bill for $16.7 million.

Composers Who Pull Our Strings

Even if you're living in a soundproof box, you've probably heard of these guys. But can you list one thing about any of them that you didn't see in *Amadeus* or *Immortal Beloved*? Improve your repertoire.

_01:: Bach: Placing His Faith in Music

The granddaddy of all the great composers is Johann Sebastian Bach (1685–1750), who lived during the baroque period and influenced all composers after him. In his day Bach was revered not as a composer but as an organist—and his flying feet on the organ pedals attracted tourists and gawkers from all over. He was also incredibly prolific. (See sidebar Just the Facts, page 184.) In Bach's day, most music was written for a single occasion; nobody ever thought of performing it more than once. Many a Bach masterpiece was saved from certain oblivion immediately before being used for wrapping fish (or toilet paper). Bach was extremely religious, and he wrote much of his music to express his faith. Among his magnificent masterpieces are the *St. Matthew Passion*, the B-minor Mass, the six Brandenburg Concertos, and forty-eight preludes and fugues for keyboard. (In his day, these keyboard pieces were played on some form of organ or harpsichord—the piano hadn't been invented yet.)

_02:: Mozart: The Prodigy Son

Born in Austria, Wolfgang Amadeus Mozart (1756–1791) was a boy genius—so much so that his father took him out of school for weeks at a time, dragging him all around Europe to showcase his talents in the violin, piano, and composition. Mozart was the quintessential composer of the classic period in music. His works show perfect proportion and restraint. Mozart wrote 41 symphonies, 27 piano concertos, 5 violin concertos, numerous sonatas, and an awesome bunch of operas, including *The Marriage of Figaro*, *Don Giovanni*, and *The Magic Flute*. Although he couldn't remain a child prodigy forever, he never lost his amazing gifts. He could compose a piece of music in a few minutes, and often did. Music spoke to him from some higher place; all he had to do was write it down. But despite some popular successes, Mozart died a pauper at age 35 and was buried in an unmarked mass grave.

_03:: Beethoven: The Original Deaf Jam

Impetuous and hot-tempered, German composer Ludwig van Beethoven (1770–1827) wrote music that burned with an inner fire. He carried sketchbooks with him and polished his musical ideas until they shone with an unprecedented intensity. His Fifth Symphony is one of his most recognized works, with that famous (and violent) "duh duh duh DAAAAAAAH" rhythm, often described as "fate knocking on the door." The movie *Immortal Beloved*—while not completely accurate—gives us an enlightening look at Beethoven's personality and a brilliant sampling of his music. He holds a special place in the musical pantheon: many musicians consider him the ultimate composer. In Boston's legendary Symphony Hall, one word is emblazoned above the concert stage: "Beethoven."

_04:: Brahms: The Boy from the Brothel Makes Good

As a kid, Johannes Brahms (1833–1897) made his living playing the piano in houses of ill re-

pute. (How many composers can say that?) As he grew up, Brahms perfectly combined the restraint and structure of the classic style with the strong emotions of the Romantic. His pieces are put together as perfectly and intricately as a jigsaw puzzle, and yet they also have overwhelming emotional force. He became known as the successor to Beethoven—a reputation that saddled him with an incredible feeling of responsibility. Notoriously self-critical, he destroyed dozens and dozens of pieces before they ever saw the light of day. He didn't publish his first symphony until he was 43 years old. (By that age, Mozart had written 41 symphonies and been dead for 8 years.) Among his most beautiful pieces are all four of his symphonies, his intermezzi for piano (especially opus 118), his violin concerto, and his two piano concertos.

_05:: Dvořák: Bohemian Rhapsodies

If any composer represented the common people, it was Antonin Dvořák (1841–1904). Born in a small town in Bohemia (now part of the Czech Republic), Dvořák was surrounded by farmers and tradespeople as a child. He studied music with village schoolmasters and played in a local band. It was Johannes Brahms (see above) who "discovered" Dvořák and championed his music. Dvořák's gift for melody and musical inventiveness took him far—specifically, to America, where he became director of the National Conservatory in New York. While in the United States, he wrote one of his best-known works: the Symphony no. 9 (subtitled *From the New World*). But even at the height of his fame, Dvořák maintained a nostalgic love for his native Bohemia. A rustic, folksy quality can be found in almost every piece he ever wrote. Dvořák was one of the composers who started a *nationalist* trend—writing classical music based on the folk tunes of his homeland.

_06:: Verdi: Songs in the Key of Strife

Some musicians think that the Italian Giuseppe Verdi (1813–1901) was the greatest opera composer who ever lived. Verdi (whose full name means "Joe Green" in Italian) had an immense talent for creating some of the catchiest, most hummable melodies ever written for the human voice. Even today, Verdi's operas are favorites for that reason—and also because they tackle such primal human subjects as love, sex, jealousy, passion, murder, and more sex. Verdi was a master of dramatic pacing that still keeps his audiences on the edge of their seats. Among his 28 masterful operas are *La Traviata*, *Il Trovatore*, *Rigoletto*, *Otello*, and, most beloved of all, *Aïda*—that grand drama set in Egypt, complete with an elephant-laden triumphal march.

_07:: Tchaikovsky: The Great Communicator

If ever a composer deserved to be called Romantic, it was the Russian composer Peter Tchaikovsky (1840–1893). Emotionally, Tchaikovsky was a mess—neurotic, insecure, intense, overly sensitive, easily depressed, and easily elated. But luckily, he had the talent to express those feelings with glorious melodies. Tchaikovsky mastered the art of direct communication with his audience. When you hear his pieces, there's nothing between him and you; you feel as if you know the guy, and you like him. His music came to the attention of a wealthy widow, Nadezhda von Meck, who sent him a monthly allowance so that he could compose freely—on the condition that they

---

Myths and Misconceptions

THE 3 YOU GOT WRONG ABOUT OPERA

OPERA SINGERS ARE FAT.

Every misconception has its kernel of truth. Big voices do tend to come in big bodies. And some great singers have big appetites. But fat is absolutely not a prerequisite for a powerful voice. Some of the strongest singers of all time—like Birgit Nilsson, the great Wagnerian soprano—were just *big-boned*.

OPERAS ARE LONG.

Again, yes, *some* of them are. Wagner wrote a handful of doozies that stretch well past midnight. But most great operas—including Verdi's masterpieces—aren't much longer than your run-of-the-mill epic movie.

WHEN AN OPERA CHARACTER IS DYING, SHE SINGS ABOUT IT FOR 10 MINUTES.

When you go to an opera, this might strike you as the ultimate in ridiculousness. The heroine is dying of consumption. The villain has been stabbed. How could they possibly summon the strength to *breathe*, let alone sing a whole 10-minute song, ending on a high D? Here's the answer: the song they sing, called an aria, is meant to convey the feeling inherent in a single instant. Imagine using a microscope to examine the minutest details of that instant. That's what an aria does. For those "10 minutes," time actually stands still. As for the high D—yeah, well, that's nuts.

never meet. When Tchaikovsky dedicated his Fourth Symphony "To My Best Friend," he was referring to her. Tragically, Tchaikovsky died at age 53 from cholera. (For years scholars have debated whether or not he purposely drank a glass of contaminated water in order to kill himself.) His credits include *Romeo and Juliet* and the ballets *Swan Lake, Sleeping Beauty*, and, most famous of all, *The Nutcracker*.

_08:: Debussy: Great First Impressions

The French composer Claude Debussy (1862–1918) brought about a new revolution in classical music. He tried to do with his music what the impressionist painters were doing with art—evoking the impressions of sights, sounds, fragrances, and even tastes. To do this, Debussy threw away traditional harmony and invented his own combinations of notes. Needless to say, he flunked out of the Paris Conservatory. He is celebrated for inventing the "whole tone scale"—that gauzy up-and-down scale you hear played by a harp whenever a character on TV has a flashback. Debussy's first important piece was *Prelude to the Afternoon of a Faun*, which caused a stir for its way-

out harmonies. Years later a ballet set to the music caused as much of a stir for its racy choreography. His most evocative piece is the extraordinarily powerful three-movement work *La Mer* (The Sea), an incredible tour de force of imagery. When you hear the music, you can hear the howling of the wind, smell the salt air, feel the ocean spray on your face, and experience the first signs of motion sickness.

_09:: Copland: An American Original

American composer Aaron Copland (1900–1990) is beloved because he created, for the first time, a truly American sound. His music echoes the sounds of the great outdoors—the Wild West, the rolling hills of Appalachia, and even the bustle of New York City. By far Copland's best-known work (and the most recognized piece of American classical music) is *Appalachian Spring*. This music, originally written for ballet, tells the story of a young couple setting up a house and beginning their new life together. Copland also scored big with *Fanfare for the Common Man*, a short piece for brass and percussion that gets ripped off in nearly every Olympic theme you've ever heard.

Bandleaders Who Made Swing the Thing

It's true: swing existed even before there were Gap commercials. Way back in the 1930s, with the Depression raging and Prohibition ending, people started looking for a release—they found it in swing.

_01:: Benny Goodman

In 1934 jazz clarinetist Benny Goodman, the "king of swing," became a regular on a national radio show that featured the three popular dance themes of the time: traditional, Latin, and big band. Goodman used these broadcasts to feature a new jazz-oriented sound called swing, integrating African American jazz sounds into traditional dance band music. Goodman and his band always played last on the show, usually after midnight, when most people east of the Rocky Mountains were already in bed. When the band went on national tour, it played to small audiences—until reaching California, where radio fans lined up for blocks. Based on that solid fan base, Goodman's reputation and musical stylings quickly grew. Because Goodman was white, he was given more opportunities to use his media savvy—unusual among African American swing bands of the time—to help bring swing to the masses.

_02:: Count Basie

While working the vaudeville circuit in the 1920s, William "Count" Basie got stranded in Kansas City, Missouri, when his tour fell apart. The rough-and-tumble frontier town turned out to be a hotbed for jazz, though, and by 1929 Basie had joined Kansas City's leading jazz band. After moving the band to New York City in 1936, he renamed it Count Basie and His Orchestra. Freddie Green on guitar, Walter Page on bass, Jo Jones on drums, and Basie on piano made up the rhythm section at the heart of the band. The four took the prevailing bluesy jazz melodies and created fast-moving, polished versions, fusing blues and ragtime into a jazz style that evolved into swing. Basie continued to innovate his style to meet the times, but creating and popularizing swing stands as his greatest contribution to music.

_03:: Duke Ellington

Duke Ellington didn't invent swing, but he definitely made it "the thing." During his lifetime Ellington composed close to 2,000 works that ranged from big band swing music to opera. In the 1920s Ellington and his band began performing at the Cotton Club in Harlem. Their regular appearances on radio broadcasts from the Cotton Club quickly gained them a national audience and an international reputation. In 1932 Ellington composed "It Don't Mean a Thing (If It Ain't Got That Swing)," correctly anticipating that swing would quickly become a national obsession. Like

Goodman, Ellington could attract a large national radio fan base of both black and white

dance audiences looking for fun during the Depression-ridden, post-Prohibition 1930s.

Classical Tunes You Know from the Movies

Classical music is the perfect movie backdrop: lots of emotion, without those pesky lyrics that conflict with the plot. Here are five hummable tunes you'll recognize from the silver screen.

_01:: That Tune from *Die Hard*

Ludwig van Beethoven's Ninth Symphony is one of the most thrillingly triumphant pieces ever written, so naturally Hollywood exploits it whenever possible. The symphony begins in a somber and severe minor key; the composer seems to be struggling mightily against fate. But in the final section—for the first time ever in a symphony—a chorus and soloists join in, singing the "Ode to Joy" (*"Freude, schöner Götterfunken . . ."*). This theme brings the music from darkness to light, and the symphony ends in a titanic blaze of optimistic glory. Several film directors have made use of the extreme emotions of this piece in their films—from *A Clockwork Orange* to *Die Hard*. And Audi once released a hilarious commercial where a bevy of crash-test dummies comes to life, singing the "Ode to Joy" in tribute to a particularly safe car.

_02:: That Tune from *Moonraker*

Peter Tchaikovsky's wildly popular symphonic poem depicts in musical notes Shakespeare's beloved story of star-crossed lovers.

The piece, *Romeo and Juliet*, has long been a favorite on the concert stage, but nowhere has it enjoyed more success than in movies and on TV. The lush, soaring love theme from *Romeo and Juliet* seems to come up every time two characters fall in love. And in many cases the music swells onscreen when two unlikely characters fall in love (as in the James Bond movie *Moonraker*, when the evil steel-toothed character, Jaws, falls for a similarly scary-looking woman).

_03:: That Tune from *Apocalypse Now*

When German composer Richard Wagner (1813–1883) wrote his "Ride of the Valkyries" for his opera *Die Walküre*, he was depicting mythical, powerful god-women riding winged horses, swooping down over the battlefield, scooping up fallen soldiers, and carrying them up to Valhalla to defend the gods. But film director Francis Ford Coppola had an even better use for this music. This is the piece that Robert Duvall blares from the helicopters in *Apocalypse Now* as soldiers swoop down and attack a Vietnamese village. In this context, the music is more than awesome—it's absolutely horrifying. This is one of the most effective uses of preexisting classical music in all of moviedom—second only to the following example.

_04:: That Tune from *2001*

German composer Richard Strauss (1864–1949) wrote the opening of *Also sprach Zarathustra* ("Thus Spake Zarathustra") to depict the awe of a primal sunrise—which inspires the prophet and thinker Zarathustra to come down from his self-imposed exile in the mountains to begin enlightening the masses. You know this music: three long notes ascending in the trumpets, followed by an enormous "da-DAAAAH" for the whole orchestra, followed by pulsing in the kettledrums. Director Stanley Kubrick used Strauss's music three times in his movie *2001: A Space Odyssey*—also to accompany a moment of enlightenment. You hear it at the very beginning, "The Dawn of Man," where one ape realizes that he can use a bone as a weapon and elevates himself above all other apes; in the middle, when astronauts discover that Great Black Monolith on the moon; and at the end, when the Star Child is born. Don't ask us what it means—we don't know. But, man, is it primal.

_05:: That Tune from *10*

Bolero by French composer Maurice Ravel (1875–1937) is nothing but a single melody, repeated over and over, to a simple Spanish rhythm. The piece begins simply, with an innocent flute playing the melody quietly over a hushed snare drum. Over the next 15 minutes, the sound grows and grows (making a crescendo) and ends with an overwhelming, monstrous climax. Not surprisingly, the piece has long been associated with sex. Director Blake

Edwards took advantage of this fact in his movie *10*. Everyone knows the scene where Bo Derek and Dudley Moore finally have their romantic moment, accompanied by this seductive number, with hilarious results.

THE MOST PROLIFIC COMPOSERS BY THE NUMBERS

Johann Sebastian Bach (1685–1750) composed so much music that it would take several decades just to copy it all down. Among many other things, he wrote over 250 church cantatas and 371 chorales. He also had 20 children (as far as he knew).

Antonio Vivaldi (1678–1741) wrote nearly 500 concertos. (Some people think they all sound alike.) He also wrote more than 40 pieces for chorus and orchestra, 50 operas, and 100 pieces for orchestra alone. Not bad for a priest.

Franz Joseph Haydn (1732–1809), the inventor of the symphony, composed at least 104 of them. (By contrast, Brahms wrote 4.)

Franz Schubert (1797–1828) wrote over 600 songs. And he wasn't even nominated for a Grammy.

Richard Wagner (1813–1883) wrote the world's longest opera—*Die Meistersinger von Nürnberg*, clocking in at over 5 hours. (And that's a comedy!) Meanwhile, Darius Milhaud's *The Deliverance of Theseus* holds the record for the shortest opera, at just 7 minutes and 37 seconds. (One of your authors has beaten that record, but the *Guinness Book* has yet to recognize it.)

Rock Gods Who Died at 27

Over the years many rockers chanted the "hope I die before I get old" mantra from the Who's "My Generation." But why have so many left us at age 27? (Jimi Hendrix also belongs on this list—check out his story on page 260.)

_01:: Jim Morrison (1943–1971): The Lizard King

Unlike the Beatles, Jim Morrison and the Doors explored the darker side of rock with lyrics focusing on violence and death. Between 1967 and 1970, the Doors poured out such hits as "Light My Fire," "Riders on the Storm," and "Hello, I Love You," but by 1969 Morrison's alcohol and drug problems provoked erratic concert performances often interrupted by drunken confusion, culminating in his arrest for indecent exposure and public drunkenness at a Miami concert. Physically and emotionally drained and facing legal problems, Morrison moved to Paris to recuperate. On July 3, 1971, he was found dead in his bathtub, a victim of a heart attack. Due to the secretive and confusing circumstances surrounding his death and burial, many fans refuse to believe that Jim Morrison is really dead and buried in a Paris cemetery.

_02:: Janis Joplin (1943–1970): Hard-Edged Soulstress

The gritty, R&B-infused vocals and legendary hard living of white soul singer Janis Joplin revived the role of the female blues singer in contemporary rock music. As the lead singer of Big Brother and the Holding Company,

Joplin scored a number of hits in the mid-1960s such as "Piece of My Heart," "Ball & Chain," and "Summertime," and she mesmerized the crowd at the 1967 Monterey Pop Festival with her now legendary performance. But shortly after completing the recording of her classic rock album *Pearl*, Joplin was found dead of a heroin overdose in a Hollywood hotel October 4, 1970. While the drug overdose is listed as the official cause of death, many feel that the years of living life at light speed took its toll on Joplin.

_03:: Kurt Cobain (1967–1994): Rock's Reluctant Prince

The life of Kurt Cobain, the lead singer/songwriter for Nirvana and one of the founders of the Seattle grunge movement in the early 1990s, was one of contradictions. His anti-establishment message became the rallying cry for a new generation of youth, but as the band became more popular and successful, Cobain became increasingly depressed, saying that fans were missing his message. Between May 1993 and April 1994 Cobain overdosed at least three times and often threatened suicide. Police were called to Cobain's home in March 1994 when he locked himself in a room with a revolver, and Cobain then checked himself into a Los Angeles hospital for treatment. He stayed only two days. A little over a week later Cobain was found dead in a room above his garage with a shotgun wound to the head.

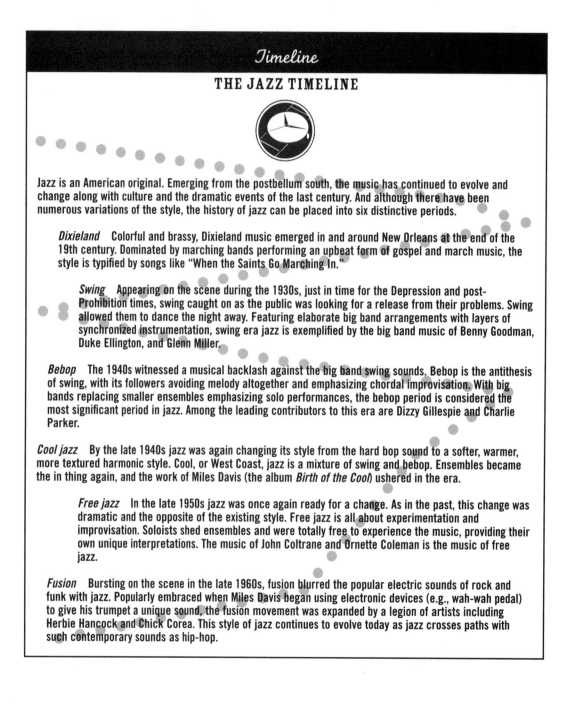

Timeline

THE JAZZ TIMELINE

Jazz is an American original. Emerging from the postbellum south, the music has continued to evolve and change along with culture and the dramatic events of the last century. And although there have been numerous variations of the style, the history of jazz can be placed into six distinctive periods.

Dixieland Colorful and brassy, Dixieland music emerged in and around New Orleans at the end of the 19th century. Dominated by marching bands performing an upbeat form of gospel and march music, the style is typified by songs like "When the Saints Go Marching In."

Swing Appearing on the scene during the 1930s, just in time for the Depression and post-Prohibition times, swing caught on as the public was looking for a release from their problems. Swing allowed them to dance the night away. Featuring elaborate big band arrangements with layers of synchronized instrumentation, swing era jazz is exemplified by the big band music of Benny Goodman, Duke Ellington, and Glenn Miller.

Bebop The 1940s witnessed a musical backlash against the big band swing sounds. Bebop is the antithesis of swing, with its followers avoiding melody altogether and emphasizing chordal improvisation. With big bands replacing smaller ensembles emphasizing solo performances, the bebop period is considered the most significant period in jazz. Among the leading contributors to this era are Dizzy Gillespie and Charlie Parker.

Cool jazz By the late 1940s jazz was again changing its style from the hard bop sound to a softer, warmer, more textured harmonic style. Cool, or West Coast, jazz is a mixture of swing and bebop. Ensembles became the in thing again, and the work of Miles Davis (the album *Birth of the Cool*) ushered in the era.

Free jazz In the late 1950s jazz was once again ready for a change. As in the past, this change was dramatic and the opposite of the existing style. Free jazz is all about experimentation and improvisation. Soloists shed ensembles and were totally free to experience the music, providing their own unique interpretations. The music of John Coltrane and Ornette Coleman is the music of free jazz.

Fusion Bursting on the scene in the late 1960s, fusion blurred the popular electric sounds of rock and funk with jazz. Popularly embraced when Miles Davis began using electronic devices (e.g., wah-wah pedal) to give his trumpet a unique sound, the fusion movement was expanded by a legion of artists including Herbie Hancock and Chick Corea. This style of jazz continues to evolve today as jazz crosses paths with such contemporary sounds as hip-hop.

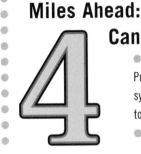

Miles Ahead:
Candidates for the Miles Davis Cosmic Jazz Combo

Pure jazz is the perfect syncopation of sound, and the following four artists are the soul of syncopation. With this cosmic combo in place, somewhere in the universe cats are grooving to jazz that's out of this world.

_01:: John Coltrane: Sax

John Coltrane almost single-handedly introduced the tenor saxophone to jazz. His groundbreaking style of playing long notes in a piercing, screaming manner coupled with his talent for improvisation has become the standard for jazz saxophonists today. After leaving the navy in 1947, Coltrane moved to Philadelphia, where he played in a number of bands, including Dizzy Gillespie's. In 1955 he joined Miles Davis's group and over the next six years gained an international reputation as the premier tenor jazz saxophonist. Always experimenting, Coltrane moved to the free jazz style in the 1960s, which allowed him to develop his unique sound even further and create music that was unquestionably pure Coltrane.

_02:: Thelonious Monk: Piano

Growing up in New York City, Monk began taking piano lessons at age 5 and by 13 was so accomplished that the Apollo Theater banned him from the weekly amateur contest because he'd won too many times. Along with Charlie Parker and Dizzy Gillespie, Monk created the jazz style called bebop in the early 1940s. By 1945 Monk's innovative form of bop stretched so ahead of its time that most other bebop players thought he was crazy; however, the style remained in vogue for the next 25 years. During his career, Monk played with many of the greats, including fellow cosmic combo members John Coltrane, Miles Davis, and Dizzy Gillespie. Classic pieces like "Round Midnight," "Straight No Chaser," and "Blue Monk" have been praised for their depth, complexity, and innovation.

_03:: Dizzy Gillespie: Trumpet

John "Dizzy" Gillespie was the heart and soul of bebop jazz. After moving to New York City in 1937, Gillespie jammed with the hottest jazz bands before he joined Cab Calloway's orchestra in 1939. During a session with Lionel Hampton, Gillespie became the first musician to record in the new bebop jazz style. Later, with Charlie Parker, he perfected the new jazz style, which took the place of swing and remained the primary force in jazz until Miles Davis's cool jazz movement replaced it in 1948. By the 1950s Gillespie transitioned from big bands to smaller combos, where he aided the development of upcoming players like John Coltrane. Gillespie's musical style and unique appearance—puffed cheeks, goatee, black horn-rimmed glasses, and beret—became the symbols of modern jazz and its rebellious nature.

_04:: Miles Davis: Bandleader

While best known for his trumpet work, Davis was an innovative bandleader and composer. Unlike the high-energy bebop style of Dizzy Gillespie, the West Coast cool jazz style that Davis created relied on phrasing and timing restraint. Davis's unique use of note placement and silence led to an intimate form of improvisation. Davis also had a knack for recruiting fantastic sidemen: he performed with Thelonious Monk in 1954 and formed a quintet with John Coltrane in 1955. In fact, almost every modern jazz great seemingly emerged from one of his bands, including Wayne Shorter, Herbie Hancock, Freddie Hubbard, and Chick Corea. Always pushing jazz forward, Davis formed an experimental quintet in the early 1960s that drifted from traditional jazz to avant-garde material to funky keyboard fusion. Even though this dismayed Davis's critics, the fans loved it.

2 Reasons Why Motown Saved America

The British are coming! The British are coming! Thank God for Hitsville, U.S.A.

_01:: The Sound Track for a New America

The growth of the black movement after the Civil Rights Act of 1964 happened just when rock and roll was ready for something new. Baby boomers hit young adulthood, bringing with them different attitudes, ideals, and disposable income. Building on the late 1950s doo-wop and girl group phenomena, Berry Gordy borrowed $800 from his family and founded Motown Records. Gordy intended to groom young black artists to be accepted by mainstream America. In this way, black rock and roll became more polished and acceptable to a wide spectrum of listeners. Not only did this appeal to the older adult audience, but it created the love songs for an entire generation. Most importantly, it became a subtle impetus for racial integration, with a young and powerful generation of black and white baby boomers sharing not only the same music but also the same attitudes and behaviors.

_02:: Motown Was America's Only Defense against the British Invasion

With the arrival of the Beatles in 1964, American rock and pop music became British. British music, dress, and style permeated all aspects of American culture, and British groups dominated Top 40 lists, radio play time, and record sales. Even most American bands sounded British. Only one rock genre survived and thrived during this onslaught: Motown. Between 1964 and 1967, Motown scored 14 number one singles and 46 Top 15 hits on the pop charts while also producing huge hits on the R&B charts. In 1967, at the pinnacle of Motown's success, 75% of its releases made the charts. Motown music peacefully coexisted with British rock because both evolved from the same African American roots. Motown even became the "safe" music for parents and older adults who had decried black rock and roll as "jungle music" just a few years earlier.

The Great Divides:
Breaks in Classical Music

If you think all classical music sounds the same, it's time to get your ears checked . . . or you could study up on the differences.

_01:: Baroque: Ornamental Floss

The earliest classical music you are likely to hear in concert comes from the baroque era (from about 1600 to 1750). The artists, painters, architects, and composers of this period filled their works with fancy little swirls and curlicues. Although baroque music might sound tame to us now, back then it was seen as highly expressive—and its complex melodies, running up and down, were seen as extremes of emotional abandon. Some of the superb composers of the baroque period were Antonio Vivaldi, George Frederick Handel, and Johann Sebastian Bach. At one time or another all of the baroque composers worked either in a noble court, in a rich man's house, or in the Christian church.

_02:: Classic: A Return to Form

All of the music in the first half of this chapter is called classical music, but just to confuse you, one of the time periods within classical music is known as the classical period (from about 1750 to 1825). The classical period was an overreaction to the excesses of the baroque—a pendulum swing in the opposite direction. Whereas baroque music had been florid, extravagant, and emotional, the classical style was sparer, more reserved, and more controlled—a return to the clean, perfectly proportioned ideal of ancient Greece. (Think white marble temples, and you'll get the idea.) Great composers of the classical period include Franz Joseph Haydn, Wolfgang Amadeus Mozart, and, in his early years, Ludwig van Beethoven. All of them wrote music in certain forms: symphonies (which Haydn basically invented), sonatas for one or two instruments, and concertos for a solo instrument with orchestra.

_03:: Romantic: A Heartfelt Response

If the restraint of the classical period had been a reaction to baroque emotion, the Romantic period (from about 1825 to 1900) was a counterreaction. In Romantic music, what mattered most was personal expression. Not surprisingly, some of the most popular music in the world comes from this period. In Romantic music you often find huge orchestras, extremes of loud and soft, and enormous passionate outbursts. To express this emotion, Romantic music often makes use of different harmonies—stretching our sense of "what key we're in" almost to the breaking point. The music sometimes seems to be crying, as in the last movement of Peter Tchaikovsky's Sixth Symphony (*Pathétique*). Because the expression of individual feelings was so important, a lot of concertos for solo instruments with orchestra were written during this period. The most celebrated composers of the Romantic period include Robert Schumann, Frédéric Chopin, Johannes Brahms, Peter Tchaikovsky, Franz Liszt, Richard Wagner, Richard Strauss, Gustav Mahler, and Antonin Dvořák.

_04:: Twentieth Century . . . and Beyond

Around 1900 composers began to break all the rules. There was no longer one reigning style—the new rule was "anything goes." After stretching harmony almost to the breaking point, composers such as Arnold Schoenberg (1874–1951) decided to break it completely. Now nothing was in any key at all—the music

---

Alphabet Soup

4 SINGER TYPES FROM THE WORLD OF OPERA

castrato [kuh-STRAH-toe]: *n* A male singer, castrated in the early years of his life, in order to prevent his voice from changing. In centuries past a castrato's voice was prized for its combination of male strength and female beauty. The most famous castrato of all time was Farinelli, who became extremely rich off his rare talent. As you can read in 6 Classical Scandals Straight from the Tabloids on p. 174, the composer Franz Joseph Haydn narrowly escaped this particular career path.

heldentenor [HEL-den-teh-NOR]: *n* The tenor (high-voiced male singer) in a dramatic opera who has a *huge* voice—big enough to trumpet over a large orchestra, knocking the audience back into their seats. A heldentenor (literally, "heroic tenor") can be found most often in operas by Wagner.

mezzo [MET-soh] *soprano*: *n* Literally, "half soprano." This is a woman whose voice—and pay—is significantly lower than a (high-voiced) soprano's.

prima donna [PREE-muh DON-na]: *n* A soprano, literally the "first lady." This is the woman who plays the heroine in an opera. Throughout history, this first lady has often been demanding to the point of ridiculousness. As a result, the expression "prima donna" is often used to refer to people who think the world revolves around them. Also known as "diva" (literally, "goddess").

---

sounded dissonant, as if all the notes were wrong. Much of the time this music was cold and unemotional, almost as if composed by a computer. Meanwhile, the composer Igor Stravinsky brought about other innovations: weird rhythms that change every second, keeping you off balance; strange combinations of instruments; and music that's in more than one key at a time (different instruments playing in different keys simultaneously). These challenging styles, believe it or not, persisted in classical music until the very late 20th century—and now the pendulum has begun to swing again. In the first decade of the 21st century, serious classical composers are once again writing beautiful, emotional melodies, constant rhythms, and harmonies that we can get our ears around. Contemporary music is now more audience-friendly than it has been in a long time.

Skirts Who Shook the Music World

Who says girls can't rock? The following women took sound to the extreme, blasting music past its traditional boundaries and breaking every convention along the way.

_01:: Grace Slick

With her powerful vocals, strong lyrics, and "up against the wall" political activism, Grace Slick was the voice of the 1960s San Francisco music scene. A former model, Slick joined Jefferson Airplane in 1965 as its lead singer and songwriter and quickly started using her songs and performances to ignite audiences to her causes—she was one of the first rock voices against the military-industrial complex and the war in Vietnam. Slick's "everything goes" peace-and-love lifestyle kept her in the eye of the public and the authorities; on at least one occasion she was arrested for public disorder when she incited the concert crowd to turn on the police in attendance. Rumor also has it that Slick the prankster tried to drop LSD into the punch bowl at her college reunion (also attended by one of President Nixon's daughters).

_02:: Joan Baez

Baez was one of the first artists in the 1960s to speak out against racism, social injustices, and the war in Vietnam. Not only did this revitalize folk music but it actually helped to create the protest music of the later 1960s and 1970s. During the 1960s, Baez helped start the career of Bob Dylan by recording his songs and sharing concert billings with him. As Baez's preoccupation with the war in Vietnam grew, so did her political activism: she founded the Institute for the Study of Non-violence and married David Harris, a student antiwar protestor jailed for draft evasion. Using her three-octave voice to spread her message, Baez has remained politically active, and her influence is still felt today in the music of the Indigo Girls and Mary Chapin Carpenter.

_03:: Chrissie Hynde

After moving from Ohio to London in the mid-1970s, Hynde co-founded the Pretenders and quickly became the prototype female punk rocker. During a time when British punk rock was male dominated, Hynde overcame the barriers and gave punk rock accept-ability to a larger audience. Her punk-tough stage presence, appearance (bangs hanging over her eyes), and witty, biting lyrics quickly made Hynde one of the most assertive female singers in rock and roll and a model for many artists who followed. Not one to shy away from a cause she believes in, Hynde still maintains her strong, assertive nature both on and off stage and has inspired a new generation, including Sheryl Crow.

Political Moments in Rock and Roll

You've heard of the separation between church and state, but what about rock and state? Here are rockers who used their power to make heavy political statements.

_01:: Frank Zappa and the Mothers of Prevention

Ah, the birth of being carded to buy a CD! In 1985 a group of four Washington, D.C., mothers founded the Parents Music Resource Center (PMRC) in an attempt to curb sexually explicit lyrics in contemporary music. Tipper Gore, wife of then-senator Al Gore, and Susan Baker, wife of Secretary of the Treasury James Baker, were two of the four founders. The PMRC persuaded the Senate Committee on Commerce, Science, and Transportation (including senior member Al Gore) to convene a hearing on truth in packaging on record albums. While notable musicians like Frank Zappa and John Denver were summoned to the stand, Dee Snider of Twisted Sister was singled out for questioning, especially by Senator Gore. The PMRC accused Twisted Sister of advocating sadomasochism, bondage, and rape in their song "Under the Blade." In turn, Snider accused the PMRC of reading into the lyrics of songs, insisting that the song "Under the Blade" was written for Twisted Sister's guitarist, who was going into surgery and was afraid of the operation.

_02:: Sinead O'Connor Takes On the Pope

The Irish singer started making waves back in 1990 when she refused to perform at a New Jersey concert after "The Star-Spangled Banner," but her best-known public stance took place on *Saturday Night Live* in 1992. After she performed the Bob Marley song "War" (a bit of a scandal in itself), she proclaimed, "Fight the real enemy!" and tore up a picture of Pope John Paul II in front of the national television audience. NBC received over 5,400 letters and calls; the National Ethnic Coalition of Organizations hired a steamroller and crushed her albums, tapes, and CDs on Sixth Avenue in New York City; and two weeks later she was booed throughout her performance at a Bob Dylan tribute concert at Madison Square Garden. When reruns of that *SNL* show air, a sans-Pope rehearsal tape is substituted.

_03:: John, Yoko, and Bed-In for Peace

John Lennon and Yoko Ono knew better than to expect a paparazzi-free wedding, so they used the press to advance their peace movement cause. On March 20, 1969, Lennon and Ono were married and the next week, in what was surely the strangest honeymoon of all time, held the first Bed-In for Peace in the presidential suite at the Amsterdam Hilton. In May they attempted to resume the bed-in in the United States, but the U.S. government refused them entry because of earlier drug charges. Instead, the bed-in took place in Montreal at the Queen Elizabeth Hotel. In front of a crowd of friends, supporters, and 50 reporters, John and Yoko stayed in bed for a week growing their hair for peace. During the week, they had recording equipment brought in and recorded the antiwar anthem "Give Peace a Chance."

_04:: Bob Dylan and the Hurricane

In 1967 Rubin "Hurricane" Carter, a successful professional boxer, received a life sentence for the murder of three people in a bar in Pat-

terson, New Jersey. Carter proclaimed his innocence and said he was the victim of a racist court and corrupt white policemen. Carter's memoirs, *The Sixteenth Round*, written during his imprisonment, caught Bob Dylan's attention, and Dylan wrote the song "Hurricane" about the case and staged two benefit concerts to raise money for Carter's defense. The first

---

Myths and Misconceptions

EVERY BREATH YOU TAKE

With the emergence of new wave rock in the early 1980s, British group The Police fused punk, reggae, and jazz into a musical style that set the direction for the next evolution of rock. In 1983 The Police released the ballad "Every Breath You Take," which became their biggest hit. While most people viewed it as a beautiful love song, that couldn't be further from the truth. The group's lead singer, Sting, has stated that the song is really about a guy stalking his ex-girlfriend. With lyrics like "every breath you take/every move you make/every bond you break/every step you take/I'll be watching you," how could so many be so wrong? Over the years another story has surfaced about the meaning of the song. Since The Police were known for making political statements, people have come to wonder if the song wasn't subtle social commentary on what the group thought was ever-increasing interference by government into private lives. After all, it was 1983—1984, and as irony would have it, drummer Stewart Copeland's father was an ex-CIA agent. George Orwell would have been proud.

concert took place in Madison Square Garden on December 8, 1975, and the second at the Astrodome in Houston, Texas, on January 26, 1976. Two months after the Houston concert, the New Jersey Supreme Court ordered a retrial for Hurricane Carter, but Carter was once again convicted and returned to prison. Finally, in 1985, Carter was released after his lawyers proved that Carter had been denied his right to a fair trial in his earlier cases.

_05:: Madonna's Prayer

Madonna's lyrics, concerts, and video performances have fueled her career and, in many cases, her critics. The 1989 video to "Like a Prayer" is the perfect example. In the video Madonna witnesses the murder of a white woman and the arrest of an innocent black man in a church, replete with religious imagery including stigmata and burning crosses. A statue of a black saint (the black man accused of the murder) comes alive when she kisses his feet. As expected, Madonna's message was lost in the public outcry over the overt erotic and perceived sacrilegious overtones of the video. Hundreds of calls and letters were sent to the networks asking the video to be removed from airplay. The video

was censured by the Vatican, and Pepsi-Cola canceled a multimillion-dollar endorsement deal with Madonna (she'd already been paid, though).

_06:: Bob Marley Gets Up, Stands Up

Marley interlaced social commentary with reggae sounds and became a major force in Jamaica's turbulent and sometimes deadly politics. During the hotly contested 1975 national elections, Marley agreed to give a concert in support of Jamaica's prime minister, Michael Manley. On the night prior to the scheduled concert, Marley was wounded in a failed assassination attempt, but he went on to play the concert the next night with his arm in sling. In an attempt to bring about reconciliation between the warring political factions in a Jamaica, Marley held a concert in 1978 that brought together Prime Minister Manley and opposition leader Edward Seaga. During the concert, both men joined Marley on stage and shook hands, an incredible development in Jamaica at the time. For his efforts, Marley received the United Nations' Peace Medal the following year. Rock's most visible spokesperson for peace and brotherhood died of cancer in 1981 at age 36.

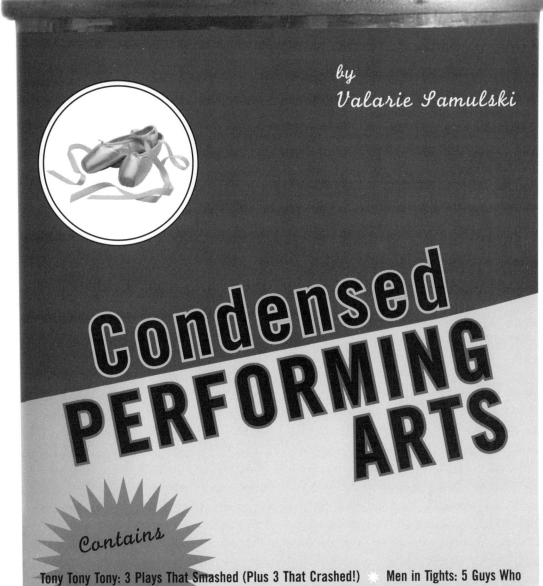

by
Valarie Samulski

Condensed PERFORMING ARTS

Contains

Tony Tony Tony: 3 Plays That Smashed (Plus 3 That Crashed!) ✳ Men in Tights: 5 Guys Who Sent the Dance World Spinning ✳ Men in Skirts?: 3 Traditions of Theatrical Cross-Dressing ✳ 6 Broadway Originals Now Available at Blockbuster ✳ 5 Barefoot Beauties Who Gave Birth to Modern Dance ✳ All the World's a Stage: 5 Traditional Theater Forms ✳ Pirouette Quartet: 4 Prima Ballerinas You Need to Know ✳ Taking It to the Street: 5 Tricks of the Trade for Aspiring Sidewalk Stars ✳ 5 Dance Styles Meant to Bring You Closer to God ✳ 3 Performance Artists Who Scare Us ✳ 6 Sexy Dances That Will Leave You Drooling ✳

Tony Tony Tony:

3

Plays That Smashed (Plus 3 That Crashed!)

Sometimes there's a fine line between *Mame* and lame. A few of these shows hit the Great White Way running, while others stumbled right from the start.

The Hits
_01:: *Cats* (1982–2000)

Who would've guessed that a bunch of human-size felines singing could make Broadway magic? Based on a book of poems by T. S. Eliot called *Old Possum's Book of Practical Cats*, the show was also unusual because it didn't have any dialogue. Entirely dependent on the music of the ubiquitous Andrew Lloyd Weber and spectacular dancing, *Cats* ran on Broadway for 18 years at the Winter Garden Theatre and eventually became the show people loved to hate before closing in 2000. Theatergoers and critics could never agree on the merit of this mighty but mindless spectacle. Reviewer Clive Barnes probably captured the ambivalence best when he said that the play was "breathtakingly unoriginal yet superbly professional."

_02:: *Deathtrap* (1978–1982)

Deathtrap, the longest running mystery play on Broadway, is a perfect example of how to steal from Shakespeare—in this case, drafting a play within a play—for stage success. Written by Ira Levin (who also wrote *A Kiss before Dying*), *Deathtrap* tells the story of a celebrated writer of Broadway thrillers suffering a dry spell, who plots to murder his student and steal the student's script to sell as his own. In a combination of suspense and humor, Levin confuses the audience with plot twists and references to his own play as it's being performed before delivering a surprise ending. *Deathtrap*, despite belonging to a rather obscure Broadway genre (the mystery play), had a story line that earned four Tony Award nominations and a film venture in 1982, starring Christopher Reeve and Michael Caine.

_03:: *Metamorphoses* (2002–2003)

Say it with us now: "More is more." Especially on Broadway. Fabulous dance routines and interesting stories aren't always enough. So, what exactly could push Ovid's Greek myths over the top? Sometimes you just have to throw in a swimming pool. And that's exactly what *Metamorphoses* did: The stage was transformed into a 27-foot-wide pool of water. It wasn't the first time that a swimming pool had been created onstage (the 1952 musical *Wish You Were Here* also had aquatic scenic design), but it was the first time audiences experienced anything of that scale. Who knows? By the next half century we might see actual tidal waves on stage.

The Flops
_01:: *Breakfast at Tiffany's* (1966)

There has to be some substance behind the hype if a Broadway play is going to make it. The famous movie *Breakfast at Tiffany's* (1961) crashed and burned on Broadway, despite being the most anticipated musical of the season. Based on Truman Capote's novella, the play starred two glamorous television names: Mary Tyler Moore and Richard Chamberlain. However, during the first preview, the author himself was quoted as saying, "I don't like the score or the leading lady," and members of the audience actually talked back to the actors and walked out. When the show closed prematurely, the producer, David Merrick, joked that "Tiffany's the jeweler promised to pay off the loss. Their competitor, Cartier's, wanted me to keep it open to damage Tiffany's."

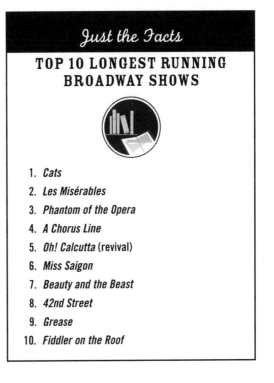

Just the Facts

TOP 10 LONGEST RUNNING BROADWAY SHOWS

1. *Cats*
2. *Les Misérables*
3. *Phantom of the Opera*
4. *A Chorus Line*
5. *Oh! Calcutta* (revival)
6. *Miss Saigon*
7. *Beauty and the Beast*
8. *42nd Street*
9. *Grease*
10. *Fiddler on the Roof*

_02:: *Miss Moffat* (1974)

Even Bette Davis couldn't pull off this Broadway save. At 66, she quit the play *Miss Moffat* and explained, "I'm too big a star to be giving a poor performance, which I'm now doing." Though she starred in the film of the same name in 1945, by 1974 she was too old to play the part, appearing visibly uncomfortable onstage and interrupting herself midsong to ask where she was. While the producer, Joshua Logan, would have liked to have placed all the blame on Bette's shoulders (especially since she had previously bailed on two other plays), the play itself was past its prime, struggling with a less-than-stellar score and frequently awkward lyrics.

_03:: *Superman* (1966)

Is there really a Superman curse? Closing after only four months in performance, it seemed as if "It's a bird . . . It's a plane . . . It's Superman" just wasn't meant to grace the stage. However, the writers, David Newman and Robert Benton, knew that the Superman comic book phenomenon should be milked somewhere, so they persevered and wrote a screenplay. *Superman*, the movie, became a series of films and a cross-marketer's dream, spawning clothing, dolls, and a television series. For the Hollywood bound, sometimes bombing on Broadway is just the beginning.

Men in Tights:
Guys Who Sent the Dance World Spinning

Not that there's anything wrong with that. The male contingent of dancers may be small, but a few fantastic guys have ignored the "twinkle toes" comments long enough to dazzle audiences.

_01:: Bill "Bojangles" Robinson
(1878–1949)

Mr. Bojangles, the father of tapology, began his dance career on street corners and in local taverns. By the age of 11, Bill Robinson was hired by a vaudeville headliner, and soon after, he was playing shows everywhere from Broadway to Hollywood to Harlem's Cotton Club. Best known for his delicate, crisp percussions executed in strict tempo and even shift, Robinson often talked to his audience and his feet, as if surprised by the rhythm chattering below. In fact, it was this squabbling characteristic that earned him the nickname Bojangles. Clearly jealous, Robinson's contemporaries complained that he could do the easiest routine in the world and get away with it simply because of his charm and charisma.

_02:: George Balanchine (1904–1983)

The most famous ballet master and choreographer of the 20th century, George Balanchine left a legacy of 425 works, 60 full-length ballets, and one of the foremost dance companies in the world (plus a few brokenhearted ballerinas). As a child, George Balanchine was offered admission to the Russian Imperial Ballet

School on a fluke while accompanying his sister to an audition. He had his heart set on joining the Imperial Naval Academy, but alas, their rolls were full, so George accepted the ballet gig. At 16 he created his first piece, *La Nuit*, and continued choreographing at every opportunity. After forming his own troupe of young dancers, Balanchine decided to leave Russia, traveling through Europe and then arriving in the United States in 1933. Once there, he founded the New York City Ballet and cofounded the School of American Ballet, where the making and marrying of ballerinas became his specialty. (Balanchine was romantically involved with several of his ballerinas and married at least three, including Maria Tallchief.)

_03:: Ted Shawn (1891–1972)

The first men to appear on the modern dance scene arrived by hitching a ride on the skirts of women. Ted Shawn intended to be a minister; he took up ballet only to help the temporary paralysis in his legs from an earlier illness. But in 1911 he saw modern dance pioneer Ruth St. Denis perform, and it changed his world. Just three years later Ted auditioned for her, made his big debut as her partner, married her, and then helped her cofound the Denishawn School and Company. Ted did the majority of teaching and choreographing at Denishawn until he broke away in 1929 to form his own company, Ted Shawn and His Men Dancers group. The company helped encourage dancing for men in colleges throughout the United States, and Shawn's repertoire grew to include 185 dances and 9 major ballets.

_04:: Alvin Ailey (1931–1989)

Alvin Ailey felt his first artistic stirrings at the age of 14 when he saw Katherine Dunham perform. Soon after, Ailey began studying at the first racially integrated dance school in California and joined its affiliated company, the Lester Horton Dance Company, in 1950. He took classes in studios all over the city of New York, searching for other dancers like himself. Eventually he formed his own dance company, which performed pieces to blues and gospel music and celebrated the heritage of African Americans. Ailey's work introduced African Americans to modern dance and introduced other people to the art and culture of African Americans. Ailey died in 1989, but his company is still among the most successful in the world.

_05:: Fred Astaire (1899–1987)

The most famous of all dancing men was a spry Nebraskan named Fred Astaire. He began his career as a tagalong little brother to his sister, Adele. At the age of six, he started performing with her in vaudeville shows, and the duo was one of the highest paid performance groups of the time. During their 27 years of performing partnership, they appeared in 10 Broadway musicals and enjoyed huge success in London. By 1932 Adele was ready to retire and Fred was faced with refashioning his career. Turning to film, he became the biggest star of the Hollywood musical era, with credits including seven highly successful films featuring his famed partnership with Ginger Rogers. He is the best-preserved choreographer because of his work on film, which includes 212 musical numbers and 133 fully developed dance routines.

Men in Skirts?:

Traditions of Theatrical Cross-Dressing

Even before there was Boy George, cross-dressing had its place in performance, stretching back to when holy men dressed up as women to merge with an androgynous god. Springboarding from this spiritual precedent, dramatic gender-bending around the world has evolved, with interesting and often shocking variations.

_01:: Japanese Kabuki Theater

Early Kabuki theater was a forum for female eroticism and prostitution, which soon blurred the boundaries between women's on-stage and "backstage" talents. After authorities forbid women to perform the theater style, men took over in 1629, performing the male and female parts. Both the Chinese and the Japanese dramatic cross-dressing traditions have developed highly refined techniques and detailed codes of movement, dress, and makeup. The Peking Opera of China and the Kabuki theater are the most popular classical theater forms in their respective countries today, and both have earned a global reputation.

_02:: Shakespearean Drama

Can you imagine watching Romeo profess his love to a boy in a wig on a balcony? In Shakespeare's time, even the most famous European dramatic traditions were initially performed by all-male casts. Sixteenth-century English society believed that the stage was no place for a woman, so all of the female Shakespearean roles were played by boys or young men. It wasn't until 1660 that the first woman, Margaret Hughes, appeared on a London stage, playing the role of Desdemona in *Othello*.

_03:: Paris Opera Ballet

Leave it to the French to throw a feminine twist into onstage gender-bending. The 19th-century danseur was a ballerina who impersonated male roles from the corps all the way to romantic leads. It turns out that the Paris Opera Ballet was actually a front for glorified prostitution during the 1830s, and women playing masculine roles became an erotic enticement, especially since the pas de deux (romantic duet) occurred between two women. The danseur usually exposed the most flesh onstage, with legs and buttocks revealed in tights or breeches instead of hidden beneath skirts. A splendid figure was a prerequisite for the position.

Broadway Originals Now Available at Blockbuster

Give 'em their regards; these shows made the jump to the big screen, creating a unique genre of American theater known as the Hollywood musical.

_01:: *Broadway Melody* (1929)

The first Hollywood musical wasn't ever an actual play. Produced by MGM, which became the greatest studio for musical films, *Broadway Melody* was simply a movie about two Broadway chorus girls in love with the same Broadway star. For audiences, the fact that it had never been a live theater show was lost amid the excitement of witnessing the very first all-singing, all-talking, all-dancing entertainment extravaganza on film. Charting the way forward from the era of silent films, *Broadway Melody* was extraordinarily original in content and craft, providing invaluable advances in sound production techniques. It was no surprise that it won the Academy Award for Best Picture in 1929, becoming the first musical film to receive that honor.

_02:: *Anything Goes* (1934)

The first real Broadway musical to be made into a film was Cole Porter's *Anything Goes* (1934). The play was the quintessential 1930s Broadway show, complete with a Depression era escapist story line that sailed the characters from New York to England on an Atlantic ocean liner. When the story traveled to the cinema, it was actually filmed twice, 20 years apart, and starred Bing Crosby both times. Yet despite its double effort, *Anything Goes* enjoyed less success as a movie than it did as a

play. It seemed that the show didn't transfer well to the screen, perhaps because only three of Cole Porter's original songs were retained in the film. However, this practice of cutting and changing the original scores from stage to screen became a precedent for the many movie musicals that would follow.

_03:: *West Side Story* (1957)

It wasn't until the late 1950s and '60s that popular Broadway plays actually began to experience equivalent success on the silver screen. *West Side Story*, a modern recapitulation of Shakespeare's *Romeo and Juliet* set in New York City, was highly successful on Broadway as the brainchild of the famed choreographer Jerome Robbins, lyricist Stephen Sondheim, and composer Leonard Bernstein. It was made into a United Artist movie in 1961, filmed on location in the streets of New York. While the exciting choreography and virile dance sequences remained consistent between the stage and screen, *West Side Story* started another trend in movie musical production that blurred the boundaries between theater and film stars. Three of the main roles in the movie were vocally dubbed, seeing as the film stars recruited for the roles couldn't quite match the singing talents of their Broadway counterparts. Despite the lip-synch factor, *West Side Story* won Best Picture in 1961.

_04:: *My Fair Lady* (1956)

My Fair Lady shared a similar backstory. The play was a revised version of George Bernard Shaw's *Pygmalion* (1913). Opening on Broadway in 1956, it also harkened to the familiar themes of a classic: a Cinderella story, in which a lower-class girl is transformed into a lady of society. While Julie Andrews played the stage role to much acclaim, MGM didn't choose her for the movie version they produced in 1964. The part went to Audrey Hepburn, whose voice was then dubbed by the same Marni Nixon who had sung for Natalie Wood in the movie version of *West Side Story*. Maybe it was Marni who deserves all the credit, since *My Fair Lady* also won Best Picture in 1964.

_05:: *The Sound of Music* (1959)

As for Julie Andrews, she rebounded quite nicely the following year with a role in one of the greatest movie musicals of all time. *The Sound of Music* was a Rodgers and Hammerstein creation that opened on Broadway in 1959. When 20th Century Fox made it into a movie in 1965, it not only won Best Picture but also dethroned *Gone with the Wind* at the box office. Even today, it's hard to imagine a child unfamiliar with the Von Trapp family version of "Do Re Mi." In this way, *The Sound of Music* showed that moving pictures expanded the art of theater beyond the elitism of the stage. Films provided a cheap and accessible way to experience dramatic art, especially for people who didn't live in urban centers.

_06:: *Grease* (1972)

A new measure of success for movie musicals was set forth in 1978 with Paramount's release of *Grease*. The Broadway play by Jim Jacobs and Warren Casey opened in New York in 1972, replete with the tragic humor of a group of 1950s teens singing and dancing to a rock-and-roll score. By the time it made it to the big screen, several songs had been changed and all of the original actors had been replaced with movie stars like John Travolta, Olivia Newton-John, and Stockard Channing. While *Grease* never won Best Picture, it became the highest-grossing movie musical of all time and was even released in Mexico as *Vaselina*. These crossovers into popular culture and high-revenue ventures mark the moment when Hollywood surpassed Broadway to become the main event in modern dramatic performing arts.

5 Barefoot Beauties Who Gave Birth to Modern Dance

Burn your bras . . . and your pointe shoes! Modern dance grew out of women's desires to reclaim their bodies at the turn of the 20th century. Rebelling against classical ballet's physical deformation of the body (pointe shoes *hurt*!) and images of women as fragile flowers, these geniuses set out to craft their own styles of movement.

_01:: Isadora Duncan (1877–1927)

Isadora Duncan's dramatic personality and proclaimed spirituality managed to draw critical attention to modern dance. Duncan set out to realign dance with nature by linking her movement to the spirit. To free up her body, she decided her corset had to go. Isadora is famed for skipping and leaping around in gauzy-thin tunics, and her dances tended to expose previously hidden areas of her form, such as the inner arm, thigh, and neck. She legitimated her aesthetic choices by saying that "Nudeness is truth, it is beauty, it is art . . . my body is the temple of my art. I expose it as a shrine for the worship of beauty." Her status as a single woman who'd had two children out of wedlock made her free-spirited sensibilities even more controversial.

_02:: Ruth St. Denis (1877–1968)

Isadora gets the credit for starting the modern-dance trend, but Ruth St. Denis made it popular. She worked her whole life in variety and vaudeville theater before she and her husband, Ted Shawn, founded the Denishawn School and Company in 1915. Not only did the school provide a seedbed for the next generation of choreographers, but its touring schedule brought dance to several American cities and small towns. While Isadora Duncan made her reputation mostly in Europe, Ruth St. Denis single-handedly brought modern dance into the American consciousness and demonstrated how dance could be an avenue to self-sufficiency for women.

_03:: Doris Humphrey (1895–1958)

Doris Humphrey began her serious dance training at the Denishawn School in 1917 and worked closely with Ruth St. Denis. In 1928 she set out to refine the sociological lens of dance when she formed her own school and company with Charles Weidman. Her explorations harnessed the power of breath and highlighted the fall and recovery of the body in relationship to gravity. As a result, she created a physical dialogue of conflict between stability and imbalance. Humphrey often described dancing as "the arc between two deaths" and maintained that "[t]here is only one thing to dance about: the meaning of one's personal experience." It's not surprising, then, that her dance themes were often concerned with examining and expressing the individual's voice in relation to the masses.

_04:: Martha Graham (1894–1991)

Martha Graham, another Denishawn student and contemporary of Humphrey, explored similar themes in her work. However, she focused more specifically on the emotional reasons for movement. For Graham, the contraction of the torso and spine was the purest form of expression, and her art was focused on creating an expressive physical language with an integrity all its own. Graham believed that "[m]ovement is the one speech which cannot lie." Both Doris and Martha were revolutionary in that they created large bodies of work cultivated from women's social and emotional perspectives, and developed original female voices that still echo through modern dance today.

_05:: Katherine Dunham (1910–)

Once the grounds of physical self-expression had been broken, modern dance exploded in new directions. Katherine Dunham used this liberation to focus specifically on the experience of African Americans, as she retraced Caribbean, West African, and South American lineages in her dance. She expanded the developing modern-dance techniques to reflect traditional movements and styles, and she's used her PhD in anthropology to research and incorporate the folklore of the African diaspora into the American consciousness. Using her art form purposefully as a means of social commentary and political activism, Dunham set a new bar for how modern dance would confront a changing world.

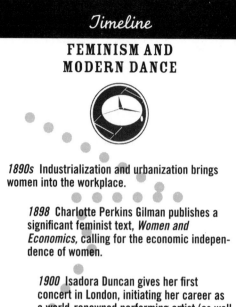

Timeline

FEMINISM AND MODERN DANCE

1890s Industrialization and urbanization brings women into the workplace.

1898 Charlotte Perkins Gilman publishes a significant feminist text, *Women and Economics*, calling for the economic independence of women.

1900 Isadora Duncan gives her first concert in London, initiating her career as a world-renowned performing artist (as well as unmarried mother) and placing herself shamelessly in the public sphere.

1915 Ruth St. Denis cofounds the Denishawn School and Company—the first American modern dance company and the first successful female business venture in performing arts in the United States.

1919 Women's suffrage groups finally secure the right to vote, giving women an official voice.

1926 Martha Graham debuts her first choreography in New York, bringing women's issues into the physical realm.

1928 Doris Humphrey forms her own company with Charles Weidman and begins an important career as a female choreographer making statements about individual voices in a collective society.

1932 Katherine Dunham begins to create a visual language through body motion to specifically communicate ideas about the African American subculture.

All the World's a Stage: Traditional Theater Forms

5

The first actors were probably primitive holy men, performing ancient religious rituals. That theatrical storytelling tradition lives on, perpetuating legends, rituals, and mysteries across the globe.

_01:: The Peruvian Chilinchili Festival

For many Native American cultures, theater has a cosmic significance, and the belief in immortality and the worship of the dead have always been essential features of religious practices. Because ancestral connections are so important, many theatrical traditions focus on re-creating those myths and legends. The Peruvian Chilinchili Festival features actors who represent the souls of the dead, while the rest of the community reacts as if the actors are actually the dead ancestors they are impersonating.

_02:: Chantways of the Navajo Indians

Native American theater also serves as a forum for communal celebrations, especially since the audience members often tend to be participants instead of just spectators. The Navajo Indians perform chantways, which are 100-hour-long celebrations involving the entire community, where no costume, word, gesture, movement, or song is left to chance. Because of the social and cultural destruction that colonization caused, theater is an essential way of preserving the ancient traditions and tribal histories.

_03:: Dō Ceremony of the Bambara People

Traditional communities in Africa use morality plays to instruct young adults about appropriate social roles. In fact, some initiation ceremonies actually simulate the death and resurrection of the initiates. Young men bid their final farewells to loved ones before their isolation period and continue to act dead for a few days upon returning to the village. In Mali, the Dō Ceremony of the Bambara people occurs every seven years at the end of the initiation period. It takes over three months to perform and features masked men speaking a private language. For African cultures, traditional theater often provides a vehicle for border crossing between life stages and spiritual states.

_04:: Javanese Shadow Theater

Shadow theater originated in China between 140 and 86 BCE and exists in Japan, Cambodia, Turkey, Egypt, and India (to name a few), but Java is the home of its highest and finest form. Javanese shadow theater began as part of ancient Malayo-Polynesian religions and incorporates themes from Javanese cosmology into elaborate puppet shows that may last anywhere from an entire night to a whole week. The showman, or *dalang*, acts as the spiritual leader in the community who possesses the ability to remember the long legends that make up the text of the performances. The *dalang* is capable of improvising at whim but also maintains the traditional movements of the ornate buffalo-leather puppets.

_05:: Japan's Nō Theater

Japan's nō theater has received as much international acclaim as the Javanese shadow theater. Originating in the late 14th century, nō theater survives unaltered as a living testimony to the values of samurai culture. In a blend of shamanistic traditions and Buddhism, nō plays emphasize spiritual energy over actual dialogue or movement. Performing with utmost simplicity, nō actors are highly respected in Japanese society, and their art form is passed down from father to son in organized stages and hierarchical progression. This theater of the warrior class isn't only a Japanese status symbol; it's also come to be known throughout the world as one of the most highly refined theatrical arts.

Pirouette Quartet:
4 Prima Ballerinas You Need to Know

So, you think prima ballerinas are just girly-girls who twirl through the air to pretty music? Actually, being a prima ballerina requires training more grueling than that of your average linebacker. And the better the ballerina, the more effortless it looks.

_01:: Marie Taglioni (1804–1884)

Marie Taglioni was born into a family of Italian dancers, choreographers, and ballet masters. Under the watchful eye of her father, Marie perfected a new and graceful method of rising up onto the tips of her toes and balancing there while executing the steps of her dances. Then, in 1832, she changed dance when she starred in *La Sylphide*. The ballet has come to be acknowledged as the first exhibition of pointework, and it earned her much praise. Marie's perfection and fantastic performance of this new technique in combination with the overall lightness, ease, and grace of her dancing style earned her the title of the first great romantic ballerina. Her romantic nature, however, didn't quite carry beyond the stage. She petitioned for divorce in 1835 when her husband, Count Gilbert de Voisins, tried to end her dancing career.

_02:: Anna Pavlova (1881–1931)

While Marie Taglioni set the precedent for the ethereal otherworldliness that's become the ballerina's hallmark, her Russian successor catapulted ballet into the international spotlight. Enrolling in the Imperial Ballet School at the age of 10, Anna Pavlova began her professional career at 16, and dreamed of following in Marie's footsteps. Performing throughout Europe to popular acclaim, her travels eventually brought her to the United States, where each of her performances received a standing ovation. America, along with the rest of the world, was taken by Pavlova's virtuosic technique blended with her sensuous charm. She created a dance style so lyrical that it appeared to be a bodily song. Undoubtedly, Pavlova's most famous solo was *The Dying Swan*, choreographed for her to the music of Saint-Saëns, which showcased her highly emotional dancing. The performance secured her reputation as the greatest interpretive ballerina and remains unsurpassed even today.

_03:: Margot Fonteyn (1919–1991)

The national ballet tradition that nurtured Russian greats like Anna Pavlova didn't exist in other places. In fact, British ballet was rather unimportant on the international scene until Margot Fonteyn began to grace its stages. Born in 1919, Margot began to study dance at the age of 4 in local classes in Surrey, England. She eventually enrolled in the Sadler's Wells School in London and made her first solo debut with the Vic-Wells Ballet (which evolved into the Royal Ballet) while she was still a student. At 16 she became the company's first prima ballerina and began her long career of international acclaim. It wasn't until 1949, however, when she made her New York debut in *Sleeping Beauty*, that Margot's faultless line and lyric musicality brought legitimacy to the British ballet. Her status as Britain's greatest ballerina continues even today, especially since Fonteyn never formally

retired but chose instead to make a graceful exit from England's Royal Ballet instead.

_04:: Maria Tallchief (1925–)

America was a rather late bloomer in the production of homegrown dancing divas. Elizabeth Marie Tallchief was born on an Osage Indian reservation in Oklahoma in 1925. When her dance talent became apparent, her mother took her to California, where she encountered two of Europe's most famous ballet lineages. (One of her teachers had worked directly with Enrico Cechetti, the great Italian ballet master who codified an entire ballet technique, and the other, Bronislava Nijinska,

---

Inventions and Innovations

SHOES THAT GO STRAIGHT TO THE POINTE

Before Marie Taglioni stunned her audiences with pointework in 1832, ballerinas actually gave their performances in high-heeled shoes. But as the art of rising up and balancing oneself on the tips of the toes became a staple of ballet, new shoes became a necessity. In their earliest form, they arrived as satin slippers reinforced with cotton wadding, glue, and starch. Today's pointe shoes, however, are made with many layers of cloth (linen, felt, canvas, etc.) held together by special glue, though they feel much like wooden boxes. Of course, ballerinas have all kinds of tricks for breaking them in, including slamming them in doors, banging them with hammers, and soaking them in water, all in the course of becoming a podiatrist's worst nightmare.

was a famous Russian ballerina and ballet choreographer in her own right.) At 17 Tallchief moved to New York City, where she was almost immediately apprenticed to the Ballet Russe de Monte Carlo and chose *Maria* as her new stage name. It was at the Russian Tea Room in New York that her life intersected with the great ballet choreographer George Balanchine, whom she eventually married.

Their artistic collaboration contributed to the formation of the New York City Ballet. In 1949 Maria Tallchief danced the lead role in *Firebird* with such blazing speed, energy, and brilliance that it became the pinnacle of her success. She was the first true star of the New York City Ballet and the first world-famous ballerina who did not train in Europe or make her reputation there.

Taking It to the Street:
5 Tricks of the Trade for Aspiring Sidewalk Stars

Entire subcultures of people make their living as performers but have never set foot on a stage. For these sidewalk stars, busy thoroughfares in tourist hot spots provide the best display for talent.

_01:: Sword Swallowing

Sword swallowing originated among the magicians and priests of India as a demonstration of their invulnerability and connection with the gods. The art form was eventually undertaken by people in Greece, China, Japan, and across Europe, and made its American debut in 1817. The dangerous challenge of pushing steel blades down the throat requires a developed control of the gag reflex and an esophageal muscular strength capable of holding the sword in place. Because the blades are dulled, it is actually the peril of pushing the sword too far into the body and rupturing internal organs rather than the slicing of flesh that causes most injuries. Despite sword swallowing's popularity in sideshows and circuses throughout the 1900s, today there are fewer than 50 remaining performers worldwide.

_02:: Contortion

Contortionists first appeared in the pictorial and sculptural work of ancient Egypt, Greece, and Rome. Contrary to popular belief, there's no such thing as being double-jointed. The term is more like a slang word used to describe the extreme flexibility exhibited by contortionists, which is actually the result of constant stretching. While certain people may be born with a higher proportion of muscle to tendon, which increases flexibility, contortionists have also developed the ability to relax the antagonistic muscle groups involved in an action. This loosens their joints and extends their range of motion. In India, Yogic philosophy developed an entire physical practice that promotes the kind of relaxation and balance necessary to assume seemingly impossible postures. Today you don't even have to be lucky enough to catch a street show where someone crams herself into a small box; just stop by any yoga studio and check out the aspiring contortionists trying to put their legs behind their heads.

_03:: Juggling

Many performers of seemingly impossible feats attribute their abilities to hours of practice and impenetrable mental focus. Juggling has even been credited with a Zen-like quality. The trick is discovering your own perfect inner rhythm, which depends on the length, weight, size, and shape of the different parts of your body and their proportional relationship to the whole. The greatest skill of the juggler, however, is cultivated ambidexterity, which promotes rhythmic coordination between the two sides of the body and brain. Most importantly though, juggling masters claim that you have to cultivate a state of mind and being that allows for fluidity of release, lets the balls drop, allows them to land in your hands, and demonstrates the patience of return.

_04:: Mime

If they aren't busy thrilling us or demonstrating a higher level of consciousness, street performers perpetually endeavor to make us laugh. Mime, the art of silent acting, existed as three recognizable traditions in the 1800s: the Oriental, Italian, and French schools. While

Oriental mime stayed closely connected to the traditional theater in China and Japan, Italian mime eventually evolved into the circus clown acts of today. It was the French mime Marcel Marceau, however, who helped establish mime as an art form in and of itself. The French style requires extraordinary balance, control, flexibility, strength, and coordination

---

Strange but True

STREET-FAIR TRIVIA

Brad Byers holds the official world record for the most swords swallowed. On August 13, 1999, he swallowed and turned ten 28-inch swords. In 2002 the first Annual Sword Swallowing Convention was held, and 19 delegates swallowed a total of 50 swords simultaneously.

Female hormones actually increase physical flexibility while male hormones reduce it, which may explain why many of today's contortionists are women.

Due to their ambidexterity, Leonardo da Vinci, Michelangelo, Muhammad Ali, Willie Mays, and Michael Jordan all could have been master jugglers in addition to their other famed vocations.

Mime was one of the earliest mediums of self-expression, giving preverbal people a way to communicate.

Ventriloquism is thought to be the explanation behind the famous oracle at Delphi in Greek mythology.

to subtly mimic human motions and create a physical landscape of illusion.

_05:: Ventriloquism

Ventriloquists pushed illusion in the opposite direction by developing vocal techniques that allowed them to speak without moving their lips or jaw. In fact, they've actually traced their lineage from ancient Egyptian and Hebrew civilizations to the early Romans and Greeks. Capitalizing on the fact that hearing is the least reliable sense, ventriloquists use controlled breathing; refined speech mechanics; and the relaxation of the face, lips, and throat to project their voice into their inanimate partners. Edgar Bergen was America's most famous ventriloquist, though not necessarily one of the greatest. While he couldn't prevent his lips from moving, audiences overlooked the fault because it seemed he really believed in his dummy partner, Charlie McCarthy. The friendship between Edgar and Charlie made them stars of radio, television, nightclubs, and movies. When Charlie was finally retired to the Smithsonian Institution in 1978, he left with the humor that had endeared him to audiences for years, claiming, "Well, at least I won't be the only dummy in Washington."

Dance Styles Meant to Bring You Closer to God

If you're looking to attract some heavenly bodies to the dance floor, maybe you just need to refine your moves. The following styles were designed to drive dancers toward religious ecstasy.

_01:: Sufis, or Whirling Dervishes

One of the most common ways to transcend to the spiritual realm using movement is to induce a trance. In the eighth century Islamic mysticism began developing in the Middle East in a sect known as the Sufi order. Following the practices of their founder, Mawlawiyah Rumi, the Sufis, or whirling dervishes, developed complex rituals designed to send them into religious ecstasy and mystical union with God. Dance was used as a means for uprooting man's foot from the terrestrial and transporting him toward the celestial. As Sufi dervishes spin they must expand their awareness to include several dimensions at once: consciousness of their own physical axis, inward pronunciation of God, awareness of where they are in space, and constant connection to the religious lineage. As their minds open to accommodate this simultaneity and their bodies engage in continuous circles, they find new spiritual consciousness and express their infinite love of God.

_02:: Yoruba Sacred Dance

In west Africa, the Yoruba people believe that dance is a way to bring one "nearer the time of the gods on earth." Their dances consist of complex rhythmic structures emphasized by the relationship between dancers and drummers. And as the dancer begins to express a myriad of rhythmic patterns, she simultaneously opens herself to receive the presence of a deity. The possessed dancer is described as being mounted by the deity, and she becomes the vessel for expressing the essence of its power and delivering messages to the community. Yoruba spiritual practices use dance as a way to communicate with the different representations of God, where dancers are thought to capture and spread the energy of God that is present in all things.

_03:: Vodun

The mass relocation of African people during the era of slavery caused a deprivation of family, community, and homeland, and created the need for spiritual systems that linked people to their ancestors. As a result, several branches of spiritual practice evolved in the New World that were rooted in Yoruba tradition. The most well-known derivative of Yoruba spirituality is vodun, Haiti's system of concepts describing the relation of humankind to ancestors and the natural and supernatural forces in the world. The sacred dances of Haiti were designed to open the body and consciousness for possession by the deities. In fact, the intensity of these interactions with deities can be so great that it requires an intervention with the *maison*, a particular dance that shifts the energy from religious to sexual ecstasy, to break the possession and purge the deity.

_04:: Brazilian Candomblé

Brazil also has its own version of the Yoruba spiritual tradition. Candomblé is based on the worship of nature deities (similar to those of Yoruba and Vodun traditions) that are paired with Roman Catholic saints. On the day of the patron saint, there are public ceremonies where song, drumming, and dancing are employed as attractive forces to the spirits, and trances are induced so that dancers can reenact spiritual myths under the deities' direction. The African origins of dancing divination have evolved even further in Brazil with the umbanda tradition—one of the first conscious attempts to create a national popular religion by combining Yoruba sacred dance with Native American and spiritualist practices.

_05:: The Shakers

Believe it or not, Christianity had it own version of ecstatic dancing despite a reputation as one of the world's most physically repressive religions. The Shakers, a Christian sect that existed during the late 18th and early 19th centuries, developed a repertoire of dances designed for worship. Their founder, Ann Lee, proclaimed that "[d]ance is the greatest gift that ever was made for the purification of the soul." In fact, as a sect that practiced celibacy, the Shakers believed that skipping, shouting, falling, and turning were all effective methods for "shaking" out the evils of carnal desire. It was by dancing that the Shakers believed they made themselves worthy of God. Whatever the specific motivation or actual discipline, people have found dancing to be a transformative and transcendent experience for millennia.

Performance Artists Who Scare Us

Performance artists are supposed to push our limits, but some go past the unexpected and into the unbelievable. Not only would we never do these things, but we would never think of them in the first place.

_01:: Allan Kaprow

If you were an audience member at Allan Kaprow's performances, chances are, you were also a participant. In 1967 Kaprow created a piece called *Self-Service*, which featured (1) people in New York standing on empty bridges and watching cars pass until 200 red ones went by (fun), (2) people in Boston tar-papering several cars in a parking lot, and (3) people in Los Angeles driving into filling sta-tions in cars that erupted with white foam from the windows. He intended the random-ness of these activities to question the iden-tity and value of each action as art and focus close attention on their enactment and the idea of performing in general. Do you get it?

_02:: Carolee Schneemann

Carolee Schneemann, one of the most famous female performance artists, has focused her

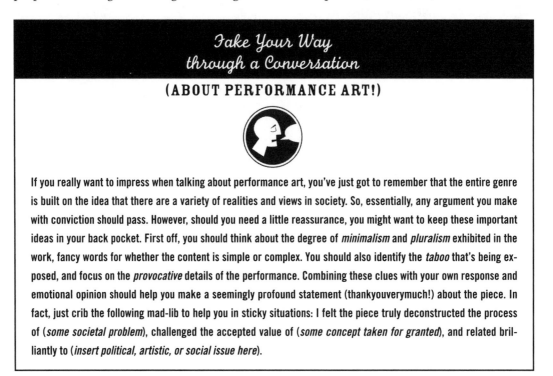

Fake Your Way through a Conversation

(ABOUT PERFORMANCE ART!)

If you really want to impress when talking about performance art, you've just got to remember that the entire genre is built on the idea that there are a variety of realities and views in society. So, essentially, any argument you make with conviction should pass. However, should you need a little reassurance, you might want to keep these important ideas in your back pocket. First off, you should think about the degree of *minimalism* and *pluralism* exhibited in the work, fancy words for whether the content is simple or complex. You should also identify the *taboo* that's being ex-posed, and focus on the *provocative* details of the performance. Combining these clues with your own response and emotional opinion should help you make a seemingly profound statement (thankyouverymuch!) about the piece. In fact, just crib the following mad-lib to help you in sticky situations: I felt the piece truly deconstructed the process of (*some societal problem*), challenged the accepted value of (*some concept taken for granted*), and related bril-liantly to (*insert political, artistic, or social issue here*).

work on gender issues. Her piece *Interior Scroll* (1975) featured Schneemann standing naked on a table and ritualistically painting herself with mud until she began to extract a paper scroll from her vagina and read from it. For Schneemann, this action was the embodiment of the various potentials of the female reproductive organ. She thought of her vagina "physically, conceptually: as a sculptural form, an architectural referent, the sources of sacred knowledge, ecstasy, birth passage, transformation." Creating pieces laced with subversive feminism, Schneemann uses her body as a representation of the larger social world.

_03:: Chris Burden

Chris Burden is the best-known American body artist. His work explores different means of self-mutilation; in past pieces he's dragged himself bare-chested through broken glass or shot a bullet through his arm. His 1974 piece, *Trans-Fixed*, featured Burden being nailed to the back of a Volkswagen and displaying his pseudo-crucifixion on the street. When it comes to performance art, we may never completely understand it, but it's certain that we'll at least have a response.

Sexy Dances That Will Leave You Drooling

OK, so we said dancing was all about religious ecstasy and preserving history. Very fine goals. But, we admit, almost every dance has a little something to do with sex.

_01:: Belly Dancing

Belly dancing, one of the oldest dance forms, is an expression of the process of creating and transmitting life through the act of giving birth. In fact, it existed thousands of years before Christ in countries as far apart as India and Spain. Temple dancers in India and in the Middle East actually used sex as a worshiping tool, and their dancing provided a release of energy that enabled them to unite with the divine spirit. Migrating populations of Gypsies eventually became the most famous belly dancers, including the Ghawazee of Egypt and the Cengi of Turkey. Flourishing in the harems

of the Middle East, belly dancing was performed by women for their own sex as a celebration of procreative power. Today it's still a popular living art practiced by a wide variety of people across the world.

_02:: Samba

One of the reasons Brazil holds the unofficial title of sexiest nation is because of its national dance, the samba. It was derived from a Congolese-Angolan dance known as *umbigada*, where soloists would swing their hips and stamp their feet in the middle of a circle, calling the next soloist forward with the thrust of the belly button. The female *sambista* assumes her sexuality via a whirlwind of the hips and thrusting, circular movements emphasizing the pelvis and buttocks. And she (deservedly) attracts attention for her frenetic exuberance and elation in liberating her sexual impulses. Beginning as a traditional dance called *samba de roda*, the samba was eventually popularized into several hybrid versions that have become a hallmark of Brazil's Carnaval and an international symbol of sexiness.

_03:: Argentine Tango

Once dance becomes a couple's event, sexual passions are expressed with exciting tension. The Argentine tango was the first social dance with overt sexuality to make the worldwide sweep. Originally a dance of the brothels, it became popular and stylized between 1907 and 1913 due to Parisian enthusiasm. The tango is based on the interlacing of legs and balancing of bodies as they strike one another, where the movements are joined in a way that melds two bodies into one. Author Angela Rippon captured it best when she described the tango as "a sensual coupling, forged by raw emotion. The closest thing you'll find to a vertical expression of the horizontal desire."

_04:: Cancan

The French, it seems, had a weakness for salacious dances. In the 1840s an acrobatic form of the quadrille, called the cancan, was introduced. Originally danced by couples, the excessive display of ankles that occurred when women kicked up their petticoats was simply shocking. After waning in the 1880s as a popular social dance, it was adopted and adapted by professional dancers in dance halls and

cabarets, including the Moulin Rouge. The cancan quickly became a burlesque profession characterized by black stockings, high heels, garters, lace panties, and kicks with wide-spreading legs.

_05:: American Burlesque

American burlesque began as a frivolous appeal to the animalistic side of man and a forum for displaying female beauty. It all happened quite by accident when a group of stranded ballet dancers were incorporated into a vaudevillian musical extravaganza called *The Black Crook*. It didn't take long for producers and performers to realize the potential of scantily clad dancers parading onstage. Burlesque evolved through the era of minstrel shows and entered a golden age in 1905. The standard format included variety acts and bits mingled with musical numbers, and performed with bawdy humor by beautiful women. Burlesque flourished with honky-tonk flare, making its home in half beer hall–half brothel establishments, where Mae West soon became its biggest star.

_06:: Striptease

By the 1920s Broadway had more nudity than burlesque theater, so the novelty of the striptease was introduced. The Minsky brothers were the first to glorify the tease at their National Winter Garden Theater on the Lower East Side of New York City, which was considered to be the high temple of American burlesque. By the 1960s there were more than 8,000 women in America making their living as go-go dancers, and by the 1970s male strippers had formed their own contingent. Eventually, however, the comedy, the tease, even the stripping began to disappear from this performance art form. Instead, blatant nudity and pornographic undertones replaced what was once a more subtle and silly form of sexual expression. While there are varying levels of comfort with sexual expression, dance can often provide a way to balance our desire and need for such expression against the perils of overexploiting our sexuality.

by
William Irwin

Condensed PHILOSOPHY

Contains

11 Quotes You Probably Heard in Your Graduation Speech ✳ 4 Great Books That Won't Put You to Sleep ✳ Behind the Philosophy: 9 Bad Boys of Thought ✳ 3 Eastern Sages Who Leave the West Behind ✳ Philosophy Doesn't Grow on Trees, but It Does Have 6 Branches ✳ 3 Isms Finally Put in Their Place ✳ Thinking Positive!: 5 Feel-Good Philosophies ✳ 3 Bad Catchphrases (and the Philosophies behind Them) ✳ Name-Dropping 101: 3 Schools of Thought That Will Impress the Opposite Sex ✳

11

Quotes You Probably Heard in Your Graduation Speech

Oh, the advice you'll get. Between all the lectures, scolding, and parental nagging you've probably been subject to, chances are some of these quotes should sound familiar by now. But do you actually know what they mean?

_01:: "The unexamined life is not worth living."—Socrates (470–399 BCE)

Socrates' belief that we must reflect upon the life we live was partly inspired by the famous phrase inscribed at the shrine of the oracle at Delphi, "Know thyself." The key to finding value in the prophecies of the oracle was self-knowledge, not a decoder ring. Socrates felt so passionately about the value of self-examination that he closely examined not only his own beliefs and values but those of others as well. More precisely, through his relentless questioning, he forced people to examine their own beliefs. He saw the citizens of his beloved Athens sleepwalking through life, living only for money, power, and fame, so he became famous trying to help them.

_02:: "Entities should not be multiplied unnecessarily." —William of Ockham (1285–?1349)

Commonly known as Ockham's razor, the idea here is that in judging among competing philosophical or scientific theories, all other things being equal, we should prefer the simplest theory. Scientists currently speak of four forces in the universe: gravity, the elec-

tromagnetic force, the strong nuclear force, and the weak nuclear force. Ockham would certainly nod approvingly at the ongoing attempt to formulate a grand unified theory, a single force that encompasses all four. The ultimate irony of Ockham's razor may be that some have used it to prove God is unnecessary to the explanation of the universe, an idea Ockham the Franciscan priest would reject.

_03:: "The life of man [is] solitary, poor, nasty, brutish, and short." —Thomas Hobbes (1588–1679)

Referring to the original state of nature, a hypothetical past before civilization, Hobbes saw no reason to be nostalgic. Whereas Rousseau said, "Man is born free, and he is everywhere in chains," Hobbes believed we find ourselves living a savage, impossible life without education and the protection of the state. Human nature is bad: we'll prey on one another in the most vicious ways. No doubt the state imposes on our liberty in an overwhelming way. Yet Hobbes's claim was that these very chains were absolutely crucial in protecting us from one another.

_04:: "I think therefore I am."
—René Descartes (1596–1650)

Descartes began his philosophy by doubting everything in order to figure out what he could know with absolute certainty. Although he could be wrong about *what* he was thinking, *that* he was thinking was undeniable. Upon the recognition that "I think," Descartes concluded that "I am." On the heels of believing in himself, Descartes asked, What am I? His answer: a thinking thing (*res cogitans*) as opposed to a physical thing extended in three-dimensional space (*res extensa*). So, based on this line, Descartes knew he existed, though he wasn't sure if he had a body. It's a philosophical cliff-hanger; you'll have to read *Meditations* to find out how it ends.

_05:: "To be is to be perceived (*Esse est percipi*)." Or, "If a tree falls in the forest and no one is there to hear it, does it make a sound?"
—Bishop George Berkeley (1685–1753)

As an idealist, Berkeley believed that nothing is real but minds and their ideas. Ideas do not exist independently of minds. Through a complicated and flawed line of reasoning he concluded that "to be is to be perceived." Something exists only if someone has the idea of it. Though he never put the question in the exact words of the famous quotation, Berkeley would say that if a tree fell in the forest and there was no one (not even a squirrel) there to hear it, not only would it not make a sound, but there would be no tree. The good news is, according to Berkeley, that the mind of God always perceives everything. So the tree will always make a sound, and there's no need to worry about blipping out of existence if you fall asleep in a room by yourself.

_06:: "We live in the best of all possible worlds."—Gottfried Wilhelm Leibniz (1646–1716)

Voltaire's famous novel *Candide* satirizes this optimistic view. And looking around you right now you may wonder how anyone could actually believe it. But Leibniz believed that before creation God contemplated every possible way the universe could be and chose to create the one in which we live because it's the best. The principle of sufficient reason holds that for everything, there must be a sufficient reason why it exists. And according to Leibniz the only sufficient reason for the world we live in is that God created it as the best possible universe. God could have created a universe in which no one ever did wrong, in which there was no human evil, but that would require humans to be deprived of the gift of free will and thus would not be the best possible world.

_07:: "The owl of Minerva spreads its wings only with the falling of the dusk."—G. W. F. Hegel (1770–1831)

Similar to "vision is 20/20 in hindsight," Hegel's poetic insight says that philosophers are impotent. Only after the end of an age can philosophers realize what it was about. And by then it's too late to change things. It wasn't until the time of Immanuel Kant (1724–1804) that the true nature of the Enlightenment was understood, and Kant did nothing to change the Enlightenment; he just consciously perpetuated it. Marx (1818–1883) found Hegel's apt description to be indicative of the problem with philosophy and responded, "the philosophers have only *interpreted* the world differently, what matters is to *change* it."

_08:: "Who is also aware of the tremendous risk involved in faith—when he nevertheless makes the leap of faith—this [is] subjectivity . . . at its height." —Søren Kierkegaard (1813–1855)

In a memorable scene from *Indiana Jones and the Last Crusade*, Indy deduced that the final step across his treacherous path was a leap of faith. And so it is in Kierkegaard's theory of stages of life. The final stage, the religious stage, requires passionate, subjective belief rather than objective proof, in the paradoxical and the absurd. So, what's the absurd? That which Christianity asks us to accept as true, that God became man born of a virgin, suffered, died, and was resurrected. Abraham was the ultimate "knight of faith" according to Kierkegaard. Without doubt there is no faith, and so in a state of "fear and trembling" Abraham was willing to break the universal moral law against murder by agreeing to kill his own son, Isaac. God rewarded Abraham's faith by providing a ram in place of Isaac for the sacrifice. Faith has its rewards, but it isn't rational. It's beyond reason. As Blaise Pascal said, "The heart has its reason which reason does not know."

_09:: "God is dead." —Friedrich Nietzsche (1844–1900)

Well, you might not hear this one in a graduation speech, but you'll probably hear it in college. Actually, Nietzsche never issued this famous proclamation in his own voice but rather put the words in the mouth of a character he called the madman and later in the mouth of another character, Zarathustra. Nevertheless, Nietzsche endorsed the words. "God is dead" is often mistaken as a statement of atheism. It is not, though Nietzsche himself was an atheist. "Dead" is metaphorical in this context, meaning belief in the God of Christianity is worn out, past its prime, and on the decline. God is lost as the center of life and the source of values. Nietzsche's madman noted that he himself came too soon. No doubt Nietzsche, too, thought he was ahead of his time in heralding this news.

_10:: "There is but one truly serious philosophical problem, and that is suicide."—Albert Camus (1913–1960)

Camus's solution to *the* philosophical problem was to recognize and embrace life's absurdity. Suicide, though, remains an option if the absurdity becomes too much. Indeed Camus's own death in a car crash was ambiguous. Was it an accident or suicide? For Camus, the absurd hero is Sisyphus, a man from Greek mythology who is condemned by the gods for eternity to roll a stone up a hill only to have it fall back again as it reaches the top. For Camus, Sisyphus typified all human beings: we must find meaning in a world that is unresponsive or even hostile to us. Sisyphus, Camus believed, affirms life, choosing to go back down the hill and push the rock again each time. Camus wrote, "The struggle itself toward the heights is enough to fill a man's heart. One must imagine Sisyphus happy."

_11:: "One cannot step twice in the same river."—Heraclitus (ca. 540–ca. 480 BCE)

Heraclitus definitely isn't alone here. His message was that reality is constantly changing; it's an ongoing process rather than a fixed and stable product. Buddhism shares a similar metaphysical view with the idea of *annica*, the

Fake Your Way through a Conversation
(WITH CORRECT PRONUNCIATION!)

If you fumble with a philosopher's name, nothing you say afterward will sound credible. So, learn to pronounce these names correctly, then start worrying about their ideas.

(George) Berkeley is properly pronounced like Charles Barkley (bark-lee). This name is commonly mispronounced "burk-lee," like Berkeley, California, which, ironically, is named after George Berkeley.

(Friedrich) Nietzsche is commonly mispronounced as "nee-chee." The correct pronunciation is "nee-ch-ya" and rhymes with "pleased ta meetchya." "Pleased ta meetchya, Neechya." Say it!

Lao-tzu (born ca. 604 BCE) is spelled several different ways in English transliteration from the Chinese. But no matter how you spell it, the proper way to pronounce it is "lau" (sounds like "ouch")-"dsuh." The stress goes on the first syllable.

(Charles Sanders) Peirce (1839–1914) is commonly mispronounced as "peer-s." The correct pronunciation is "purse," which is somewhat funny because Peirce rarely had a penny in his purse. Oddly, Peirce took his middle name, Sanders, as an anglicized form of Santiago, or "St. James," in honor of a fellow pragmatist, William James (1842–1910), who helped him out financially.

(Ludwig) Wittgenstein (1889–1951) is a name that demands authentic German pronunciation, and there are plenty of ways to slaughter it. Here's one that embodies all of them, "wit-jen-steen." The correct pronunciation is "vit" (rhymes with bit)-"ghen" (rhymes with Ken)-"shtine." The first name is pronounced "lude-vig." If you think it's hard to pronounce his name, try reading his *Tractatus*.

claim that all of reality is fleeting and impermanent. In modern times Henri Bergson (1859–1941) described time as a process that is experienced. An hour waiting in line is different from an hour at play. Today contemporary physics lends credence to process philosophy with the realization that even apparently stable objects, like marble statues, are actually buzzing bunches of electrons and other subatomic particles deep down.

Great Books That Won't Put You to Sleep

Reading philosophy has been known to cure insomnia, but these books will actually keep you awake at night . . . thinking . . . we swear!

_01:: Plato's *Republic*

Plato's *Republic* raises the questions, What is justice? And what is the just society? If given the ring of Gyges, which makes a person invisible while wearing it, most people would do immoral things they could not get away with otherwise, but in the just society, a person would have no such use for the ring. Plato thus gives his design for a utopia in which all men and women are equal but in which they are assigned roles based on the part of their psyche that dominates them. Warriors are dominated by spirit, workers by appetite, and guardians (philosopher kings) by reason. Children are raised communally with no knowledge of who their biological parents are, which makes everyone the child of the previous generation and the sibling of the members of his or her generation. Plato goes on to suggest that the epics of Homer should be banned as they provide false and corrupting images of the gods, and that the rigorous education of the guardians should culminate in the study of philosophy. Only rulers who understand what justice truly is will be able to implement it in governing society.

_02:: Aristotle's *Nicomachean Ethics*

Aristotle's *Ethics* addresses the question, What is the good life? Aristotle (384–322 BCE) argues that human flourishing, or becoming our best, results from using reason to govern our actions and feelings. The flourishing person possesses the virtues and good character traits that allow him to act rightly in any situation. Each virtue is a mean, a perfect balance point between two extremes, an excess and a deficiency. For example, courage is the mean between the excess, rashness, and the deficiency, cowardice. Virtue is learned through repeated practice, experiencing situations that call for acting virtuously. Ideally, Aristotle argues, practice makes acting virtuously become automatic. And in the highest form of friendship, peers reinforce the virtues in one another, making one another better.

_03:: Descartes' *Meditations on First Philosophy*

Descartes begins philosophy anew, suspending belief in everything he had taken to be true, seeking one thing he could know with absolute certainty, and using it to serve as the foundation on which to build all philosophical knowledge. Suspending belief based on his five senses and even belief in simple mathematical truths (because he could be dreaming them), Descartes discovers he cannot possibly suspend belief in his certainty that he thinks. And because he thinks, he exists. After playing with this notion for a while, Descartes reasons that the body is a physical thing that works like a machine, subject to the laws of nature, and thus is not free. The part of him that thinks, however, the mind, is not physical and thus free. We are left, though, with a question that continues to perplex philosophers: How can a nonphysical mind interact with a physical body?

_04:: Nietzsche's *On the Genealogy of Morals*

Nietzsche attempts to unravel and expose traditional morality by investigating etymology, the origin of moral terms. *Good*, he finds in his study of various languages, originally meant "godlike," and actions were considered good when done by those who were powerful, godlike. The English words *noble* and *classy* remind us that originally those who were powerful were considered good. *Bad* originally meant "common" or "simple," and those who were not powerful and the actions they took were thus deemed bad. The English words *base*, *poor*, and *villain* ("from the village") remind us that originally the bad were the powerless. This original morality, in which the chief virtue was power, Nietzsche calls the master morality. With the rise of Christianity comes the rise of the slave morality, in which the chief virtues are love and compassion and the propaganda tells us that "the meek shall inherit the earth." This moral reversal was born from the resentment the low and the slavelike felt for the powerful. As a result, what was good came to be called evil and what was bad came to be called good. Nietzsche didn't wish for a re-

Strange but True

HOW WAKING UP EARLY KILLED DESCARTES

They say getting up early won't kill you, but that may not be true. René Descartes never had a real job. After college he traveled throughout Europe, much of the time as a gentleman volunteer in the army, a pretty cushy gig requiring no actual combat. In his thirties Descartes retired to the Netherlands, not for weed and hookers, but for peace and toleration. And he often spent his mornings in bed, philosophizing a little and sleeping a lot. Descartes enjoyed success as a philosopher, mathematician, and scientist, his works drawing the attention of the powerful and the intelligent. One of the powerful who admired Descartes' work was Queen Christina of Sweden, who repeatedly invited him to join her court and instruct her in philosophy. Descartes repeatedly declined the offer, calling Sweden "the land of ice and bears." In 1649, finding himself flat broke, he finally broke down and accepted the queen's offer. When he arrived, Descartes discovered to his horror that Queen Christina—who could stand barefoot in the snow—wanted philosophy lessons at 5 a.m. Rising at the ungodly hour and trudging through the elements killed Descartes. The formal cause of death was pneumonia, but we all know the early wake-up call was to blame.

turn to the master morality but looked for a new morality that went beyond good and evil.

Behind the Philosophy: Bad Boys of Thought

9

You'd think that a philosopher could reason out the best way to behave, right? But you'd be wrong, very wrong.

_01:: Socrates, the Barefoot Bum

Notoriously ugly, clad in one coat long beyond its years, and always shoeless, yet possessed of charisma that made the youth swoon, Socrates was a fixture in the marketplace of Athens. There he would engage people with the Socratic method, beginning with a question that seemed straightforward and easy enough to answer, such as, What is virtue? Never content with the first answer, his irony and follow-up questions would inevitably lead to contradictions or admissions of ignorance on the part of his interlocutors. Socrates rubbed some people the wrong way, though, and was brought to trial on trumped-up charges of impiety and corrupting the youth. Defiant to the end, Socrates suggested that the proper sentence for his "crimes" would be free meals at the public expense, as he had done the city good. The jury gave him a hemlock cocktail instead.

_02:: Diogenes, a Cynic's Cynic

Always suspicious of society and philosophers, Diogenes (died ca. 320 BCE) would stop at nothing to make a point. He once ripped the feathers out of a live chicken to disprove Plato's account of human beings as the only featherless biped. Asked once what wine he liked best, his cynical response was "other peoples'." Alexander the Great, intrigued by stories about Diogenes, sought him out and announced, "I am Alexander the Great. What can I do for you?" "Stand back—you block my light" was Diogenes' response. While the ordinary person would have lost his head after such an insult, Diogenes was admired all the more, as the great conqueror said, "If I were not Alexander, I would be Diogenes."

_03:: Peter Abelard (1079–1144), the Castrated Cleric

Sex scandals are nothing new to the Catholic Church. Take the case of Abelard, the influential medieval philosopher who, ironically, did important work in ethics and logic. The young cleric fell in love with a beautiful young girl named Héloïse, whom he was supposed to be tutoring, and they married secretly, though they lived apart. Héloïse's uncle, however, mistakenly thought Abelard had discarded Héloïse by placing her in a convent, and he took revenge by having servants castrate Abelard in his sleep. Abelard woke up and things were never the same between him and Héloïse (needless to say, things were never the same between his legs either). The ill-fated pair were, however, reunited in death, buried together at Père Lachaise cemetery in Paris and immortalized in song by Cole Porter: "As Abelard said to Eloise, 'Don't forget to drop a line to me, please'" (from "Just One of Those Things").

_04:: Marx: Big Heart, Skinny Wallet

Unable to find work as a philosophy professor, Karl Marx (1818–1883) plotted a revolution. Working intermittently as a journalist and largely relying on the charity of friends, Marx lost many apartments and even some children for lack of financial resources. Declaring religion "the opiate of the masses," Marx found no solace in a better world to come, but instead sought to change the one he inhabited. "A specter is haunting Europe," he said, "the specter of communism. The workers of the world have nothing to lose but their chains." History reveals that Marx didn't adequately anticipate capitalism's ability to shift and change to avoid the revolution, as later workers' movements won concessions in the form of labor laws, the welfare state, and five-day work weeks. So, the next time you sleep late on a Saturday, make sure to give props to the man who made the dream of the weekend off a reality.

_05:: Arthur Schopenhauer, Poodle-Loving Pessimist

The ultimate pessimist, Schopenhauer (1788–1860) viewed reality as a malicious trap, believing we live in the worst of all possible worlds. A notorious misogynist, Schopenhauer once pushed a woman down a flight of stairs. Grudgingly, he paid her regular restitu-

Pure Genius

THALES OF MILETUS

Thales of Miletus (ca. 624–546 BCE), the first Western philosopher, set the standard for absentminded professors to come. Lost in thought, gazing at the sky, Thales fell into a well. Ridiculed as an impractical dreamer, Thales set out to show that philosophers could do anything they set their minds to, including amassing wealth. One winter, using his knowledge of meteorology and astronomy, Thales predicted a bumper olive crop for the coming season. He cornered the market on olive presses in Miletus and made a fortune when the olive harvest met his expectations. Remarkably, Thales predicted the solar eclipse of 585 BCE. He also measured the height of the Egyptian pyramids using their shadows. Thales is perhaps best known for arguing that water is the basic source element, that ultimately all things are made of water. He also argued that "all things are full of gods and have a share of soul," a poetic rendering of the insight confirmed by much later science that all matter is always in motion.

tion for her injuries until her death, when he recorded in his journal, "The old woman dies, the burden is lifted." Schopenhauer despised noise but inexplicably had a fondness for something more odious, poodles. A series of disposable poodles were his constant companions for most of his life. Not a pleasant academic colleague, Schopenhauer resented the success of Hegel, whose philosophy he thought was the worst kind of nonsense. Perhaps planning to undo Hegel, Schopenhauer scheduled his course lectures at the same time as Hegel's. The result, however, was an early retirement for Arthur.

_06:: Nietzsche: A Bad Boy Who Wasn't

One might think he railed against the corrupting influence of Christianity and declared "God is dead," because of his own misery (Nietzsche suffered from migraine headaches and poor digestion, topped off with bouts of insomnia). But the guy whose autobiographical *Ecce Homo* includes such chapters as "Why I Am So Wise," "Why I Am So Clever," and "Why I Write Such Good Books" was actually an unassuming, mild-mannered man. His belief in "the will to power" as the most basic human drive finds little reflection in his own life outside his fantasies. Though he fancied himself a warrior and a ladies' man, Nietzsche's military service was brief and unspectacular, and he never had a lover. As a bad boy in college, he may have visited a brothel or two, though. One theory suggests that the insanity that cut his career short and institutionalized him for the last 11 years of his life was the result of untreated syphilis.

_07:: Heidegger, Nazi Sympathizer

Though he originally planned to become a Catholic priest, this philosopher of being was far from holy. He carried on an extramarital affair with his gifted student Hannah Arendt, who later fled Germany to avoid persecution as a Jew. This might seem a peccadillo, except that Martin Heidegger was an anti-Semite who embraced the rise of Hitler's Third Reich. Notoriously, Heidegger had his dedication page in his *Being and Time* removed in subse-

quent printings of the book, as it paid homage to Edmund Husserl, his former teacher, a Jew. At a time when intellectuals should have risen up, Heidegger sank to the lowest common denominator. What's worse, he never recanted or apologized.

_08:: Bertrand Russell, Cambridge Casanova

An innovator in mathematics and logic, and one of the founders of analytic philosophy, at first blush Russell sounds like a dry guy. Yet his life was anything but dull. Plagued by bouts of terrible depression as a young man, Russell learned to cultivate a zest for life. This heavy-drinking, pipe-smoking professor was notorious for having affairs with his friends' wives. He rejected organized religion with his famous essay "Why I Am Not a Christian," but nonetheless had a passion for social justice, flirting with runs for political office and doing jail time for political protest, that last time at age 94. Notably, Russell was a leading intellectual voice against the war in Vietnam.

_09:: Michel Foucault, the Marilyn Manson of Philosophy

Always the outsider, Foucault (1926–1984) was the voice of the marginalized and oppressed, notably as a supporter of and inspiration for the Paris student uprisings of 1968. Making use of Nietzsche's insights on the nature of power and the method of historical investigation and exposure known as genealogy, Foucault challenged the legitimacy of dominant cultural structures. Suspicious of institutions, in works such as *Madness and Civilization*, *The Birth of the Clinic*, and *Discipline and Punish*, Foucault called for the abolition of prisons and asylums. Himself a homosexual, Foucault challenged our idea of what is normal in *The History of Sexuality*. As a visiting professor at Berkeley, Foucault frequented the San Francisco bathhouses and developed a passion for S&M. Though he kept his disease a private matter, he was the first (and to date only) major philosopher to die of AIDS.

Eastern Sages Who Leave the West Behind

The line between philosophy and religion isn't clearly drawn in the East. As a result, these thinkers go straight to the heart of fundamental human concerns in a way not often matched in the West.

_01:: Confucius: If the Mat Was Not Straight the Master Would Not Sit

Believing that the way of earth was out of line with the way of heaven and that societal order was necessary for personal order, the Chinese sage Confucius (551–479 BCE) stresses the importance of harmony in five basic relationships: ruler and minister, father and son, elder brother and younger brother, husband and wife, and friend and friend. There are three primary elements in Confucian ethics: jen, li, and chih. Jen calls for compassion and reciprocity: "What you do not want done to yourself, do not do to others." Li, or rituals like ancestor veneration, cultivate individual moralities and indicate our place in the cosmos. And jen and li come together in chih, a kind of individual integrity in which one lives virtuously and authentically in thought and action.

_02:: Lao-tzu and the Tao of Who?

In the *Tao te Ching* Lao-tzu sets forth a profoundly optimistic philosophy, calling for harmony with what is good, i.e., nature and our own original nature. We become sages by following the Tao, or the way. As Lao-tzu states, the universe has a natural way running through it like the current in a river, which we must simply get in touch with and follow. His teaching, wu-wei, calls for action by nonaction (effortless action), as when an athlete "in the zone" moves with effortless grace, or as nonviolent protest defeats the most stubbornly active opposition. Lao-tzu goes on to say that attempting to understand how the Tao works is actually counterproductive and trying to define and name the Tao is futile: "The Tao called Tao is not Tao."

_03:: Nagarjuna (ca. 150–250 CE), the Happy Medium

Despite the Buddha's silence on metaphysical issues, later Buddhist philosophers, notably Nagarjuna, wondered about the reality of the world. Nagarjuna applied the doctrine of the Middle Way, not going to extremes, denying the extreme view that reality is solely material

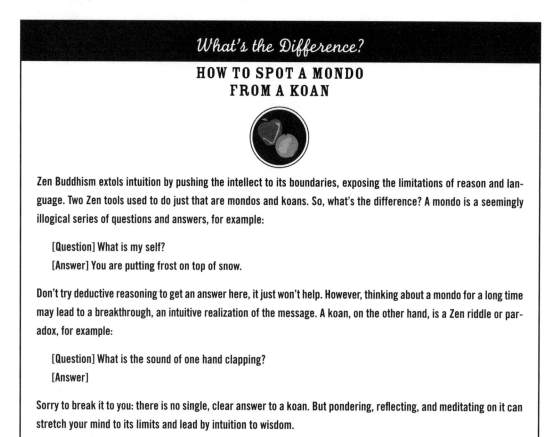

What's the Difference?

HOW TO SPOT A MONDO
FROM A KOAN

Zen Buddhism extols intuition by pushing the intellect to its boundaries, exposing the limitations of reason and language. Two Zen tools used to do just that are mondos and koans. So, what's the difference? A mondo is a seemingly illogical series of questions and answers, for example:

[Question] What is my self?

[Answer] You are putting frost on top of snow.

Don't try deductive reasoning to get an answer here, it just won't help. However, thinking about a mondo for a long time may lead to a breakthrough, an intuitive realization of the message. A koan, on the other hand, is a Zen riddle or paradox, for example:

[Question] What is the sound of one hand clapping?

[Answer]

Sorry to break it to you: there is no single, clear answer to a koan. But pondering, reflecting, and meditating on it can stretch your mind to its limits and lead by intuition to wisdom.

and denying the opposite extreme that there is no material reality. The interdependence of all things on all things implies that everything is sunya—empty—and thus the same. There are no opposites; such concepts mislead us. There is no birth or death, destruction or permanence, unity or multiplicity, coming in or going out. Because, like all things, nirvana is sunya and the cycle of suffering—samsara—is sunya, they are not in essence different. Nirvana involves liberation from concepts, thus seeing nirvana and samsara as the same.

Philosophy Doesn't Grow on Trees, but It Does Have Branches

6

Just as science divides its labor among branches such as biology, chemistry, and physics, philosophy too divides itself into specialized branches.

_01:: Metaphysics: We're Not Talking Tarot Cards Here

Metaphysics isn't just for crystal-carrying Capricorns any more. The most basic question of metaphysics is, What is real? To answer the question, metaphysics also asks, How can we distinguish what is real from what is not real? And are there different degrees and types of reality? Metaphysics considers the reality of the mind, space, time, free will, and God. Some philosophers, such as Plato, have argued that the reality we take in through our senses is just a pale shadow of a higher, more perfect reality. By contrast, other philosophers, such as David Hume (1711–1776), have argued that the only reality is that which we take in through our senses; all else is sheer fantasy. The truth may lie somewhere between those answers, but you can decide for yourself.

_02:: Epistemology: When You've Gotta Have the Truth

You come to a fork in the road and on a hunch choose the path that leads you to your destination. Did you know it was the right path? You had a true belief about which was the right path, but you didn't *know* it was the right path. Why? Because you didn't have justification or evidence, just a hunch. Episte-

mology, the study of knowledge, traditionally defines its subject as true, justified belief. But what counts as justification? Does the justification have to arise from the proper causal relations outside of us? Or does it have to arise from proper reasoning within us? What yields knowledge? Reason alone? The testimony of our senses alone? Both acting together? And can we ever have enough justification to claim knowledge of anything?

_03:: Ethics: A System Not Employed by Enron and Not Available from Microsoft

In opposition to relativism, which tells us that ethical standards are individually or culturally determined, philosophers seek universal ethical standards. Virtue theorists, such as Aristotle, argue that cultivating character traits such as patience, temperance, and courage through repeated practice leads to the good life and to the good person who can be counted on to do the right thing no matter what situation arises. Natural law theorists, such as Thomas Aquinas (1225–1274), argue that there are objective moral laws just as surely as there are objective physical laws. Intentionally killing innocent people, for example, goes against the law of nature. Utilitarians,

X-TREME UTILITARIANISM

Jeremy Bentham (1748–1832), a major figure in modern utilitarianism, may have taken his theory to the extreme. Utilitarianism holds that we should act in a way that produces the greatest good for the greatest number of people. So, for example, while not paying my taxes might produce the greatest good or happiness for me personally, it will not produce the greatest good for my fellow citizens. And so my selfish desire to evade tax payment is over-ridden by the greater good supporting the public welfare. The question does arise, however, What should a good utilitarian do with his body when he dies? While in most cases it may be best to cremate or bury them, Bentham had his own take, having his body embalmed and preserved at University College, London (though things went miserably wrong with his head, which has been replaced with a wax replica). Bentham's motivations are unclear, but perhaps he thought that it's tougher to engage the ideas of past philosophers when their bodies are absent. Although Bentham's corpse never did inspire much further philosophical dialogue, according to rumor it does make an appearance at college council meetings, the minutes for which supposedly record Bentham as present but not voting.

that reason dictates that we should act only in a way, in which we would want everyone else to act.

_04:: Political Philosophy: Lots of Debate but No Parties

Despite the shameful actions of politicians past and present, Plato and Aristotle considered ethics and politics inseparable. The good person and the good society depend on one another. In his *Republic* Plato raises the question of the legitimate role of the government and calls for the abandonment of democracy in favor of a protosocialist state, an ideal developed much later by Karl Marx. Thomas Hobbes viewed the government as an over-bearing presence, a Leviathan, but one to which we must submit for our own protection. According to John Locke (1632–1704), all men are born with the inalienable rights to life, liberty, and property, and through the social contract, we form governments to protect those rights. Libertarian philosophers of today see the protection of those rights as the only legitimate function of governments. By contrast, communitarian philosophers argue that governments must take care of their citizens in the spirit of community, thus justifying, among other things, the welfare state. Other topics of discussion in political philosophy include justice, fairness, punishment, globalization, the family, paternalism, and autonomy.

such as John Stuart Mill (1806–1873), argue that we should judge actions right or wrong on the basis of the greatest happiness principle: act so as to produce the greatest good (i.e., happiness) for the greatest number. The categorical imperative of Immanuel Kant tells us

_05:: Aesthetics: Hey There, Beautiful!

"Beauty is in the eye of the beholder," some say, but philosophers from Aristotle to Kant and beyond have searched for objective standards by which to judge the beauty of art and nature. "There's no accounting for taste," some say, but philosophers, such as Hume, attempt to do just that. Anyone who's ever sampled both Hershey and Godiva chocolate can tell you the Godiva chocolate tastes better. While some food, painting, and music may be acquired tastes, the beauty of nature is readily apparent to a child. Why? Why do we seek beauty and value art? How can we find truth and meaning in art? And do the intentions of artists govern how we should interpret their work? It's all there in aesthetic debate.

_06:: Logic: It's Elementary, My Dear Watson

Logic comes naturally for Vulcans like Mr. Spock, but humans need to specify and study the rules of proper reasoning that take us from the premise of an argument to its conclusion. There are two types of logical reasoning or argument: deductive and inductive. Despite what your seventh-grade science teacher said, the difference between the two does not depend on moving from general premises to a specific conclusion or vice versa. A deductive argument is one in which the premises are intended, if true, to guarantee the truth of the conclusion. A deductive argument in which the reasoning accomplishes this is called valid, and if its premises are indeed true as well, it's called sound. An inductive argument is one in which the premises are intended to provide support, but not

Strange but True

MOTION IS IMPOSSIBLE— ZENO'S PARADOXES

The Greek mathematician Zeno of Elea (ca. 495–ca. 430 BCE) attempted to show that space and motion were impossible. It would take too long to explain and examine all the paradoxes, but one will illustrate his basic argument. Zeno asks us to imagine a runner moving from point A to point B. If we assume that the line from point A to point B contains an infinite number of points, then the runner must reach the halfway mark before he reaches the end. But before he reaches the halfway mark, he must reach a point halfway to that, and so on. Between each of these halfway points, there are an infinite number of points. Here comes the paradox: How can the runner traverse an infinite series of points in a finite time interval? Using this same principle, Zeno showed that an arrow in flight does not move and that Achilles can never outrun a tortoise if the tortoise has even the slightest head start. In short, if we can divide something at all, we can divide it ad infinitum.

absolute proof, for the conclusion, and an argument that produces likely support is called strong.

Isms Finally Put in Their Place

Struggling to find the philosophy that's just right for you? Why not take a little inspiration from your surroundings.

_01:: Stoicism: When You're on the Porch

Stoicism takes its name from the Greek word *stoa*, meaning "porch," as the original stoics gathered on a *stoa* in Athens. This folksy source of the name speaks to the very practical concern of stoicism—how to live a tranquil life in the midst of a chaotic world. Stoicism, a philosophy embraced by both the former slave Epictetus (ca. 50–ca. 135) and the emperor of Rome Marcus Aurelius (121–180), counsels self-control, detachment, and acceptance of one's fate. Stoicism holds that the events of the world are out of our control and fated to be. Our minds, however, are free and so our reactions to and feelings about what happens to us and in the world around us are under our control. We can live with peace of mind under any and all circumstances so long as we adjust our minds to accept things as they are. This does not mean we should never take steps to change things, but we should realize that ultimately we have only influence, never control, over things outside our own minds.

_02:: Cynicism: When You're in the Doghouse

Cynicism takes its name from the Greek *kynikos*, related to our word *canine*. The most famous Cynic, Diogenes, chose to live outside of Athens in a tub and in the company of dogs, whom he found nobler than the residents of the city. The Cynics scorned and distrusted the values and ways of society, and Diogenes displayed this attitude with philoso-

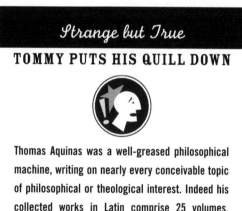

Strange but True

TOMMY PUTS HIS QUILL DOWN

Thomas Aquinas was a well-greased philosophical machine, writing on nearly every conceivable topic of philosophical or theological interest. Indeed his collected works in Latin comprise 25 volumes. Strangely, though, Aquinas stopped writing altogether in December 1273, three months before his death. Ill health was not to blame. Rather, at prayer one evening Aquinas had a mystical experience, and afterward is said to have remarked, "All I have written seems like straw to me." This was not to say that his previous writing and commitment to faith seeking understanding was without value, just that by comparison with the awe-inspiring vision he had, his writing and projects seemed the stuff of animal beds.

phy in the form of performance art. He would walk through the marketplace of Athens carrying a lighted lantern in the middle of the day and, when asked what he was doing, would reply that he was looking for an honest man. None could be found by his lights.

_03:: Thomism: When You're in the Pulpit (This One Has Mass Appeal)

The philosophy of Thomas Aquinas (1225–1274) is the most significant contribution to Catholic philosophical thought. Following the guiding dictum of medieval philosophy, "faith seeking understanding," Aquinas believed that faith gives the answers to questions of theological and philosophical importance, and

philosophical reasoning makes sense of those answers where possible. His major work, the *Summa Theologica*, is *the* landmark work of medieval philosophy, and every major medieval philosopher after Aquinas studied, commented on, and felt the influence of his work. In 1879 Pope Leo XIII declared Aquinas to be *Aeterni Patris* ("of the Eternal Father"), and to this day his metaphysics and natural law ethics are an important source of Catholic theology. Thomism isn't merely a historical entry in the story of philosophy but a vibrant and continuing school of thought. Notable 20th-century Thomists include Etienne Gilson (1884–1978), Jacques Maritain (1882–1973), and Bernard Lonergan (1904–1984).

5 Thinking Positive!: Feel-Good Philosophies

If contemplating life has you down in the dumps, maybe it's time you justified your existence with some peppy reasoning. Chin up, kid. Here are a few feel-good philosophies to get you grinning again.

_01:: Eat, Drink, and Be Merry! with Epicureanism

Today an epicure is a gourmet, and as his detractors had it, Epicurus (341–270 BCE) indulged in extravagant pleasures of food, drink, and sex. Nothing could be further from the truth. Epicurus lived in a kind of hippie commune called the Garden and subsisted on a modest diet of water, cheese, vegetables, and the occasional glass of wine. With

no belief in an afterlife, Epicureanism holds that pleasure is the highest good in this life and there is no fear of punishment in an afterlife. Simple pleasures taken in moderation are best. In fact, some pleasures are unnatural and unnecessary, for they return more pain than pleasure in the long run. Just watch any VH1 *Behind the Music* episode to see why Epicurus is right about the pain of overindulgence.

_02:: Seize the Day! with Existentialism

Existentialism may conjure images of a French recluse smoking stinky cigarettes and despairing at the meaninglessness of it all, but this just ain't right! Existentialism generally prescribes a seize-the-day attitude and offers consolation in the face of the void. Some existentialists, such as Kierkegaard and Marcel (1889–1973), have actually been committed Christians, hopeful of salvation. Heidegger and Karl Jaspers (1883–1969) rejected the label of existentialism, but Sartre embraced it and defined it as the doctrine that "existence preceded essence," which means that we have no given nature but can create a nature for ourselves. The common bond of philosophies that fall under the heading of existentialism is a focus on lived individual existence rather than grand systematic theoretical speculation.

_03:: It's All Good! with Relativism

"Everything is relative," they say. Relativism is the belief that there are no universal standards for what is true, right, good, beautiful, etc. Standards are determined by the individual or the culture. Varieties of relativism include moral (right and wrong are relative), epistemological (truth is relative), aesthetic (beauty is relative), and metaphysical (reality is relative). Cultural relativism asserts that accepted standards differ among cultures and individuals. This claim is undoubtedly true. But whether differing cultural and individual standards can all be correct is another matter. A simple version of relativism runs into the problem of being self-contradictory. If, for example, I believe that it is wrong for anyone to fly kites on Sunday and you believe everyone has an absolute duty to fly kites on Sunday, relativism must hold that we're both right. But logically speaking, we can't both be right.

_04:: It's the Thought That Counts! with Rationalism

Rationalism is the belief that some, perhaps all, knowledge can be obtained through reason alone. Some rationalists take the senses to be less reliable than reason, while others distrust the senses completely. The most ancient rationalist, a Greek philosopher named Parmenides (born ca. 515 BCE), argued that according to reason and despite what our senses tell us, change and multiple beings are impossible. So, there is only one being and it never changes. Parmenides' student Zeno elaborated on this thesis by arguing through a series of paradoxes that motion, a kind of change, is impossible. Descartes is the most important modern rationalist. He begins his philosophical system by acknowledging that the senses sometimes deceive us and so should not be trusted. Happily, he goes on to discover that reason unaided by the senses yields certain knowledge that "I exist."

_05:: Share the Wealth! with Marxism

While many know that Groucho said he'd never want to belong to a club that would have him as a member, few know that Karl declared, "I am no Marxist." Even in Karl's lifetime Marxism was interpreted and applied in many ways beyond Marx's original vision. Karl Marx argued that the story of human civilization is best understood as a history of economic class conflict. Asserting that previous philosophers had merely interpreted the world, Marx's goal was to change it. The contemporary class conflict Marx pointed to was that between the workers and the capitalists: the owners of the means of production. In *The Communist Manifesto*, Marx and his co-author, Friedrich Engels (1820–1895), conclude with the cry "workers of the world unite." The pair called for a workers' revolution that would ultimately lead to a communist society guided by the principle "from each according to his ability, to each according to his need." Significantly, Marxism has been applied to literary theory as a way of reading literature in terms of class conflict. Notable Marxists who interpreted Marx in light of their own political concerns include György Lukács (1885–1971), Louis Althusser (1918–1990), the later Jean-Paul Sartre, and Herbert Marcuse (1898–1979).

3 Bad Catchphrases (and the Philosophies behind Them)

Sure, you've seen the bumper stickers, or overheard annoying conversations where someone would mutter an overused phrase, then wave a hand in the air, expecting a high-five. But who knew they were really spouting philosophy?

_01:: Show Me the Money! (Pragmatism)

Pragmatism focuses on questions that make a difference to the way we live and seeks answers that have a "cash value." This stands in direct contrast to abstract concerns that have no clear payoff. A distinctly American product, pragmatism's three chief figures are C. S. Peirce (1839–1914), William James (1842–1910), and John Dewey (1859–1952). Rejecting the correspondence theory, which holds that a belief is true if it corresponds to the way things actually are, and the coherence theory, which holds that a belief is true if it fits in with the rest of our beliefs, the pragmatic theory of truth holds that something is true if it works. For James, free will and God are true because they are ideas that work to make our lives better. Pragmatism's most enduring legacy, Dewey's theory of education, makes children active learners in a classroom that is a laboratory in which they can openly follow and explore their interests.

_02:: Not! (Nihilism)

Taking its name from the Latin *nihil,* meaning "nothing," nihilism is the general term applied to the belief that nothing is objectively meaningful. Existentialists are often mischaracterized as nihilists. Nietzsche, for example, predicted that with the "death" of God—the loss of belief in what is central—the 20th century would face an unprecedented threat of nihilism. Nietzsche did not advocate nihilism, but rather warned against it and urged the creation of new, more vibrant beliefs. The absurdity of actually adopting nihilism is played for laughs in the offbeat Hollywood comedy *The Big Lebowski*, in which the hero, "the dude," is hounded by nihilists.

_03:: There's More Than One Way to Skin a Cat (Pluralism)

Pluralism subscribes to the old, now politically incorrect, adage, "there's more than one way to skin a cat." Rejecting relativism as giving away too much, pluralism remains wary of absolute universal standards. Not just any view of right and wrong, truth, beauty, etc., can be right. But more than one view can be right. Obviously, there's more than one way to get from New York to Chicago. Similarly, religious pluralism holds that despite their differences, all true religions are in touch with the same ultimate reality. Other forms of plural-

---

Strange but True

AVOID THE BEANS (AND OTHER PYTHAGOREAN THEOREMS)

The name Pythagoras (ca. 580–ca. 500 BCE) probably resonates in your mind because of distant memories of geometry or music class. He is known primarily as the person who connected mathematics to music; in fact, for Phythagoras, all is number. His passion for mathematics was expressed in a mystical way. For example, he thought that the number 10 was sacred, and he often had his disciples spend days contemplating a number or a geometric figure. His mysticism, however, included some strange taboos. Here is a partial list of the rules of the Pythagorean school:

One must not eat beans
One must not pick up what has fallen
One must not touch a white rooster
One must not break bread
One must not step over a crossbar
One must not stir the fire with iron
One must not eat from a whole loaf
One must not pluck a garland
One must not sit on a quart of anything
One must not eat the heart of anything
One must not walk on highways
One must not allow swallows to nest on one's roof
One must not look in a mirror beside a light

Bertrand Russell called Pythagoras intellectually one of the most important men who ever lived and one of the most interesting and puzzling men in history.

ism suggest there's more than one way to do the good, know the truth, conceive the beautiful, or experience reality. Though it's motivated by practicality and tolerance, pluralism may itself give away too much. At least that's what absolutists, believers in single universal standards, would say.

Name-Dropping 101:
Schools of Thought That Will Impress the Opposite Sex

3

If you want to swing and cruise in the hippest intellectual atmospheres, your cocktail party cheat sheet better include some of these words.

_01:: Feminism: Something in the Way She Thinks

Feminism argues that from its beginning, Western philosophy has been a boys-only "reindeer game." The dominant views and approaches of philosophy have been distinctly male, marginalizing, at times outright excluding the female perspective. Metaphysics has sought a stable, phallic account of reality and has privileged mind and intellect (associated with the male) over body (associated with the female). Epistemology has sought to establish knowledge on the basis of rigid justification rather than explore the insight and intuition that make knowledge possible. Ethics has centered around male conceptions of objective duty rather than understanding ethical decisions as really being made in contextual relationships. The most activist issue of feminism is the political and civil rights of women, who were so long deprived of such rights as voting and owning property. Today political femi-

nism addresses issues of sexual harassment, domestic violence, the continuing inequality of women's rights in the third world, and more subtle forms of gender inequality such as the corporate glass ceiling.

_02:: Deconstruction: Razing a Good Point

Deconstruction simply means that the meaning can never be clear. Jacques Derrida (1930–), the father of deconstruction, played on the French words for *differ* and *defer* to coin the term *différance*, implying that meaning is derived from difference. Further, in Derrida's logic, meaning is never fully present but is always deferred or postponed. There is always something to come next that can destabilize the meaning we thought was there. Derrida looks for metaphors, wordplay, footnotes, and other marginal comments that suggest a meaning other than that intended by the author. So, to deconstruct a novel, a film, or anything else is not just to analyze its parts but to show how it contains inconsistencies that actually subvert its intended meaning.

_03:: Postmodernism: Truthless People

Though the term *postmodernism* has almost as many meanings as users, in general, philosophers of postmodernism are concerned with the implications of a new era that began with the loss of Enlightenment ideals. Postmodernism holds that we have come to the end of "totalizing narratives" such as science, Chris-

tianity, and Marxism, none of which can be taken seriously as telling the whole story or truth. All our knowledge is piecemeal, fragmented, and perspectival—and no one can see or describe the big picture. With mass production and simulation, with the *Mona Lisa* available on everything from postcards to mouse pads, with artificial flavors and the growth of virtual-reality technology, the nature and value of what is "real" is always called into question.

by
Richard A. Muller

Condensed
PHYSICS

Contains

4 Reasons to Have Your Physics Super-Sized ✳ 6 Swashbuckling Physicists (and Their Beautiful Minds)* ✳ Glowing Concerns: 5 Ways Radioactivity Lights Up Your Life ✳ Really Big Bangs!: Huge Explosions We're Actually Glad About ✳ 8 Scary Warnings That Could Have Been Placed on This Book ✳ 5 Miserable Screwups by a Famous Physicist ✳ 1 Nobel Prize That Should Never Have Been Awarded ✳ Say It Ain't So!: 4 Things Einstein Got Wrong ✳ 9 Laws of Physics That Don't Apply in Hollywood ✳ 2 Reasons Physics Doesn't Work in the Real World ✳

*Written by mental_floss

Reasons to Have Your Physics Super-Sized

Physicists love to use the term *super*. For some unexplained reason, they find the term superior to its synonyms, such as *big*, *great*, or *fantastic*. From superclusters to supernovas to supergravity to superheavy elements, physics is simply littered with the prefix. In fact, some day people may identify 20th-century physics ideas by the word's overuse, just as we can spot movies made in the 1940s by their frequent use of the word *swell*. The following are just a few of the ways the word *super* has attached itself to physics phenomena.

_01:: Superconductors

We like conductors: after all, they carry electricity into our homes so we can watch bad reality TV. In the name of cooler and better, in 1911 Heike Onnes discovered the property of superconductors—materials such as lead and mercury, which have no resistance to electricity when cooled near to absolute zero ($-459.67°F$). If an electric current starts flowing in a loop of superconductor, it will continue to flow forever. So, what's the catch? You have to keep it near $-459.67°F$—and that's extremely hard to do. Everyone got excited when high-temperature superconductors were discovered in the 1980s, but even those had to be kept at the temperature of liquid nitrogen. If and when we discover a superconductor that works at room temperature, our homes and countries will all be rewired with the superior wire.

_02:: Supersymmetry

Physicists classify all elementary particles into two groups, called fermions and bosons, based on their spin. Electrons, protons, and neutri-

nos are considered fermions, while photons, gravitons, and gluons make up the boson camp. Prior to the theory of supersymmetry, these two classes of particles were considered to be quite different from each other. But the theory of supersymmetry romantically assumes that all particles come in pairs, with a boson for every fermion, and vice versa. In a sense, these pairs are actually two aspects of the same particle. If supersymmetry turns out to be true, then it could be the final unification of physics. Unfortunately, there are no known supersymmetric pairs, so the theory may be superfluous.

_03:: Superstring Theory

This is a theory that is even more far out than plain supersymmetry. In superstring theory, the ultimate fundamental particle from which all others are made is called a string (because of its geometry). And depending on how this string vibrates, it becomes an electron, a neutrino, a graviton, or a quark (the fundamental unit inside the proton and neutron). In ordinary string theory, the particles with different spin rates are different strings; in superstring theory, they are the same. How can that be? The string has a more complicated geometry than the string you use to tie a package, with many extra spatial dimensions, typically 10 . . . not an easy thing to visualize. Super-string theory is considered superlative because it solves many of the mathematical problems that plagued particle theory—in particular, annoying infinities that wouldn't go away. But beware—there is no experimental evidence that string theory is true, i.e., that it represents physical reality rather than just superficial mathematics.

_04:: The Super

The Super is the name for the original version of the hydrogen bomb, and American nuclear physicist Edward Teller (1908–2003) worked for years trying to figure out how to make one work. The original model consisted of a stick of hydrogen ignited at one end by an ordinary atomic fission bomb, like the one dropped on Hiroshima. The hydrogen would ignite into fusion and burn down the stick. So, to make a bigger bomb, just make the stick longer, right? Nope. Calculations showed it wouldn't work, as it would cool down too much and put itself out. It was only when Teller discussed the problem with Stanislaw Ulam (1909–1984) that they came up with the solution: to compress the hydrogen using gamma radiation. That became the new design, and the Super was superseded.

6 Swashbuckling Physicists (and Their Beautiful Minds)

OK, so most physicists probably wouldn't be mistaken for Indiana Jones. But just because they don't tote snapping whips or fancy hats, it doesn't mean their stories don't get passed around. Here are the true tales of six colorful physicists you ought to know.

_01:: Albert Einstein (1879–1955)

Sure, you know all about Uncle Albert's famous equations, his knack for the violin, his love of sailing, or maybe even that he was offered the presidency of the newly created Israel in 1952. But did you know that he was a notoriously bad dresser? That's right, unkempt hair and all, Albert Einstein was a poster boy for unruly appearances. In fact, he was so underdressed on one occasion (a reception with the emperor of the Austro-Hungarian Empire no less) that he was mistaken for an electrician because of his work shirt. Not surprisingly, Albert also disliked extravagance, claiming that luxuries were wasted on him. Despite his intellectual celebrity status, the Nobel Prize winner refused to travel in anything but third class.

_02:: Nikola Tesla (1856–1943)

Tesla dreamed up AC current, won technical disputes with Edison, had ideas stolen from him by Marconi, and designed the tesla coil (that lovely spinning thing you find sparking light in every mad scientist's lab). But even more intriguing than all of this were his peculiarities. Nikola Tesla's personal life was one of crippling obsessions: washing his hands endlessly, counting every item on a dinner table before tucking in, and maintaining a hatred for earrings and other round objects. But perhaps most unusual was his fondness for pigeons. Tesla was so smitten by one bird in particular that when it passed away, he wrote, "Yes, I loved her as a man loves a woman, and she loved me. . . . When that pigeon died something went out of my life. . . . I knew my life's work was over."

_03:: Richard Feynman (1918–1988)

A real live wire of the science world, Richard Feynman was a giant in his field. One of the most famous physicists of the 20th century, Feynman contributed heavily to the Manhattan Project, won a Nobel Prize for his work in quantum electrodynamics, and contributed key insights as a member of the presidential team investigating the NASA *Challenger* disaster. He was also well known for banging away on his bongos whenever he got the chance and for trying to perfect the art of picking up women (from college parties to red-light districts). If you'd like some insight into his mischievous personality, though, consider how he let the great minds working on the Manhattan Project know that their classified documents weren't exactly safe. Feynman studied up a bit on safecracking, stole a few combinations, then picked the government locks with ease, taking nothing from the vaults. Instead he left amusing notes for the officials, letting them know just how good their security was.

_04:: Stephen Hawking (1942–)

Well known for authoring *A Brief History of Time*, the world-renowned theoretician has made his greatest contributions in the physics of black holes. He was also elected one of the Royal Society's youngest fellows and selected to Cambridge's Lucasian post, a professorship of mathematics once held by Isaac Newton. While all signs point to genius, that doesn't mean Hawking is always right. Back in 1975, he made a bet with Kip Thorne of Caltech that Cygnus X-1 did not contain a black hole. (The prize was a subscription to a racy magazine.) In 1990, when Hawking decided the evidence against him was overwhelming, he conceded in a waggish manner: he had a friend break into Thorne's office and steal the recorded terms of the bet. Hawking signed his defeat, then sneaked it back in for Thorne to find later. In the following months Thorne also received his promised issues of *Penthouse*.

_05:: Fay Ajzenberg-Selove (1926–)

As a little girl, renowned physicist Fay Ajzenberg-Selove had a knack for engineering. When she became bored with simple electronics, she turned to her true love—physics—but her path was far from easy. Her family fled Hitler's reign, and during the escape her father distributed small knives to each of his children, showing them how to slit their wrists in the event that they were caught. The experience was chilling, but surviving the Holocaust

Myths and Misconceptions
EVERYTHING YOU THOUGHT YOU KNEW ABOUT PHYSICS (BUT WERE AFRAID TO ASK)

Black holes don't suck things in, despite what you see on *Star Trek*. If we replaced the sun with a black hole of equal mass, the earth's orbit wouldn't change. It's only when you get very close to the surface of the black hole that the gravity becomes intense.

Einstein didn't make the atom bomb possible by showing that $E = mc^2$. The discovery of radioactivity had already shown that there was a million times more energy available than in ordinary chemical reactions, and the discovery of the chain reaction made fission power practicable. Einstein's equation just explains where the energy is coming from; it played no role in the development of atomic bombs or nuclear reactors.

Explosive detectors at airports don't detect hidden explosives. In fact, there's no reliable way to detect explosives remotely. The explosive detectors at work are just really fancy X-ray machines that look for suspicious shapes and wires. A chemical swipe can detect residual explosives on the outside of luggage but not the explosives within.

gave Ajzenberg-Selove tremendous courage for her later battles with sexism. In the 1950s Fay was invited by colleagues at Princeton to use some of the university's equipment for her experiments. The chairman of the physics department at Princeton, however, had a rigid rule: No women in the building. She ignored the warning, slinking through the halls late at night and conducting her experiments till the wee hours of the morn.

_06:: Archimedes (ca. 287–212 BCE)

Archimedes, of "give me a long enough lever and a place to stand, and I'll move the earth" fame, is also well known for popularizing the term *eureka*. The famous Greek mathematician, physicist, and inventor lived most of his life in Syracuse, where he was under the patronage of the royal family. The emperor asked him to de-termine whether a crown was pure gold, and the answer struck Archimedes while he was bathing. When the water started overflowing, he realized the crown's density was the key. He took the crown, placed it in water, and noted how much water was displaced. Then he took the crown's exact weight in pure gold and re-peated the process (surprise, surprise—the numbers were different). Supposedly, Archim-edes was so excited by his flash of bathtub in-spiration that he continued flashing: he jumped out of the tub and ran home nude, shrieking, "*Eureka!*" (or "I found it!") in delight.

Glowing Concerns:
5 Ways Radioactivity Lights Up Your Life

The word *radioactivity* always seems to bring up a number of glowing concerns. But maybe it's time you got over your fears and warmed up to the idea. Here are some reasons to grin about radioactivity.

_01:: If You Aren't Radioactive, You Just Ain't Livin'

The carbon dioxide in the air contains one part in a trillion of radiocarbon, which is ra-dioactive and produced by cosmic rays from space. Plants, of course, take in this carbon, so then they become radioactive. If you eat plants or animals that eat plants, then *you* be-come radioactive. So, why is this important? When you die, the radiocarbon will begin to decay. In 5,730 years half the radiocarbon will be gone. In another 5,730 years half of that will be gone. Because scientists can measure the age of ancient bones by measuring how much of the radiocarbon is gone, if a bone is not measurably radioactive, that means that its owner has been dead at least 50,000 years.

_02:: Radioactivity Helps You Get Your Drink On

It isn't that the Bureau of Alcohol, Firearms, and Tobacco tests alcoholic beverages for ra-dioactivity. What is surprising is that it rejects any alcohol that doesn't show radiation as "unfit." What's the reason? Any alcohol that has zero radioactivity must have come from very old carbon, and that usually means the alcohol has been manufactured from fossil fuels. After burial for 100 million years, the radiocarbon in the original organisms decays, and Congress has decreed that such alcohol may not be legally consumed. The argument that it's unfit probably has more to do with politics than with science, since there's no scientific reason why fossil fuel alcohol would be any worse than alcohol from grapes.

_03:: The Hills Wouldn't Be So Alive

Mountains come from the collision of large tectonic plates on the surface of the earth. Nobody knows what makes these plates move, but a reasonable guess is that the very slow flow of rocks (if they go slowly enough, they behave like fluids) is driven by the heat of radioactivity in the earth's depths. So, if it weren't for the fabulous effects of radioactivity, the plates wouldn't have moved, and those hills Julie Andrews and the Von Trapp family are so eager to sing about would never have existed.

_04:: You Might Be Speaking French

This is also related to the movement of the plates, discussed in the previous paragraph. About 100 million years ago, Europe and North America were one continent. And if you look on a modern map, you can still see how the continents once fit together. But the flow of rock, possibly driven by radioactivity, sent the continents apart. As a result, we have Europe and the United States. Why should we be thankful for radioactivity? Well, without it, the United States and France would probably be next-door neighbors!

Strange but True
FACTS AND PHYSICS

Chocolate chip cookies have 15 times as much energy as the same weight of TNT. (TNT is used as an explosive because it can release energy quickly, not because it has a lot.)

Compared to the rest of the atom, the nucleus is as small as a mosquito in a football stadium.

When you look at the sun, you aren't seeing it the way it is. You are seeing it the way it was eight minutes ago. If it blew up seven minutes ago, you wouldn't know immediately. (It takes light, and anything traveling at the speed of light, that long to travel the 93-million-mile distance.)

The speed of light is only 1 foot per computer cycle (assuming you have a 1 GHz computer). That's the same as 186,000 miles per second. That's why computers have to be small—so they can retrieve data as fast as they can think.

A meteor carries 100 times as much energy in its motion as does an equal weight of TNT in its explosion. (That's why an asteroid or comet hitting the earth had enough energy to kill the dinosaurs and most other life 65 million years ago.)

_05:: Ain't No Sunshine When There's No Radioactivity

The sun is driven by a process called fusion, which is actually a series of reactions that requires short-lived radioactive intermediaries to undergo a kind of radioactivity called beta decay. Simply stated, without radioactivity, the fusion on the sun could not proceed, and the sun would have cooled off billions of years ago. And guess what: without the sun, plants and animals wouldn't be here, and you wouldn't have that killer tan.

Really Big Bangs!:
Huge Explosions We're Actually Glad About

Baking soda and balloon explosions in the bathroom = bad; creation of the world = good.

_01:: Starting Off with a Bang

In 1948 physicist George Gamow said that the universe began as an explosion billions of years ago. The overwhelming majority of scientists today agree with him, but originally some thought the idea was a bit of a joke. A rival of Gamow's, the noted astronomer Fred Hoyle, ridiculed the theory and gave it the hokey name big bang theory—and of course the name stuck. The explosion produced all the hydrogen and most of the helium that fuels our stars and the sun. Some speculate that the big bang actually created space and maybe even time. And it's continuing to happen: all of the galaxies are flying away from one another in just the pattern predicted by the theory. But don't worry. There can never be an explosion to exceed the big bang; it involved all the energy of the universe.

_02:: From Stars to Supernovas

Sometime between 4 and 5 billion years ago, a giant star burned hydrogen and helium from the big bang and cooked them into carbon, oxygen, and nitrogen—the ashes of fusion. These remained buried in a star for millions of years until the star suddenly exploded, increasing its brightness by a billion for about a month and expelling all its ashes into space. We call those explosions supernovas, and they happen pretty frequently. One occurs in the Milky Way (our galaxy) about once every hundred years. Our own lucky star formed from the blobby ashes of a supernova, and presto! 4.6 billion years later it became the sun. A nearby little blob became the earth. So, you see, we really are all made of stars.

_03:: Lowest Comet Denominator

About 200 million years ago mammals evolved from reptiles. (And you were upset about the monkey rumors!) The mammals were small, had mediocre brains, and were always outfought and outthought by the bigger, smarter lizards. Finally, about 65 million years ago, a large comet or asteroid—the size of San Francisco—crashed into the earth. Its energy of motion was 100 times greater than we would have gotten from an equal mass of dynamite, and when it hit, that energy was turned into heat, causing the greatest explo-

sion that life has ever known. All the large animals were killed, including all the large lizards known as dinosaurs. A few of the smaller lizards, including some birds, survived, as did a few of the smaller mammals. Plants soon came back, and the mammals discovered that their terrible tormentors, the horrible dinosaurs, were all gone. Long live the mammals!

Scary Warnings That Could Have Been Placed on This Book

We dare you to keep reading!

_01:: This Book Is Radioactive

Paper contains carbon from trees, and such carbon contains the radioactive isotope carbon 14 at a concentration of about one part in a trillion. If that number seems small, then think about this one: there are about 100 trillion of those radioactive atoms. Every minute, about 100 of them decay (i.e., explode), releasing an energetic beta ray with an energy up to 156 thousand electron volts! And it's all true. It's just that it takes a lot more radioactivity than that to do harm. Of course, you're also partially made out of carbon, so you're radioactive too. In fact, the book and you also contain a whole host of other radioactive elements, including small amounts of potassium, uranium, and thorium.

_02:: Keep Out of Reach of Antimatter for Fear of Explosion

That's right! If this book were to come into contact with an equal amount of antimatter, it would likely explode, releasing an energy equivalent to 20 million tons of TNT. So would anything else. Contact with antimatter releases all the energy stored in the mass of the nucleus. That's why there appears to be no antimatter around. We think that all the original antimatter in the big bang was annihilated. Fortunately, there was a slight excess of matter, and that's why we're here. We can make antimatter, but it takes enormous power to do so. To make enough antimatter to annihilate this book would take the energy equivalent of 20 million tons of TNT.

_03:: Shocking: Parts of This Book Are Electrified at over 1 Million Volts

Should you be worried? For a heavy element, 1 million is a typical voltage near a nuclear surface. In fact, that's what keeps the electrons tightly bound to it. Voltage is dangerous only when there is no nearby electron to cancel it, because of the high energy that an electron can pick up from the attraction. But in this case the electron is already orbiting the nucleus, so there's no danger. The voltage would be 1 million volts only in a tiny region close to the nucleus.

_04:: Reading This Book Could Contribute to the Ultimate Heat Death of the Universe

Any work you do, be it manual or intellectual, requires the conversion of chemical energy into work and heat, and that increases the entropy (the disorder) of the universe. That's the third law of thermodynamics, but many people don't realize that the disorder you contribute consists of infrared radiation sent off to distant space. Locally, your entropy is actually decreased every time you learn something. There's a widespread belief that the gradual increase in entropy will eventually lead to complete disorder. This would be very cold, but for historic reasons it's still called a heat death. We don't know if this is in our future, but our own contributions will be negligible.

_05:: Parts of This Book Could Fly Off at Greater Than 60 Million MPH without Warning

The fastest electrons are those in the inner orbits of the heaviest elements, such as lead and uranium, which exist in microscopic amounts

---

Pure Genius

ENRICO FERMI

Though Fermi is virtually unknown to the public, he's considered by many in the field to be a contender for the greatest physicist of the 20th century, along with Albert Einstein. Unlike Einstein, though, Fermi made major experimental discoveries as well as theoretical ones. But while many might scoff at placing Fermi and Einstein on the same pedestal, we've got plenty of proof to back the claim up. Most common particles (the electron, the proton) are called fermions thanks to Fermi's theory. The Fermi level determines the behavior of transistors and computers. The Fermi pressure keeps stars from collapsing. His discovery of the surprising behavior of slow neutrons made nuclear reactors possible, and he built the first one, under Stagg Field in Chicago. The Fermi mechanism explains cosmic radiation. The Fermi theory explains how radioactive elements emit electrons. Fermi won a Nobel Prize, and so did four of his students. His reactor made the production of plutonium practical, and he's been called the father of the atom bomb. The highest award in the U.S. for a scientist is the Fermi Award. Fermilab was named after him. The 100th element is named fermium in his honor. And his photo has appeared on a U.S. stamp, strangely, with an incorrect equation on the blackboard behind him. Get the idea?

---

in all materials, including this book. Those electrons have a nominal velocity of about 10% of the speed of light. (The speed of light is usually given as 186,284 miles per second, or 671 million miles per hour.) If the nucleus were to suddenly vanish (e.g., by antimatter annihilation from a rare cosmic ray), then the electron would fly off with that velocity. But don't worry about it. In doing so, the electron wouldn't cause any more harm than the cosmic rays that are constantly penetrating your body anyway.

_06:: If This Book Is Moved Horizontally, the Type on This Book Will Become Narrower

This is a consequence of special relativity. According to the theory, any object in motion will become shorter by a factor of gamma (it's called the Lorentz contraction). We won't bore you with the equation; just know that the shortening, which is real (it's observed in laboratory experiments), is important only when the velocity is comparable to the speed of light. So just don't move the book around at the speed of light, and everything will be just fine.

_07:: The Weight of This Book Will Increase Significantly If It Is Moved Rapidly

Another consequence of special relativity, this increase in mass is noticeable only if you're moving the book rapidly. By rapidly, of course, we mean near the speed of light. However, if you choose to move the book around 67 miles per hour, then the mass will increase by only one part in 100 trillion. And while that may not sound like much, it's the same mass you would get by adding half a trillion carbon atoms to it. So, be careful not to throw your back out when hot-rodding with that bag full of books!

_08:: This Book Might Spontaneously Disappear and Reappear in the Middle of Your Stomach

One of the great, fun things about science is that everything has a probability. For example, the probability is greater than zero that you will pole-vault over the moon tomorrow. Tunneling is a theory in quantum mechanics that explains the passing of a particle through a seemingly impenetrable barrier without a cause that is explainable by classical physics. The probability of it happening to an entire book, over a distance of several centimeters, is so low that it will not happen, on average, in many trillions of years. But physics can't say that it won't happen, only that it's not very likely.

Miserable Screwups by a Famous Physicist

Oh, that Lord Kelvin (1824–1907). Sure, he made fundamental contributions to the theory of heat. And thermodynamics. And he had that temperature scale named after him. But really, when you make blunders this big, it's definite proof everyone's entitled to a few mistakes.

_01:: The Earth Is Young

When Darwin published his "Origin of Species," Kelvin came to the conclusion that it was a mistake. He convinced Darwin that the earth could not be more than 100 million years old (as Darwin had said in the book) because there was no process that could have kept the sun burning that long. In fact, we now know that the earth is 4.6 billion years old, 46 times Kelvin's limit. But Darwin was so awed by Kelvin's self-confidence that he removed his discovery from subsequent editions of his manuscript. In fact, Darwin's deduction for the age of the earth should have been taken as an indication that Kelvin's model of the sun was wrong. Now we know that the sun derives its heat from nuclear fusion, a process that hadn't yet been discovered.

_02:: The Earth Is Shrinking

So, how did mountains come about? Kelvin's belief was that mountains grow because of the reduced space on a shrinking earth. Unfortunately for his theory, the earth isn't shrinking, at least not a significant amount. Kelvin thought the earth must be shrinking because of all the heat coming from the interior, and he argued the point vigorously. Kelvin believed that the heat came from two sources: from primordial energy from meteor impact and from the continuing compression of rocks by the earth's gravity. What he didn't know was that the earth was so old that little primordial heat was left, and that present-day shrinkage from gravity is negligible. We now know that the heat comes from radioactivity in the rock, but again, radioactivity hadn't yet been discovered when Kelvin was making his explanations.

_03:: Airplanes Won't Work

Kelvin is often quoted as saying, circa 1899, that "heavier than air flying machines are impossible." But he knew that birds flew, so this is certainly a paraphrase at best. Perhaps more accurate is the version "the aeroplane is scientifically impossible." Giving him the benefit of the doubt, we can interpret his statement to mean "a commercially useful aeroplane is impossible." He might have said such a thing based on his mastery of thermodynamics; no motor that existed at that time could produce the required power with low weight. In fact, the engines built by the Wright brothers (four years later) were innovative, and the need for better airplane engines drove much of the subsequent engine development.

_04:: Radio Has No Future

Kelvin is reported to have said this in 1897. And while this sounds like typical arrogance today, he probably said it because he believed that radio would offer no realistic alternative to the proposed transatlantic cable, which he was backing. People undoubtedly were bugging him about Marconi's recent experiments showing that signals could travel through the air, thus making his transatlantic cable unnecessary. In fact, the cable proved enormously important, as radio waves travel poorly across the Atlantic. So, in a sense, he was right. What Kelvin didn't anticipate was the enormous growth of radio as a form of entertainment and as a way of conveying news to the populace.

_05:: Physics Is Dead

Near the turn of the 20th century, Kelvin asserted that virtually all the physics there was to know was known and that as an academic discipline, physics had almost completed its work. The outstanding problems of his lifetime had been the theory of heat, to which he had made many of the greatest contributions, and the theory of electromagnetism, which had been put in completed form by Maxwell. Kelvin admitted that there were a few loose ends, especially the blackbody radiation problem (the theory of heat radiation led to a prediction of infinite radiation—clearly not true) and the puzzling results of the 1887 Michelson-Morley experiment (where the duo tried to detect the motion of the earth by detecting differences in the speed of light in two directions). Kelvin was sort of right: the physics we now label classical physics was mostly complete, while the two puzzles he mentioned opened the door to modern physics. The blackbody radiation problem led Planck to hypothesize that radiation emission is quantized, and that led to quantum mechanics. The Michelson-Morley experiment, on the other hand, led to the theory of relativity.

1 Nobel Prize That Should Never Have Been Awarded

What's more depressing than spending your entire life in a lab and never winning a Nobel Prize? How about spending your entire life in a lab, winning the Prize, and then finding out your award-winning research was completely wrong!

_01:: Enrico's Error

Enrico Fermi received a Nobel Prize in physics "for his demonstrations of the existence of new radioactive elements produced by neutron irradiation." Of course, Fermi had done so much Nobel Prize–quality work that it's unfortunate that he won for one of his rare mistakes. We now know that the "new" radioactive elements discovered by Fermi were not new radioactive elements (presumably beyond uranium), as he had stated, but rather fission fragments, or pieces of the original nucleus. The same year Fermi was given the prize, two other physicists (Lise Meitner and Otto Frisch) performed the same experiment and correctly described the results as fragments from fission. Fermi's other great work is described in the sidebar on p. 248. Fermi's stature, however, goes so far beyond the Nobel Prize that very few physics professors are even aware of his gaffe.

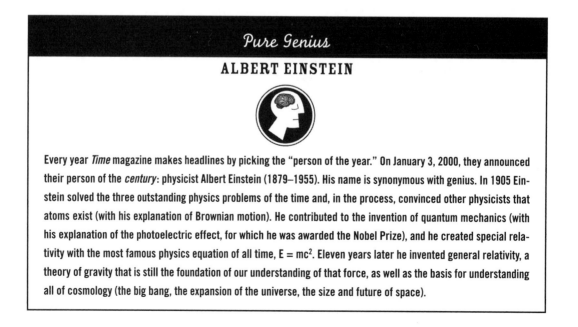

Pure Genius

ALBERT EINSTEIN

Every year *Time* magazine makes headlines by picking the "person of the year." On January 3, 2000, they announced their person of the *century*: physicist Albert Einstein (1879–1955). His name is synonymous with genius. In 1905 Einstein solved the three outstanding physics problems of the time and, in the process, convinced other physicists that atoms exist (with his explanation of Brownian motion). He contributed to the invention of quantum mechanics (with his explanation of the photoelectric effect, for which he was awarded the Nobel Prize), and he created special relativity with the most famous physics equation of all time, $E = mc^2$. Eleven years later he invented general relativity, a theory of gravity that is still the foundation of our understanding of that force, as well as the basis for understanding all of cosmology (the big bang, the expansion of the universe, the size and future of space).

Say It Ain't So!:

4 Things Einstein Got Wrong

Einstein's mistakes make a great point: in order to be right about anything important, you have to be willing to be dead wrong.

_01:: God Throws Dice

Einstein was one of the founders of quantum mechanics. His explanation of the photoelectric effect showed that light itself is quantized, and it was this work that won him his Nobel in 1921. (He didn't get it for relativity, which was more controversial.) Yet as quantum mechanics developed, he refused to believe what became a central tenet: that all events could be described only in terms of probability. Einstein summarized this by his famous statement, "God does not throw dice." According to quantum mechanics, two absolutely identical radioactive atoms will probably decay at different times. Einstein believed that there must be something hidden inside the nucleus, a hidden variable that was different for the two. Very sensitive statistical tests performed by experimentalists have shown that he was wrong. There aren't any hidden variables, at least not the simple kind.

_02:: Hubble Trouble

When Einstein developed his theory of gravitation, usually called general relativity, he found a problem. The universe, which he thought was static, could not be static according to his equations. Instead of predicting that the universe was changing, he modified his equations to introduce a cosmological constant that would support his theory. When physicist Edwin Hubble discovered that the universe was not static but was expanding, Einstein called his cosmological constant "the greatest mistake of my life."

_03:: Constant Hassles

Einstein effectively abandoned his cosmological constant when he learned of Hubble's discoveries. Ironically, calling this a mistake made for the second greatest mistake of his life! In the late 1990s Saul Perlmutter and his group at Berkeley discovered that the cosmological constant was not zero but was causing the universe to accelerate. Their result was soon confirmed by another group. So, had Einstein stuck to his guns, he could have been given credit for predicting one of the great scientific findings of the last 10 years—the accelerating universe.

_04:: A Field Day with Field Theory

Einstein spent the latter decades of his life trying to find a unified field theory that would illuminate a connection between gravity and electricity. In 1920, when he was in his forties, he decided to devote his career to

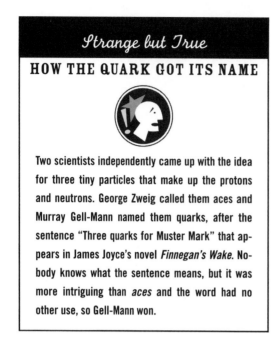

Strange but True

HOW THE QUARK GOT ITS NAME

Two scientists independently came up with the idea for three tiny particles that make up the protons and neutrons. George Zweig called them aces and Murray Gell-Mann named them quarks, after the sentence "Three quarks for Muster Mark" that appears in James Joyce's novel *Finnegan's Wake*. Nobody knows what the sentence means, but it was more intriguing than *aces* and the word had no other use, so Gell-Mann won.

unifying the theories of gravity and electromagnetism. He was so far ahead of his time that his major effort in this problem was doomed to failure. Although his work is full of mathematical insights, Einstein passed away before realizing his error. In the late 1960s and early 1970s, physicists Steven Weinberg, Abdus Salam, and Sheldon Glashow (and others) finally succeeded where Einstein couldn't—in unifying electromagnetism with the weak force—not the gravitational force that Einstein had worked on. The weak force is the force that makes for most radioactivity. It wasn't even known at the time Einstein began his work, so he couldn't have guessed that he was unifying the wrong forces.

9 Laws of Physics That Don't Apply in Hollywood

In general, Hollywood filmmakers follow the laws of physics because they have no other choice. It's just when they cheat with special effects that we seem to forget how the world really works.

_01:: Those Exploding Cars

When you're watching an action flick, all it takes is a crash, or maybe a stream of leaky gasoline that acts like a fuse, and suddenly, bang! You see a terrific explosion that's complete and violent. But gasoline doesn't explode unless mixed with about 93% air. Gas-induced car explosions were discovered on film relatively recently (you don't see them in the old black-and-white movies), and now audiences

just take them for granted. In general, there's no need to rush out of a crashed car, risking injury, because you fear an imminent explosion—it's probably not gonna happen.

_02:: Sound That Moves at the Speed of Light

Hollywood always gets this one wrong. On film, thunder doesn't follow lighting (as in real life, because sound is slower); they occur simultaneously. Similarly, a distant volcano erupts, and the blast is heard immediately rather than five seconds later for each mile. Explosions on the battlefield go boom right away, no matter how far away spectators are. Even a small thing, like the crack of a baseball player's bat, is simultaneous with ball contact, unlike at a real game.

_03:: Everything Is Illuminated: The Myth of Radioactivity

Films would have you believe that radioactivity is contagious and makes you glow in the dark. Where did this idea come from? *The Simpsons*? Perhaps, but the truth is that the most common forms of radioactivity will make you radioactive only if the radioactive particles stick to you. Radioactivity is not contagious. If a person is exposed to the radioactive neutrons from a nuclear reactor, then he can become slightly radioactive, but he certainly won't glow. And because radioactive things emit light only when they run into phosphor—like the coating on the inner surface of a TV tube— you don't really need to worry.

_04:: Shotgun Blasts and Kung Fu Kicks Make Targets Fly across the Room

With the string of new kung fu films out (they run the gamut from *The Matrix* to *Charlie's Angels*), you just can't escape the small matter of bad physics. Yeah, the action scenes look great and all, but in reality momentum is conserved, such that every action has an equal and opposite reaction. So, when you see a gal kick someone across the room, technically the kicker (or holder of a gun) must fly across the room in the opposite direction—unless she has a back against the wall.

_05:: Legends of the Fall

We aren't surprised when the cartoon character Wile E. Coyote runs off a cliff and is suspended there momentarily before he falls. But in the movies, buses and cars shouldn't be able to jump across gaps in bridges, even if they go heavy on the accelerator. The fact is, a vehicle will fall even if it's moving at a high speed. During the 1989 San Francisco earthquake, a driver saw a gap in the bridge too late and, probably inspired by movies, accelerated to try to make it across. Unfortunately, the laws of physics were not suspended, and he fell into the hole and crashed on the other side. Movies with special effects should come with a warning: "Laws of physics are violated in this movie. Don't try these stunts at home."

_06:: The Sounds of Science

All across the silver screen, you'll catch people screaming as their car flies in slow motion across the gap in the bridge. The problem, though, is that their voices don't change. In reality, if you slow down motion by a factor of two, the frequency of all sounds should drop by an octave. Women will sound like men, and men will sound like Henry Kissinger. Sound is an oscillation of the air. Middle C, for example, is 256 vibrations per second. If time is slowed down, there are fewer cycles per second, and the resulting sound is lower in pitch.

_07:: Shell Shock! Exploding Artillery Shells That Blow Straight Up

In movies, shells tend to kill only the person standing directly over them. It seems like a waste of artillery, since—if you believe the movies—each shell can't kill more than a single rifle bullet can. But in real life, artillery shells blow out in all directions, killing people all over. Movie directors like to have their actors running through a field of such shells, but they don't want their actors killed, so they arrange for underground explosions in holes that blow straight up, missing anyone who's more than 5 feet away.

_08:: The Sparking Bullet

Sparking bullets are a relatively recent invention in movie special effects. The gimmick provides a way of letting the audience know that the bullet just barely missed its target. In real life, sparks do occur when you scrape steel or other hard metals on hard surfaces (such as brick) because little pieces of the brittle material are heated to glow and fly off. The problem here is that bullets are generally made of lead because it's dense and soft, and you don't want the bullets scarring the steel of the gun barrel. Ever notice that no sparks fly from the front of the gun? That's because you're seeing lead bullets.

_09:: Sound Travels in Space

This is the granddaddy of all scientific complaints about space movies. For instance, in space the hero shouldn't be able to shout out instructions to the other astronauts from a spot several yards away. The movie *Aliens* corrected this misimpression with its tagline: "In space, nobody can hear you scream." And it's true. Sound is the vibration of air, and it's sensed when the air makes your eardrums vibrate. But try to forget this rule as soon as possible; it'll wreck a good many movies for you.

Reasons Physics Doesn't Work in the Real World

Admit it: you think physicists have it all figured out. But the fact is, some of the best theories just don't work anywhere but on the blackboard.

_01:: Science Friction: F = ma
(Force = Mass × Acceleration)

Sure, this fundamental equation of physics is simple to memorize, but it's virtually useless in real life. In fact, engineers almost never use it. The reason? Friction—that awful complication that keeps physics demonstrations from working. So, how do you calculate friction? If you ask an engineer, he'll give you an empirical co-efficient that he measured from previous experiments. But the truth of it is that physics is useless for most everyday phenomena. That's why physicists like to confine their research to atoms, nuclei, and space. In these realms, friction is either absent or it behaves according to simple rules. Anything that doesn't obey simple rules in physics is labeled "engineering," "chemistry," or something else.

_02:: Light Concerns

The speed of light is about 186,284 miles per second. But when light goes through air or glass, it slows down. Einstein assumed when he made his theory of general relativity that everyone would know he was referring to the speed of light *in a vacuum*. Because light is thought to have no mass, it'll always move at this fundamental speed. The concern here, though, is that if we discover someday that light has a very small but non-zero rest mass, then even light would never travel at the speed of light. Who knows? If that happens, we might have to rename the fundamental speed the Einstein velocity.

by
Christopher
Smith

Condensed
POP CULTURE

Contains

6 Musicians Who May (or May Not) Have Choked on Vomit or a Ham Sandwich ✳ Comic Gold: 7 Comic Books Worth Stealing from Grandma's Attic ✳ 8 Films Worth Sneaking Past Customs ✳ 6 Album Cover Artists Who Wear Their Art on Their Sleeves ✳ Keeping It Reel: 6 Directors Whose Names Have Become Adjectives ✳ 5 Pop Culture Story Lines Plucked from the Classics ✳ 7 Classic TV Episodes That Should Be Sent into Space to Demonstrate to Aliens What We Earthlings Call "Funny" ✳ 6 Tricky Lyrics You'll Never Get Wrong Again ✳

Musicians Who May (or May Not) Have Choked on Vomit or a Ham Sandwich

What can we learn from the tragic deaths of all these talented people, taken from us far too soon? Stay the hell out of London.

_01:: Tommy Dorsey (1905–1956)

The first musician to die the archetypal rock-and-roll death was actually a trombonist. Tommy Dorsey and his clarinetist brother, Jimmy, were two of the biggest bandleaders of the swing era. The quarrelsome brothers split up in 1935 but reunited in 1953. The reunion would be short-lived, however. Tommy, a famed heavy eater, choked on vomit in his sleep at his country home in Greenwich, Connecticut, on November 26, 1956, thanks to a huge dinner with sleeping pills for dessert. It was just a week after the bone-slinging Lithuanian's 51st birthday.

_02:: Jimi Hendrix (1942–1970)

Much mystery surrounds the day guitar god Jimi Hendrix finally kissed the sky. But the facts are these: Jimi spent the night of September 17–18, 1970, in London, partying with a German girlfriend, Monika Danneman. At 3:00 a.m. she fixed Jimi a tuna fish sandwich, and they went to bed. She awoke around 10:20 the next morning to find Jimi with vomit around his mouth and nose, unable to wake up. He was rushed to St. Mary Abbott's Hospital, but en route he choked on his own vomit. He was pronounced DOA, the official cause listed as "inhalation of vomit

due to barbiturate intoxication." The strange death also falls under the category of 3 Rock Gods Who Died at 27 (see page 185 for the rest of the list).

_03:: Eric "Stumpy Joe" Childs (1945–1974)

One of the many ill-fated drummers of the legendary (and completely fictional) British rock band Spinal Tap, John "Stumpy" Pepys—also known as the Peeper—died in a bizarre gardening accident that the police said was "best left unsolved." Two drummers, Mick Shrimpton and Peter "James" Bond, fell victim to spontaneous combustion. But the most bizarre death would have to be that of Childs, who, his bandmates sadly recall, choked on *someone else's* vomit. The originator of the vomit remains unknown because "you can't really dust for vomit."

_04:: Bon Scott (1946–1980)

When Ronald "Bon" Scott, hard-drinking Scottish front man of seminal rock group AC/DC, died, his band was on the verge of exploding internationally with the release of *Highway to Hell* (file under: Chillingly Prophetic Album Titles). But on February 19, 1980, after a night of heavy drinking, Scott passed out in the backseat of a friend's car in London. While speculative causes of his death have ranged from alcohol poisoning to hypothermia, the true cause was—you guessed it—asphyxiation by inhalation of vomit. The band replaced him with Brian Johnson and recorded *Back in Black*, one of the greatest rock albums of all time, as a tribute to their fallen comrade. (The album included, ironically, a toast to the high life, "Have a Drink on Me.")

_05:: John Bonham (1947–1980)

Many consider Led Zeppelin's John "Bonzo" Bonham the greatest rock drummer ever to pick up sticks. He was also, unquestionably, one of the greatest drinkers. The binge that finally sent him up the Stairway to Heaven occurred September 24, 1980, during which he reputedly downed 40 shots of vodka in four hours. Sometime during the night at Jimmy Page's home in Windsor, England, he vomited in his sleep and choked. Bassist John Paul Jones found him dead the next morning, and Led Zeppelin called it quits three months later. Some sources list alcohol poisoning as the cause of his death—a logical assumption, considering his blood alcohol content was a staggering 0.41. To put that in perspective, consider this: at 0.30, most people slip into a coma.

_06:: "Mama" Cass Elliot (1941–1974)

One of the most famous of all musicians to die by choking actually did not. Since her death in a London hotel room on July 29, 1974, the

What's the Difference?
RAP VS. HIP-HOP

There's no easy answer to this one. Some maintain that rap is a kind of music, whereas hip-hop is a lifestyle, one that includes rap, break dancing, DJ-ing, and graffiti art. Rap pioneer and sage KRS-One says simply, "Rap is something you do, but hip-hop is something you live." Others insist that hip-hop is a musical style distinct from rap, for very specific reasons: hip-hop has a particular beat and uses scratching and "breaks" (samples). Just as heavy metal fans would never confuse a speed metal act with a hair band, true aficionados feel the same way about rap and hip-hop. They insist that rapping over a soul or heavy metal track could never be hip-hop. In other words, all hip-hop is rap, but not all rap is hip-hop.

legend has grown that Elliot, whose girth was as famous as her voice, died by choking on a ham sandwich. This, like all things pork, is not kosher. An autopsy determined that she died of heart failure due to fatty myocardial degeneration, a condition caused by her obesity. The ham sandwich legend grew from the fact that one was found on her bedside table. The sandwich was unresponsive to investigators' questions about its involvement in the singer's death.

Comic Gold:

7 Comic Books Worth Stealing from Grandma's Attic

Hey, Grandma never liked to read comics anyway, right?

_01::, _02:: Action Comics #1 (June 1938)

This is it, the comic book Holy Grail, the one that introduced the world to Superman. The cover bears the famous—if somewhat crude—drawing of Superman smashing a car against a rock. Written and drawn by Jerome Siegel and Joe Shuster, the comic introduced Superman as "Champion of the oppressed, the physical marvel who had sworn to devote his existence to helping those in need!" The last survivor of the doomed planet Krypton (duh), Superman could "leap ⅛th of a mile; hurdle a 20-story building . . . raise tremendous weights . . . run faster than an express train . . . and nothing less than a bursting shell could penetrate his skin!" Superman was so popular, he became the first character to get his very own comic book. Superman #1 hit newsstands in the summer of 1939. The Man of Steel has held up pretty well, you could say.

Action Comics #1

Cover price in 1938: 10¢
Estimated top value today: $350,000

Superman #1

Cover price in 1939: 10¢
Estimated top value today: $210,000

_03:: Detective Comics #27 (May 1939)

Less than a year later, an artist named Bob Kane decided to create a caped superhero of his own, one much darker, more mysterious, and more "human" than the squeaky-clean Superman. His creation: Batman. Unlike the campy '60s TV version of the character, the Batman in this first issue was a dark, vengeful crusader who stalked the night (he watches as a bad guy plunges into a vat of acid), presaging the hero's reemergence in the 1980s in *The Dark Knight Returns*. Perhaps this darkness was a reflection of the dread of war looming on the horizon in 1939? The cover proclaimed, "Starting this issue: The amazing and unique adventures of THE BATMAN!" and promised "64 pages of action!"

Cover price in 1939: 10¢
Estimated top value today: $300,000

_04:: Marvel Comics #1 (October 1939)

In 1939 a comic book house called Funnies Inc. approached pulp fiction publisher Martin Goodman with a proposal to provide him with ready-made comic book artwork. All he had to do was publish it. Seeing the kind of cash Action Comics and others were raking in, he agreed, and Marvel Comics was born. The first

Fake Your Way through a Conversation

THE LOWDOWN ON MARVEL AND DC

To the uninitiated, a comic book is a comic book. But to fans and collectors, the world of superheroes is divided into two camps: Marvel and DC. So, to avoid any embarrassing faux pas at your next comic book soiree, here's your handy guide to the two universes.

MARVEL COMICS

Founded: October 1939 (formerly Timely Comics)

Names to Drop: Stan Lee, Martin Goodman, Jack Kirby, Joe Simon, John Romita

Heroes: Captain America, Iron Man, Spider-Man, Thor, Namor the Sub-Mariner, Silver Surfer, Wolverine, Daredevil, the Punisher, Elektra

Villains: Dr. Octopus, the Red Skull, Kingpin, Dr. Doom, Magneto

Teams: The Avengers, X-Men, The Fantastic Four

Famous Green Guys: Green Goblin, the Lizard, the Incredible Hulk (who was originally gray)

Conversation starters: "I think I liked the Hulk better in his original gray." "Nobody could draw Iron Man like Jack Kirby!" "Mary Jane never looked hotter than when McFarlane was penciling *Spider-Man*. Meow!"

DC COMICS

Founded: 1934 (formerly New Fun Comics)

Names to Drop: Harry Donenfeld, Bob Kane, Frank Miller, Alan Moore, Jerome Siegel, Joe Shuster

Heroes: Superman, Batman and Robin, Wonder Woman, Hawkman, the Flash, Aquaman, Swamp Thing

Villains: Lex Luthor, the Joker, the Riddler, the Penguin, Darkseid, Catwoman

Teams: Legion of Super-Heroes, Justice League of America, Legion of Doom

Famous Green Guys: Green Lantern, Green Arrow

Conversation Starters: "I think Aquaman could totally perch-slap Sub-Mariner in an underwater fight, don't you?" "Which one had the scarier Joker—*Arkham Asylum* or *Batman: The Killing Joke*?" "Meanwhiiiiile, back at the Hall of Justice . . ."

issue introduced three legendary Marvel characters: the Sub-Mariner of Atlantis, prince of the Deep; the Human Torch (a different Human Torch than the one that would become part of the Fantastic Four 22 years later—let's not get them confused); and Ka-Zar the Great, a man who lived in the jungle among apes (strangely similar to another popular ape man whose name had a lot of the same letters).

Cover price in 1939: 10¢

Estimated top value today: $250,000

_05:: Batman #1 (Spring 1940)

After appearing in 13 issues of Detective Comics, Batman and his new sidekick—Robin the Boy Wonder (introduced in Detective Comics #38)—were so popular, they got their very own comic book. *Batman* began as a quarterly, but that wasn't enough for fans. Neither was a bimonthly. So, before long, readers could get a new Batman adventure every month. The first issue introduces two of Batman's most legendary nemeses: the Joker and Catwoman. More than 63 years and over 600 issues later, Batman is still fighting villains—as well as his own demons—on the streets of Gotham City.

Cover price in April 1940: 10¢
Estimated top value today: $100,000

_06:: All-American Comics #16 (July 1940)

How many times has this happened to you? Man finds alien metal lantern. Man makes ring out of lantern. Man presses ring to lantern. Man has incredible superpowers over everything. Except wood, obviously. That's the story in All-American Comics #16, a book published tangentially under the DC Comics umbrella. When regular guy Alan Scott made his ring, the superhero created was, of course, the Green Lantern. The idea of an everyday schmoe just lucking into superhero-ness proved incredibly popular. A similar idea struck gold in 1962 when a young nerd named Peter Parker got bitten by a radioactive spider (see below).

Cover price in 1940: 10¢
Estimated top value today: $115,000

_07:: Amazing Fantasy #15 (August 1962)

The word bubbles on the cover say it all: "Though the world may mock Peter Parker, the timid teen-ager . . . it will soon marvel at the awesome might of . . . SPIDER-MAN!" And writer Stan Lee (pseudonym of Stanley Martin Lieber) and artist Mike Ditko could not have been more right. Spider-Man was the first comic book hero to be a regular teenager, going through the same things his readers were dealing with: shyness, insecurity, a crush on a pretty girl, and trouble with the popular jock (Flash Thompson). No wonder people of all ages are still true believers.

Cover price in 1962: 12¢
Estimated top value today: $42,000

Films Worth Sneaking Past Customs (Note: *Crouching Tiger, Hidden Dragon* Not Included)

A trip across an ocean can add cachet and panache and a lot of other French words to just about anything. Even Jerry Lewis. And nothing makes you look classier than knowing a thing or two about foreign film. Here are some of the most *essentiel*.

_01:: *Un Chien Andalou* (France, 1928)

What do you get when you combine two of the greatest surrealist minds of the 20th century (Luis Buñuel and Salvador Dali) and throw in a heaping helping of existential ennui? You get *Un Chien Andalou*, one of the most bizarre, disturbing, and controversial films ever made. Thank God it's only 17 minutes long. A mishmash of unlinked dreamlike sequences, each prefaced with a meaningless time marker ("Eight years later . . . ," "Around 3 o'clock in the morning . . ."), the film challenges the very concept of film itself. Its most infamous image is its first, in which Buñuel himself sharpens a straight razor on a strop, then uses it to slash a woman's eyeball, an image paralleled by a sliver of cloud moving across a full moon. This leads to a string of unrelated images just as haunting: grand pianos full of rotting animal corpses that turn into dead priests, ants crawling out of a hole in a man's hand. You get the idea. The title (which means "An Andalusian Dog") has no reference in the film.

_02:: *M* (Germany, 1931)

Silence of the Lambs. Psycho. Seven. They all have their roots in *M*, Fritz Lang's expressionist masterpiece about a serial child killer. Lang anticipates Kubrick in his use of sound (and silence): the murderer whistles Grieg's cheery but ominous *Peer Gynt* before he kills. And, like Hitchcock, Lang terrifies you by what you *don't* see: a child's off-screen murder is symbolized by a balloon stuck in phone lines. Peter Lorre portrays killer Hans Beckert, who was based on a real child killer called the Monster of Düsseldorf. His scene before a mock court of his criminal captors, pitiful and pleading that he can't help himself, stands as one of the all-time great performances. And to think the Nazis almost suppressed *M* because they suspected its original title—*Murderers among Us*—referred to them.

_03:: *Seven Samurai* (Japan, 1954)

Like many Japanese products, this movie took an idea from America, improved on it, and was then remade in America. Akira Kurosawa's epic *Seven Samurai* drew inspiration from American Westerns by directors like John Ford. Ironically, it was eventually remade as a Western: *The Magnificent Seven*. Kurosawa's film is the magnificent story of seven out-of-work warriors coming together to help a village tormented by bandits in chaotic 16th-century Japan. The film combines epic sweep and personal detail to produce an incredibly rich story of real depth and power. And like all good heroic epics involving lots of guys (translation: *Spartacus*), it's vaguely homoerotic.

_04:: *The Seventh Seal* (Sweden, 1956)

Ah, Ingmar Bergman. No one else could make death, the black plague, rape, lost faith, metaphysical pondering, and chess all look so darn good. Max von Sydow plays a knight facing a crisis of faith. When Death (a white-faced figure in a hooded black cloak, lampooned in *Bill and Ted's Bogus Journey*, of all places) comes for him, the knight challenges him to a game of chess, during which he gives Death the third degree about the nature of God and all that. The film's last shot is its most famous: Death leads a line of people, silhouetted against a cloudy sky, in a final dance, uniting them all in the final equality of mortality. The shot was not planned: the dancing characters are actually grips and gaffers dressed up and ad-libbing.

_05:: *La Dolce Vita* (Italy, 1960)

Federico Fellini's *La Dolce Vita* is a symbol full of symbols. Marcello Mastroianni plays Rubini, a frustrated writer and wannabe playboy. Over a series of seven days and nights, Rubini prowls Rome's Via Veneto in search of "the sweet life." Each night is, both literally and figuratively, a descent into decadence, darkness, self-indulgence, and futility. Each dawn brings an ascension into light, self-discovery, shattered illusions, and regret. Packed with symbolism (a statue of Christ suspended from a helicopter; the seven hills of Rome = seven days and nights = the seven

---

Alphabet Soup

SOME LINGO FROM THE BACK LOT

Abby Singer [AB-ee SIN-gur]: *n* The second-to-last shot of a day of filming. The real Abby Singer, a production manager for numerous films and TV series, often called out, "Only one more shot," signaling to cast and crew that the workday was almost over. But the director frequently trumped him, asking for more takes or another shot. The Abby Singer is followed by . . .

martini [mar-TEE-nee]: *n* The very last shot of the day is called the martini because, the director hopes, the only shot left is a nice Bombay Sapphire.

Alan Smithee [AL-in SMIH-thee]: *n* A pseudonym used when a director wants nothing to do with the finished film, having lost creative control due to extensive reediting, studio meddling, or other interference. Directors can appeal to the Directors Guild of America (DGA, their union) to have their name taken off the film. If the appeal is successful, the name is replaced with Alan Smithee, the only pseudonym the DGA allows for directors, although writers, producers, and even actors have used it. John Frankenheimer, Dennis Hopper, Sam Raimi, and many others have all chosen to "Smithee" their films. So, get up and leave the theater if the opening credits say "An Alan Smithee Film." Or "Directed by Kevin Costner."

MOS [EM OH ES]: *adj* Describes a scene shot without live sound, such as panoramic landscapes or the like. Hollywood legend links the origin of MOS to Austrian actor and director Erich Von Stroheim, whose accent turned "without sound" into "mit-out sound."

deadly sins) and strange characters, *La Dolce Vita* depicts the sweet life as it is: a pretty, empty illusion.

_06:: *The Discreet Charm of the Bourgeoisie* (France, 1972)

This one is a doozy. Spanish filmmaker Luis Buñuel serves up this scathingly hilarious piece of social commentary with his trademark heapin' helpin' of surrealism. The plot—what there is of it—involves a group of hoity-toity types whose dinner plans keep getting interrupted by increasingly strange events. For example, the army marches through their party. The movie is a fable, a parable about the empty lives of the well-to-do and their detachment from real life. And it's actually funny.

_07:: *La Grande Illusion* (France, 1937)

Directed by Jean Renoir, this film portrays the relationship between French soldiers and their German captors in a World War I prisoner-of-war camp. Using innovative slow pans and long tracking shots, Renoir paints a picture of post-World War I Europe in microcosm: the aristocratic French and German officers commiserate about the looming death of Europe's rigid class system, while the enlisted men of both sides share their dreams about returning to live in a new, egalitarian, peaceful world. But the title reveals Renoir's attitude about the notion of war having the power to ultimately correct society's wrongs: it's simply an illusion.

_08:: *Trainspotting* (UK, 1996)

OK, so it's not *technically* in a foreign language. *Boot et mate as bloody wail beh!* The Scottish accents in director Danny Boyle's heroin-addled morality tale-slash-comedy-slash-antidrug manifesto are as thick as Edinburgh fog. One disco scene is actually subtitled. But the images in the film—the baby crawling on the ceiling, the harrowingly realistic heroin binges, the kitten sitting by the body of a toxoplasmosis victim—are unforgettable. Love it or hate it, *Trainspotting* can't be ignored. Extra trivia tidbit: the title refers to a curious British hobby. Trainspotters spend hours on train platforms meticulously recording the type and numbers of passing trains. Sound like a pointless waste of life? So's heroin.

6 Album Cover Artists Who Wear Their Art on Their Sleeves

Every art form has its giants, and album covers are no different. Some of the designers were so prolific, so recognizable, that their work became as famous as the bands themselves.

_01:: Hipgnosis

It sounds like "hypnosis" but, like, it's more about "gnosis," knowing spiritual truth, y'know? Only, like, more "hip." The name helps explain the distinctive style of Hipgnosis, a British design trio led by the prolific Storm Thorgerson. Hipgnosis covers combine enigmatic, symbolic images with a disturbing sense of timeless isolation. Consider the naked children on Led Zeppelin's *Houses of the Holy* or the empty black shape on *Presence*, the black eye bars on AC/DC's *Dirty Deeds (Done Dirt Cheap)*. And most of Pink Floyd's unforgettable covers, like the fiery handshake on *Wish You Were Here* or *Dark Side of the Moon*'s iconic prism. All classics. All instantly recognizable. And all Hipgnosis. Far out.

_02:: Neon Park

The pseudonym of quirky painter Martin Muller, Neon Park produced offbeat paintings for bands of all stripes, most notably Little Feat (some of his covers featured cakes on swings or ducks dressed up like Hollywood pinups). His bizarro style became popular after the equally unique Frank Zappa and his band, the Mothers of Invention, chose Neon Park's work for the cover of *Weasels Ripped My Flesh* (1970). The cheery cartoonlike drawing of a white-bread father figure tearing his smiling face to bloody ribbons is the most famous example of the strange work of Neon Park.

_03:: Andy Warhol

Album covers were just one more medium for which pop art legend Andy Warhol changed the rules. He brought an interactive sense of fun to his covers. The Rolling Stones' 1971 classic *Sticky Fingers* featured a well-endowed man in tight jeans that had a real working zipper (contrary to legend, the dong behind the denim is *not* Mick Jagger's). The zipper left its mark on the album cover genre. Unfortunately, it also left its mark on the record itself (right in the middle of "Sister Morphine"). Warhol was also responsible for the peel-away banana on 1976's *The Velvet Underground & Nico*. The man just had a way with phallic symbols.

_04:: Pen & Pixel Graphics

Yo, for all the straight up hip-hop impresarios who want CD covers drippin' wit Benjamins, Bentleys, and plenty of bling bling, Pen & Pixel graphics is da shizznit. The Houston design firm all but defined the look of rap albums of the late '90s and beyond. Pen & Pixel's

SO WHAT REALLY IS IN THAT BRIEFCASE IN *PULP FICTION*?

You know the scene. Vincent opens the briefcase, an orange glow bathes his face, and he stares in wonder. But what the hell is it? One of the most popular theories among fans and trivia nerds is that the briefcase contains the stolen soul of Marsellus Wallace. I mean, it's so obvious: the lock combination is 666. The briefcase is way too light to contain gold or Tarantino's hoped-for Oscar (another theory). And if it was the stolen diamonds or severed ear from *Reservoir Dogs* (two more theories), why would it be orange? Further, Marsellus has a Band-Aid on the back of his head, because everyone knows that's where the Devil takes your soul (a fact not actually in any recognized religious text). Of course, it's a nice theory but completely unsubstantiated by anyone remotely involved with the film. Cowriter Roger Avary said the original contents—diamonds—were too boring, so the briefcase became just "an intriguing MacGuffin" with nothing in it. Somebody had the orange light bulb idea, and the mystery was born. So, what's the best answer for what's in the suitcase? The one Tarantino actually came up with: two light bulbs and some batteries.

diamond-studded type treatments, metallic inks, and exaggerated photographs of fur-clad, jewel-encrusted rap artists have graced tons of rap albums, including *Da Game Is To Be Sold,* *Not To Be Told* by Snoop Dogg and Master P's *Da Last Don.* And like so many distinctive styles, theirs have also inspired a lot of blatant imitation. Or is it just "sampling"?

_05:: Reid Miles

Many cover artists have defined the look of a band, sometimes even a decade. The work of Reid Miles defines a legendary record label and an entire genre of music. From 1956 to 1967, Reid Miles produced hundreds of striking graphic covers for jazz artists on the Blue Note label including Freddie Hubbard, Jimmy Smith, and Art Blakey. Miles brought the graphic sensibilities of his commercial-art background to bear on his covers, using bright colors, clean type, and cropped black-and-white or duo-tone photos to evoke the moods of the music. His style, still imitated to this day, defined what cool looked like.

_06:: Honorable Mentions: Illustrators and the Bands Who Love Them

For some bands, their name on the front means one particular artist's name in the liner notes. For example, if you see YES over an other-worldly dreamscape, dollars to doughnuts the art is by Roger Dean. Prog-rock supergroup Asia liked him too. How about the Coca-Cola-esque Chicago logo? Of its more than 20 iterations, the original and 13 others were by John Berg. All those gruesome portraits of theatrical metal masters Iron Maiden's horrific mascot, Eddie, are the work of Derek Riggs. Journey's winged scarab beetle? Veteran designer Jim Welch.

Keeping It Reel:

6 Directors Whose Names Have Become Adjectives

When it comes to film, it's not enough to be good. You've gotta have style, meaning that film school schlubs everywhere will do their best to mimic your work.

_01:: Stanley Kubrick (1928–1999)

It's impossible to label Kubrick with a single genre, ranging as he did from historical epic to horror to sci-fi to war to black comedy about war. His films were always masterful and thought provoking. But the keys to being Kubrickian are deliberate pacing, a sense of contradictory emotion (claustrophobia caused by open spaces, complete silence shattered by loud noises, horrific images shot beautifully), and storytelling without words. Also, a director can be called Kubrickian when he is being his most difficult; Stanley Kubrick was legendary for his perfectionism, his need for control ("It is essential for one man to make a film"), and his exhaustive shooting, sometimes demanding 50 or 100 takes to get a scene just right.

Kubrick at his most Kubrickian: *Dr. Strangelove* (1964), *2001: A Space Odyssey* (1968), *A Clockwork Orange* (1971), *The Shining* (1980), *Eyes Wide Shut* (1999).

Spielberg at his most Kubrickian, at least until the last 10 minutes: *A.I.: Artificial Intelligence* (2001), a project conceived by Kubrick but shot (and killed) by Spielberg.

_02:: Ingmar Bergman (1918–)

For serious film buffs, Swedish director and writer Ingmar Bergman is God. His films are slow burns of pain and raw emotion, wrenching in their realism and jarring in their stark beauty. Bergmanesque films smolder with emotional tension, intellectual gravitas, symbolism, and religious imagery. If you're planning to see a film described as Bergmanesque, bring your tissues and prepare to think about things like love, death, your relationship with your father, and the nature of God. The 2001 drama *In the Bedroom* (directed by Tom Field) was considered very Bergmanesque. For younger or less sophisticated viewers who prefer explosions and poop jokes to naked emotional drama, *Bergmanesque* can be mistakenly used interchangeably with *boring*.

Bergman at his most Bergmanesque: *The Seventh Seal* (1957), *Cries and Whispers* (1972), *Scenes from a Marriage* (1973), *Fanny and Alexander* (1982).

_03:: Robert Altman (1925–)

While not all of his films necessarily fall into the category, Altman's films are often multi-character studies that portray the many layers of human social interaction with equal parts humor and venom (2001's *Gosford Park*, for example, had 30 speaking roles). Altman is renowned for his technique of giving all the actors in a scene their own microphones and encouraging them to ad-lib, mixing the results into a symphony of half-heard conversa- tional snippets, muttered insults, and naked confessions. But below it all, Altmanesque films demonstrate an understanding of the human condition and a contempt for pomposity and social castes. No wonder he is such an outspoken critic of the Hollywood system and considered a maverick.

Altman at his most Altmanesque: *M*A*S*H* (1970), *Nashville* (1975), *The Player* (1992), *Gosford Park* (2001).

Altman at his least Altmanesque: *Popeye* (1980).

_04:: Federico Fellini (1920–1993)

Like Bergman's, Fellini's films are full of symbolism and personal reflection. His Oscar-winning masterpiece *8½* is a painfully honest autobiographical study of a film director suffocated by success. But what has come to be most Felliniesque about Fellini's films are his characters. Through his lens, life was a carnival, a circus parade of bizarre characters whose very surrealism makes them all the more real—midgets, clowns, whores, circus folk, or even circus-clown-midget-whores. Think of the cover of the Doors' album *Strange Days*. That is, visually speaking, the essence of Felliniesque.

Fellini at his most Felliniesque: *La Strada* (1954), *Nights of Cabiria* (1957), *La Dolce Vita* (1960), *8½* (1963), *Juliet of the Spirits* (1965).

_05:: David Lynch (1946–)

There is a temptation to describe anything unexplained or bizarre as Lynchian. But the term implies something much more. To be truly Lynchian, a film or event must juxtapose something incredibly bizarre and unexplainable with something else completely mundane—

Pure Genius

ALFRED HITCHCOCK

The son of a greengrocer from Leytonstone, London, Alfred Hitchcock (1899–1980) directed his first film, *Number 13*, at the age of 23. After several hits in England (including *The Man Who Knew Too Much*), he moved to Hollywood. He had trouble finding a studio to hire him until David O. Selznick chose him to direct *Rebecca* (1940). It won Best Picture. Despite never winning an Oscar for any of his next 37 films, Hitch did receive the Irving Thalberg Memorial Award for lifetime achievement in 1967. His acceptance speech? "Thank you."

Hitchcock's films show his particular penchant for blondes. But his most famous technique was the use of a MacGuffin, an object that propels the action but has no real bearing on the story's outcome. Classic Hitchcock MacGuffins are the true identity of the spy in *North by Northwest* or the stolen $40,000 in *Psycho*. Other directors have used MacGuffins, like the contents of the briefcase in *Pulp Fiction*. Quentin Tarantino borrowed another page from Hitch's book: the cameo appearance in his own films. Hitchcock showed up in every film he made from *The Lodger* in 1926 until his last, *Family Plot*, in 1976.

like finding a severed ear in a perfectly mani-cured suburban lawn, as in *Blue Velvet*. Lynch likes to set his absurd happenings in the most white-bread small towns (he hails from Missoula, Montana), thereby increasing their strangeness and their universality at the same time. Lynch's weirdness is very self-conscious, very calculated, which is what makes it so creepy. Through people and places that (we hope) are nothing like us and our world, he shows us the worst parts of ourselves.

Lynch at his most Lynchian: *Eraserhead* (1977), *Blue Velvet* (1986), *Twin Peaks* (TV, 1990), *Lost Highway* (1997), *Mulholland Drive* (2001).

_06:: Alfred Hitchcock (1899–1980)

You may think that defining the characteristics of a director dubbed "the master of suspense" would be a no-brainer. But Hitchcock's mastery goes deep. In almost 70 films, Hitchcock drew suspense from ordinary objects (who knew birds or shower curtains could be so terrifying?), from strained romantic relationships, and, most of all, from viewing the characters' reactions to violence rather than the violent acts themselves. No one could draw more terror from a single gaze than Hitchcock. As the master himself once said, "Film your murders like love scenes, and film your love scenes like murders." Many films are Hitchcockian—*Body Double, Dead Again, What Lies Beneath, Frantic*—but none of them are Hitchcock.

Hitchcock at his most Hitchcockian: *Rope* (1948), *Dial M for Murder* (1954), *Rear Window* (1954), *Vertigo* (1958), *North by Northwest* (1959), *Psycho* (1960), *The Birds* (1963).

5 Pop Culture Story Lines Plucked from the Classics

Why come up with a new plot line when you can recycle? Better yet, steal from a source with a built-in fan base.

_01:: *West Side Story* (1961) = William Shakespeare's *Romeo and Juliet*

This one's pretty common knowledge, and the parallels aren't hard to see. Instead of Romeo and Juliet, the star-crossed lovers are Tony and Maria. Instead of fair Verona you've got not-so-fair Spanish Harlem. Similarly, Shakespeare wasn't allowed to have a woman play the part of Juliet, and for some reason studios couldn't find a Hispanic actress to play the part of Maria. Instead of two warring families (Capulets and Montagues), you've got two warring gangs. And instead of wordy soliloquies and gut-wrenching violence, you've got finger-snapping tunes and dynamite dance choreography. And instead of them both dying, only Tony gets it. After all, how can you kill Natalie Wood?

Fake Your Way through a Conversation
(WITH A STAR TREK FAN!)

Say a Trekker (the polite term) approaches you with amorous intentions: "You're the most beautiful carbon-based life-form in the Alpha Quadrant. Would you care to join me for a Romulan ale? May I store your number in my tricorder?" Here's a quick primer for your convenience. If you're in a pinch, though, you can always say your Prime Directive prevents you from dating dweebs.

Aliens, Not-So-Friendly—the Borg, Jem'Hadar, Cardassians, Klingons (sometimes), Q Continuum: In the original series, the warlike Klingons were *the* bad guys. But sometime between then and *The Next Generation*, an uneasy truce came into effect. One of them, Worf, even joined the crew of the *Enterprise*. The Ferengi (big-eared merchant aliens that bear a strange resemblance to NBA star Reggie Miller) were too comical to be the new bad guys. Enter the ultimate menace, the robotic Borg, stalking the galaxy in giant cubes assimilating entire planets into their Collective: "You will be assimilated. Resistance is futile." The super-hottie on *Star Trek: Voyager*? That's ex-Borg babe Seven-of-Nine.

Kirk and Picard: The two big-name captains of the starship *Enterprise*. James Tiberius Kirk (William Shatner) commanded *Enterprise NCC-1701* in the original series and the first seven films. Jean-Luc Picard (Patrick Stewart) commanded several *Enterprise*s in *The Next Generation* and the later films.

"Live long and prosper": A Vulcan blessing/salute, accompanied by a hand sign: fingers spread in a V formation, thumb out, both ad-libbed by Leonard Nimoy. He derived it from a common blessing from rabbis to their congregation. The gesture symbolizes the letter *shin*, the first letter of the word *Shadai*, a secret Hebrew name for God.

Prime Directive: The guiding principle of all Starfleet interactions with alien species. The main clause: "No Starfleet personnel may interfere with the healthy development of alien life and culture."

Stardate: The way of marking time that replaced AD as the standard. There's a complicated method for determining stardate (SD), but here's a good one to know: SD 40759.5 = October 4, 2363 = commissioning date of the starship *Enterprise*.

Starfleet: The military arm of the United Federation of Planets, an alliance including Earth and over 150 other planets.

Tachyon pulse: An emission of a special kind of energy that seems to solve all kinds of problems, from temporal anomalies to subspace rifts. If that doesn't work, usually an *inverse* tachyon pulse does the trick. It is a common deus ex machina solution in the Trek series.

Warp speed: As Mach 1 is the speed of sound, Warp 1 is the speed of light.

_02:: *O Brother, Where Art Thou?* (2000) = Homer's *Odyssey*

So, you say you can't see the parallels between the George Clooney vehicle and Homer's epic poem of Odysseus' 10-year voyage home from the Trojan War? Look closer: three escaped convicts undergo a long journey from prison to get home, having lots of obstacles thrown in their way. The Sirens (three singing, bathing beauties on rocks) lure the men into trouble; they run afoul of a giant Cyclops (John Goodman as eye-patched Big Dan Teague). Rather than hiding under sheep, as in the *Odyssey*, they hide under Ku Klux Klan robes. And when the main character, Ulysses (Odysseus' name in the Roman version of the tale), returns home, he finds his wife being courted by another. One character, a gubernatorial candidate, is named Homer Stokes. And, well, both titles start with the letter *O*. However, scholars haven't been able to find a mention of Dapper Dan Hair Pomade in the original text.

_03:: *Rent* (1996) = Puccini's *La Boheme*

These two line up almost scene for scene. The original followed a group of starving artists in 1830s Paris. The musical is about a group of starving artists in 1990s Greenwich Village with Americanized versions of the original's names (Rodolfo the poet = Roger the musician; Marcello the painter = Mark the filmmaker; Mimi the seamstress = Mimi the exotic dancer; Benoit the landlord = Benny the landlord). Instead of tuberculosis, *Rent*'s characters are dealing with another plague: AIDS. And a whole lot of them are gay. Late composer Jonathan Larson even uses pieces of dialogue and music from the opera and doesn't hide it. Roger repeatedly plays a snippet on his guitar that Mark dismisses for sounding too much like "Musetta's Waltz" from the opera.

_04:: *Star Trek II: The Wrath of Khan* (1982) = Herman Melville's *Moby Dick*

No, seriously. It does. Well, kind of. In *Moby Dick* a man's relentless pursuit of (and hatred for) his nemesis, a plump white whale, drives him to the edge. Ditto for the movie, only in this case the nemesis is a plump white William Shatner. References to *Moby Dick* occur throughout the movie (the book itself is on the shelf in Khan's ship *Botany Bay*). Khan's dialogue mirrors much of Captain Ahab's: "Thar she blows!" becomes "There she is!" Both men chase their prey because "he tasks me." Both vow to chase their quarry "around Perdition's flames." And Khan's last words are lifted directly from Captain Ahab: "From Hell's heart I stab at thee! For hate's sake I spit my last breath at thee!"

_05:: *Clueless* (1995) = Jane Austen's *Emma*

Never has such a seemingly brainless movie linked itself so closely to such a thoughtful book. But *Clueless* is actually a rigidly faithful retelling of Austen's romantic coming-of-age tale. Emma becomes Cher, the pampered, ditzy teenager with a heart of gold. The parallels are many, including her friendship with a social outcast, her matchmaking (a teacher and a guidance counselor instead of Mr. Weston and Miss Taylor), and imagined overtures from an unavailable male (in Emma it's for social reasons; in *Clueless* it's because he's gay). An adventure in a carriage becomes a failed driving test, and Gypsies that threaten Emma are replaced by a couple of reckless guys at the mall. One main difference: Alicia Silverstone is much, much hotter than any Austen character. Ever.

Note: Similar parallels occur between the 1999 film *10 Things I Hate about You* and Shakespeare's *The Taming of the Shrew*. The titles even rhyme.

7 Classic TV Episodes That Should Be Sent into Space to Demonstrate to Aliens What We Earthlings Call "Funny"

Some moments on TV are universally funny no matter whom you ask. But just what makes a show funny—is it the writing, the delivery? We're not sure, but we know it when we see it.

_01:: *Seinfeld*—"The Contest" (1992)

Of all *Seinfeld*'s memorable moments—Poppy peeing on Jerry's couch, George's "shrinkage," the Soup Nazi—"The Contest" stands out as an instant classic. The titular contest is a bet between Jerry, George, Kramer, and Elaine about who could go the longest without masturbating (or, in one of the series' many classic catchphrases, being "master of your domain"). All are tempted: George watches a silhouetted nurse give a woman a sponge bath, Jerry is dating a virgin, and Elaine does aerobics behind John-John Kennedy. But the first to succumb is Kramer, who, after watching a nudist in her apartment, slams his money down with an emphatic, "I'm out!"

_02:: *The Mary Tyler Moore Show*— "Chuckles Bites the Dust" (1975)

It's a premise straight out of Greek drama or Shakespeare: a parading elephant tramples to death a circus clown in a giant peanut suit. At first horrified by others' reactions to Chuckles's tragic death, Mary can't keep from giggling all through his funeral. Ted's solemn eulogy featuring a timeless quote from Chuckles—"A little song, a little dance, a little seltzer down your pants"—sends her over the edge. The scene turns bittersweet when a mourner reminds Mary that Chuckles would've wanted her to laugh. With that, her giggling turns to heartfelt tears.

_03:: *The Dick Van Dyke Show*—"That's My Boy???" (1963)

The brainchild of comic legend Carl Reiner, *The Dick Van Dyke Show* was known for its spot-on timing and sharp writing. The "That's My Boy???" episode builds around a flashback: Rob (Dick Van Dyke) is absolutely certain that he and Laura (Mary Tyler Moore) brought the wrong baby home from the hospital. To settle the matter once and for all, Rob invites the other couple to their home for dinner. When he

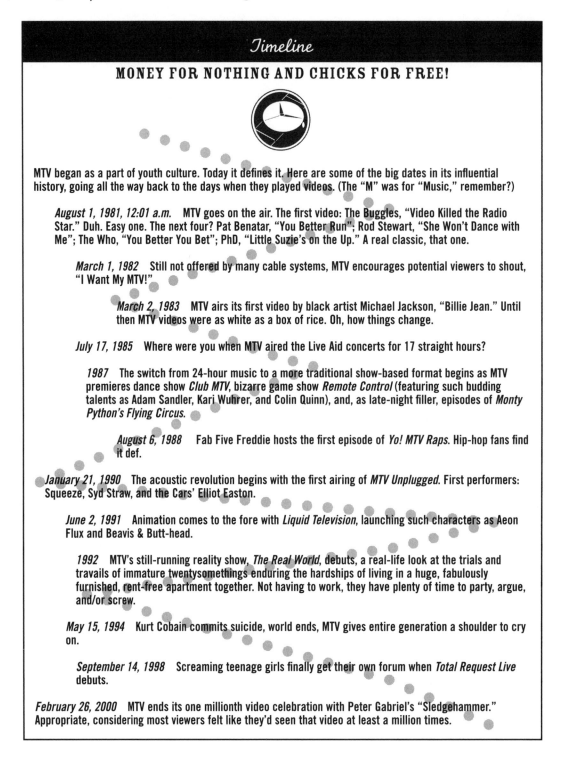

Timeline

MONEY FOR NOTHING AND CHICKS FOR FREE!

MTV began as a part of youth culture. Today it defines it. Here are some of the big dates in its influential history, going all the way back to the days when they played videos. (The "M" was for "Music," remember?)

August 1, 1981, 12:01 a.m.   MTV goes on the air. The first video: The Buggles, "Video Killed the Radio Star." Duh. Easy one. The next four? Pat Benatar, "You Better Run"; Rod Stewart, "She Won't Dance with Me"; The Who, "You Better You Bet"; PhD, "Little Suzie's on the Up." A real classic, that one.

March 1, 1982   Still not offered by many cable systems, MTV encourages potential viewers to shout, "I Want My MTV!"

March 2, 1983   MTV airs its first video by black artist Michael Jackson, "Billie Jean." Until then MTV videos were as white as a box of rice. Oh, how things change.

July 17, 1985   Where were you when MTV aired the Live Aid concerts for 17 straight hours?

1987   The switch from 24-hour music to a more traditional show-based format begins as MTV premieres dance show *Club MTV*, bizarre game show *Remote Control* (featuring such budding talents as Adam Sandler, Kari Wuhrer, and Colin Quinn), and, as late-night filler, episodes of *Monty Python's Flying Circus*.

August 6, 1988   Fab Five Freddie hosts the first episode of *Yo! MTV Raps*. Hip-hop fans find it def.

January 21, 1990   The acoustic revolution begins with the first airing of *MTV Unplugged*. First performers: Squeeze, Syd Straw, and the Cars' Elliot Easton.

June 2, 1991   Animation comes to the fore with *Liquid Television*, launching such characters as Aeon Flux and Beavis & Butt-head.

1992   MTV's still-running reality show, *The Real World*, debuts, a real-life look at the trials and travails of immature twentysomethings enduring the hardships of living in a huge, fabulously furnished, rent-free apartment together. Not having to work, they have plenty of time to party, argue, and/or screw.

May 15, 1994   Kurt Cobain commits suicide, world ends, MTV gives entire generation a shoulder to cry on.

September 14, 1998   Screaming teenage girls finally get their own forum when *Total Request Live* debuts.

February 26, 2000   MTV ends its one millionth video celebration with Peter Gabriel's "Sledgehammer." Appropriate, considering most viewers felt like they'd seen that video at least a million times.

opens the door to greet them, he (and we) learn for the first time that they are black. Van Dyke's priceless expression of shock, embarrassment, and relief caused one of the longest laughs by a studio audience in TV history.

_04:: Ed Ames's "Frontier Bris" on *The Tonight Show with Johnny Carson* (1965)

When singer-actor Ed Ames appeared on *The Tonight Show* on April 29, 1965, he and Johnny Carson thought it might be fun to show off his tomahawk-throwing skills, which he'd learned for his part on TV's *Daniel Boone*. Proudly declaring, "This is how you take care of an enemy," Ames hurled a tomahawk across the studio and embedded it, handle up, directly in the crotch of a man-shaped outline. The audience's and host's roars of laughter—which lasted several minutes—are television legend, as is Carson's perfect ad-lib: "Gee, Ed, I didn't even know you were Jewish!"

_05:: *I Love Lucy*—"Lucy Does a TV Commercial" (1952)

I Love Lucy erased any doubt that the sitcom would dominate prime time. Retail stores even changed their open-late night to Thursday from the traditional Monday, because everyone stayed home Monday to watch *Lucy*. Lucy and Ethel's adventure in a candy factory, the birth of Little Ricky, and Lucy's trouble in a grape-stomping vat are all classics. But when Lucy tries to shill a highly alcoholic "health tonic" called Vitameatavegamin, it's an absolute scream. Drunk after four takes, she slurs through the product's name, misses the spoon, then chugs right from the bottle. It's a brilliant showcase of Lucille Ball's impeccable

timing and fluid physicality. Besides, showing someone getting drunk on a network sitcom in 1952 was pretty ballsy.

_06:: *Sanford and Son*—"Fred Sanford, Legal Eagle" (1974)

Frequently when a sitcom tries to take on serious social issues, the result comes off hamfisted and sappy. But Norman Lear's shows—*All in the Family, The Jeffersons, Sanford and Son,* and others—did it masterfully. One of the most daring examples is this episode of *Sanford and Son*, which first aired on January 11, 1974, during the show's third season. When Lamont receives an unfair traffic ticket from a white policeman, Fred decides to serve as his lawyer. Fred, famous for his great lines (to Aunt Esther: "I'm calling you ugly; I could push your face in some dough and make gorilla cookies!"), cracks off a doozy here. He accuses the cop of ticketing only black people. When the judge responds that justice is blind to color, Fred snaps back: "Look around here; there's enough niggers in here to make a Tarzan movie!" The studio audience howled. And white America squirmed.

_07:: *The Simpsons*—Pick 'Em

The Simpsons is like sex or pizza. When it's good, it's great. And when it's bad, it's still pretty good. Dozens of the show's more than 300 episodes are worthy of consideration. But which one to pick? Homer's stint as Mr. Plow or Bart's as Mr. Burns' heir? Marge's gambling problem or one of Sideshow Bob's murderous plots? Perhaps the episode that best encapsulates the show's brilliance, its crackling writing, its incredible cast of characters, and its references to—and skewering of—all pop culture is in fact *two* episodes: "Who Shot Mr. Burns?"* Airing in May and September of 1995, the shows parodied the "Who Shot JR?" phenomenon of *Dallas* 15 years earlier to hilarious effect. Even Tito Puente is a suspect.

*It was Maggie, by the way, although the show produced several alternates to confuse snoops.

6 Tricky Lyrics You'll Never Get Wrong Again

Here are some of the trickiest lyrics in pop music, spelled out and explained for all you driver's seat soloists.

_01:: That "Leonard Bernstein" section of "It's the End of the World as We Know It (and I Feel Fine)" by R.E.M., 1987

"The other night I dreamt of knives, continental drift divide. Mountains sit in a line. Leonard Bernstein. Leonid Brezhnev, Lenny Bruce and Lester Bangs."

Great. So, what's it mean?

Very little. But here's who all those guys whose names start with *L* are:

Leonard Bernstein: American composer and conductor whose most famous musicals include *On the Town* (1944) and *West Side Story* (1957).

Leonid Brezhnev: President of the Soviet Union from 1977 to 1982. As a member of the Presidium (or Politburo), he pronounced the Brezhnev Doctrine, which gave the USSR the authority to roll tanks into any Warsaw Pact country where "communism was threatened." Hence, the Prague Spring of 1968.

Lenny Bruce: Groundbreaking American comedian whose outspoken, obscene political humor got him in trouble with the government.

Lester Bangs: Outspoken rock critic for *Creem* magazine, who railed against the pretensions of hippie musicians and extolled the virtues of raw, iconoclastic rock and roll.

_02:: That Weird Last Line of "One Week" by Barenaked Ladies, 1998

"Birchmount Stadium, home of the Robbie."

Great. So, what's it mean?

Birchmount Stadium is a sports venue affiliated with Birchmount Park Collegiate school in Toronto, Canada. The Robbie is a soccer tournament held at the stadium. The song line is taken directly from a sign outside the stadium.

_03:: Some of the Garbled Lines in "Rock the Casbah" by the Clash, 1982

"The muezzin was a-standin' on the radiator grille."

"But the Bedouin they brought out the electric camel drum."

"Sharif don't like it, Rockin' the Casbah, Rock the Casbah."

Great. So, what's it mean?

muezzin: A Muslim crier who calls the faithful to prayer five times a day. He calls from towers attached to the mosque, called minarets.

Bedouin: A member of one of the nomadic desert tribes of North Africa, Syria, and Arabia.

sharif: Can be used to describe a descendant of the prophet Mohammad through his daughter Fatima, or the chief magistrate of the holy city of Mecca. In this context, a Moroccan ruler or prince.

casbah: The citadel and palace of a North African sovereign.

_04:: Some Lines from That Middle Part of "Bohemian Rhapsody" by Queen, 1975

"Scaramouche, Scaramouche, will you do the Fandango."

"Bismillah! No we will not let you go."

"Beelzebub has a devil put aside for me, for me, for me."

Great. So, what's it mean?

Bohemian: Originally referred to someone from the Czech region of Bohemia, or Gypsies. Today it can be either a wandering vagabond or, more commonly, an artistic or literary person who disregards conventional lifestyles.

rhapsody: A rambling, disconnected series of sentences or statements composed under excitement, with no natural connection.

Scaramouche: A cowardly braggart and boastful buffoon, used as a stock character in Italian commedia dell'arte.

fandango: A provocative Spanish courtship dance in 3/8 or 6/8 time; performed by a man and a woman playing castanets.

bismillah: Arabic for "In the name of Allah." In daily speech it is a way of expressing truth or sincerity, similar to "With God as my witness" or the like.

Beelzebub: Today, another name for Satan. In Milton's *Paradise Lost*, he was one of the fallen angels, second to Lucifer in power. The name comes from Baalzebub, a Philistine god of Ekron. Also called Baal in the Old Testament. *Baal-zebub* means literally "lord of the flies" or, some say, "dung-god."

_05:: What about That "Hippopotamus of Love" or Whatever in "The Joker" by the Steve Miller Band, 1973?

"Some people call me Maurice, 'cuz I speak of the pompatus of love."

Great. So, what's it mean?

No matter how you spell it—*pompatus, pompetous,* or *pompitude*—you won't find it in a dictionary, because it's not a word. It's actually a corrupted form of yet *another* made-up word. It comes from an obscure 1954 R&B tune by the Medallions called "The Letter" in which singer/songwriter Vernon Green croons about the "puppetutes of love." Turns out "puppetute" was Green's made-up word to refer to "a secret paper-doll fantasy figure who would be my everything and bear my children." So from "puppet" we get "puppetutes." And Steve Miller, a huge old-school R&B fan, borrowed the line for his song 19 years later. But, since he didn't know the right word, approximated it as close as he could. Thus, "pompatus."

_06:: The Granddaddy of Them All: What the Hell Is That "Douche" Line in "Blinded by the Light" by Manfred Mann's Earth Band, 1976?

"Blinded by the light, revved up like a deuce, another runner in the night."

Great. So, what's it mean?

deuce: '60s slang for a 1932 Ford, or "deuce coupe." Note: Don't blame Manfred for the bizarre lyrics. They were written by Bruce Springsteen.

by
Shane Pitts &
Royce Simpson

Condensed
PSYCHOLOGY

Contains

5 Common Myths about Human Behavior ✳ 3 Famous Studies That Would Be Illegal Today ✳ 5 Funny Psychology Experiments (Both Ha-Ha *and* Peculiar!) ✳ To Sleep, Perchance to Dream: 4 Insights on Snoozing ✳ 6 Mind-Bending Ailments ✳ 3 Crazy Kid Conundrums (That Are Somehow Still Cute) ✳ 6 Reasons You're an Unreasonable Reasoner ✳ Saying One Thing but Meaning Your Mother: 9 Thoughts on Freud ✳ 3 Rational Explanations for Disorderly Conduct ✳ 4 Fascinating Fetal Feats ✳ Shrink Rap: 4 Giants of Psychology Discussed in Plain English ✳

Common Myths about Human Behavior

Maybe Malcolm X said it best: "You've been hoodwinked. You've been had. You've been took. You've been led astray, led amok. You've been bamboozled." Face it, kid. Someone lied to you, and it's time you got the truth.

_01:: You Use Only 10% of Your Brain

Undoubtedly, you've heard this one, but it's just not true—we use it all. While the origin of the myth isn't known, there are several lines of evidence that expose it as false. Maybe what people mean is that only 10% of our neurons are essential or are used at a given time? That's not true either. Brain imaging techniques such as fMRI (functional magnetic resonance imaging) clearly show that the brain doesn't just sit there while we engage in many activities. Think about it from an evolutionary perspective: the brain comprises only about 5% of total body mass but consumes 20% of the body's oxygen and glucose. It makes little survival sense for a species to develop a large, energy-hungry organ to use only 10% of its capacity.

_02:: Listening to Mozart Will Make Your Child Smarter

The so-called Mozart effect is a good example of a scientific finding being distorted by the media through hype not warranted by the research. It all started when researchers reported that after exposure to a selection of Mozart's music, college students showed an increase in spatial reasoning for about 10 minutes on tasks like putting together pieces of a jigsaw puzzle. Note first that the research was done on college students, not infants, and that the effect was very brief. In addition, no one's been able to replicate the research. The increase in spatial reasoning, it turns out, can be generated by any auditory stimulation (e.g., listening to a short story or other types of music) that keeps people alert while being tested. However, none of this has stopped eager parents—spurred on by fantastic claims from unscrupulous companies—from purchasing Mozart CDs for their babies.

_03:: Subliminal Advertising Will Make You Buy Stuff

Maybe you've heard of the "Drink Coke and eat popcorn" study. Supposedly, these words were flashed outside of patrons' awareness on a movie screen, and this induced them to buy more Coke and popcorn. Not only was that "study" never published, but it was later exposed as a hoax—a publicity stunt by an advertising executive. In over 200 published studies, there is no clear evidence of subliminal messages persuading anyone to buy or do anything. In one study, participants listened to tapes with classical music embedded with subliminal messages designed to increase either their self-esteem or their memory. At the end of five weeks, participants completed self-esteem scales and memory tests. Did the

Just the Facts

THE AMAZING NERVOUS SYSTEM

Average number of neurons in the brain: 100 billion

Number of synapses (neural connections): 60 trillion, give or take a few billion

Average loss of neurons: 85,000 per day (≈31 million per year)

Brain weights (in grams): human: 1,300–1,400; sperm whale: 7,800; hippopotamus: 582; chimpanzee: 420; cat: 30; hamster: 1.4

According to the *Guinness Book of World Records* the world's heaviest human brain weighed 5 lb. 1 oz. The lightest healthy brain weighed 1 lb. 8 oz.

Rate of neuron growth (early pregnancy): 250,000 neurons per minute

Neurons can transmit information at over 200 miles per hour.

During the first three years of life, 75% of brain growth is completed.

---

tapes work? No. They had no real effect on memory or self-esteem. But those who thought they were exposed to memory tapes, for example, believed they had improved regardless of the actual content of the tape.

_04:: That Whole "Hot-Hand" Thing in Basketball

Sports fans, players, and coaches attest to the fact that players perform in streaks. They pre-dict that it's more likely for a player to make his next shot if he has made his previous two or three shots rather than missing them. But as it turns out, streak shooting is an illusion. Statistically, NBA players are no more likely to make shots after hitting previous shots. The shooting percentages after one, two, or three misses and after one, two, or three hits are virtually identical. The same is true for free throws. Likewise, players' own perceptions of being "hot" or "cold" are not predictive of their shooting performance. Lots of factors go into hitting a shot, including player skill, the defense, and so on, but the "hot hand" is just an illusion.

_05:: The Right Brain and Left Brain Function Separately

The idea is that the right and left hemispheres of the brain are highly specialized and that each one has a separate mode of thinking and stream of consciousness. The two hemispheres are somewhat specialized for various tasks, but it's a drastic oversimplification to assume that various mental functions are completely handled by one hemisphere or the other. The superiority of one hemisphere over another on most mental tasks is very modest. In normal individuals, the two hemispheres work in concert on all tasks. Likewise, even patients who've had their brain hemispheres disconnected generally experience a unity of conscious experience. Despite popular opinion, there's no research that links being left- or right-brained to musical ability, occupational choice, or other personal preferences. And, no, you can't educate the two sides separately.

Famous Studies That Would Be Illegal Today

What happened to the good old days, when a scientist could just rustle together some test subjects and let loose in the lab? You know, without having to worry about petty humane things . . . like ethics!

_01:: Stanley Milgram's Obedience Studies

In this Yale University study, participants were told they were part of an experiment on the effects of punishment on learning. They were instructed to teach another participant (the "learner") a list of words and, whenever the learner made a mistake, deliver an electric shock via a generator with levers labeled in 15-volt increments (up to 450 volts—where the label read "Danger: Severe Shock" and "XXX"). The learner (who, unknown to the participant, was not actually receiving shocks) became increasingly vocal, at one point even screaming, "I can't stand the pain! Get me out of here!" Because the experimenter urged the participants to continue, nearly 65% of them continued to obey the experimenter to deliver the maximum 450 volts. The participants weren't sadistic, Milgram argued, just socialized to obey authority figures.

_02:: Stanford Prison Experiments

In the summer of 1971 Philip Zimbardo put Stanford University students in jail. Students, who volunteered and were paid, were randomly assigned to be either a guard or a prisoner. The prisoners were surprised at their homes, handcuffed, and taken by police cruiser to a makeshift jail in the basement of the psychology department. There they were stripped of their personal belongings and given smocks, nylon caps, and identification numbers. The uniformed guards were simply told to enforce the rules. In just a few short days, the guards began to devise sadistic and degrading rituals for the prisoners, many of whom became depressed, anxious, or apathetic. Although they knew that this was just an experiment, all of the guards and prisoners adopted their roles, completely overriding their own individuality. The outcome was so dramatic, the experiment was stopped after only six days.

_03:: Little Albert

John Watson and Rosalie Rayner conducted one of the most famous and controversial studies in psychology using an 11-month-old boy who came to be known as Little Albert. With Little Albert, Watson demonstrated that many fears are conditioned through an association with other fearful situations. Before the experiment, Little Albert was a normal baby who was afraid of loud noises but not much else. Little Albert loved playing with small animals until Watson taught him to become afraid of a white rat by repeatedly banging a steel rod with a hammer whenever

Albert was given a white rat to play with. Little Albert's fear generalized to other similar objects, such as Watson's white hair and a Santa Claus mask. Watson clearly demonstrated that fears could be conditioned, but his methods have been roundly criticized, especially since the conditioning was never reversed.

Funny Psychology Experiments (Both Ha-Ha *and* Peculiar!)

Forget the comedy clubs and must-see sitcoms. If you're looking for a really good time, you can always get your giggles at the campus psych department.

_01:: How Long Is That Line? Asch's Studies on Conformity

You're sitting at a table with six strangers (who are all privy to the study) and are shown two cards, one with a single line and another with three. You are to say aloud which of the three lines on the second card is the same length as the line on the first. The three lines are not close in length, so the judgment is straightforward. The first two rounds are uneventful, with everyone agreeing on the match, but on subsequent rounds, one by one, the others clearly say the wrong answer. What would you do? If you were like most of Solomon Asch's subjects in his 1951 and 1956 studies, at least part of the time you too would say the wrong answer. Why? In many cases we conform to group norms out of a need to be accepted or a fear of rejection.

_02:: Pavlov: That Name Should Ring a Bell

Ivan Pavlov, a Nobel Prize–winning physiologist, conducted experiments that formed the basis of what is now known as classical conditioning. While studying the digestion of dogs in the early 1900s, Pavlov noticed that they would begin to salivate *before* they were presented with food to eat. Through numerous experiments, Pavlov discovered that almost any stimulus (for example, a metronome or a buzzer) could come to elicit the salivary response if the stimulus had been reliably paired with food in the past. In a typical experiment, Pavlov would present meat powder to a dog while a metronome was ticking so that eventually just hearing the metronome would cause the dog to salivate. Pavlov's work was influential because it detailed the process by which learned associations are made.

_03:: Help! The Smash-Hit Psychology Study by Latané and Rodin

Under what circumstances will people in an emergency situation receive help? In a 1969 study by Bibb Latané and Judith Rodin, a female researcher greets a male participant and asks him to complete a questionnaire. The researcher then leaves to go to an adjacent room. After a few minutes there is a crash, and the female researcher screams, "Oh, my God, my foot . . . I . . . I . . . can't move it." Do you think the man helped? Would you? The determining factor seemed to be the presence of other people. About 70% of the men facing this situation alone helped the woman, but when a pair of strangers were confronted with the emergency, only 40% of the time did either person offer help. This counterintuitive finding illustrates the bystander effect: as the number of people witnessing an emergency increases, the likelihood that any given person will help decreases.

_04:: The Case of the Mathematical Horse: Clever Hans

In 1907 a horse named Clever Hans caused quite a stir in Germany when he and his owner toured the country, amazing crowds with the horse's mathematical prowess. Yes, Hans could add, divide, convert fractions to decimals, and even do simple algebra. Clever Hans would tap out with his hoof the correct answer in response to a question from his owner. Many scientists observed Hans and couldn't explain the ability. Enter psychologist Oskar Pfungst, who used controlled conditions to observe Hans. Pfungst discovered that Hans couldn't answer the questions if the questioner didn't know the answer. Likewise, Hans didn't answer questions correctly if he couldn't see the questioner. When people asked Hans a question, they made subtle, involuntary changes in posture such as leaning forward and then raising their head as Hans approached the correct answer. Hans started tapping when someone leaned forward and stopped when they changed pos-

Strange but True
A MAN WALKS INTO A BAR

On September 13, 1848, Phineas Gage's life changed forever. Gage, a railroad supervisor in Cavendish, Vermont, was blasting rock to make way for a new section of tracks when an accident sent tamping rod shooting through his skull. The rod was traveling so fast that it exploded through his left cheek and continued out the top of his head. Amazingly, Phineas survived the accident, but in many ways he was never the same. Before the accident Phineas was considered thoughtful by his friends and colleagues and was well-liked. But after the accident he became noticeably impulsive, foul-tempered, and rude. In fact, his friends commented that he was "no longer Gage." The Phineas Gage case continues to fascinate scientists today because it provides insight into the relationship between the workings of the brain and personality. Sadly, Gage never fully recovered from that fateful day and was reduced to working as a circus sideshow.

ture again. Hans was clever but not mathematical.

_05:: Child's Play: A "Touching" Experiment

Over 80,000 nurses practice therapeutic touch (TT), a technique designed to heal by influencing the patient's "human energy field." The healers claim to detect a human energy field when passing their hands over the afflicted regions of the patients and to transfer their energy to the patients. A nine-year-old girl, Emily

Rosa, decided to put these claims to the test. As described in her article, published in the *Journal of the American Medical Association* in 1998, Emily had 21 TT practitioners place their palms face up through slots in a screen, which prevented them from seeing their hands. On each of the trials, Emily randomly selected one of the practitioner's hands and hovered her hand palm down a few inches above the subject's palm. The subject had to detect Emily's energy field by identifying where her hand was placed. The practitioners were no better than chance at correctly locating Emily's hand, being correct only 44% of the time.

To Sleep, Perchance to Dream:
Insights on Snoozing

Hey, hey, hey! Before you go ahead and hit that snooze button for the 11th time, maybe it's time you think about what you're doing. Here are four things you should know about sleep.

_01:: Riding the Sleep Cycle

Think all sleep's the same? Actually, a 10-minute catnap is quite different from a 10-hour zonk. In stage 1 (about 10 minutes) you may imagine flashes of bright lights or have the distinct sensation of falling, which leads to a full body jerk (you've probably seen people doing it while napping on an airplane). During stage 2 you might talk incoherently, but don't worry—you're unlikely to divulge state secrets. While in the deeper sleep of stages 3 and 4, brain activity is at its lowest point, and you're most likely to sleepwalk during stage 4. At the end of stage 4 you cycle back up through the stages, except as you exit stage 2 you enter REM (rapid eye movement) sleep, when most dreams occur. As the night progresses you spend progressively less time in stages 3 and 4 and more time in REM sleep.

_02:: We All Dream a Little Dream

Many people simply don't remember their dreams, but when awakened during a REM period, those who claim not to dream typically report dreaming. People who consistently recall dreams tend to wake just as they exit the last REM period of the night, whereas others may wake up too long after their last REM period to recall much. Dreams do occur in all stages of sleep, but they're more prevalent and much more vivid during REM sleep. Dreams about falling, being chased, repeatedly failing to do something, flying, rejection, and being unprepared or late for an important event are common. Contrary to popular Freudian assumptions about the hidden sexual and aggressive content of dreams, most dreams are overtly and directly related to our everyday lives and concerns.

_03:: While You Were Sleeping: The Role of External Stimuli

Have you ever heard your alarm clock go off but continued sleeping and dreamed you were on a train or were hearing a car horn? Subjects who have water sprayed on their hands during REM sleep and are later awakened tend to report water-related dreams—waterfalls, leaky roofs, etc. Your brain doesn't "shut off" during sleep. It's simply in a different state from wakefulness. So, please don't put your roommate's hand in a glass of warm water during the night. Though we may incorporate some external stimuli into our dreams, we don't remember information conveyed to us during sleep. It's unfortunate but this means you won't be able to learn Spanish on tape while you snooze.

_04:: The Contagious Yawn

Everyone yawns, including in utero fetuses, some reptiles, birds, and most mammals. Fatigue and boredom certainly aren't the only reasons we yawn. One hypothesis is that yawning serves similar functions as stretching. Both activities increase blood pressure and flex muscles and joints. If you try to stifle a yawn, just as when restraining a stretch, the yawn is not very satisfying. A part of the brain, the hypothalamus, appears to be integral to yawning. It contains a number of chemicals that can induce yawns, some of which surge at night and when awakening. Yawns are catching, but there is little understanding of why they are contagious. One possibility is that at one time in our evolutionary history, yawns served to communicate changing environmental or internal bodily events to members of a social group.

Mind-Bending Ailments

Brains are pretty scary to begin with: they're pinkish gray, they're lumpy, and they blank out at the most inappropriate times. But what would happen if your brain really turned on you?

_01:: That's No Friend of Mine

Do your friends and family feel like strangers? You might be suffering from Capgras' syndrome, a rare condition in which family, close friends, or items of personal significance seem like imposters. What gives? When you see a familiar face, you don't just recognize the face; you also experience some sort of emotional reaction to it. Capgras' delusion arises when there's a disconnection between these two brain functions. You can identify your father's face and know it's familiar, but since there's damage to the pathways between face recognition and emotional reaction, you experience no jolt of emotion. Since it doesn't *feel* like your father, the man must be an imposter!

_02:: I Can't See, but I Can Slam-Dunk

Believe it or not, people with blindsight are blind due to cortical damage, but they can still unconsciously "see" some aspects of their environment. One famous patient, D.F., couldn't read the big E on the eye chart or identify how many fingers a doctor was holding up right in front of her, but she could put an envelope through a slit in the wall with a high degree of accuracy. How is that possible? There's more than one way to see. The "what" pathway is responsible for recognizing what an object is—for instance, is it a wolf or a banana? The "where or how" pathway determines where objects are and how to navigate and interact with them. Without visualizing the "what," people with blindsight are still able to figure out the "where."

_03:: Not for Weak Stomachs

Picture living your life under a strobe light. That's what it feels like to suffer from akinetopsia, or motion blindness. This very rare condition results from selective loss of motion perception because of damage to certain areas of the brain (the temporoparietal cortices). Patients with motion blindness can identify stationary objects and have no problems with other aspects of vision, but moving objects inexplicably seem to appear in one position and then another. For instance, when crossing the street, cars that at first seemed far away could suddenly be very near. And liquid pouring from a pitcher into a cup might look frozen until the cup finally overflowed, allowing the patient to infer that it was full.

_04:: Better Than Peyote

Can you imagine tasting music or smelling the color red? Most of us can't (or at least don't re-

---

Strange but True

THE HISTORY OF FRONTAL LOBOTOMIES

Many of us remember Nurse Ratched from the book and movie *One Flew over the Cuckoo's Nest*. This cold-blooded villain controlled the mental ward in part because it was understood that she had the therapies of shock treatments and frontal lobotomies at her disposal. Unfortunately, there was a time in our history when the use of frontal lobotomies to treat psychiatric disorders such as schizophrenia was as much fact as fiction. During a frontal lobotomy, a sharp object was inserted into the frontal lobes of the brain and moved back and forth to destroy tissue. The 1940s and 1950s represented the heyday of frontal lobotomies, with nearly 40,000 people receiving the treatment in the United States alone. One man in particular, Walter Freeman, worked tirelessly—traveling the country performing lobotomies and preaching about their effectiveness (while reportedly driving his "lobotomobile"). The advent of psychotropic drugs as well as a recognition that most patients did not improve after their surgery produced a sharp decline in the use of lobotomies during the 1960s. In very rare circumstances more precise psychosurgeries are performed today but generally only as a last resort.

---

member), but those with synesthesia can and do. Just as the word *anesthesia* means "no sensation," *synesthesia* means "joined sensation." For some reason, stimulating one sense triggers perceptions in another sense. For example, a bright light might seem loud, the sound of a bagpipe sour, the color after sex a static silver. No one's sure of the cause, but there are a few hypotheses. Some experts think that crossed wires in the brain cause the problem (the path to the taste buds gets hooked up to the sense of hearing path, for example), while others believe that it's a lack of inhibition (the natural pathways that squelch irrelevant sensory input just aren't working properly).

_05:: The Man without a Face

Prosopagnosics have no trouble recognizing noses, ears, eyes, chins, and so on, but they can't seem to fuse them together into a coherent, whole face. In extreme cases, they can't even recognize their own faces in the mirror. Prosopagnosia results from damage to structures just below the ears, stretching toward the back of the skull (otherwise known as the inferotemporal cortex). Dr. P, a famous case in the annals of neuropsychology, searched for his hat as he was departing his physician's of-

fice only to reach out and grab his wife's head and try to lift it off! Not being able to recognize faces clearly, he apparently mistook his wife's head for a hat.

_06:: Rent *Memento* and You'll Understand

If you haven't seen *Memento*, check it out. The main character suffers from damage to the hippocampus (one of the memory centers of the brain) and loses the ability to form new long-term memories (his pre-accident memories stay intact, though). Anterograde amnesiacs live life as though constantly waking from a dream. Leonard, the *Memento* character, takes to tattooing himself because he can't trust the people around him to tell the truth—even if they did, he'd just forget a few minutes later anyway. Strangely, sufferers of this condition can learn new tasks (for example, they improve while taking, say, tennis lessons), but they assume every lesson that it's just beginner's luck.

3 Crazy Kid Conundrums (That Are Somehow Still Cute)

Why do advertisers love to use kids in commercials? Kids can get away with things that would make an adult look stupid or smarmy—it's all about seeing things from a kid's perspective.

_01:: I'll Give You Five Shiny New Nickels for That Paper Dollar

If you've been around preschoolers and children up to the age of six or seven much, you may have heard something like, "Please cut

the pizza into lots of slices, I'm really hungry," or you may have seen an older child "exchange" five nickels for one paper dollar—much to the delight of the younger sibling. One reason for these cute behaviors is that preschoolers tend to lack what psychologists call conservation. They fail to understand that properties of an object, such as number or volume, don't change despite changes in the object's appearance. They tend to focus on only one dimension of an object at a time. With the pizza example, the child is focused on the number, but not the size, of the slices.

_02:: Enough about You; Let's Talk about Me

Preschoolers tend to be egocentric, meaning they assume that others share their point of view. Humorous examples are plentiful. Playing hide-and-seek with a three-year-old, you may find him standing in plain view with his eyes covered. If you ask one of your two preschool girls if she has a sister, she will say, "Yes." If you then ask her if her sister has a sister, she may look confused and say, "No!" because she can't see herself from her sister's perspective. Egocentrism also explains why many young children stand in front of the TV. They can see, so everyone else must also be able to see. Egocentrism also helps explain "collective monologues," in which two preschoolers apparently are taking turns talking to each other, but it's clear that they're not talking about the same things.

_03:: I Saw Mommy Kissing Santa Claus

Preschoolers sometimes have difficulty distinguishing appearance from reality. When daddy puts on the Santa outfit, to a five-year-old, he *is* Santa. If a mother puts on a costume mask in front of her four-year-old, he may become confused and bawl, assuming that his mother is now a green, wart-faced monster. By around age four or five, children develop what psychologists call a "theory of mind," which is when the child begins to understand that others have mental states (beliefs/desires) of their own that influence how they behave.

Reasons You're an Unreasonable Reasoner

You're not crazy, really. Just highly unreasonable. But don't worry about it; we don't blame you at all. We blame your illogical brain.

_01:: I Must Be Psychic!

You're driving down the road, and a song comes on the radio that you were just humming in your head. The phone rings, and it's the long-lost friend you were just thinking of. These incidences seem strange, maybe even mystical to most of us. But such incidences can be explained by the illusory correlation— the tendency to perceive a relationship between two events that are independent. When these surprising coincidences occur, we tend to remember them very well, but how often are we thinking about that song and it doesn't come on the radio, or how often does the song come on the radio when we're not thinking about it? The tendency to notice the hits and forget the misses can lead to some bizarre and erroneous beliefs, such as the full moon causing abnormal behavior.

_02:: My Point Exactly!

False beliefs are often maintained by a strong confirmation bias, or the tendency to seek information that confirms our preexisting beliefs rather than information that may disconfirm them. This bias becomes more than academic when social issues are considered. For instance, if someone believes that African Americans are hostile, that Republicans have the best agenda, or that a coworker is always wrong about everything, that person will seek information that confirms those beliefs and rarely examine, remember, or notice disconfirming evidence. The more this happens, the more firmly entrenched the false beliefs become.

_03:: It's All So Clear!

The availability bias occurs when our judgments are based on information that is vivid and memorable rather than reliable. Your opinion about an auto purchase may be more influenced by your salient knowledge of one friend who has a Honda that's frequently in the auto shop rather than on reliability information based on thousands of consumer experiences. Similarly, especially after televised airplane crashes, people overestimate the risk of flying by commercial airline compared with car travel. The gun lobby tries to focus consumers on vivid cases of home intruders, when the facts are that vastly more gun deaths in the home are due to accident and suicide

What's the Difference?

CLINICAL PSYCHOLOGIST, PSYCHOTHERAPIST, PSYCHOANALYST, AND PSYCHIATRIST

Sure, they sound interchangeable, but there are definite distinctions between clinical psychologists, psychotherapists, psychoanalysts, and psychiatrists. So, how do you tell them apart? A *clinical psychologist* has typically earned a PhD or PsyD in psychology and has completed an internship. The term *psychotherapist*, or therapist, is a generic term that may be applied to anyone who delivers therapy. Its use is unregulated in most states. The term *psychoanalyst* is associated with those who deliver psychoanalytic (Freudian-like) therapy. A *psychiatrist* is a medical doctor who has specialized in mental disorders after completion of basic training in medicine. Only psychiatrists can prescribe medications. Others who deliver therapy may include licensed social workers (LSWs), pastors, rehabilitation counselors, and anyone who has obtained a license to deliver therapy (an LPC—licensed professional counselor). People in these occupations typically have at least a master's degree in psychology or social work.

than to criminal intruders. The ease and vividness with which something comes to mind are no substitute for careful evaluation.

_04:: I'm Due for a Win!

Which of the following sequences of six coin tosses is most likely: (1) HHHTTT, (2)

HTTHTH, (3) HHHHHH? Most people pick the second sequence, though the three sequences are equally likely. People choose the second sequence because of a mistaken belief that if a process is truly random it should always look random—even in small runs. This belief can lead to the gambler's fallacy: people become more likely to bet on black numbers after a roulette wheel has come up red five times in a row. They believe that black must be "due." Of course, the five previous spins or coin tosses or lottery numbers have no bearing at all on the sixth.

_05:: Which Came First—the Chicken or the Pig?

It's almost irresistible to assume that since two variables are correlated, one must cause the other. One survey of elderly Americans noted a correlation between the amount of coffee the couples drank and the frequency of their sexual activity. The author suggested that the stimulants in the coffee might cause this increased sex drive. Before you run out and raid Starbucks, let's consider this further. There could be a third, unknown, factor. Or there could be a number of other variables related to both coffee drinking and sexual behavior—such as health, social activity, and so on. Even if we're sure that one caused the other, we can't be sure by using correlational research alone if A causes B or B causes A. Correlation is not causation.

_06:: The Glass Is Half Full!

Seemingly simple things have a way of subtly influencing our reasoning. Framing effects occur when the way an issue is worded influences a judgment or decision. For example, people think condoms are effective in controlling the spread of HIV or AIDS when condoms are said to have a 95% success rate but not when they have a 5% failure rate. People prefer meats that are 85% fat free compared to 15% fat. People sometimes make health choices based on wording. For example, people choose to use sunscreen if the message is framed in terms of a gain ("Using sunscreen increases your chances of maintaining healthy, young-looking skin") rather than in terms of a loss ("Not using sunscreen decreases your chances of maintaining healthy, young-looking skin").

Saying One Thing but Meaning Your Mother: Thoughts on Freud

Sigismund Schlomo Freud (aka Sigmund Freud) and his psychoanalytic theory have had an enormous impact on 20th-century culture, but his influence on psychological science is hotly contested. He's been described as a visionary, a genius, and an intellectual giant. On the other hand, some people just think he was a quack.

_01:: The "Talking Cure"

One of Freud's most significant contributions may very well be the emphasis he placed on talking about one's problems as a means of alleviating them. Talking with a therapist is still a widely used format of therapy today. (People generally do not lie down on couches, though.) The details of the therapeutic process are typically not Freudian unless you go to an analyst, but the general format is similar. The acts of creating a relaxing atmosphere and gaining acceptance are still integral parts of psychotherapy.

_02:: What Lies Beneath

Freud's most enduring idea is the role of the unconscious. Psychologist widely accept his general idea of the mind as an iceberg with the submerged unconscious playing a role in much of human behavior. Many empirical studies have demonstrated that we are often unaware of why we think or behave as we do and that we process extensive amounts of information outside conscious awareness. While some argue that unconscious processes account for most of our behavior, there's considerable dis-

agreement on the role the unconscious plays in human behavior.

_03:: Defense Mechanisms

A few of the ego defense mechanisms articulated by Freud and especially by his daughter Anna have received some empirical support over the years. Reaction formation, a defense mechanism in which one changes unacceptable impulses into their opposites, has garnered some support. Examples of reaction formation include a racist who behaves overly friendly toward someone of color or a young boy who derides a girl he really likes. However, defense mechanisms tied to Freud's ideas on "instinctual energy" such as displacement (shifting sexual or aggressive urges toward a less threatening target) have received very little support. Further, it seems that the basis of most defense mechanisms are not fuming, unacceptable impulses as Freud contended, but rather our motives to maintain our self-image.

_04:: The Role of the Unconscious

Whether Freud's ideas about the unconscious appear on a "contributions" or a "criticisms" list depends on whether we're speaking in generalities or specifics. Freud's ideas, in general, about behavior being influenced by the unconscious are well supported. The specifics of his views are another matter. Freud saw the unconscious as an analytically sophisticated, seething cauldron of repressed sexual and aggressive urges that controls nearly every thought and behavior. It was a place where boys harbored sexual feelings for their mothers and aggression toward their fathers, and little girls wrangled with feelings of inadequacy because they didn't have penises. Empirical research on the unconscious does not bear out this idea of the unconscious. Rather, research reveals a vast but simple, unanalytical information processor in which ordinary stimuli and tasks are handled.

_05:: After-the-Fact Explanations

One of the most damaging criticisms of Freud's psychoanalytic theory is that it provides explanations for behavior after the fact but predicts little about those behaviors in advance, which makes aspects of the theory unfalsifiable and therefore more akin to a pseudoscience than a science. If you are angry at your mother for remarrying, you illustrate the theory that "you have an unresolved Oedipal complex resulting in jealousy toward this new father figure." If you are not upset but rather quite happy about the marriage, you again exemplify his theory because you're "demonstrating a reaction formation" (see p. 294). A scientific theory must specify in advance observations that would contradict the theory if they were to occur. It's convenient that no behavior can ever contradict Freudian theory.

Strange but True

FREUD FUN FACTS!

Sigmund Freud's father, Jakob, was 20 years older than his young mother, Amalia. Freud had half-brothers very close to Amalia's age and a nephew older than he was. In fact, there may have been intriguing dynamics between his young attractive mother and his older half-brothers, of which Sigmund was likely aware.

Freud was a gifted student who was barely 10 years old when he entered high school. He began his studies in law before becoming more interested in medicine, and enrolled in medical school at 17. He received his medical degree at 25, specializing in clinical neurology.

Patients who visited Freud reclined on a small couch during therapy. He sat behind them because he couldn't bear to be stared at by his patients.

Freud never won a Nobel Prize in medicine or anything else for that matter. His only major award was the Goethe Prize for literature.

Freud was an unabashed cocaine advocate who regularly ingested the drug and gave it to his sisters, friends, and patients. He even published six articles describing its benefits. Freud avoided cocaine addiction but was clearly addicted to nicotine. He chain-smoked cigars, averaging 20 a day. He developed cancer of the palate and jaw at age 67 and underwent a series of 33 operations. He continued to smoke cigars until his death in 1939.

_06:: Ambiguous, Nebulous Concepts

Psychoanalytic theory falls short partly because many of the core concepts are too ambiguous and nebulous to be measured. For instance, how do you compute an id, castration anxiety, or penis envy? How do you know whether the latent, hidden content of interpreted dreams is valid and reliable? Science uses operational definitions, which means that variables and concepts are defined in terms of the operations or procedures used to measure them. Many central Freudian concepts, such as repression, are not measurable and are therefore untestable.

_07:: Overemphasis on Sex

Freud's ideas were a product of his time, so it's no surprise that his theory has been heavily criticized for its overemphasis on sexuality. Freud saw the expression or repression of sexual motivations as major, even primary, determinates of human behavior. Freud's dogged attachment to this idea was relayed in a letter to follower Carl Jung: "My dear Jung, promise me never to abandon the sexual theory. That is the most essential thing of all. You see, we must make a dogma of it, an unshakable bulwark." Some of Freud's original followers, such as Carl Jung and Alfred Adler, parted company with him in part because they viewed his ideas on sexual motivations as extreme and unnecessary to explain human behavior.

_08:: Biased Observations

Critics of Freud say that his theory was built on biased, nonobjective, and even fabricated observations of only a handful of patients. There is ample evidence that Freud pressured patients into accepting, for example, his suggestions that they had been abused. He subjected his patients to leading questions and may have planted ideas in their memory. Likewise, historical analyses show that Freud distorted many of his case studies to fit with his theory irrespective of the facts of the cases and regardless of what patients did or didn't say. A related criticism is that Freud's ideas were developed based largely on a very small, self-selected sample of wealthy, upper-class, 18- to 20-year-old, mentally unstable, single women from Victorian Vienna.

_09:: Bad Test Results

Of those specific psychoanalytic concepts that have been tested empirically, few have fared well. The structural theory—id, ego, and superego—has not received empirical support. The idea of progression of development through oral, anal, phallic, and genital psychosexual stages and the linking of adult personality characteristics to psychosexual stages of child development have no empirical underpinnings. The Oedipal complex, where a boy has sexual impulses toward his mother and comes to view his father as an unwanted rival, has likewise received no empirical support. Many psychologists suggest that Freud is of historical interest only and that a science of mind and behavior must move on without him.

Rational Explanations for Disorderly Conduct

While most people have a general understanding of what OCD (obsessive-compulsive disorder), depression, and schizophrenia are, the following disorders may be new to most.

_01:: Dissociative Fugue: Home Sweet Home, I Think?

Like Betty Sizemore, the title character in the film *Nurse Betty*, people with this disorder have complete amnesia and suddenly leave their home and work and may start a new life. They may also assume a new identity. The disturbance may last for hours, days, or even months. Neither the victim nor those around him or her are typically aware of the disorder. Fugues typically occur after extreme stress, such as severe marital quarrels, loss of a cherished job, combat, or natural disasters. The sufferers typically recover, are disoriented, and are eager to return home. They usually don't have much recollection of their altered lives. The disorder is very rare, with less than 0.2% of the American population experiencing it, and not much is known about the cause.

Stump the Expert

THE SCIENTIFIC PURSUIT OF CONSCIOUSNESS

Consciousness is one of the most profound puzzles of existence, and it's a cutting-edge topic of investigation among psychologists, biologists, neuroscientists, and others. How is it that lower-level physical processes in the brain give rise to the subjective, conscious experience of the color green or of the agony of an intense headache or of the resonating sound of a cello? Why should they give rise to experience at all? Some experts argue that explanations of consciousness are beyond the realm of science; others disagree. One of the more promising hypotheses for how consciousness arises comes from John Searle, who maintains that consciousness is a biological phenomenon caused by lower-level processes in the brain. He claims that as an emergent property, the processes and elements within the brain cause consciousness, but it's not a property of any individual elements and cannot be explained simply as a summation of the activity of those elements. For example, consider a cup of coffee. The liquidity of the coffee is explained by the behavior of the molecules that compose it, but none of the individual molecules are liquid. Consciousness, like the liquidity of brewed coffee, is a property that emerges from the behavior of many individual elements that cannot be reduced to or explained by any single element in the system.

_02:: Frottage (Unwanted Touching)

Frotteurism, from the French *frotter*, "to rub," involves the rubbing of one's genitals against a nonconsenting, unsuspecting person. A frotteur may rub his penis against the buttocks or thighs of women in a crowded public place such as a bus or subway. The frotteur tends to choose places that afford easy escape, such as crowded sidewalks or buses that make frequent stops. He may board a bus several times a day during rush hour in search of multiple victims. Frotteurs are typically men, between 15 and 25 years of age, and the behavior generally begins in adolescence. The impersonal nature of the sexual contact seems to be important to the frotteur. The number of the attacks may be considerable. In a large-scale study, researchers found that frotteurs in their sample averaged 901 victims during the course of their disorder.

_03:: Delusional Disorder: Brad Pitt Is So in Love with Me

Individuals with erotomanic delusional disorder, also known as de Clerambault's syndrome, are under the delusion that another person is in love with them. The person they have the delusion about is typically of higher social status and unattainable due to marriage or celebrity. The person with the disorder is often convinced that the sought-after individual is the one who initiated the relationship despite little or no contact between the two. Sometimes the disorder spirals into stalking, harassment, assault, and/or kidnapping. The most notorious case of this disorder involved John Hinckley Jr., who attempted to assassinate former President Reagan to capture the attention of actress Jodie Foster.

Fascinating Fetal Feats

It's amazing to realize how young you were when you first came to your senses—your five senses, that is. Sure, it might take us a little longer than most species to walk around or even lift our own heads, but that doesn't mean we're late bloomers in every department.

_01:: Taste and Smell

At 13 to 15 weeks, fetuses have taste buds that look like a mature adult's. Whether fetuses can taste the liter a day of amniotic fluid they ingest is not known, but we do know that premature infants and newborns prefer sweet tastes to sour tastes. Some researchers think that amniotic fluid serves as a flavor appetizer or precursor to breast milk. Newborns show a distinct preference for the smell of their mother over that of a stranger. A one-week-old will orient significantly more toward a gauze pad from its mother's bra than a pad from another nursing mother.

_02:: Hearing

Despite their insulated environment in the womb, fetuses can hear. They will jump at the sound of a slammed door or other loud noises. Newborns will fling their arms in the air and open their eyes wide when startled by a loud noise. As with smell, a newborn will display a preference for the sound of his or her own mother's voice. The newborn will suck more vigorously on a pacifier to turn on a recording of the mother's voice compared to that of a strange woman's similar voice. A 20-week-old will orient toward the sound of his or her own name more than that of similar-sounding other names. Newborns are particularly sensitive to high-pitched and melodic sounds and human voices. It's little wonder that people in all cultures speak to infants in the slow-paced, high-pitched, melodic, simple "motherese," or baby talk, that attracts the infant's attention.

_03:: Learning, Memory, and Language

In addition to displaying memory for their mother's voice, newborns show memory for other stimuli as well. In one study, mothers read passages from one of three different stories to their babies during the last six weeks of pregnancy. Shortly after birth, newborns donning headphones sucked faster or slower on an electronic pacifier to activate recordings of the story they had heard in the womb rather than a new story. Displaying a sensitivity to language, newborns not only prefer the sound of their own mother's voice but tend to prefer that voice when she speaks in her native language rather than a foreign language. By six months of age, infants from different-speaking countries show different auditory brain mappings, which helps explain why related languages (Spanish and French, for example) are easier to learn than dissimilar ones.

_04:: Vision

Despite popular myths, newborns can see, though they are very nearsighted. They can focus best on objects that are seven or eight inches away. A few hours after birth, newborns can tell the difference between light and dark shades and can track slow-moving objects. Newborns show a marked preference for complex patterns with lots of contrast—especially human faces. They stare much longer at complete, correctly featured faces compared to other complex stimuli, including face patterns with features rearranged. It seems as though newborns are especially attuned via evolutionary forces to attend to significant social stimuli in their environment.

Shrink Rap:

4 Giants of Psychology Discussed in Plain English

Who said psychologists don't have superpowers? Between these four brainiacs, your head could be shrunk down to nuthin' in no time flat.

_01:: Carl Gustav Jung (1875–1961)

A one-time close companion and disciple of Freud, Jung was Freud's heir apparent until their split over theoretical differences in 1914. Jung's version of psychoanalysis was built around the collective unconscious—ancestral experiences common to all humans. The contents of this unconscious, or archetypes, are innate psychological predispositions that converge ancestral experiences around common themes such as the anima (the representation of woman in man) and animus (man in woman). Jung focused heavily on the dreams and on the development of the self, which he viewed as the unifying core of the psyche. For inspiration, Jung delved into history, religion, mythology, mysticism, and archaeology. His most enduring contribution has been that of a typology of personality most popularly captured in the Myers-Briggs Type Indicator, which classifies people as introverts or extroverts, for example.

_02:: Jean Piaget (1896–1980)

The influence of Piaget's theory and work on child cognitive development has been compared to Shakespeare's influence on English literature. Born in Switzerland, Piaget was a precocious child, publishing a small article by age 10. He published 20 papers before receiving his doctorate in 1918 at age 21 and eventually published over 40 books and 100 articles on child psychology alone. Piaget is most famous for his stage theory of intellectual development, in which children sequence through four distinct stages of cognitive development: sensorimotor, preoperational, concrete operational, and formal operational. Piaget likened children to little scientists constantly conducting experiments on their environment as they actively seek information to better understand the world.

_03:: B. F. Skinner (1904–1990)

Burrhus Frederic Skinner was one of the most influential psychologists of his generation and is almost as well known to the public as to the scientific community. Skinner is best known for his research demonstrating the effects of reinforcers and punishers on behavior. It was his belief that virtually all behaviors are the result of environmental consequences; stated simply, behavior that is reinforced (or rewarded) will be more likely to be repeated, while punished behavior will be less likely to be repeated. So, according to Skinner, we may watch movies, eat chocolate cake, and even love our parents because these things supply us with ample reinforcement. While much of Skinner's research used pigeons and rats, often in controlled experimental chambers called Skinner boxes, his principles are regularly applied to humans using a technique called behavior modification.

_04:: Carl Rogers (1902–1987)

Carl Rogers was one of the pioneers of the humanistic approach in psychology. The humanistic perspective differs from Freud's psychoanalysis and Skinner's behaviorism in that individuals are assumed to be responsible for their actions rather than at the mercy of unconscious motives or environmental forces. The role of the therapist is to provide a supportive, nonjudgmental atmosphere while helping clients take responsibility for their betterment. Rogers's method of therapy reflected his belief that all individuals have an innate self-actualizing tendency, or a desire to understand their true selves and be the best they can be. Rogers believed that a complete understanding of the self can be obtained only when individuals are loved and respected unconditionally. The humanistic approach in psychology reached its heyday during the 1960s and '70s, but many of Rogers's views on human nature, and especially his client-centered therapeutic techniques, continue to be influential in psychology.

by
Greg Salyer

Condensed RELIGION

Contains

5 Unusual Creation Stories ✳ 5 Religious Rituals That Hurt Like Hell ✳ Mmm-Mmm God: 4 Ways to Be Religious While Having Sex ✳ 8 Steps to Founding a World Religion ✳ 6 Versions of Heaven ✳ Abandon All Hope, Ye Who Enter Here: 7 Versions of Hell ✳ 6 Women Who Shaped World Religions ✳ 3 (or 3 Million) Famous Gods ✳ Straight from the Cutting Room Floor: 6 Texts That Didn't Make It into the Bible ✳

5 Unusual Creation Stories

If tales of Adam and Eve or earth being a seven-day job leave you yawning, here are a couple of alternative creation myths that have human beings arriving with flair.

_01:: If at First You Don't Succeed . . .

Like many gods, the Mayan deities created life on earth to be worshiped by it, and like many gods, they began with animals. As we know, with the exception of parrots, animals can't talk. The gods were displeased because they couldn't understand the animals' praise (or growls, as it were). Of course, when the gods are displeased, bad things happen, as in you might become food for a greater creation. Initially, that creation was a man of mud. He had mud for brains and eventually melted in the rain. Man, version 2.0, involved a being constructed of wood, but he had wooden expressions, so the gods felt unloved. Finally, the gods created human beings that were just like gods, knowing and seeing everything the gods did. Guess how long that lasted?

_02:: Bumba and His Digestive Problems

An unusual creation story from the Boshongo people of sub-Saharan Africa includes a high god who created the world by vomiting. As is often the case, the world begins in watery darkness, and Bumba, the only being in existence, is alone. He "wretches and strains" until he vomits up the sun. The sun dries up some of the water, and the earth begins to emerge. Next, Bumba vomits the moon and stars so that the night has lights as well. Finally, in one last regurgitative effort, Bumba

vomits animals and men. One of the men "was white like Bumba." This line indicates that the story was written down after contact with Europeans (and therefore contact with writing).

_03:: New and Interesting Uses for Masturbation

In the Egyptian Book of the Dead (1550 BCE), two major gods (Shu, the god who separated the earth and sky, and Tefnut) are born in a most unusual fashion: "When I rubbed with my fist, my heart came into my mouth in that I spat forth Shu and expectorated Tefnut." It would seem that these two divinities were created by one god's act of masturbation. Although it's not surprising to find sexual imagery in sacred texts, you just don't see many references to masturbation. In regard to the creation of humankind, the text reads, "I wept tears, the form of my Eye, and that is how mankind came into existence." Hey, we'll take the poetic with the raunchy.

_04:: I Don't Know, Do You?

This marvelous story comes from the oldest Hindu sacred text, the Rig Veda, and offers an interesting counterpoint to Western worry about the "true" story of creation. In this hymn, the author asks the same questions that others ask about creation but doesn't worry too much about the answers. He begins: "The

Timeline

'CAUSE YOU GOTTA HAVE
FAITH, FAITH, FAITH!

Here's a quick primer to when religious movements first got their big breaks.

125,000–30,000 BCE   The Neanderthals kick things off with possible burial rituals.

30,000 BCE   Cro-Magnon moves things forward with cave paintings and figurines.

7,000–3,000 BCE   The Neolithic age brings with it agricultural revolutions, fertility religions, and megaliths (e.g., Stonehenge).

3000–1500 BCE   Hinduism's Vedas appear in their oral form, Judaism's Abraham (1900–1700 BCE) makes his presence felt, and early elements of Shinto arrive on the scene.

1500–1000 BCE   Good age for religious texts. As the Egyptian kingdoms flourish, the Egyptian Book of the Dead hits shelves, while Hinduism's Vedas also make their way into print (1500 BCE). Judaism's superstar Moses (ca. 1300 BCE) also hits the scene.

1000–500 BCE   Definitely big years for religious movers and shakers. Zoroastrianism's Zoroaster (ca. 1100–550 BCE), Judaism's King David (1010–970 BCE), Taoism's Lao-tzu (ca. 600–500 BCE), Confucianism's Confucius (ca. 551–479 BCE), Buddhism's Siddhartha Gautama Buddha (563–483 BCE), and Jainism's Mahavira (599–527 BCE) all make their mark.

500 BCE–1 BCE   Christianity's Jesus Christ (ca. 4 BCE–30 CE) makes a memorable entrance.

1 CE–500 CE   As the Mayans make their presence felt (300), this era turns out to be huge for Christianity. Paul's ministry (ca. 50–60) explodes on the scene, the Gospels are revealed (ca. 70–95), and the religion gets a huge endorsement as it becomes the state religion of Rome (313). Looking eastward, Mahayana Buddhism emerges, and the religion known as Shinto formally picks up its name.

500–1000 CE   Islam's Muhammad (ca. 570–632); Buddhism: national religion of Tibet (700s); Christianity: pope rules Church and state (800–1100); Islam: dominates much of the world (750–1258).

1000–1500 CE   The Aztec and Inca empires flourish in the Western hemisphere (1325–1470), as Islam manages to expel Christian crusaders (1300) in the Middle East. Zen Buddhism hits the scene in Japan (13th century), and the Spanish Inquisition begins (1478). Sikhism also finds a founder in Guru Nanak (1469–1504).

1500–2000 CE   Big years for Christianity as the Protestant Reformation takes place (1521). The Baha'i religion is established in 1863. Jews are severely persecuted during the Holocaust, and Israel becomes a state in 1948.

nonexistent was not; the existent was not at that time. The atmosphere was not nor the heavens which are beyond. What was concealed? Where? In whose protection? Was it water? An unfathomable abyss?" The only thing for certain in this story seems to be that there was darkness in the beginning, or rather "darkness within darkness." But a spark of desire born on the sea of darkness sets things in motion and creation begins. Or does it?

_05:: The Woman Who Fell from the Sky

According to the Iroquoian legend "The Woman Who Fell from the Sky," a young woman journeys to another village, and there she meets a magician, the most prominent man in the village, and asks to be his wife. After she passes a series of strenuous and painful tests, he agrees. She soon realizes that a beautiful tree has drawn her there to be impregnated, and one day she spreads her legs to receive a blossom that falls lightly onto her vagina. Meanwhile, the magician is in dire straits because the village is suffering a drought, and some of the elders suggest that his new bride might be to blame. They plot to bury her under the tree, but when they lift it up, there's no hole in the earth, only an expanse of blue. The curious woman agrees to jump, and at that moment she becomes the woman who fell from the sky. Her offspring now populate the earth.

5 Religious Rituals That Hurt Like Hell

Religious rituals aren't just day-to-day affairs, like brushing your teeth. They're highly organized and symbolic efforts to place the body in touch with the sacred. In fact, a good number of religious groups agree that pain can help achieve this goal. Here are a few of the most painful exercises undertaken to achieve contact with the sacred.

_01:: Circumcision

Circumcision is practiced by a number of cultures all over the globe and has been throughout history. But why? The Ndembu of Zambia explain the ritual by way of a story of a boy who was accidentally circumcised while playing among sharp grasses. The name of their ritual is *Mukanda*, which means "to heal and make strong." Some sociologists and anthropologists have come up with a variety of explanations for circumcision: (1) to mark captives, (2) to attract the opposite sex, (3) to indicate tribal affiliation, (4) to maintain hygiene, (5) to increase sexual pleasure, (6) to cut the ties to the mother (the rite is usually performed by older men), (7) to test bravery, (8) to sacrifice, (9) to symbolically castrate, and (10) to simulate menstruation. No one really knows (or agrees on) the answer, but that doesn't keep people from snipping away.

_02:: The Sun Dance

The Sun Dance is a sacred ritual performed by a number of Plains Indians as a reflection of the cosmos and an offering of thanks for the life and aid given by the spirits. The ritual is situated around a pole ceremonially placed in the center of a specially built lodge. The dancers enter the lodge and begin moving up and down on the balls of their feet while blowing eagle whistles and looking beyond the top of the center pole and into the sun. They fast and dance for four days, and some of them drink only what is provided from the sky. As if that doesn't sound painful enough, the young men attach themselves to the pole by piercing their skin with bones wrapped with leather. The leather is tied to the center pole, and the men lean back and stretch their skin in hope of earning special blessings from Wakan Tanka, or the Great Mysterious. Ultimately, the men stretch their skin until it breaks.

_03:: Bloodletting

Bloodletting has been called the mortar of life for Mayan culture, a powerful and sophisticated civilization that existed in what is now Guatemala for about 1200 years, beginning in 300 BCE. Gods, kings, and priests all practiced it, and it became a prominent rite of passage in Mayan culture. So what was it? Let's say a king was ascending to the throne. He would take the spine of a stingray or a blade made of obsidian and perforate his penis. Then he would draw a rope through the wound so that the blood would run down the rope to bits of bark that were lying on the ground. Once the blood had saturated the bark, the king would burn it, and a sacred serpent would appear in the smoke to provide instructions for the king.

_04:: Human Sacrifice

While it's not as widespread as some cartoons and films might suggest, human sacrifice does

---

Fake Your Way through a Conversation

THE BUDDHIST ESSENTIALS

While Buddhism is relatively popular in the West, many people don't understand its full scope. Buddhism refers to the founder, Siddhartha Gautama, who was given the title of Buddha, or Enlightened One, after he received his enlightenment under a bo tree. The Buddha taught the "Middle Way," that is, a path that is neither hedonistic nor ascetic. The Middle Way is essentially the eightfold path of right view, intention, speech, action, livelihood, effort, mindfulness, and concentration. The basic teaching of the Buddha is called the Four Noble Truths: (1) Life is suffering, (2) Suffering is caused by desire, (3) Desire can be broken, (4) Desire can be broken by following the eightfold path. There are several sects of Buddhism, but two divisions predominate: Theravada and Mahayana. Theravada claims to follow the essential teachings of the Buddha and emphasizes life in the *sangha*, or monastic community. Mahayana Buddhism is the more expansive tradition that spread into China and Japan. It includes belief in bodhisattvas, or divine helpers, who have delayed their achievement of Nirvana so that they can help all living beings.

---

exist in the world's religions. The Aztecs, in particular, gave this exchange some horrific twists. Victims were kept in cages by the community temple and fed and taunted by the locals. At the time of the killing ceremony, victims were dressed in elaborate regalia, paraded through the streets, and forced to perform established routines before they ascended the pyramid to die. At the top, priests would place a victim over the altar so that the victim's chest would protrude for the ritual. Another priest would then drive a knife into the chest and drag out a beating heart, which was then raised to the sun before the gathered people. The body would fall off the altar, then roll down the steps of the pyramid, where it would be carried away for dismemberment.

_05:: Seppuku

The term for ritual suicide is *hara-kiri* (often mispronounced in America thanks to a number of World War II films), or *seppuku*, which involves ritual disembowelment. Because hara-kiri is a ritual suicide, there is a clear set of rules to follow that align with the Bushido code, such as refraining from any emotional expression. While seppuku was restricted to men, women performed *jigai* when they were dishonored, a slicing of the jugular vein. The seppuku ritual was often arranged by the victim himself and watched by family and officials. He would first recite his shame and ask the audience for the honor of witnessing his seppuku and then stab himself deeply below the waist and turn the knife upward (showing no emotion). After drawing out the knife, he would offer his neck to the presiding executioner (an honored position).

Mmm-Mmm God:
4
Ways to Be Religious While Having Sex

Thanks in part to theologians from St. Paul to the Puritans, westerners have a difficult time connecting sex and religion, except in terms of sin. But sex may be the oldest religious expression, and many religious traditions recognize sexuality as central to their understanding of the sacred. Here are four ways to get some God in your groove.

_01:: Tantrism

If you've seen the term *tantric* before, you were probably looking at a sex manual or reading about Sting, but the word is actually a religious one found in Hinduism and other Eastern religions. Tantrism includes a variety of rituals that focus on transcending dualities in hopes of achieving a holy union with the primal nature of this universe. Deep, eh? In the most advanced form of Tantrism, ritualistic sex was used as a vehicle for this transformation, along with other practices that were considered forbidden. Unlike our current sex manuals, however, Tantrism indicated that there were severe karmic consequences for practicing tantric sex just for pleasure. The idea was to transcend such mundane concerns as sleeping or eating and use them as symbols of a greater union. The vehicle for this transformation, however, was the thing that was to be transcended—in this case, sex.

_02:: Mysticism

You wouldn't expect medieval monks and nuns to have a sex life, but many of their writings suggest that their desire for union with God takes on erotic qualities. The type of mysticism, espoused by Bernard of Clairvaux, William of St.-Thierry, and others, emphasizes the divine union of God and humans, or spiritual marriage. As such, there is a kind of intercourse associated with this union that is, well, mystical, and much was made of the notion of believers as the bride of Christ. Women mystics were especially interested in love-mysticism, and writers like Teresa of Avila, Catherine of Siena, Theresa of Liseaux, and Julian of Norwich wrote about God in a way that had more prudish readers squirming in their chairs.

_03:: The Song of Solomon

One of the most curious texts in the Bible is called the Song of Solomon, or the Song of Songs. It's nothing less than an erotic love poem and contains some of the most explicit sexual imagery in the Bible. For example, verses 7:7–8 read, ". . . your stature is like a palm tree, your breast like its fruit. I will climb up into the palm tree. I will take hold of its fruit." Scholars have struggled to make sense of this bit of biblical erotica by calling it an allegory of God's love or a statement on marriage, but the word God is never mentioned in this text, and it certainly isn't about marriage—it's about sex.

_04:: Shinto

The most ancient writings of Japan, the Kojiki (712 CE), explain the origins of the Japanese islands and reflect a much older oral tradition that has to do with the rhythms of nature, especially fertility and rebirth. In fact, the two main gods in the story, Izanagi and Izanami, have so much sex in the beginning that their offspring populate heaven and earth. The Shinto world, then, is dependent upon sexuality, and as such, sexuality is considered natural and good, and to have sex is to reflect the work of the gods.

8 Steps to Founding a World Religion (✳ = required, others optional)

Does your mom think you're special? Was your childhood boring and uneventful? Have you ever gone to extremes, been rejected by your friends, or been misunderstood? You could start your own religion! Be sure to read the fine print, though.

_01:: Have a Miraculous Birth

An eventful entrance is a surefire sign that you're going to have an eventful life, and Siddhartha Gautama, or the Buddha, shows just how it's done. There were signs in the heavens and on his body at the boy's birth, and a wise man (they're everywhere) predicted that the infant would become either a great ruler or a great enlightened one. The name Siddhartha means "one who attains the goal." In fact, as we know from Christianity, a miraculous conception doesn't hurt either. In the Buddha's case, he came to his mother in the form of a dream that a white elephant impregnated her by entering her right side.

_02:: Have an Uneventful Childhood*

With some exceptions, it seems that founders of the world's religions have a relatively normal childhood. This fact works well in terms of the "plot" of the leader's life because it allows potential followers to see them much like themselves, as well as covering up those embarrassing childhood incidents that don't really go with leading a world religion. Can you imagine pictures of Buddha, Jesus, or Muhammad in the bathtub, or getting scraped up on the playground? An uneventful childhood sets the stage for an eventful adulthood.

_03:: Go to Extremes*

Again, the Buddha is a perfect example. Kept from the suffering of life by his father, who wanted him to be a ruler instead of a religious figure, Siddhartha went from being a pampered pet to the greatest ascetic who ever lived. Asceticism, the belief that the body must be punished or denied for spiritual liberation, was the prevailing religious practice in India at the time, and the Buddha took this already extreme practice to new heights. It was said that at one point he could touch his backbone through his stomach, and he learned to live on one grain of rice per day. Of course, he eventually realized that such extremes—hedonism and asceticism—were just that, and he preached the Middle Way.

_04:: Be Rejected by Your Peers*

It seems that founders of the world's religions generally have to be rejected in one form or another. This can occur because they're weird, offensive, belligerent, or some combination of the above. In the case of Muhammad, his new religion was bad for business. His anti-idolatrous stance made it hard to sell idols along the Arabian trade routes, and the businessmen were not amused (are they ever?). Similarly, the Buddha's ascetic friends rejected him when they saw that he had abandoned their way, and of course Jesus was called a blasphemer by the religious leaders of the day and punished as a criminal. So cheer up! If people just don't seem to like you or think you're weird, there may be eternal glory in your future as a founder of a world religion!

_05:: Disappear for a While

A pretty good strategy in a number of areas (such as when you don't pay your taxes), the founders of world religion usually find that having lost years or days adds to their mystery and suggests that they have had experiences that are unique. Not a bad line on the résumé for the job. Consider Jesus, who spent 40 days and nights in the desert being tempted and came out of the experience ready to begin his work. St. Paul spent 14 years in the Arabian Desert before he became the apostle to the Gentiles and converted the world to Christianity. Moses too ended up tending sheep in the desert before he had that conversation with the burning bush and demanded that Pharaoh let his people go.

_06:: Die—the More Strangely the Better*

The Buddha died from eating bad mushrooms, Muhammad expired from eating poisoned lamb, and Jesus was hung on a cross. If your birth was special, then your death had better be spectacular. Of course all the founders have to die, and some, like Abraham, live long and full lives before they meet their maker. A

Strange but True

FOUNDERS FROM NONTRADITIONAL FAMILIES

Confucius, Moses, and Muhammad—three significant men in three significant religions. Sure, they lived in vastly different times and places, but they do share one trait: they each are products of single- or no-parent childhoods. Confucius lost his father shortly after he was born, and he claimed that the difficulties he and his mother faced enabled him to do the kind of work a noble would never have to consider. He did note, however, "It is not hard to chafe at poverty." The story of Moses is one of the most dramatic in the Hebrew Bible, or Old Testament, and the drama begins at birth and lasts to his death. Moses was born at a time when Pharaoh had declared that all male children born to the Hebrews were to be killed, so Moses' mother hid him for three months but eventually had to do something more drastic. The solution? She put him in a basket along the Nile River, and Pharaoh's daughter found him and raised him as her own son. As for Muhammad, he was born in 570 CE, but his father was already dead when he emerged from the womb. Even more tragic, his mother died when Muhammad was six years old. From then on, Muhammad stayed first with his paternal grandfather, then with his uncle Abu Talib, and like many other founders, he grew up in poverty.

bizarre death, however, puts a fine point on the unique life of a founder and makes for a dramatic ending to the story (plus guaranteed TV-movie success).

_07:: Live Again*

As we know, sequels can be good or bad, but they're never quite the same as the original. If you want to found your own religion, it really helps to be resurrected or live again in some fashion. The Buddha did it by passing into Nirvana, a state free from desire and suffering. Jesus had a more active post-death existence, proving himself to the doubtful Thomas and eventually judging the living and the dead. More important, perhaps, the second life of the founder promises a second life for the followers. Best to keep the details of this second life as murky as possible lest it appear to resemble this life too much, but promises of a new body and a cool place to live work well.

_08:: Watch Your Followers Misconstrue Your Teachings, Sometimes to the Point of Bloodshed*

There is always a crucial moment in the life of a religion when the founder dies (or just goes away). What to do then? When the founder is alive, there is opportunity for him to correct misinterpretations, adjust expectations, and comment on current events, but when he's gone, these functions are usually replaced by ethical systems that purport to get at the founder's teachings. Legend has it that a split occurred in the followers of the Buddha only one day after his death. Before a year was up, they had to call a council to sort things out, which didn't work. Soon there were 4 sects of Buddhism, and within 10 years of the Buddha's death, there were 16. The problem is that the death of the founder leaves a power vacuum, and history has proven that we are all too willing to fill that vacuum with our own ideas about what the founder meant, and all too often we are willing to prove our point with the point of a gun.

Versions of Heaven

Ah, heaven. Marx called it a carrot used by the wealthy to keep us working hard for little money. After all, the real rewards are supposed to come much later. But despite what Marx had to say, the notion of a happy afterlife won't quite go away. Here are six pleasant resorts the righteous can look forward to in the afterlife.

_01:: Heaven: Judaism

As one of the oldest and most influential religions in existence, Judaism might be expected to be the source of our most profound notions of heaven, but it isn't. In fact, there is no clear indication of a heaven or afterlife in the Jewish scriptures at all, which leads to a lot of debate on the subject. Two typical positions are those of the Pharisees, who believed that there was an implied notion of an afterlife, and the Sad-

---

Stump the Expert

THE PROBLEM OF EVIL

One of the most vexing problems in religion is the existence of evil, and the problem can be summarized in a series of propositions:

1. God is omnipotent, or all-powerful.
2. God is omniscient, or all-knowing.
3. God is omnipresent, or everywhere.
4. God is benevolent, or all-good.
5. Evil exists.

Logically, one of these statements must be false. Why? Because a god who has all the characteristics of propositions 1–4 cannot allow evil to exist. That does not mean of course that believers in God cannot hold all these beliefs; they often do. What it means is that they cannot hold them philosophically; they must resort to some kind of mysticism or lack of faith in the mind's ability to understand the world in order to hold them. Both of these options are unavailable to philosophers. Other believers, wanting to maintain their philosophical integrity, have rejected one of the four propositions (usually the first). But the revered St. Augustine tried a different approach: he rejected the fifth proposition. Augustine knew that if evil exists, and if God is the creator, then God had to create evil, so he argues that evil is "the absence of the good" and has no independent existence. It can, however, help us to appreciate the good by showing us what the absence of the good entails. Though he was trying to provide a solution to the problem of evil for Christians, some of them felt that Augustine's measures sacrificed too much of the Christian worldview since the fight against evil is central to their beliefs.

---

ducees, who pointed out that there was no biblical evidence of such. Over the millennia, Jews have come to believe in various versions of heaven, some of which occur after the Messiah comes and involve the righteous dead coming back to life. Still, overall, Judaism is more concerned with life in the here and now.

_02:: Paradise: Zoroastrianism

It was the ancient Persians who gave us the word *paradise*, which means a walled garden or park, and Zoroastrianism in particular gave

us notions of the afterlife that were adopted and/or adapted by Jews, Christians, and Muslims. Zoroastrianism is also interesting because, unlike other religions, it claims that everyone will eventually get to heaven, though it might take awhile. The paradise of Zoroastrianism is attained the fourth day after death by crossing the Bridge of the Separator, which widens when the righteous approach it. (See the next section for what happens to the wicked.) The righteous soul crosses the bridge and is met by a beautiful maiden who is the physical and feminine embodiment of all his good works on earth. He is then escorted into the House of Song to await the Last Day. On this day, everyone will be purified and live in a new world absent of evil and full of youthful rejoicing.

_03:: Heaven: Christianity

The Christian notion of heaven is one of singing and rejoicing before God in a "new heaven and a new earth." It also reflects Christianity's roots in Judaism because this new heaven contains a city called New Jerusalem. There are elaborate descriptions of the city in the book of Revelation. New Jerusalem has a wall and 12 gates, and on each gate is the name of one of the tribes of Israel along with an angel. There are also 12 foundations, 1 each for the 12 apostles. In fact, we even know the size of the New Jerusalem: 1400 miles square with a 200-foot wall. The structure itself is made of all kinds of precious stones, some of which have not yet been identified on this earth. There is a river of "the water of life," which flows from God's throne, and trees of life line the banks of the river and produce fruit every month. Believers will have God's name written on their foreheads, and all pain, tears, and death will disappear forever.

_04:: Paradise: Islam

The Islamic version of heaven is a paradise for those whose good works have outweighed the bad as determined by the straight path laid out in the Quran. Heaven is a garden where the faithful lie upon couches in a climate-controlled environment surrounded by "bashful, dark-eyed virgins, chaste as the sheltered eggs of ostriches." They will drink from crystal goblets and silver vessels as "immortal youths" hover about them looking like "scattered pearls." The believers will be clothed in green silk and brocade and will wear silver bracelets, and they will "drink a pure draught" drawn from Allah's own source as a reward for their striving and patience.

_05:: Moksha: Hinduism

Eastern religions don't really have notions of heaven like those in the West. Instead, they usually offer some kind of release from illusion and suffering in the present world. The Hindu Upanishads are philosophical portions of the Vedas, Hinduism's oldest sacred text, and in them the notions of the self and afterlife are developed. According to the Upanishads, our actions connect us to this world of appearances, which is in fact illusory. What is real is Brahman, the ultimate reality that transcends our sensory experiences. Unfortunately, we live in ignorance of Brahman and act according to our illusions. This action (karma) causes us to participate in the cycle of death and rebirth (samsara—see next section) from which it's difficult to escape. Thus, if you can escape your ignorance and realize that ultimately you are not you but Brahman itself, then you can achieve release from the cycle of death and rebirth. This release is called moksha.

_06:: Nirvana: Buddhism

One of the four noble truths of the Buddha is that suffering is caused by desire, the desire to have but also the desire to be. Desire is *tanha*, or a burning that keeps us caught in the web of illusion that is our ego. The Buddha taught that desire is a flame that burns us, causes suffering, and keeps us tied to the cycle of death and rebirth because the flame continues burning into the next life. What we hope for is Nirvana, or the extinguishing of that flame, which is also the end of suffering.

7 Abandon All Hope, Ye Who Enter Here: Versions of Hell

Walt Whitman wrote that "the fear of hell is little or nothing to me," but he was Walt Whitman. For most religious people, the fear of hell is a powerful motivation to believe in a faith, avoid sin, and generally behave. Here are seven pretty effective motivational scenarios.

_01:: Hell: Judaism

As with their view of heaven, Jews have an ambiguous version of hell. The Hebrew Bible makes little mention of it except as a place where the spirits of the dead reside (Sheol). There is, however, the term *Gehinnom*, which refers to a valley in which children were reportedly sacrificed to the god Molech. Eventually, this valley became a refuse dump that was constantly burning, which provided a powerful metaphor for a place to send sinners. In later Judaism, hell is the place of punishment for unbelievers, but according to the rabbinical texts, they will probably stay there for no more than a year.

_02:: The Chinvat Bridge: Zoroastrianism

The Bridge of Separation, as it's also known, is the one that all people must walk after they die. For the righteous it broadens and leads to a beautiful maiden, but for the less than righteous, it turns on its side and becomes like a razor. The ancient god Mithra is there with a scale to balance the good and evil deeds done during one's lifetime, and if evil deeds prevail, then the soul is tormented by an old hag before it falls off the bridge into hell. The torments of the evil go well beyond Dante's imagination and focus on punishments directly related to their evil deeds. Zoroastrian hell may be the most horrific of all, and a text called the Vision of Arda Viraf describes it in all its gory glory. Fortunately, everyone eventually leaves Zoroastrian hell. They are purified and join the righteous in the reign of the god Ahura Mazda.

_03:: Hades: Greek

Hades is actually the name of the lord of the dead and ruler of the netherworld, but the name became so associated with the place that the two merged, so Hades is also the place the dead go. Hades rules this world with Persephone—whom he abducted from the earth-goddess Demeter—and a number of other figures such as Thanatos, Hypnos, Charon, and Cerberus. Hades represents the place of eternal punishment for evildoers, where the sinners are put on horrifying display. Such examples include Tityos bound while a vulture eats his liver, Tantalus thirsty and hungry but unable to eat the fruit just above his head or drink the water at his feet, and Sisyphus forced to push a rock up a hill only to have it roll back again for eternity.

_04:: Hell: Christianity

Christian hell seems at one level to be a combination of the Jewish idea of Gehinnom, where there is eternal burning, and Hades, where there is eternal punishment. In fact, the Greek word for *hell* in the New Testament is often *hades*, and Jesus uses the word *Gehenna* (a version of *Gehinnom*) to indicate the place for sinners where the fire is not quenched and the worm does not die. The book of Revelation indicates that those whose names are not found written in the Book of Life are thrown into the lake of fire. In fact, Death and Hades themselves are thrown into the lake of fire in the end. In addition to these texts, Dante did much to embellish the Christian notion of hell in his *Inferno*.

_05:: Hell: Islam

The Quran, the sacred text of Islam, usually speaks of heaven and hell in the same passage, perhaps in order to provide a dramatic contrast. Hell is often described as "an evil resting place" and the "Fire." But fire is just the beginning of the torment in hell because the fire is like a wall enclosing the wicked, and when they cry out, they are showered with water as "hot as molten brass," which scalds their faces. It gets worse. The unbelievers wear garments of fire and are lashed with rods of iron, and if they try to escape, they are dragged back and told to "taste the torment of the Conflagration."

_06:: Samsara: Hinduism

Again, the Eastern religions have a very different notion of the afterlife, although in some sects of Hinduism, Buddhism, and Taoism, there are heavens and hells that are similar to Western ideas of the same. Hindu hell, however, is traditionally a continuation of life on earth called samsara. Samsara is the endless cycle of death and rebirth that is the result of our ignorance of the ultimate reality of the universe. The word means "to wander across," as in lifetimes, and samsara is the result of karma or actions taken in this life that will determine the nature of one's rebirth and the caste one is born into.

_07:: The Bardo: Tibetan Buddhism

One of the most detailed and elaborate depictions of the afterlife is from the Tibetan Buddhist text Bardo Thodol, or the Tibetan Book of the Dead. As the title suggests, the book deals with dying or, more accurately, with the state of Between, and there are many "betweens": birth and death, sleeping and waking, waking and trance, and three others within the death-rebirth between. The Bardo Thodol teaches that after death, the soul exists in the Bardo for 49 days in a between that can lead to Nirvana or back into rebirth. One of the factors that influences the soul's ultimate location is the dying itself. A good death tends to push the soul toward enlightenment, while a bad death can move it toward rebirth in the world. Tibetan Buddhists thus spend a lot of time and energy in helping the dying.

Women Who Shaped World Religions

If you haven't noticed it already, women don't play a prominent role in the world's religions. There are plenty of reasons for this, including patriarchy, sexism, and fear on the part of men. But there are significant moments when women appear in religion, and when they do, the effect is usually powerful. Here are some famous and not-so-famous women who shaped world religions.

_01:: Buffalo Woman: Lakota

The story of Buffalo Woman is that of a Lakota sacred figure who comes to the people in a time of starvation and shows them how to use the sacred pipe. In the end she walks away and becomes in turn a black, a brown, a red, and a white buffalo calf. Just after she

disappears, buffalo come in great numbers and give themselves willingly to the people, thus setting the stage for a long and harmonious relationship between the buffalo and the Lakota in which the former provide everything the latter need. The appropriate response of the Lakota is to perform the sacred pipe ceremony, which reminds them of all their relations and of Wakan Tanka, or the Great Mysterious.

_02:: Isis: Egyptian

Isis and her famous brother-husband, Osiris, were two of the most powerful gods in the ancient world, and Isis in particular was worshiped in Egypt and throughout the Mediterranean for centuries. She was also a favorite goddess of the Romans. Isis worship withstood the growth of Christianity and remained viable until the sixth century CE. Her qualities and attributes are those of the Great Mother, especially in her fertility symbolism. The daughter of the sky goddess Nut and the earth god Neb, Isis was often represented by a cow, and her power was considered great, especially for warding off evil.

_03:: Lilith: Judaism

The story of Lilith is one that has animated contemporary religious feminism because Lilith was a rebel, a woman who wanted to define her own sexuality and was punished for it. According to rabbinic legend, Lilith was Adam's first wife, and she refused to lie beneath him during intercourse because she too was made of dust and should not have to be in an inferior position. When Adam tried to take her by force, she uttered the secret name of God and fled to the desert. Later Jewish tradition (and superstition) has Lilith as a demoness who lives in the desert and gives birth to 100 demons a day. She also visits and strangles infants and sexually assaults men who sleep alone. Lilith's punishment and characterization are seen by some contemporary feminists as the result of male reaction to female independence.

What's the Difference?
SEPARATING THE SUNNIS FROM THE SHIITES

Like every religion, Islam has its different expressions, and these days it's become increasingly important to understand the differences between them. Most Muslims are Sunni (about 85%). They consider themselves to be in line with the most ancient understanding of Islam and focus their attention on the Quran and community and family life. The Shiites were formed as a result of a schism in Islam, one that initially concerned leadership succession but grew into a full-fledged theology of its own. Shiites believe that revelation can continue through the imams, religious leaders who speak for God, and these imams never die but wait in hiding to return to earth. There are either 7 or 12 imams, depending on the tradition. Shiites also have a messiah figure, called a Mahdi, who will bring justice to the earth. Because their first leader, Ali, was murdered, Shiites tend to understand martyrdom as a high expression of faith. Interestingly, Shiites tend to mistrust the Quran since it does not mention their leader.

_04:: Khadija: Islam

Khadija was unusual in the world of ancient Arabia. She was a 40-year-old woman who owned her own caravan. She was also a widow when she met a deeply religious and influential man named Muhammad, who was 15 years her junior. Soon Khadija became his only wife in a culture that permitted polygamy, and they were married for 25 years. Khadija's influence on Muhammad was enormous: She provided money and wisdom to a tortured orphan who was struggling with painful and strange visions. Her wealth alone enabled Muhammad to pursue his religious vocation, and Khadija was one of the first converts to the new religion of Islam.

_05:: Amaterasu: Shinto

Amaterasu is the sun goddess of Japan. This is unusual in itself since solar deities are usually male (Egypt is another exception). But in spite of that, the goddess has been extraordinarily influential. Amaterasu is so highly integrated into Japanese society that her emblem, a rising sun, adorns Japan's national flag. There is also a national Japanese holiday devoted to her; the Great Festival of the Sun Goddess is celebrated on July 17 with all-day street processions and parties. Amaterasu is also known as the ancestor of Japan's imperial family; consequently, all royal families in Japan trace their lineage back to her. Even today, an important part of the Japanese coronation ceremony takes place at the temple at Ise where Amaterasu is believed to reside.

_06:: Mary: Christianity

As the mother of Jesus, Mary is the most important saint in Catholicism, and reverence for her began early in the history of Christianity. She became the emblem of the pain of love in having to see her son crucified for the world, and her title as "bearer of God" elevated her to a status where she is seen as reigning with her son in heaven. Considered immaculately conceived—or born without sin—Mary was said to be taken directly to heaven upon her death. The Catholic use of the rosary is an expression of Mary's importance to the faith since it entails meditation on various aspects of the life of Jesus and Mary and includes the Ave Maria, or Hail Mary.

(or 3 Million) Famous Gods

While not all religions have deities (e.g., Confucianism, Taoism, Buddhism), gods do play an important role in the world's religions. Their personalities are varied, but they usually represent human ideals in some form and thus are recognizable to us. At the same time, they're certainly more than human and thus are objects of fear, reverence, and worship. Here are three gods everyone should know.

_01:: Yahweh

Yahweh is an approximation of the secret name that God gave to Moses as he spoke from the burning bush. Yahweh is also called Jehovah, and when the name is used in most bibles, it appears as small capitals to distinguish it from the other names of God, such as Elohim or Adonai. The reason Yahweh or Jehovah is an approximation is that the ancient Hebrews refused to pronounce the name for fear of taking it in vain, which is one of the Ten Commandments. Apparently, the name

Myths and Misconceptions

FIVE MYTHS ABOUT THE BIBLE

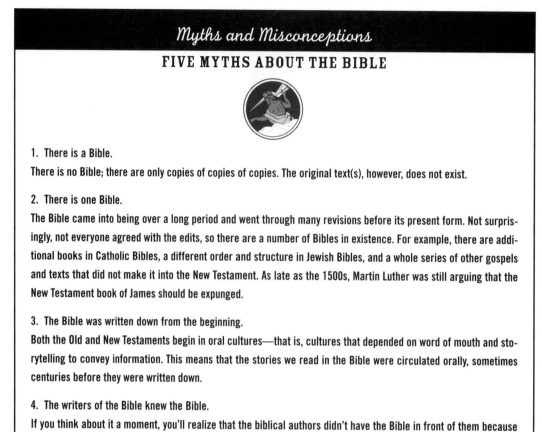

1. There is a Bible.
There is no Bible; there are only copies of copies of copies. The original text(s), however, does not exist.

2. There is one Bible.
The Bible came into being over a long period and went through many revisions before its present form. Not surprisingly, not everyone agreed with the edits, so there are a number of Bibles in existence. For example, there are additional books in Catholic Bibles, a different order and structure in Jewish Bibles, and a whole series of other gospels and texts that did not make it into the New Testament. As late as the 1500s, Martin Luther was still arguing that the New Testament book of James should be expunged.

3. The Bible was written down from the beginning.
Both the Old and New Testaments begin in oral cultures—that is, cultures that depended on word of mouth and storytelling to convey information. This means that the stories we read in the Bible were circulated orally, sometimes centuries before they were written down.

4. The writers of the Bible knew the Bible.
If you think about it a moment, you'll realize that the biblical authors didn't have the Bible in front of them because it was still being developed. Often biblical writers show absolutely no awareness of other biblical texts. One exception of course is that the authors of the New Testament knew the Old. But Paul, for example, cannot refer to the Gospels because they weren't written down when he was writing. In fact, the Gospels weren't written until 40 to 70 years after Jesus died and was resurrected and some 20 years after Paul's first letters.

5. The author is the author.
Ever wonder how Moses wrote about his own death? Well, he probably didn't. Ever wonder how Paul got so many bylines in the New Testament? He probably shouldn't have. Our notions of authorship are relatively new, and during the time when the Bible was being composed, it was common for people to write using more famous or authoritative people's names.

was pronounced once a year by the high priest on the Day of Atonement, or Yom Kippur, but since that ceremony hasn't taken place for 2,000 years, the correct pronunciation's been lost. Add to this the fact that written Hebrew from this period didn't have vowels, and there's even more confusion. The name of this god, then, appears as YHWH or JHVH in English. Whatever the pronunciation, Yahweh is a unique god who acts in history on behalf of the Jewish people, such as when he led them out of slavery in Egypt.

_02:: The Hindu Pantheon

Hinduism, in addition to being the oldest of the recorded religions, has also given us a pantheon that is enormous and diverse. There is a god or goddess to help with anything in life, but Hindus are typically devoted to one god in particular. This god or goddess might be Parvati, a princess who nurtures her subjects, or Ganesha, the elephant-headed god who helps solve everyday problems, or a whole host of others. Three gods in particular, however, have received the most attention in Hinduism, and they are sometimes called the Trimurti, or "three forms." Brahma is considered the creator god, Vishnu is the preserver, and Shiva is the destroyer. Hindus do not, however, separate these functions as easily as one might think since each of the gods serves some of these functions.

_03:: Mithra

Mithra is an ancient god who appears in Persia and reached the zenith of his popularity in Rome. Older than Jesus by several centuries, the legend of Mithra has him being born of a virgin on December 25 and visited by shepherds and magi. He had 12 disciples, healed the sick, and cast out devils, and was often depicted as a lion or lamb. Mithra rose again around the vernal equinox (March 21) and later ascended into heaven. Obviously, there is some speculation that Christianity was a new kind of Mithraism. Mithra is associated with the bull because of a legend where he captured and then sacrificed a sacred bull, and from this sacrifice came everything that was good in the world. Mithra also appears in Zoroastrianism as the god who weighs a person's deeds on a scale.

6 Straight from the Cutting Room Floor: Texts That Didn't Make It into the Bible

That's right! If you've been looking for the director's cut of the Bible, with all the extra features, you've come to the right place. The reasons why these texts were cut vary, but they generally have to do with the prevailing theological and cultural concerns at the time the Bible was being assembled. Regardless, here are some texts that some people never wanted you to know about.

_01:: Susanna and the Elders (Daniel and Susanna)

Though it sounds like a '50s girl group, it's actually a wonderful little story that includes a beautiful woman unjustly charged and a young Daniel (of lion's den fame) who defends her with great cunning. Susanna was the wife of Joachim, a rich and honored man who was often consulted by the elders for his wisdom. Two of these elders began to lust after Susanna, and one day, while she was bathing in the garden, the two lecherous elders, who had

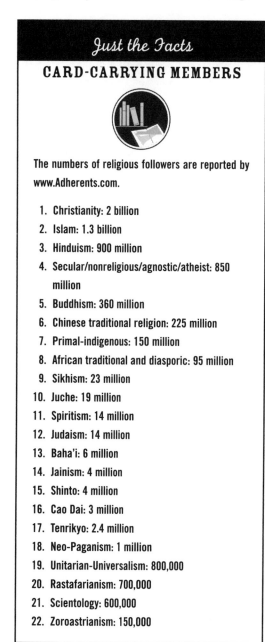

Just the Facts

CARD-CARRYING MEMBERS

The numbers of religious followers are reported by www.Adherents.com.

1. Christianity: 2 billion
2. Islam: 1.3 billion
3. Hinduism: 900 million
4. Secular/nonreligious/agnostic/atheist: 850 million
5. Buddhism: 360 million
6. Chinese traditional religion: 225 million
7. Primal-indigenous: 150 million
8. African traditional and diasporic: 95 million
9. Sikhism: 23 million
10. Juche: 19 million
11. Spiritism: 14 million
12. Judaism: 14 million
13. Baha'i: 6 million
14. Jainism: 4 million
15. Shinto: 4 million
16. Cao Dai: 3 million
17. Tenrikyo: 2.4 million
18. Neo-Paganism: 1 million
19. Unitarian-Universalism: 800,000
20. Rastafarianism: 700,000
21. Scientology: 600,000
22. Zoroastrianism: 150,000

said, and as Susanna was being led away to be killed, a young man named Daniel called out that she was innocent. He proved it by questioning the men separately and asking under which tree in the garden Susanna had consorted with this man. When the men gave two different answers, they were killed and Susanna spared.

_02:: Judith

In another story about a powerful woman, Judith is a beautiful widow who is also a powerful warrior. Judith lives in Bethulia, which is being attacked by the hated Assyrians. Led by the Assyrian king's best general, Holofernes, the army captures the water supply, and the elders of Bethulia decide that they have five days before they must surrender. Judith, however, is having none of it. Until this point, she'd been in mourning for her dead husband, but now she removes her mourning clothes and dresses herself to be alluring. She then leaves the city and hands herself over to the Assyrians surrounding it. Holofernes is impressed with her and asks her to dine with him hoping to seduce her, but he gets drunk and passes out. Judith takes his sword and cuts his head off. Then she returns to the Hebrew camp and orders that the head be placed on the wall. When the Assyrians see it, they are routed by the Hebrews, and everyone praises God and Judith. While the story isn't included in Bibles, it has been the subject of several works of art.

_03:: Tobit

Tobit is another story of Jews in exile. In this case the main character, Tobit, is a man who has fallen on hard times in addition to being in exile. Part of his difficulty comes from trying

hidden themselves there, asked her to have sex with them or they'd tell everyone that they'd seen her with another man. Susanna bravely refused to sin with the men and chose to face execution instead. The men did as they to be righteous under the reign of Sennacherib and other kings. In particular, Tobit buries the dead left behind by the evil king in direct opposition to him. He is blind and poor, but his fortunes change when his son Tobias and the archangel Raphael begin to work on his behalf. In the process, Tobias, gets a wife, the widow (seven times) Sarah. On their wedding night, Tobias and Sarah are attacked by a demon, but Tobit's pennance has paid off. The archangel Raphael has already forewarned the family, clueing Tobias in to a unique way of repelling the demon using fish guts and a scent that would repel any hound of hell.

_04:: The Infancy Gospel of Thomas

This gospel, which is very different from the Gospel of Thomas, is a narrative containing a number of stories about the childhood of Jesus. The Bible is silent on Jesus' childhood except for a brief mention of a visit to the Temple, but the Infancy Gospel of Thomas tells us that Jesus could be quite an unruly child with a temper and the power to act on it. For example, in one story Jesus is making clay figurines of birds by a creek on the Sabbath. When he is reproached by an elder, Jesus claps his hands and tells the birds to fly away—and they do. When he is run over by a boy in the street, he tells the unfortunate boy that he will continue no longer. The boy falls down dead. Of course, Jesus does do some good things in this gospel. When his father, Joseph, a carpenter by trade, cuts a board too short, Jesus is able to stretch it for him.

_05:: The Gospel of Mary

This isn't Mary the mother of Jesus but Mary Magadalene, the woman from whom seven devils were cast. She is generally represented as a sinner whom Jesus saved. In this gospel, however, the disciples are anxious and fearful about going out to preach the gospel because if the ruling powers killed Jesus, surely they'll kill them too. Mary Magdalene stands up in their midst and tells them to be of good cheer and to remember the words of Jesus. Peter encourages her to continue because "we know that the Savior loved you more than other women." Mary goes on to describe her mystical vision of Jesus and their secret conversation, but Andrew and Peter turn on her and argue that Jesus would never have revealed such secrets to a woman. Levi (Matthew), however, comes to Mary's aid and reminds them once again that Jesus loved her more than them. They then go out and preach.

_06:: Acts of Paul and Thecla

The Apostle Paul was a traveler, and as travelers can, he got into some interesting situations. This text describes Paul preaching in a church (a house, really) of one of his friends. He is described as "a man small in size, bald-headed, bandy-legged, well-built, with eyebrows meeting, rather long-nosed, full of grace." Thecla, a virgin betrothed to a man named Thamyris, sits by her window, listening to Paul preach, and she finds that she cannot tear herself away. For three days and nights, she sits there without eating until her fiancé is called to deal with her. Thamyris makes inquiries as to this man Paul because Thecla "thus loves the stranger." His friends suggest having Paul brought up on charges of teaching heresy, and so it is done. Thecla, however, follows Paul and wallows on the ground where he is imprisoned. Paul is scourged, and Thecla is ordered to be burned, but when the fires reach her, she is not consumed.

Contributors

Will Pearson and **Mangesh Hattikudur** met as freshmen at Duke University. Cleverly ignoring the lures of law school and investment banking, the pair cofounded *mental_floss* magazine and have been grinning ever since. This is their first book.

When she's not flossing, **Elizabeth Hunt** works in the publishing department of the International Reading Association. Previously she worked as the project coordinator of the book *Watch It Made in the USA, 3rd Edition.* This is Liz's second project with Mangesh—they met while working on their high school newspaper, *Tiger Pause*.

Founded in 2001, *mental_floss* **magazine,** currently available at newsstands everywhere, has received rave reviews in a variety of publications including the *Washington Post*, the *Chicago Tribune, Entertainment Weekly,* and *Newsweek.* The publication is regularly featured on *CNN Headline News*, and was named one of the top ten new magazines of 2001 by *Library Journal.*

Alexei Bayer, a coauthor of *mental_floss's* economics column "Know Your Dough," is a New York-based economist and writer contributing to a number of national publications and *The Globalist* Web site. He writes a column for *Vedomosti,* Russia's leading business daily.

Karen Bernd, Ph.D., is a professor of biology at Davidson College in Davidson, NC. A molecular biologist by training, Bernd has authored pedagogical material to help others integrate animations and current research in their biology courses, and her research has been published in leading scientific journals.

Robert Cumming is an art critic and writer. Initially a curator in the Tate Gallery Education Department, he went on to become the founder and chairman of the renowned Christies Education programs in London, New York, and Paris. He writes extensively for the British and American press, including *mental_floss,* and his bestselling art books have been translated into thirty different languages worldwide. He lives in Buckinghamshire, UK, with his wife and two daughters.

Curry Guinn is a researcher in artificial intelligence at RTI International in Research Triangle Park, NC, and an adjunct assistant professor at Duke University. His current research focuses on developing synthetic humans that converse, display emotion, and react to the world according to their personality.

Former newspaperman and sometime college journalism instructor **Peter Haugen** is the author of *World History for Dummies*. A contributor to *mental_floss*, he writes regularly for *History* magazine and is working on a history of biology in the 20th century. He lives in Madison, WI, with his wife and two sons.

Bill Hauser, Ph.D., is currently an assistant professor of marketing and an adjunct professor of sociology at the University of Akron in Akron, OH. After two decades of directing market research for Fortune 500 companies, Bill is currently fulfilling his lifelong dream of teaching, research, and writing.

William Irwin is associate professor of philosophy at King's College in Wilkes-Barre, PA. He is the editor of *The Matrix and Philosophy*, *The Simpsons and Philosophy*, *Seinfeld and Philosophy*, and *The Death and Resurrection of the Author?* He is the author of *Intentionalist Interpretation* and the coauthor of *Critical Thinking*.

Martin W. Lewis is a lecturer in international relations at Stanford University. He was educated at the University of California at Santa Cruz (B.A. in environmental studies) and the University of California at Berkeley (Ph.D. in geography). He is the author (or coauthor) of several books, including *The Myth of Conti-*

nents: A Critique of Metageography and *Diversity Amid Globalization: World Regions, Environment, Development*.

Richard A. Muller is a professor of physics at the University of California at Berkeley. His research includes astrophysics, geophysics, elementary particles, and climate. He has received a MacArthur Prize and the NSF Alan T. Waterman Award. He currently teaches a course called "Physics for Future Presidents."

Shane Pitts is a cognitive psychologist at Birmingham-Southern College in Birmingham, AL. His primary research interests are memory distortions, social cognition, and stereotyping. He enjoys art, basketball, spending time with his girlfriend, and diet Mountain Dew (not necessarily in that order). He isn't as good a swimmer, but is younger and taller than exactly one other author of the psychology chapter in this book.

Greg Salyer teaches English at Longwood University in Farmville, VA, and has taught courses in literature, philosophy, and religion for twelve years. He is the author of *Leslie Marmon Silko*, a critical introduction to the Native American writer's work, and the editor of *Literature and Theology at Century's End*. He has published numerous articles on Native American and contemporary literature, religion, and film, and is currently working on a book on Native American writer Louise Erdrich.

Valarie Samulski is a choreographer, dancer, and writer exploring the intersection of social, cultural, and political vertices in the arts. A summa cum laude graduate of Duke University, she is now teaching and performing throughout the United States, and makes her home in Fort Greene, Brooklyn.

Dr. Joe Schwarcz is a chemistry professor and director of the McGill University Office for Science and Society. He has received numerous awards for teaching as well as for interpreting science for the public. He writes a regular newspaper column entitled "The Right Chemistry" and is the author of four books.

Kenneth Silber is a writer based in New York City and coauthor of *mental_floss*'s economics column "Know Your Dough." Silber writes frequently for TechCentralStation.com. His articles have appeared in various publications, including *Book, Commentary, National Review*, the *New York Post, Reason*, and *Skeptical Inquirer*.

Royce Simpson received his Ph.D. in Experimental Psychology from the University of Alabama in 1992. He is currently an associate professor at Spring Hill College in Mobile, AL, where his teaching load includes courses in cognition, learning & behavior, and social psychology. His current research interests include an examination of gender differences in autobiographical memory.

Pop culture contributor **Christopher Smith** works as an advertising writer for The Richards Group in Dallas, TX. His own 30- and 60-second contributions to pop culture include award-winning spots for Motel 6 and many others. He is also a veteran performer with Dallas's Ad-Libs Improv Comedy Troupe. A native of upstate New York and graduate of Penn State, he lives in Dallas with his wife, Heather, and their baby daughter, Clara.

Scott Speck, conductor, regularly leads orchestras in the United States and around the world. He has conducted at the Kennedy Center, San Francisco's Opera House, the Paris Opera, and London's Royal Opera House at Covent Garden. Scott is the coauthor of three of the world's bestselling books on the arts: *Classical Music for Dummies, Opera for Dummies*, and *Ballet for Dummies*.

John Timpane is the Commentary Page editor for the *Philadelphia Inquirer*. He is also a musician, a poet, and the author of *Writing Worth Reading* (with Nancy H. Packer), *It Could Be Verse*, and *Poetry for Dummies*.

Exclusive offer for
CONDENSED KNOWLEDGE READERS!

If you liked *Condensed Knowledge*, you're going to love *mental_floss* magazine. Hip, quick, quirky, and fun, *mental_floss* is the perfect antidote to dull conversations. Jam-packed with fascinating facts, lucid explanations, and history's juiciest secrets, *mental_floss* uncovers everything from black holes to the Dead Sea Scrolls, and laces it with just enough wit to keep you grinning for weeks. So, go ahead and pick up a copy. And an hour later, when your kids are tugging at your pant legs and your spouse is burning dinner, and you're busy wondering just where the time went, you'll realize that *mental_floss* doesn't just make learning easy, it makes it addictive.

Save 50% off the cover price of this wonderful magazine. Go to www.mentalfloss.com/condensedknowledge or complete and mail the form below.

Please enter my subscription to mental_floss magazine immediately!

___ 6 issues (1 year) $14.95

___ 12 issues (2 years) $27.95

(Canadian orders add $10.00 per year; payable in U.S. funds)

Name: _____

Address: _____

Apt / Suite #: _____

City _____ **State** _____ **Zip** _____

Check enclosed _____ **Please charge my Visa/MC** _____ **Exp:** _____

Signature _____ WHCCK

Mail this form to:

mental_floss
P.O. Box 1940
Marion, OH 43306-1940

HarperCollins*Publishers* is not a party to this offer and is not affiliated with *mental_floss* magazine.